The House of the Dead

Or, Prison Life in Siberia (1861)

*A Harrowing Journey Through Suffering,
Redemption, and the Human Soul*

A Modern Translation

Adapted for the Contemporary Reader

Fyodor Dostoevsky

Table of Contents

Preface - Message to the Reader

Rebuilding the Greatest Library in Human History

Thousands of years ago, the Library of Alexandria was the heart of global knowledge — a sanctuary where the wisdom of every known civilization was gathered and shared freely.

And then, it was lost.

Now, we're rebuilding it — and you are invited to join us.

At the Library of Alexandria, we've set out to make every book available to *every person on Earth* — not just in print, but in every language, every format, and for every reader.

Here's how we do it:

- **Deluxe Print Editions at True Printing Cost** - Order any book as a high-quality paperback, elegant hardcover, or stunning boxset — and only pay what it costs to print. No markups. No middlemen.
- **Unlimited Access to the Greatest Works** - Enjoy thousands of timeless classics — from Plato to Shakespeare to Tolstoy — in beautiful, modern eBook and audiobook editions. Read and listen without limits — for every reader, everywhere.
- **Modern Translations for Every Language & Dialect** - We're reimagining the classics in clear, accessible language — and translating them into every dialect imaginable. Everyone deserves to understand humanity's greatest ideas.

When you visit **LibraryofAlexandria.com**, you're not just accessing books — you're joining a global movement to restore, preserve, and share the wisdom of civilization.

Join us today at LibraryofAlexandria.com

Together, we'll ensure the light of human wisdom never fades again.

With gratitude,
The Modern Library of Alexandria Team

Visit:

www.libraryofalexandria.com

Or scan the code below:

Introduction

A Chronicle of Darkness and Grace:
Dostoevsky's Spiritual Awakening in a Siberian Prison

The House of the Dead is not just one of the earliest works of Fyodor Dostoevsky—it is also his most autobiographical and, in many ways, the key to understanding all that would follow in his literary and philosophical development. First published between 1861 and 1862, it was based on the four years Dostoevsky spent as a prisoner in a Siberian labor camp after his 1849 arrest and mock execution for participation in a radical intellectual circle. Unlike the more fictionalized psychological or philosophical narratives of his later novels, The House of the Dead is grounded in direct personal observation, lived experience, and deep suffering. It is both a prison memoir and a theological testimony—one that offers a profound meditation on the resilience of the human soul, the complexities of human depravity and dignity, and the mysterious paths by which grace may reach even the darkest places.

Written under the guise of a fictional narrator, Aleksandr Petrovich Goryanchikov, a nobleman sentenced to ten years of hard labor for the murder of his wife, The House of the Dead weaves together memoir, ethnography, and philosophical reflection in a collage of scenes from prison life. It presents no linear plot and offers no easy resolution. Instead, the novel immerses the reader in the harsh, soul-flattening routines of life in a Siberian prison, punctuated by small moments of extraordinary humanity—glimpses of laughter, kindness, and endurance amidst cruelty, despair, and spiritual numbness.

The setting itself is integral to the novel's meaning. Dostoevsky's Siberian penal colony is not simply a place of confinement—it is a moral and existential crucible. The men he encounters there are not abstract symbols or caricatures of vice. They are flesh-and-blood human beings, both brutal and beautiful, capable of savagery one moment and tenderness the next. In presenting these characters, Dostoevsky neither idealizes nor condemns them. Rather, he observes, with searing honesty, the contradictions of the human heart.

What makes The House of the Dead so powerful is its moral vision. It is not a story of political victimhood or of protest against the cruelty of the state (though that cruelty is unflinchingly depicted). Instead, it is a story about how suffering can strip a person down to their barest essence—and how even in that state, redemption is still possible. For Dostoevsky, prison was not just a punishment—it was a purgatory. And like all true purgatories, it was a place of transformation. He entered as a man of theories. He emerged as a man of faith.

This modern translation aims to bring Dostoevsky's early masterwork into clear, accessible language without sacrificing the intensity, nuance, or spiritual gravity of the original. The hope is that readers today—whether new to Dostoevsky or seasoned admirers— can encounter this text not simply as historical testimony, but as a living voice: one that speaks urgently and compassionately to the ongoing questions of evil, justice, compassion, and hope.

While the conditions of 19th-century Siberian prisons may seem distant, the human dynamics Dostoevsky reveals remain deeply familiar. We still struggle to understand the roots of violence. We still wrestle with the tension between punishment and forgiveness. We still debate whether people can truly change—and what it takes to awaken a soul hardened by guilt or despair. In this sense, The House of the Dead is not a relic of the past. It is a mirror, held up to our own world and our own hearts.

Witnessing Humanity in Chains: Characters, Contradictions, and Moral Survival

What makes The House of the Dead so unique among prison narratives is its refusal to either romanticize or dehumanize its subjects. Dostoevsky understood the temptation to categorize prisoners as "monsters" or "victims." But he also understood that human beings defy such simplistic classifications. In the prison yard, he found men who had committed unspeakable acts—and yet who retained, however buried, traces of innocence, kindness, and spiritual longing.

The narrator, Goryanchikov, is an outsider in nearly every way. As a nobleman, he is immediately set apart from the peasant-majority inmate population. His education, social class, and initial arrogance make him a target of suspicion and isolation. But over time, his assumptions are challenged and broken. The men he expected to hate or fear become, gradually, individuals with names, histories, quirks, and contradictions. He learns that beneath every hardened exterior is a human soul—wounded, yes, and often distorted by suffering, but not beyond redemption.

We meet a wide range of prisoners: cruel murderers, jovial thieves, petty criminals, and quiet saints. There is Shapkin, the cheerful storyteller; Akim Akimych, the absurdly fastidious and rule-bound inmate; the terrifying yet strangely childlike Aley; the haughty and philosophical convicts who debate theology and ethics; and the tormented ones who barely speak but whose eyes betray a hidden sorrow. Each character is a study in paradox—reminding the reader that evil and goodness often live side by side in the same person.

Dostoevsky's observations are intensely psychological. He explores how prison life reduces men to animals through routine, deprivation, and humiliation. Yet he also shows how moments of freedom—an unexpected act of kindness, the beauty of a Christmas performance, the warmth of a memory—can briefly lift a soul above the mud. The body may be in chains, but the spirit sometimes escapes.

The theme of degradation runs through every page. Convicts are stripped of their names, referred to by numbers, subjected to violent floggings, forced into backbreaking labor. The guards are often brutal, the hierarchy rigid, and the environment bleak. But Dostoevsky does not present these horrors in order to elicit easy outrage. Rather, he invites us to see how even in such conditions, the spark of humanity can endure. The power of the novel lies in its moral balance: it neither excuses cruelty nor despairs over it. It observes, records, and slowly builds a case for compassion—not as sentimentality, but as realism.

The narrator himself undergoes a transformation. His early detachment gives way to involvement. He begins to understand the men not as "types," but as brothers. He becomes less concerned with escaping his fate than with understanding it. Through this moral awakening, Dostoevsky dramatizes his own spiritual journey—the shift from intellectual pride to humility, from judgment to empathy, from theory to faith.

And yet, The House of the Dead does not end with a grand redemption. It ends in uncertainty. Some prisoners find peace. Others remain hardened. Some are released. Others die. Life goes on. The camp continues. And yet, in the midst of it all, Dostoevsky plants a seed of hope: that even the most broken soul can change, and that love is possible even in hell.

Suffering, Faith, and
the Seed of Dostoevsky's Later Vision

To fully appreciate The House of the Dead, it must be read not only as a standalone narrative, but as the foundation of Dostoevsky's mature moral and theological vision. In these pages, we find the embryonic themes that would later explode in full force in Crime and Punishment, The Idiot, The Brothers Karamazov, and Demons. Here we find the first iterations of Dostoevsky's conviction that suffering is the crucible of spiritual awakening, that true freedom is inner rather than outer, and that grace often comes not in triumph, but in defeat.

Suffering, for Dostoevsky, is not merely a punishment—it is a form of revelation. In the labor camp, stripped of privilege and autonomy, he encountered the mystery of human resilience. He saw how some men collapsed under pressure, while others discovered unexpected depths of endurance and compassion. He saw how faith could flicker in the most unlikely places, and how even the guilty might be more spiritually alive than those who judged them.

This insight became the bedrock of his future work. For Dostoevsky, redemption does not come through reform programs, enlightened governance, or philosophical ideologies. It comes through personal transformation—through facing one's own sin, through suffering, through confession, and through the rediscovery of love. In The House of the Dead, we begin to see this theology taking shape, raw and tentative but already compelling.

Equally important is Dostoevsky's critique of abstract moralism. In the prison, he finds that ideologies fail to account for the real complexity of human behavior. Men do not become evil because of systems. They become evil because of pride, pain, ignorance, and sometimes pure accident. And yet, the same men often harbor hidden nobility. Any attempt to reduce human beings to sociological types or to reform them through ideology alone is doomed to fail.

This is the ethical realism that underpins Dostoevsky's greatness. He sees the worst and best in people simultaneously. He believes in evil—but he also believes in grace. He knows that some wounds never heal. But he also knows that kindness, even a small act, can save a soul.

The House of the Dead may lack the dramatic plot and philosophical grandeur of Dostoevsky's later novels, but it has its own power: the power of witness. It is a record of what the author saw, felt, and endured. It is a document of spiritual rebirth. And for the reader, it is an invitation—not merely to learn about prison life in 19th-century Russia, but to reflect on the nature of freedom, dignity, and redemption in every age.

This modern translation preserves the grit, depth, and humanity of the original while making it fully readable for contemporary audiences. In a world still struggling with mass incarceration, systemic injustice, and the question of how to respond to wrongdoing, Dostoevsky's vision remains as urgent as ever.

The House of the Dead is not a novel of easy answers. It is a descent into darkness—but one that never loses sight of the light. It is a story of the worst that people can do—and of the best that they can still become. Above all, it is a testament to the enduring possibility of grace, even in a world where so much seems dead. It teaches us that beneath the chains, the ashes, and the shame, the soul still breathes. And it waits—perhaps forever—for the touch of compassion that might awaken it again.

Prison Life in Siberia

PART 1

Chapter 1
Ten Years A Convict

In the vast steppes, the mountains, and the dense forests of Siberia's remote regions, you occasionally come across small towns with a population of one or two thousand people. These towns are made entirely of wood and have an unremarkable appearance. Typically, they have two churches—one at the town's center and the other in the cemetery. In many ways, they resemble large villages near Moscow more than actual towns. Despite their size, these towns often have a full complement of officials, such as police-masters, assessors, and other minor authorities. The cold climate of Siberia is offset by the many perks of government service, making the region appealing to some.

The locals are simple folk with traditional ways and old-fashioned values that remain untouched by time. The officials in these towns, who are regarded as the local nobility, are either long-established Siberians or newcomers from Russia. Those from Russia often arrive straight from the major cities, drawn by the high salaries, extra travel allowances, and enticing opportunities for advancement. Those who manage to adapt to life here usually stay permanently, reaping rewards that make up for any hardships.

On the other hand, people who are restless or frivolous often struggle to adjust. They quickly grow bored and regret their decision to come. These individuals impatiently wait out their required three years of service, after which they request transfers and leave. Once gone,

9

they criticize Siberia and speak of it mockingly, though they are mistaken in their judgment. Siberia is a good place, not only for government service but also for many other reasons.

The climate is pleasant, the merchants are wealthy and hospitable, and there is a substantial population of Europeans who live comfortably. The young women are beautiful, with rosy complexions and impeccable morals. Wild game is so plentiful that it practically leaps into the hunter's sights. Champagne flows in abundance, and the caviar is plentiful and of outstanding quality. In short, Siberia is a land of opportunity for those who know how to take advantage of it, and many do just that.

In one such cheerful and self-satisfied town, which left me with a positive impression, I met an exile named Alexander Petrovitch Goriantchikoff. He was once a landowner in Russia but had been sentenced to second-class hard labor for murdering his wife. After serving his ten-year sentence, he quietly settled as a colonist in the small town of K——. Officially, he was registered in a nearby district, but he lived in K——, earning a living by teaching children. It is not unusual in Siberia to find exiles working as tutors. They are not looked down upon because they often teach essential skills, such as the French language, which would otherwise be nearly unknown in these remote areas.

I first saw Alexander Petrovitch at the home of an official, Ivan Ivanitch Gvosdikof, a kind and hospitable older man with five daughters. Alexander gave the girls lessons four times a week, charging thirty kopecks per lesson. His appearance intrigued me. He was very pale and thin, seemingly weak, though still relatively young—around thirty-five years old. He dressed neatly in European-style clothing. When spoken to, he would listen attentively and politely, as if considering a puzzle or secret hidden in the words. His responses were brief and carefully considered, leaving me uneasy without understanding why. Conversations with him were always strained and uncomfortable.

Curious, I asked Ivan Gvosdikof about him. He assured me that Alexander had impeccable morals, or he would never have entrusted him with his daughters' education. However, Alexander was known to be a recluse who avoided social interaction. People said he was very learned, spent much of his time reading, and rarely spoke freely. Some even thought he was mad, though this did not carry much stigma in the town. In fact, many respected him for his intelligence and believed he might have influential connections back in Russia. It was rumored that he had cut ties with his family after his exile.

Everyone in town knew his story—that he had killed his wife out of jealousy less than a year after their marriage and that he had turned himself in, which had lessened his punishment. People saw his crime as a tragedy deserving of pity rather than condemnation. Despite this, Alexander remained an outsider, only appearing in public to teach. At first, I paid him little attention, but gradually, I found myself drawn to him. There was something mysterious about him. Conversations with him were difficult; he answered all my questions politely but with such an air of finality that I hesitated to ask more. Yet, his enigmatic nature kept me intrigued.

After conversations like these, you could see signs of pain and exhaustion on his face. I remember one warm summer evening when we left Ivan Gvosdikof's house together. On a whim, I invited him to join me for a cigarette. The reaction on his face was startling. He looked frightened, became flustered, mumbled a few disjointed words, and then, after giving me an angry look, suddenly turned and fled in the opposite direction. I was left puzzled by his behavior, and later, when I saw him again, he seemed to look at me with a kind of dread. Despite this, I couldn't help but feel drawn to him.

A month later, I decided to visit Petrovitch without any real reason. Looking back, it was a foolish and inconsiderate thing to do. He lived on the far edge of town with an elderly woman whose daughter was ill with consumption. The daughter had a lively, charming little girl about ten years old.

When I entered, Petrovitch was sitting beside the child, teaching her to read. At the sight of me, he froze as if caught doing something wrong. He quickly stood up, visibly uneasy, and stared at me with a mix of fear and confusion. We both sat down, but he watched my every move as if expecting me to accuse him of some hidden wrongdoing. It was clear he distrusted me. He seemed to view me as some kind of spy, and I could almost hear him thinking, "Will you leave soon?"

I tried to make small talk about our little town and the latest news, but he either stayed silent or responded with a strained smile. It became clear that he had no interest in what was happening around him and knew little about it. Shifting the topic, I spoke of the country and its people, but his intense, uncomfortable gaze made me regret my words. At one point, I offered him some books and newspapers I had just received, but though he looked at them with longing, he refused, citing his lack of free time.

When I finally said goodbye and left, I felt a sense of relief, as if a weight had been lifted. I regretted intruding on a man who so clearly wanted to be left alone. However, the deed was done. I noticed during my visit that he had very few books, so the claim that he read extensively didn't seem true. Yet on two occasions when I passed his house at night, I saw a light in his window. What kept him up so late? Was he writing? If so, what could he possibly be writing?

I was away from town for three months. When I returned in winter, I learned that Petrovitch had died. He hadn't even summoned a doctor. By the time I got back, he was already forgotten, and his room sat empty. Hoping to learn more about him, I sought out his landlady. For twenty kopecks, she gave me a basket of papers he had left behind and admitted she had already used several sheets to light her fire. She was a gruff, withdrawn woman and offered little insight into her former tenant. She explained that he rarely worked, often going months without opening a book or touching a pen. Instead, he spent his nights pacing his room, deep in thought, sometimes talking aloud to himself.

She mentioned his affection for her granddaughter, Katia. He seemed particularly fond of her name and would always have a requiem said at church for someone's soul on St. Catherine's Day. He avoided visitors and only left his home to give lessons. Even his landlady, when she came to clean once a week, was met with a cold, distant demeanor. During the three years he lived there, they barely exchanged words.

When I asked Katia about him, she turned away, silent, and began to cry. It struck me that someone had loved this man. Taking the basket of papers, I spent the day sorting through them. Most were unimportant, just children's schoolwork. Eventually, I found a thicker packet filled with neat, delicate handwriting that abruptly stopped midway through. It seemed as though the writer had forgotten about it.

The packet contained a fragmented narrative of the ten years Alexander Petrovitch had spent in hard labor. The story was disjointed, interspersed with anecdotes and startling, grim memories that seemed to burst forth as if torn from him in moments of anguish. I read some of these fragments repeatedly, wondering if they had been written during fits of madness. Yet, his reflections on the prison, which he referred to as the "Dead-House," offered a glimpse into a world I had never imagined. The strange events he described, along with his unusual observations about the people he lived among, compelled me to read further. Perhaps I'm mistaken, but I feel these writings are worth sharing. I will publish parts of them and let the readers decide for themselves.

Chapter 2
The Dead-House

Our prison was located at the far end of the fortress, behind the earthen walls. Looking through the small gaps between the wooden stakes of the fence, all you could see was a tiny patch of sky and a high grassy mound that stretched out like the endless steppe. Day and night, sentries marched back and forth on top of it. From the very beginning, it was clear that for years on end, through those same small gaps, I would see nothing but that little piece of sky, the same grassy mound, and the same sentinels pacing back and forth. The sky wasn't directly above us but far, far away. Imagine a courtyard about two hundred feet long and one hundred and fifty feet wide, enclosed by a jagged hexagonal fence made of tall stakes driven deep into the ground. That was the outer boundary of the prison. On one side stood a large, solid gate that was always locked and constantly guarded by sentries. It only opened when the prisoners were sent out to work. Beyond that gate were light, freedom, and the world of free people. Beyond that barrier, one could imagine a magical realm, almost like a fairy tale. On our side of the fence, though, there was no such dream—only a place without resemblance to anything else. Here, everything was set, rigid, and unchanging. It was a house of living death. This is the place I want to describe.

Inside the fence, you could see a few buildings. On either side of the vast, barren yard stood two long wooden barracks, built from thick tree trunks and only one story high. These were the dormitories for the prisoners, who were divided into different groups. At the far end of the enclosure, there was a building that served as the kitchen, split into two sections. Behind that was another structure that functioned as a cellar, storage space, and barn all at once. The center of the yard, completely bare and desolate, was an open space where the prisoners lined up three times a day for roll call. They were counted and called by name every morning, noon, and evening, as well as several other times during the day if the guards were suspicious or overly meticulous. Between the buildings and the fence, there was enough room for prisoners who preferred solitude or were deeply reflective to walk when they weren't working. They would pace there, lost in thought, hidden from others' view.

When I passed them on these walks, I found it interesting to study their serious, weathered faces and try to guess their thoughts. One prisoner, in his spare moments away from grueling labor, had a peculiar habit of counting the fence stakes. There were exactly fifteen hundred of them, and he knew every single one. To him, each stake represented a day of imprisonment, and by counting them daily, he kept track of how many days he had left to serve. He felt a small bit of happiness every time he finished counting one side of the hexagonal fence, though he still faced many long years before he would be free. But in prison, one learns patience.

I remember one day when a prisoner who had served his sentence came to say goodbye to his fellow inmates. He had spent twenty years in hard labor. Some of the prisoners even recalled seeing him arrive—back when he was young, carefree, and not yet weighed down by thoughts of his crime or punishment. Now, he was an old man with gray hair and a sad, bitter expression. As he walked silently through the six barracks, he stopped at each one to pray before the icons, bow deeply to his former comrades, and ask them not to think badly of him.

I also remember one evening when a prisoner who had once been a prosperous Siberian farmer received unexpected news. Six years earlier, he had learned that his wife had remarried, a revelation that caused him great pain. That evening, she came to the prison and asked to see him, wanting to give him a gift. They spoke for only a couple of minutes, weeping together, before parting forever. I will never forget the look on his face when he returned to the barracks. In this place, one learns to endure anything.

When night fell, we had to return to the barracks, where we would be locked in until morning. It was always difficult for me to leave the open yard for the stifling barracks. Imagine a long, low room filled with the oppressive smell of unwashed bodies and poor ventilation, dimly lit by flickering tallow candles. I can't understand now how I managed to survive there for ten whole years. My bed was a simple structure made of three wooden planks. That was the only space in the room that I could call my own. In that single room, more than thirty men were crammed together.

The worst part was how long it took for the barracks to settle down at night. Four hours would pass before everyone fell asleep. Until then, the air was filled with noise—laughter, curses, the clanking of chains, thick smoke, and the overwhelming stink of our crowded, filthy lives. It was a chaotic mix of shaved heads, scarred faces, and ragged clothes.

Yes, humans are adaptable creatures—this might be the best way to define us. We can adjust to anything. In our prison, there were always around two hundred and fifty inmates. This number stayed more or less constant. When some prisoners finished their sentences, new ones arrived to take their place. A few also died while serving their time. The prisoners came from all parts of Russia, and there were even some foreigners and mountain people from the Caucasus.

The inmates were divided into groups based on the severity of their crimes and the length of their sentences. Most were civilian convicts sentenced to hard labor. These were men who had lost all their rights, rejected by society, and branded with irons to mark their disgrace. Their sentences ranged from eight to ten years, and after serving their time, they were sent to Siberian settlements as colonists.

The military convicts were different. They didn't lose their rights as civilians, unlike those in Russian disciplinary units. Their sentences were shorter, and after completing them, they returned to their units to serve in the Siberian battalions. Some of these military convicts returned later for more serious crimes. This time, they came back not

16

for a few years but for at least twenty, becoming part of the group known as the "lifers." These inmates were not deprived of their rights but were imprisoned indefinitely, tasked with the hardest labor.

There was also a special group made up of the most hardened criminals—nearly all repeat offenders. This group was essentially imprisoned for life, even if the length of their sentence wasn't specified. They were given double or triple workloads and kept in prison until extreme labor was required somewhere in Siberia. They often said to other prisoners, "You're only here for a set time. We're here for life."

I've heard that this special section was eventually abolished, and the civilian and military prisoners were later separated, with military convicts forming disciplinary units. The administration has also changed since then, so the customs I describe belong to an earlier time. It feels like a distant dream now. I still remember the evening I first arrived at the prison. It was December, and darkness was setting in. The convicts were returning from their work, and roll call was about to begin. A guard with a thick mustache opened the gate to this strange place, where I would spend so many years and experience so much. I couldn't have imagined what awaited me. For example, I could never have guessed how unbearable it would feel to never be alone, not even for a moment, for ten years. We worked under guard, slept in barracks with two hundred others—never a single moment of solitude.

Still, I had to get used to it. Among the prisoners, there were all kinds of people—accidental murderers, professional killers, petty thieves, and skilled pickpockets. Some could even steal things from a table in broad daylight. It was hard to say why or how some ended up here, but each had a story, often confusing and painful, like the haze of regret after a night of drinking.

Most of the inmates rarely spoke about their pasts. They didn't want to think about their former lives and tried to forget them altogether. Some of the murderers seemed carefree and cheerful, as if their conscience never bothered them. But others were quiet and gloomy, speaking little and keeping to themselves. It was uncommon for anyone to share their story, and even when someone did, their audience usually listened with indifference. Nothing anyone said could shock the others. "We've seen it all," they'd sometimes boast with a strange pride.

I remember one drunken convict once bragging about how he had lured a five-year-old child into a loft and then killed and dismembered the child. Usually, his stories made the barracks laugh, but this time the room fell silent, and the men shouted at him to stop. They didn't interrupt because they were outraged by his crime but because such things were considered unfit for discussion.

It's worth noting that many of the prisoners were surprisingly well-educated. At least half of them, if not more, could read and write. Where else in Russia could you find a group of two hundred and fifty men with such literacy? Some later argued that education corrupts people, but this is nonsense. Education doesn't lead to moral decay, though it does foster independence and determination, which can make life more complicated for those in authority.

Each group of inmates had its own uniform. One group wore vests that were half brown and half gray, with trousers that had one leg brown and the other gray. I recall a little girl selling scones once walking up to the convicts and laughing at their clothes. "They're so ugly!" she exclaimed. "They don't even have enough fabric to make a full outfit in one color!" The uniform consisted of gray vests with brown sleeves. Their heads were also shaved in strange patterns—sometimes with a stripe down the middle, other times shaved from ear to ear or from the forehead to the nape of the neck.

This peculiar community had a distinct appearance that made them recognizable at a glance.

Even the most commanding personalities, those who naturally stood out among the convicts, could not resist conforming to the general atmosphere of the prison.

With the exception of a few who showed childish cheerfulness—and who were universally despised because of it—most of the convicts were sullen, envious, terribly vain, arrogant, touchy, and overly formal. They believed the most important trait was to show no surprise at anything, and they aimed to carry themselves with dignity. However, even the calmest demeanor could disappear in an instant. Some prisoners, though seemingly humble to the point of servility, had true strength of character. Yet oddly, even they were often overly and irrationally vain. Vanity was the most noticeable trait in nearly everyone.

Most of the prisoners were deeply corrupt and twisted, creating an atmosphere of constant gossip and slander. Our daily life was like living in hell, an ongoing torment. Yet, no one dared challenge the prison's internal rules or traditions. Whether they liked it or not, they had to follow them. Even the most defiant individuals eventually gave in. Men who, when free, had committed shocking crimes—driven by their unchecked egos and acting as though in a frenzy—quickly realized in prison that they could impress no one. They soon fell in line, adopting the general attitude of the group and maintaining a sense of personal dignity, as if being a convict were an honorable title. There was no visible shame or regret, just an outward compliance that seemed calculated as the best way to behave. They seemed to think to themselves, "We're lost souls who failed to live freely; now we must follow the rules here."

Phrases like "If you won't obey your parents, you'll obey the whip" or "Those who refuse to sow must now break stones" were often repeated as if they were moral lessons or proverbs. But no one took them seriously; they were just empty words. None of the convicts admitted guilt for their crimes. If an outsider tried to criticize one of them, the response would be endless insults. Convicts were masters of verbal abuse, crafting their insults with an almost artistic precision. They didn't aim to offend with crude words but rather with cutting meanings and venomous undertones. Their constant quarrels only sharpened this skill.

Since they worked only under the threat of harsh punishment, many were lazy and degenerate. Even those who weren't already corrupted when they arrived quickly became so. Forced to live together against their will, they remained strangers to one another. "The devil must've worn out three pairs of shoes before he got us all together," they would joke. Intrigue, gossip, scandals, jealousy, and hatred dominated their interactions. In this idle environment, no ordinary malicious gossip could match the cruelty of these hardened criminals, whose sharp tongues were always ready.

Still, there were a few prisoners with strong, resolute characters. These men were respected, even though they didn't seek attention or pick fights without reason. They carried themselves with dignity, avoided unnecessary trouble, and followed the rules not out of principle or respect for authority but as if they had silently agreed with the administration on how to behave. This unspoken agreement benefited both sides.

The prison officials were careful in how they dealt with these men. I remember one such prisoner, known for his ferocious temper and wild instincts, being summoned for a whipping one summer day. The prisoners weren't working that day, and the adjutant—the direct overseer of the prison—was waiting in the orderly room by the main gate to oversee the punishment. This officer, a major, was a terrifying figure to the prisoners. His severity bordered on madness, and he ruled over them with an iron fist. His piercing gaze, which seemed to notice everything without effort, was especially feared. The convicts called him "the man with eight eyes." His harsh methods provoked anger among the already volatile inmates, and only the intervention of the more reasonable and well-mannered commandant prevented serious disasters. How the major managed to leave the service unscathed remains a mystery to me, though I know he was later court-martialed.

The prisoner turned pale when called but usually would submit without protest. He would lie down, endure the brutal whipping without a sound, then rise and shake it off, accepting his punishment with a kind of stoic calm. However, this time the man felt he was innocent. As he walked calmly toward the guards, he secretly slipped a shoemaker's awl into his sleeve. Sharp tools like this were strictly forbidden, and inspections to confiscate them were frequent and thorough. But it was nearly impossible to completely remove such items, as they were essential for certain tasks. If officials managed to seize them, prisoners would quickly acquire new ones.

When this incident happened, all the convicts rushed to the palisade, pressing themselves against it, their hearts pounding as they peered through the gaps. Everyone knew Petroff wouldn't submit to the flogging this time and believed it would be the end of the Major's tyranny. But just before the punishment began, the Major got into his carriage and left, delegating the task to a subordinate. "God has saved him!" the convicts muttered. Petroff endured the punishment without protest. Once the Major was gone, his anger seemed to subside. Prisoners usually obeyed up to a point, but there was always a line that couldn't be crossed. It was remarkable how these rare bursts of rebellion would emerge, often over something trivial. A man who had endured years of cruelty might suddenly snap over a minor slight. People often said such men were mad.

During all my years there, I never saw even a hint of repentance or guilt for the crimes committed. Most of the convicts seemed to dismiss concepts like honor or conscience, believing they had the right to live as they pleased. Vanity, bad influences, deception, and false pride played a large role in this. But who can say they truly understand the depths of such hearts, seemingly lost to darkness? One might expect to see at least a fleeting moment of regret or moral anguish during so many years, yet I saw none. To judge crime based on simple, ready-made ideas is impossible. The reality is far more complex. It's well known that prison or forced labor doesn't reform criminals. These systems exist merely to punish them and to reassure society. The strict routines and relentless labor only deepen their hatred, fuel their craving for forbidden pleasures, and intensify their resistance.

I'm equally skeptical of the so-called benefits of solitary confinement. While it may appear effective, it weakens a person's spirit, drains their energy, and reduces them to a hollow shell, which is then displayed as a reformed example. Such methods break the criminal's will rather than truly changing their heart. Many convicts see themselves as the victims, believing society wronged them rather than the other way around. Having served their punishment, they feel absolved in their own minds.

Of course, there are crimes that any rational person would agree are heinous and universally condemned. Yet in prison, I often heard the most horrific offenses recounted with laughter, as if they were casual anecdotes. I will never forget one particular prisoner—a former nobleman and government official—who had committed parricide. He had caused great sorrow to his father, a kind and patient man, who had tried in vain to guide his wayward son back to the right path. Deeply in debt and desperate for money, the son murdered his father, hoping to inherit his wealth. For a month, the crime went undiscovered. During that time, the man reported his father's disappearance to the authorities and carried on his lavish lifestyle. When the body was eventually found in a drain, the head had been severed and then placed back on the corpse mockingly, along with a cushion under it.

The murderer never confessed. Stripped of his noble status, he was sentenced to twenty years of hard labor. While in prison, he was careless and frivolous, though he wasn't entirely unintelligent. He lacked any sense of dignity, which made the other convicts despise him. Interestingly, his crime was never openly discussed, yet he sometimes casually mentioned his father. Once, while boasting about his family's strong health, he remarked, "My father, for instance, was never sick a day in his life—right up until he died." Such cold indifference was shocking and suggested something deeper than mere wickedness—perhaps a psychological or physical abnormality beyond current understanding. Though I doubted the truth of such a crime at first, the details shared by people from his town were too clear to dismiss. Even his own nightmares betrayed him; one night, he cried out in his sleep, "Hold him! Hold him! Cut off his head!"

Many of the convicts talked or shouted in their sleep, their dreams filled with curses, slang, and violent images of knives and axes. "We're broken," they would say. "That's why we scream in the night."

The hard labor in the fortress wasn't fulfilling work but a punishment that had to be endured. Prisoners worked the required hours and then returned to the barracks. For most, their so-called freedom brought no relief. Without some kind of personal occupation, their confinement would have been unbearable. Many of these men had lived extravagantly before prison and still dreamed of returning to that life. But being forcibly confined together, they were stripped of everything, including their dignity. Humans cannot live without meaningful work or a sense of ownership. When deprived of these, they become twisted, like wild animals. For this reason, nearly every convict took up a trade or hobby to pass the time and maintain some sense of purpose.

In summer, the long days were consumed by forced labor, leaving barely enough time to sleep. But winters were different. By regulation, the prisoners were locked in the barracks at dusk. With the long evenings stretching ahead, they turned to work. Despite rules against possessing tools, the convicts found ways to labor in secret, and the administration often looked the other way. Some men arrived without knowing any trade, but with the help of their fellow prisoners, they learned skills and became skilled craftsmen.

Among us were cobblers, bootmakers, tailors, masons, locksmiths, and gilders. There was even a Jew named Esau Boumstein who worked both as a jeweler and a moneylender. Everyone had a job and earned small amounts of money by taking orders from the town. For a man deprived of true freedom, money was a kind of tangible liberty that brought a small sense of consolation. Even if he couldn't spend it, just having it in his pocket made him feel better. However, money could always be spent, especially since forbidden things seemed even more tempting. Spirits were often available in the prison, despite strict rules. Smoking was also banned, yet everyone smoked. Money and tobacco kept the prisoners from falling into scurvy, just as work kept them from turning on one another. Without work, they might have destroyed each other like spiders trapped in a jar.

Both work and money, however, were technically forbidden. The authorities conducted strict searches, often at night, confiscating anything unauthorized. Even the most carefully hidden hoards were sometimes discovered. This was why money wasn't hoarded for long; it was usually exchanged quickly for alcohol, which explained how spirits made their way into the prison. Those caught hiding money or other items not only lost their stash but were also severely beaten.

Despite these searches, the prisoners always managed to replace their confiscated goods, and life returned to normal. The administration was aware of this. Although the situation in the prison resembled living at the foot of a volcano, the prisoners rarely protested against punishments for these minor infractions. Those without manual skills found other ways to trade and make deals. The economy inside the prison was surprisingly inventive. Items you'd never imagine having value were bought and sold. Even the smallest scraps of cloth had worth and could be bartered.

Money had an exaggerated value in this environment because of the extreme poverty. Long hours of difficult and often complex tasks might earn only a few kopecks. Some prisoners loaned money and charged high interest, creating a thriving business. Those who fell into debt pawned their meager belongings for a few coins, often at outrageous rates. If they failed to repay on time, the lenders would sell the pledged items without hesitation.

Usury thrived so much that prisoners even borrowed against government-issued items like uniforms and boots—things they needed daily. When this happened, the borrower often went straight to the supervising officer to report the hidden government property. The items were confiscated from the lender without any formalities. Surprisingly, this never caused disputes between the lender and the borrower. The usurer usually handed over the items with a resigned, almost expectant attitude, as though he understood he might have done the same in the borrower's position. If insults were exchanged, they were more a formality than genuine hostility.

Stealing was common and shameless. Each prisoner had a small box with a padlock for storing items issued by the administration, but these were often broken into. The prison was full of skilled thieves. Even a prisoner who was genuinely kind to me once stole my Bible—the only book allowed in the prison. He admitted it the same day, not out of remorse but because he pitied me when he saw me searching for it.

There were also prisoners who acted as "innkeepers," selling spirits and becoming relatively wealthy in the process. Smuggling, in particular, played a key role in bringing alcohol into the prison despite the strict surveillance. Many prisoners had been convicted for smuggling, so they knew how to evade detection. Smuggling was more than just a crime for these men; it was a calling. Like gamblers, they found excitement and purpose in the risk. Money wasn't always their main motivation. They enjoyed the challenge, the danger, and the thrill of outsmarting the system.

I recall one man who was unusually calm and gentle, never quarreling with anyone. He had been sent to the prison for smuggling along the Western Russian border. Despite his fear of punishment, he couldn't resist the urge to smuggle spirits into the prison. Although he made little profit, he kept returning to this dangerous trade, often being punished and swearing he'd never do it again. Yet after a month or so, he would inevitably give in to his passion. Thanks to men like him, spirits were always available.

Another source of support for the prisoners came from alms. The generosity of merchants, shopkeepers, and ordinary people was remarkable. They often gave small white loaves of bread or, less frequently, money. These donations made life more bearable, especially for those awaiting trial, who were poorly fed. The alms were always shared equally among the prisoners. When supplies were scarce, the loaves were divided into halves or even smaller portions to ensure everyone received something.

I remember receiving my first alms—a small coin—shortly after my arrival. One morning, as I returned from work under escort, I saw a widow and her young daughter. The mother had lost her husband, a soldier who had been sentenced by a court-martial and had died in the prison's infirmary. I had seen them once before when they came to say their tearful goodbyes. This time, the little girl whispered something to her mother, who stopped and took a coin from her basket. The girl ran up to me and said, "Here, poor man, take this in the name of Christ." She slipped the coin into my hand and returned to her mother, smiling. I kept that coin for a long time.

Chapter 3
First Impressions

During my first weeks in the prison, especially the earliest days, the experience left a deep mark on my mind. The later years, however, blended together into a hazy and jumbled memory. Some periods of that life have even vanished entirely from my recollection. What remains is a singular, overarching impression: one of constant pain, monotony, and suffocation. The memories of my first days there are still vivid, as though they happened only yesterday. This was inevitable. I distinctly recall being surprised at first by how ordinary everything seemed—nothing particularly shocking or extraordinary, nothing unexpected. It wasn't until I had spent some time in the convict prison that I began to realize how unusual and unpredictable this life truly was. That realization startled me, and I carried that sense of astonishment throughout my sentence. I never fully adjusted to the existence I was forced to lead.

Initially, upon my arrival, I felt an overwhelming sense of revulsion. Yet, strangely, the life itself seemed less unbearable than I had feared during my journey to the prison. Despite being encumbered by their iron chains, the prisoners moved about freely within the compound. They insulted each other, sang songs, worked, smoked pipes, and even drank spirits, though heavy drinking was rare. Nightly card games were a regular event. The work itself didn't seem too arduous at first, and I doubted it could truly be called "hard labor." It took me a long time to understand why the work was genuinely grueling and excessive. The difficulty lay not in the tasks themselves but in the fact that they were forced, mandatory, and performed under the constant threat of punishment. A free peasant works harder than a convict, especially in summer when they labor day and night. But a peasant works for his own benefit and toward reasonable goals, making his toil less burdensome. By contrast, the convict gains nothing from his work.

I once thought to myself that if someone wanted to destroy a man completely—if they sought to punish him in the most agonizing way and crush even the hardest criminal—it would require making his labor utterly meaningless. Imagine forcing someone to pour water back and forth between two vessels or to carry dirt from one spot to another only to immediately return it to its original place. I am convinced that after only a few days of such purposeless work, a prisoner would either take his own life or commit crimes so severe they would bring about his execution. Such punishment would be nothing but torture—an act of cruel vengeance without any corrective purpose. It would be absurd and inhuman.

When I arrived in December, it was the dead of winter, so the work in the fortress was relatively light. I had no concept of the grueling labor that awaited us in summer, which was five times as demanding. During the winter, the prisoners dismantled old government boats on the Irtitch River, worked in small workshops, cleared snow piled up against the buildings, or burned and crushed alabaster. Since the days were short, work ended early, and everyone returned to the barracks, where little remained to occupy them aside from small, personal tasks.

Only about a third of the prisoners worked diligently. The rest spent their time idling in the barracks, scheming, arguing, or insulting one another. Those who had a bit of money used it to buy spirits or gambled away their savings. This idleness, combined with boredom and a lack of purpose, drove many to these destructive pastimes.

In the prison, I came to understand one of the most unbearable forms of suffering: forced cohabitation. Living in close quarters is always difficult, but in prison, it becomes almost unbearable. Among the prisoners were men so vile that no one would willingly share a space with them. I am certain that every convict, even if unconsciously, felt the torment of this enforced proximity.

The food provided to the prisoners seemed acceptable to me. Some even claimed it was far better than the meals in other Russian prisons, though I couldn't confirm this, having never been imprisoned elsewhere. Those with money could supplement their diet as they pleased. Fresh meat was inexpensive, costing only three kopecks a pound, and wealthier prisoners often indulged in it. Most prisoners, however, made do with the standard rations.

When prisoners praised the food, they were usually referring to the bread, which was highly regarded. Bread was distributed collectively to each room rather than individually or by weight—a method that prevented constant hunger for at least a third of the convicts. The bread, renowned for its quality throughout the town, was baked in the prison's well-constructed ovens. The cabbage soup, thickened with flour, was less appealing. On workdays, it was thin and watery. What disgusted me most, though, was the manner in which it was served. Yet the other prisoners didn't seem to mind.

For the first three days after my arrival, I was exempt from work to recover from my journey. On the second day, I was taken out of the barracks to have my chains adjusted. Unlike my fellow prisoners, whose chains were made of four thick links fastened beneath their trousers, mine consisted of rings that produced a clear, distinctive clinking sound. My chains had to be worn over my clothes, which marked me out from the others.

I vividly remember my first morning in the prison. The sound of a drum echoed from the orderly room near the main entrance. Ten minutes later, the under officer came to unlock the barracks. One by one, the convicts woke and rose, shivering from the cold. By the dim light of a tallow candle, they stretched and yawned. Most of them were grumpy, their foreheads creased by marks from the irons. Some made the sign of the cross; others muttered nonsense. When the door opened, a blast of icy air rushed in. The prisoners hurried to the pails of water, taking a mouthful and spitting it into their hands to wash their faces. The water had been fetched the night before by a prisoner appointed to clean the barracks and perform other small tasks.

This prisoner, chosen by the convicts themselves, was exempt from regular work. He was responsible for inspecting the camp beds, cleaning the floors, and bringing water. The same water used for washing in the morning served as drinking water throughout the day. That morning, as the prisoners crowded around the pails, an argument broke out over one of the pitchers.

"What are you doing there with your marked forehead?" grumbled one of the prisoners, a tall, gaunt man with sallow skin. His head was

29

oddly shaped, with strange lumps that drew attention. He gave a shove to another convict, a short, round man with a cheerful, ruddy face.

"Just wait," replied the smaller man, bristling.

"What are you yelling about? You know there's a penalty if you hold up the others. Move along. Look at this monument, brothers!" The tall man sneered, gesturing toward the other. "A little calf, fattened up on the prison's white bread."

"And what do you think you are? A fine bird, huh?" shot back the smaller man.

"That's right," answered the tall one with a smirk.

"What kind of bird are you talking about?"

"You don't need me to spell it out."

"Why not?"

"Figure it out yourself."

Their eyes locked in a silent battle, each daring the other to take the next step. The smaller man clenched his fists, poised as if ready to lunge. I stood watching, curious about what would happen next. This was all new to me. I thought a fight might break out, but later I learned that these kinds of exchanges rarely ended in violence. They were more like a form of entertainment, a kind of verbal sparring that amused the others and broke up the monotony of prison life.

The tall prisoner stayed calm, his manner dignified. He knew the crowd expected him to say something, to prove he wasn't intimidated or humiliated. To preserve his standing, he had to show he was above his opponent, someone worth respecting. Slowly, he turned his head to cast a disdainful sideways glance at the smaller man. His gaze moved up and down, as though he were inspecting an insect, his expression oozing contempt. The short man grew more enraged by the second, and it looked as though he might leap at his adversary when suddenly a group of prisoners stepped in, forming a barrier between the two.

"Fight with your fists, not your mouths," someone called from the corner of the room.

"No, hold them back," said another voice. "Let's see them fight. We're real champions here, one against seven—that's our style!"

"Champions, are we?" a third voice jeered. "One of them's here for stealing a loaf of bread, and the other got whipped for nabbing a pot of curdled milk from an old woman."

"Enough, quiet down," barked a retired soldier. He was tasked with keeping order in the barracks and slept in a corner on a bedstead he'd been allowed to keep. Slowly, he sat up and began pulling on his greatcoat.

"Water, brothers, water for Nevalid Petrovitch! Water for our little brother who's just woken up," someone joked.

"Your brother? I'm no brother of yours!" muttered the old soldier. "Did we ever share a rouble's worth of spirits together?" He grumbled as he thrust his arms through the sleeves of his coat.

By now, it was time for roll call. The prisoners hurried toward the kitchen, putting on their coats as they went. They lined up, wearing their two-toned caps, to receive their bread from one of the cooks—prisoners who doubled as bakers. These cooks, like the others assigned to household tasks, were chosen by the inmates themselves. There were two cooks for the kitchen, four in total for the entire prison. They alone had access to the single kitchen knife allowed in the prison, used strictly for cutting bread and meat.

In the dining area, the prisoners clustered around tables wherever they could find space. They wore their caps and coats, cinched at the waist with leather belts, ready for the day's work. Some had kvas in front of them, dipping pieces of bread into the sour drink. The noise in the room was almost unbearable—a constant din of chatter, laughter, and movement. Yet, in the midst of the chaos, small groups gathered in corners, talking quietly and calmly, as if untouched by the surrounding clamor.

"Good morning and enjoy your meal, Father Antonitch," said a young prisoner as he sat beside an elderly man who had lost all his teeth.

"If you're not joking, then good morning to you," the old man replied without looking up, struggling to chew a piece of bread with his gum-filled mouth.

"I honestly thought you were dead, Antonitch."

"You go first, and I'll follow," came the dry response.

I sat down nearby, observing two other convicts to my right deep in conversation, both trying to appear dignified.

"I'm not really worried about being robbed," one said, "but I'm more afraid of stealing something myself."

"Rob me? That'd be a mistake. The devil himself couldn't stop me from getting even with anyone who tried," the other responded.

"But what could you do? You're just a convict, like the rest of us. We've got no standing here. You'll see, that woman will rob you blind, and she won't even bother to say 'thank you.' The money I gave her is as good as gone. Just imagine—she showed up here a few days ago! What was I supposed to do? Ask for permission to go live in Theodore the executioner's house? He's still got that place in the suburbs, the one he bought off Solomon—that crooked Jew who hanged himself recently."

"Yeah, I know the one. Solomon used to sell liquor here three years back. People called it the secret drinking shop."

"I know."

"No, you don't know. It was a completely different drinking shop."

"What are you talking about, a different shop? You've got no idea what you're saying. I can bring you as many witnesses as you want."

"Oh, you'll bring witnesses, will you? Who do you think you are? Do you even know who you're talking to?"

"Yeah, I do."

"I've beaten you up plenty of times, but I don't brag about it. So don't act so high and mighty."

"Beaten me? Nobody alive has ever beaten me, and the one who did is six feet under."

"Rotten dog of Bender!"

"May the Siberian plague eat you alive with sores!"

"May an axe split that thick skull of yours!"

The insults flew back and forth like a heavy downpour.

"Alright, they're about to fight," someone called out mockingly. "If you can't behave like decent men, at least keep quiet. Always so happy to come eat the government's bread, aren't they?"

The two were eventually separated before any blows could be exchanged. Verbal battles like these were common and mostly harmless. Trading insults was practically a pastime for the prisoners, a form of entertainment to fill their endless hours. Rarely did it escalate into actual violence, because serious fights risked the attention of the Major, who would launch an inquiry or personally intervene. That was a scenario everyone wanted to avoid, as it never ended well for anyone involved. So the men mostly limited themselves to these loud, dramatic arguments, which often ended as quickly as they began.

This behavior surprised me at first. I never would have guessed that people could find pleasure in trading insults, using them almost like a game. It wasn't just anger—it was also about pride. The men respected a skilled insulter, someone who could craft biting remarks like an artist.

Sometimes, the best at this were admired almost as much as actors on a stage.

Even during my first night, I noticed some of the prisoners eyeing me. Some hung around as though they suspected I had money, trying to win my favor by teaching me tricks, like how to carry my irons without too much discomfort. They even offered me—naturally, for a price—a small box with a lock to keep safe the items the administration had issued me and the few personal belongings I'd brought with me. But by the very next morning, those same prisoners had stolen the box, along with the money inside, and spent it on drink.

One of the thieves later became a good friend of mine, despite the fact that he continued to rob me whenever the opportunity arose. Oddly enough, he seemed genuinely sorry each time, as though he couldn't help himself. It felt like theft was second nature to him, a duty he was compelled to fulfill. I found it hard to hold a grudge against him.

These same convicts were quick to let me know that I could get tea if I wanted. They even found me a teapot to rent for a small fee and recommended a cook who, for thirty kopecks a month, would prepare meals for me if I decided to buy my own food and eat separately. Of course, they also borrowed money from me—three times on the very first day.

The noblemen who had been stripped of their titles and imprisoned alongside us were generally disliked by the other convicts. Even though they had lost all their rights and shared the same conditions, they were never fully accepted as equals.

This instinctive dislike wasn't entirely unfounded. To the common prisoners, we remained "gentlemen," even though they often mocked us for our fall from grace.

"Look at him," they'd say. "Once, his fancy carriage crushed the streets of Moscow. Now he's here picking hemp!"

They understood our struggles, even though we tried to hide them. The hardest times were when we worked together. Our physical strength simply didn't measure up to theirs, and we were more of a burden than a help. It's no easy task to earn the trust of ordinary people, especially ones as hardened as these.

Among the prisoners in the entire penal colony, only a handful were of noble birth. Among these were five Poles, whom I will discuss in more detail later. The Poles, especially the political prisoners among them, were even more disliked by the other convicts than the Russian nobles were. These Poles treated the common convicts with an aloof and disdainful politeness that barely concealed their disgust for the company they were forced to keep. The convicts were not slow to notice this attitude and retaliated in kind, treating the Poles with equal hostility and indifference.

It took me nearly two years to earn the goodwill of my fellow prisoners, but eventually, many of them grew attached to me and declared that I was a "decent fellow." There were, altogether, five Russian nobles in the prison, including myself. I had heard of one of them even before my arrival, a man widely regarded as despicable—a corrupt, vile creature who acted as an informer and spy. From the very first day, I made it clear I wanted nothing to do with him. Another nobleman was the parricide whose story I have already recounted in these memoirs. The third was Akimitch, an unforgettable and truly unique character.

Akimitch was tall, thin, and remarkably peculiar. He was not only weak-minded but also terribly ignorant. Despite this, he had a German-like attention to detail and a penchant for arguments. The convicts mocked him, yet they feared him for his easily offended, excitable, and quarrelsome nature. From the moment of his arrival, he asserted himself as an equal among the prisoners. He insulted them, fought with them, and, in his own way, maintained a strange sense of justice. Akimitch couldn't stand to see any injustice, no matter how trivial, and would insert himself into situations that didn't concern him. Yet he was painfully naïve. He would scold the convicts for being thieves and earnestly urge them to abandon their ways, as though such a change could be accomplished with a simple reprimand.

Akimitch had served as a sub-lieutenant in the Caucasus, and on the first day, he eagerly recounted to me the story of his downfall. He had started his military career as a cadet in a Line regiment, waiting patiently for his commission. Once he was finally promoted to sub-lieutenant, he was assigned to command a small fort in the mountains. A neighboring tributary prince had attacked the fort by setting it ablaze under the cover of night. Though the attack failed, Akimitch pretended not to know who was responsible and instead attributed the assault to insurgents roaming the area. A month later, he invited the prince to visit the fort under the guise of friendship. When the prince arrived unsuspectingly, Akimitch assembled his garrison and publicly accused the prince of treachery. After delivering a lengthy speech on the prince's duties and the shamefulness of his actions, Akimitch concluded his address by having the man shot on the spot.

Akimitch reported the incident to his superiors with all the details, but this act of vigilantism led to his court-martial. Though originally sentenced to death, his punishment was commuted to twelve years of hard labor in Siberia. Akimitch fully admitted that his actions had been illegal; he recognized that the prince should have been tried in a civil court. Yet he remained unapologetic, insisting, "He burned my fort. What else was I supposed to do? Thank him?"

The convicts often laughed at Akimitch, considering him somewhat mad, but they respected his skill and precision. He was remarkably talented, mastering numerous trades during his time in the prison. He could cobble shoes, craft boots, carve wood, paint furniture, and even work as a locksmith. He had a knack for observing an object and reproducing it perfectly. Through his skills, he managed to earn a modest income, selling baskets, lanterns, and toys in the nearby town.

With the money he earned, he bought small comforts like shirts and pillows and even made himself a mattress. Because he slept in the same barracks as I did, he was incredibly helpful to me during my early days in the prison.

Every morning, the convicts were assembled in two lines outside the barracks, surrounded by an armed escort with loaded muskets. An officer from the Engineers would arrive with the work supervisor to assign tasks for the day. I was sent with a group to the Engineers' workshop—a low brick building in a large courtyard cluttered with tools and materials. The workshop had separate areas for carpentry, locksmithing, painting, and forging. Akimitch worked in the painting section, where he mixed varnish, prepared paints, and skillfully painted furniture to look like expensive walnut wood.

During one of our early conversations, as I shared my first impressions of the prison, Akimitch listened thoughtfully and offered his own perspective.

"They don't like nobles here," he explained, "especially those of us convicted for political reasons. They take pleasure in provoking us, in trying to wound our pride. It's understandable, really. We're not one of them, and they know it. They've all been serfs or soldiers at some point. How could they possibly feel any sympathy for us?"

He continued, "Life here is hard, no doubt about it. But it's nothing compared to the disciplinary companies in Russia. Now, there, it's absolute hell. Men who've been through both call this place paradise in comparison. At least here, there's some order, even if it's grim. In Russia, they don't shave your head or make you wear uniforms like here. I actually prefer the shaved heads and uniforms—it's cleaner, more orderly. But some of these men hate it. What we've got here is a Babel of humanity: soldiers, Circassians, Old Believers, peasants who've abandoned their families, Jews, Gypsies—people from every corner of the empire, all crammed together to eat from the same pot and sleep on the same planks. No freedom, no privacy, no real

37

enjoyment unless you can steal a moment for yourself. And then there's always the looming reality of the prison itself, constantly hanging over us."

By then, I already knew most of what Akimitch described, but I was eager to learn about the Major, the officer who oversaw the prison. Akimitch didn't hold back in sharing his thoughts, and the picture he painted was anything but reassuring.

The Major was a spiteful, erratic man with almost unchecked power over two hundred prisoners. He viewed us all as his personal enemies, which made him especially dangerous. His temperament, coupled with his authority, created an atmosphere of fear and resentment. He was known to storm into the barracks at all hours, waking prisoners if they were not sleeping in the positions he had dictated. If someone was caught sleeping on their back or their left side, the Major would shout, "You'll sleep as I ordered!"

The convicts feared and despised him in equal measure. His flushed, angry face and piercing eyes made him a figure of dread. Everyone knew he doted on his dog, "Treasure," to an absurd degree. When the dog fell ill, the Major nearly lost his mind. At the suggestion of his servant, Fedka, he summoned a convict with veterinary skills to treat the animal. The convict, a clever Siberian peasant, later recounted the tale to his fellow prisoners with a mix of humor and disbelief.

"Treasure," the dog, lay stretched out on a cushioned sofa, his head resting delicately on a white pillow. It was clear to me at a glance that he was suffering from inflammation and needed to be bled. While I believed I could have treated him, I hesitated. What if the dog died under my care? The blame would surely fall on me. So I told the Major, "Your Excellency, I regret to inform you that you called me too late. Had I seen your dog yesterday or even the day before, I might have saved him. But now, there's nothing more to be done. He will not survive." And as predicted, "Treasure" passed away.

One day, I heard of a convict who had attempted to kill the Major. This particular prisoner had been known for years for his quiet submission and peculiar behavior. Some even believed he was insane. He had some education and spent his nights reading the Bible. Long after everyone else was asleep, he would climb onto the stove, light a small church candle, and sit reading the Gospels. He followed this routine for an entire year.

Then, out of the blue, he refused to go to work. His defiance was reported to the Major, who stormed into the barracks in a rage. But as soon as the Major entered, the convict hurled a brick he had hidden in preparation for this moment. The brick missed its mark. The convict was immediately seized, tried, and flogged. Within moments, he was carried off to the hospital, where he died three days later. In his final hours, he declared he harbored no hatred for anyone but had wanted to suffer. He wasn't affiliated with any fanatical sect, yet when his name was mentioned in the barracks afterward, it was always with respect.

Not long after this incident, I was finally fitted with the new irons. As they were being soldered on in the forge, several young women selling small white loaves began to wander in one by one. Most of them were young girls bringing bread their mothers had baked, though older women sometimes came too. Each loaf cost two kopecks, and nearly all the prisoners bought them.

Among the convicts was a carpenter, a man already graying but with a cheerful, ruddy complexion. He had tied a bright red handkerchief around his neck before the women arrived, clearly preparing for their visit. A heavyset woman with a face pockmarked from smallpox approached his workstation and placed her basket of rolls on his table. They began to chat casually.

"Why didn't you come yesterday?" the carpenter asked her with a confident smile.

"I did come," she replied boldly, "but you were gone."

"Well, they had us leave early. Otherwise, we would have met. The day before yesterday, all of them came to see me."

"Who's 'all of them'?" she asked.

"Mariashka, Khavroshka, Tchekunda, Dougrochva," he rattled off playfully, adding, "you know, the one we call 'the woman of four kopecks.'"

The exchange intrigued me, and I turned to Akimitch. "Could it be that—?"

"Yes," he answered, lowering his gaze modestly, for he was a man of strict propriety.

Indeed, such encounters did occur, though rarely and under nearly impossible circumstances. The convicts preferred to spend their money on alcohol rather than on romantic pursuits. Meeting women required an extraordinary effort: arranging a time and place, finding a secluded spot, and most challenging of all, avoiding the ever-watchful escorts. These obstacles, combined with the exorbitant costs involved, made such liaisons exceedingly rare. Still, I occasionally witnessed scenes of affection, though they were far from the romantic ideals one might imagine.

One day, while three of us were heating a brick kiln near the banks of the Irtish River, two women approached. The soldiers escorting us were lenient and paid them no mind.

"Where have you been hiding so long?" a convict called out to one of the women, clearly someone he had been expecting. "Were you caught up at the Zvierkoffs' place?"

"The Zvierkoffs?" she retorted with a dismissive laugh. "I'd sooner believe chickens have teeth than go there."

This woman, known as Tchekunda, was filthy beyond description, and her companion, the infamous "four kopecks," was even worse. Despite their appearances, the convicts treated them with surprising warmth.

"It's been a while since we've seen you," one of the men teased "four kopecks." "You look like you've lost weight."

"Maybe I have," she replied with a smirk. "I used to be plump and pretty. Now I look like I've swallowed a basket of eels."

"And you still chase after the soldiers, don't you?" he continued.

"People spread lies," she shot back. "But even if I were flogged to death, I'd still like soldiers."

"Forget the soldiers," the convict said with a grin. "We're the ones you should love. We've got money."

The absurdity of the situation was striking. Here was a convict, shackled and shaved, dressed in the two-tone prison uniform, flirting with a woman while under the watchful eye of his armed escort.

When my irons were finally secured, I bid farewell to Akimitch and returned to the barracks with a soldier escorting me. Those who did task work always returned earlier, so by the time I arrived, many convicts were already inside.

The kitchen wasn't large enough to accommodate everyone at once, so the first arrivals ate first. The cooks, elected by the prisoners, served cabbage soup and, on occasion, fried fish. I tried the soup but found it unpalatable, so I made myself some tea instead and sat at one end of the table with another convict of noble birth. Around us, the prisoners milled about, some eating quietly while others conversed in small groups.

At one table, a group of five convicts appeared to be celebrating. The cook served them soup and fried fish, and they looked at us with unusual friendliness. A tall convict entered and greeted them boisterously.

"Well, my friends from Kursk, enjoying yourselves?" he exclaimed with a grin, seating himself among them.

"We're not from Kursk," one of them replied flatly.

"Then, my friends from Tambov, perhaps?" he suggested with a grin, looking around the table.

"We're not from Tambov either," one of the men replied curtly. "Why don't you go find yourself some rich peasant if you're looking for a feast?"

"If only I could," he replied, feigning despair. "Maria Ikotishna's hiccups are eating away at my insides—otherwise, I'd be starving. But where is this rich peasant of yours?"

"Try Gazin," another convict suggested with a laugh. "Go find him."

"Gazin? Oh, he's been drinking up his fortune today. Devouring every last kopeck," the man responded with mock exasperation.

"He must have at least twenty rubles stashed away," added another convict. "Running a drinking shop is profitable, you know."

"Fine, then. If none of you will share with me, I'll have to stick to the government rations."

"Why not ask these noblemen for tea instead?" someone joked, nodding toward my direction.

"Noblemen?" a convict sitting in the shadows said in a low, somber voice. "Where do you see noblemen? They're no better than us anymore."

"I wouldn't mind some tea," said the man with the heavy lower lip, now smiling good-naturedly at me. "But I've got my pride. I wouldn't dare ask."

"I'll share some with you if you'd like," I said, motioning toward my teapot. "Would you care for some?"

42

"Would I care for some?" he echoed, his eyes lighting up as he approached the table. "Who wouldn't want tea?"

"Funny," muttered the convict with the somber tone, his gaze fixed on me. "Back when he was free, he lived on cabbage soup and black bread. Now, in prison, he needs tea like a gentleman."

"Doesn't anyone here drink tea?" I asked him directly, but he ignored me, refusing to answer.

Just then, a young prisoner entered the kitchen, carrying a net filled with white rolls. "White rolls! Fresh, hot rolls! Who'll buy?" he shouted, his voice ringing out above the din. For every ten rolls he sold, the baker rewarded him with one, which he saved for his own meal.

"I'd eat them all myself if I didn't need the money," he declared dramatically. Then, as he scanned the room, he added with a grin, "Come on, lads! Only one left for anyone who's ever had a mother!"

The absurd appeal made everyone laugh, and soon several rolls were bought.

"Well," the young man said as he pocketed his earnings, "Gazin's been drinking up a storm again. It's practically a sin, the way he carries on. And at a time like this! If the man with eight eyes shows up, we'll have to hide him."

"How drunk is he?" someone asked.

"Drunk enough to be dangerous," the boy replied. "He's completely unmanageable when he's like this."

"Will there be a fight?"

"There always is," the boy shrugged before moving on with his rolls.

Curious, I turned to my Polish neighbor and asked, "Who is this Gazin they're talking about?"

"He's one of the prisoners," the Pole explained. "He sells spirits on the side. Whenever he's made a little money, he drinks it all away. When he's sober, he's quiet and harmless, but once he's drunk, his true nature comes out. He becomes cruel and malicious, often attacking others with a knife until they wrestle it away from him."

"How do they manage that?"

"Ten men will tackle him at once," the Pole said calmly. "They beat him mercilessly until he's unconscious, then they lay him on his plank bed and cover him with a pelisse."

"But doesn't that risk killing him?"

"Anyone else would die from it," the Pole admitted. "But not Gazin. He's built like a bull. The next day, he'll get up as if nothing happened."

I paused for a moment, then asked, "Why do they seem to hoard their food but envy me for drinking tea?"

"It's not about the tea," the Pole replied, his voice dropping slightly. "It's envy, plain and simple. You're a gentleman, and no matter how hard you try to blend in, they see you as different—better. They'll look for any reason to provoke you, to bring you down. It's a kind of torment we nobles endure here. Life in this place is hard for everyone, but for men like us, it's twice as painful. You'll be judged for the smallest things—your food, your tea, anything that sets you apart. They think you have no right to those comforts, even though many of them enjoy the same privileges."

After a pause, he stood up and left the table, leaving me alone with my thoughts. His warning lingered in my mind. Already, I could feel the truth of his words settling in.

Chapter 4
First Impressions (Continued)

Hardly had M. —cki, the Pole with whom I had been speaking, left the room when Gazin, staggering and completely drunk, stumbled into the kitchen. He collapsed in a heap, oblivious to the time of day or the presence of others.

The sight of a convict so intoxicated during work hours, in a place constantly under the vigilant eye of the Major, astonished me. The Major was known for his severity, and his surprise visits could happen at any moment. Moreover, the under officer was always present, the old soldiers kept a watchful gaze, and the sentinels were ever alert. It baffled me how Gazin could be so brazen in such a tightly controlled environment. This scene challenged everything I thought I understood about life in the prison, and it took me a long time to make sense of such occurrences.

I had already observed that money held a peculiar power over the convicts. For them, earning even a few kopecks brought a sense of comfort and purpose, almost as if it served as a surrogate for the freedom they had lost. To have coins jingling in one's pocket seemed to provide a form of consolation, a feeling that life still offered some tangible reward. On the other hand, being without money cast a shadow over their spirits. Penniless convicts grew restless and despondent, and many were driven to commit reckless acts just to acquire some coins.

Yet, for all its significance, money rarely stayed in their possession for long. Confiscation by the Major during surprise inspections was common, and theft among the prisoners was rampant. The Major, upon discovering any hidden funds, would take them without hesitation. Though it was rumored that the confiscated money went toward improving prison meals, most of us doubted this claim. More often than not, convicts resorted to hiding their savings with someone they trusted, to avoid losing everything to either the Major or their fellow prisoners.

An elderly convict, known simply as "Grandfather," had become the unofficial treasurer for many of the prisoners. He was an "old believer" from Starodub, a thin, gray-haired man who carried himself with an air of tranquility that set him apart. His calm, kind demeanor intrigued me from the moment I first met him. His clear, gentle eyes seemed to radiate a quiet wisdom, and his serene smile hinted at a deep, unshakable inner strength. I often sought him out for conversation and found in him a rare combination of warmth and intelligence.

Grandfather's crime, however, seemed at odds with his character. Years ago, he had been a prosperous shopkeeper with a family he dearly loved. When the government attempted to convert the "old believers" in his town to Orthodox Christianity, he and several others rebelled. In their fervor, they set fire to the newly constructed Orthodox church. For this act, he was sentenced to hard labor and exile. He accepted his punishment with a stoic dignity, convinced that he was suffering for his faith. Though he never denied the crime, he spoke of it without hatred, as if it were a necessary sacrifice.

I often wondered how such a gentle soul could have committed such a destructive act. When I asked him about his beliefs, he never tried to argue or convert me. Unlike other "old believers," who were often argumentative and proud, Grandfather remained humble and avoided controversy. He had a lightness about him, an ability to laugh with a kind of purity that was unlike the coarse, cynical laughter of the other prisoners. His laugh was soft, clear, and almost childlike, a sound that resonated deeply with me. I came to believe that a man's laugh could reveal his true nature, and Grandfather's laughter confirmed his goodness.

The respect Grandfather commanded among the convicts was

universal, yet he carried it without arrogance. They called him "Grandfather," and he accepted the nickname without offense. His gentle influence on his co-religionists was undeniable, and even the most hardened among us seemed softened by his presence.

Despite his outward calm, it was clear that Grandfather carried a deep sadness. One night, as I lay awake in the barracks, I heard a faint, stifled sobbing. Looking around, I saw him sitting on the stove, the same spot where the devout convict who had tried to kill the Major once prayed. He was hunched over his manuscript prayer book, quietly reading and weeping. Between sobs, I heard him whisper, "Lord, do not forsake me. Master, give me strength. My poor little children, my dear little children, we shall never see one another again."

The sight and sound of his sorrow moved me in a way I cannot fully describe. In that moment, I saw not just a convict or a rebel, but a father mourning his separation from those he loved most. His pain was profound, and it lingered in my thoughts long after that night.

We often entrusted our savings to the old man known as "Grandfather." Somehow, the belief spread throughout the barrack that he was immune to theft, as though protected by an unseen force. Everyone knew he had a secret hiding spot for the money, but no one could ever discover where it was. Eventually, he revealed the hiding place to a select few, including the Poles and myself. One of the stakes in the palisade had a branch that appeared to be part of it but could actually be removed. Behind this removable branch was a hollow space where he securely stashed the convicts' savings.

Now, returning to the thread of my narrative: why didn't convicts try harder to save their money? It wasn't just the risk of it being stolen or confiscated by the authorities—it was also because prison life was so stifling that the inmates craved freedom, even if only fleetingly. Their existence was so constrained, their identities so marginalized, that the thought of splurging on a moment of indulgence—a chance to escape mentally, if not physically—felt natural to them. Some convicts would pour themselves into grueling work just to earn enough for one day of reckless indulgence. They would spend all their money in a single spree, knowing full well they'd have to start from scratch the next day.

Clothing was another extravagance for some. They would save up to buy bright, flashy shirts, uniquely patterned trousers, or belts with decorative metal clasps. On holidays, these prison "dandies" would don their finest attire, strutting around their sections of the barracks as if they were on a grand promenade. Their pride in their appearance was almost childlike, a brief respite from the dehumanizing drudgery of prison life. Yet, their new clothes rarely lasted more than a day or two; by evening, many had sold or pawned them for a fraction of their worth to fund other indulgences.

Feasts were the pinnacle of these indulgent moments. They often coincided with religious holidays or the name day of a particularly merry convict. On such occasions, the celebrant would begin his day with a ritual: placing a wax taper before the holy image, offering a prayer, and then ordering a feast. He would stock up on meat, fish, and pastries, gorging himself like a king. However, it was rare for convicts to share these meals with others. The feast was almost always a solitary affair, but the reveler would ensure that his drunken state became a public performance. After consuming vodka, he would stumble about the barracks, boasting loudly to all who would listen.

Oddly enough, drunkenness was a mark of distinction in the convict prison. Among Russians, there is often a peculiar sympathy, even admiration, for those who are drunk. In the prison, this sentiment was amplified. A visibly intoxicated man became an object of envy and respect—a figure who had, if only briefly, transcended the oppressive confines of his reality.

Music often accompanied these revelries. One convict, a deserter from the army who owned a battered violin, became the unofficial court musician for these festivities. Despite his sour expression and obvious fatigue, he dutifully followed the drunken celebrants from barrack to barrack, playing the same repetitive tunes on demand. His reluctance was evident, but when chastised—"Play! Aren't you being paid?"—he would dig into his violin with renewed vigor, as if to drown out his own frustrations.

Despite the risks involved, the drunken convicts were rarely a source of genuine trouble. If the Major arrived unexpectedly, the intoxicated men were quickly hidden away by their comrades, an act of solidarity performed without expectation of reward. The guards, too, turned a blind eye, understanding that a drunk convict was easier to manage than one harboring suppressed rage. They knew that outright prohibition of vodka would lead to unrest, so they tacitly allowed the trade to continue.

But how was the vodka procured? This was a fascinating process, and it reflected the resourcefulness and audacity of the convicts. The drink-sellers, as they were called, were prisoners who decided to make their fortune by smuggling and selling vodka within the prison walls. It was a high-risk, high-reward endeavor. At first, the seller would personally bring small quantities of vodka into the prison, selling it at inflated prices. If successful, and if they avoided detection, they would accumulate enough capital to expand their operations. Soon, they could hire assistants—other convicts willing to take the risks on their behalf.

The smuggling process was elaborate. The vodka was purchased in the town, often by a willing accomplice—a soldier, a shopkeeper, or even a woman from the outskirts. These suppliers would deliver the liquor to a prearranged hiding spot near the convict's work site. However, it was an unspoken rule that the supplier would skim a bit of the vodka for themselves, replacing what they drank with water. The convict, knowing better than to protest, would take what was given and consider himself fortunate that the deal went through at all.

The smuggler then had to transport the vodka into the prison. They used creative methods to evade detection, such as storing the liquid in tightly sealed animal intestines, which they wrapped around their bodies. The real test came at the prison gate. The smuggler had to outwit the guard, often by timing their arrival to coincide with a distracted or inexperienced sentry. A small bribe—a coin slipped into the guard's hand—could ensure safe passage.

This intricate network of suppliers, smugglers, and sellers was a testament to the lengths people would go to reclaim a shred of control over their lives. For the convicts, vodka wasn't just a drink; it was a fleeting taste of freedom, a brief escape from the monotony and despair of their existence.

The corporal carefully examines each convict as they return to the barracks, feeling over their clothing and searching them thoroughly before opening the gate to let them through. The carrier of the vodka, hoping to avoid detection, counts on the corporal's potential reluctance to inspect him too thoroughly. Yet, if the corporal is particularly sharp or suspicious, he will do exactly the opposite— conducting an even more rigorous search. If the contraband vodka is discovered, the carrier's last chance of avoiding punishment is to discreetly slip a coin into the corporal's hand, a small bribe intended to smooth the way. Often, this maneuver works, allowing the vodka to safely reach the drink-seller waiting inside.

However, there are times when the smuggler's gamble fails. If the corporal is unwilling to look the other way or if the bribe is refused, the consequences are harsh. A report is immediately made to the Major, who sentences the unfortunate smuggler to a severe flogging. The vodka is confiscated, and the smuggler's plans end in ruin. Yet, despite the punishment, the smuggler does not betray the drink-seller who employed him. This is not due to any sense of honor or solidarity but simply because betrayal would bring no benefit. The smuggler would be flogged regardless, and while it might be some consolation to see the drink-seller share in the punishment, the smuggler knows he still needs this figure for future schemes.

Denunciation, on the other hand, was common in the convict prison and surprisingly accepted. Prisoners did not harbor the kind of hatred for spies and informers that one might expect. Instead, they often befriended them. If someone had tried to explain to the convicts the moral baseness of mutual denunciation, it would have been incomprehensible to most. One particular nobleman, a man I have mentioned before, was notorious for his cowardly and cruel nature. He formed a close alliance with Fedka, the body-servant of the Major. This man would relay every detail of life inside the prison to Fedka, who in turn shared it with the Major. Everyone in the barracks knew about this arrangement, yet no one showed open hostility toward the informant or even reproached him for his behavior.

Once the vodka successfully reached the prison without interception, the drink-seller would pay the smuggler and settle accounts. The vodka, already costly to procure, was further diluted with water—often up to fifty percent—to increase profits. Once the product was ready, the drink-seller simply had to wait for his customers to arrive.

Holidays were particularly profitable. Sometimes, even on an ordinary weekday, a convict who had been saving every kopeck for months would finally come forward to indulge in a long-awaited spree. These days were often dreamt of during grueling winter nights and helped sustain them through the hardest labor. Finally, the anticipated day would arrive. With money in his pocket—neither stolen nor confiscated—he would eagerly spend it all at once. The drink-seller would start by offering vodka that was relatively pure, only diluted twice, but as the bottle emptied, more water was added until the liquor was nearly unrecognizable. The convict, however, paid an exorbitant price for this heavily diluted vodka—five or six times the amount it would cost in a regular tavern.

As one might imagine, it took many glasses of this weakened

alcohol, and a considerable sum of money, for a convict to become truly drunk. Despite this, the convicts, having lost their tolerance for alcohol, were often intoxicated relatively quickly. Once drunk, the convict might pawn or sell his new clothes to buy more vodka. If he had nothing else to sell, he would even trade the government-issued clothing he was wearing. After spending everything down to his last rag, the convict would finally collapse and wake up the next morning with a splitting headache.

If he begged the drink-seller for credit to purchase one more drink, his request would be flatly denied. That same day, the convict would return to work, starting the cycle of labor and saving once again for another debauched spree. Meanwhile, the drink-seller, if he had accumulated a significant profit—perhaps a dozen rubles or more— would procure vodka for himself. Unlike the watered-down liquor he sold to others, this vodka was kept pure. Declaring an end to trade, he would feast, drink, and hire musicians to play for him, enjoying a festival of his own making that might last several days. When his stock of vodka was depleted, he would join other drink-sellers, spending his remaining money on their liquor until nothing was left.

Even with all the care and vigilance exercised by the convicts to protect their drinking escapades, it was inevitable that the Major or another officer would occasionally discover the misconduct. The drunken convict would be hauled to the orderly room, his remaining money confiscated, and a harsh punishment inflicted. Once flogged, he would return to the barracks like a chastened animal, only to eventually resume his role as a drink-seller, the cycle beginning anew.

Among the prisoners, there were occasional individuals who sought the company of women. For a steep price, these convicts, often aided by a bribed soldier, managed to slip out of the fortress under the pretense of work and make their way to a quiet house in the suburbs. There, a secret banquet would be held, with money spent lavishly on food, drink, and the companionship of women. Such escapades required meticulous planning and carried great risk, but they were rarely discovered. Most of the soldiers involved in these schemes were themselves on a path toward imprisonment and were eager to profit from their role in facilitating the escapes. Yet, these clandestine outings were rare, given their high cost. For most convicts, cheaper and less risky means of escape—both literal and emotional—had to suffice.

At the start of my time in the prison, there was a young convict who piqued my interest almost immediately. His name was Sirotkin, and there was something uniquely enigmatic about him that drew my attention. His appearance was striking, with features that were unusually regular and pleasant to look at. He was no older than twenty-three, yet he had already been condemned to the special section—a punishment reserved for the most dangerous military criminals, sentenced to hard labor for life. Despite this fearsome designation, Sirotkin's demeanor was anything but threatening. Quiet and mild-mannered, he rarely laughed or spoke, yet his presence had a subtle gravity that set him apart. His blue eyes, fair hair, and clear complexion gave him a childlike softness that even the harshness of his shaven head could not diminish.

Though he had no particular trade or skill, Sirotkin somehow managed to procure money from time to time. He was notoriously lazy and carried himself in a perpetually disheveled manner, but he would light up like a child with joy if someone gifted him a new garment, particularly a bright red shirt. He would eagerly show it off to anyone who would look, as if it were a prized possession. Sirotkin neither drank nor gambled, and he avoided conflicts with the other prisoners. He wandered through the barracks with a calm, aimless air, his hands tucked into his pockets, lost in his thoughts. What occupied his mind, I could never tell. When spoken to, he always answered politely, in a straightforward manner, but never engaged in the idle chatter that so many of the others indulged in. His behavior was puzzling, almost childlike—especially when he spent his money on simple treats like white rolls and gingerbread, savoring them as though he were a carefree boy of seven.

Sirotkin's habits and mannerisms were unlike anyone else's in the prison. He took no interest in maintaining his clothes or boots, and if his vest tore, he would leave it that way. While others busied themselves with work or schemes, he would often stand still, arms at his sides, watching the activity around him. He had no inclination to join in, and if someone teased him or made him the target of a joke—a frequent occurrence—he would simply turn away without a word. If the mockery was particularly harsh, he would blush and quietly withdraw, avoiding any confrontation.

I often wondered how someone like Sirotkin could have ended up in the special section, reserved for the most dangerous and hardened criminals. The answer came during a period when we were both in the hospital ward, lying on neighboring beds. For the first time, I was able to engage him in a deeper conversation. He spoke with surprising openness, recounting how he had been conscripted into the military, a traumatic event that had brought his mother to tears. He described the harshness of military life, the unyielding discipline, and the cruelty of his superiors.

"But why are you here, and in the special section of all places? Surely it's a mistake, Sirotkin," I pressed him.

He looked at me with his childlike, clear eyes and replied without hesitation, "It's true, Alexander Petrovitch. I was only with the battalion for a year before I was sent here. I killed my captain, Gregory Petrovitch."

This revelation stunned me. I had heard rumors but never believed them. "How could that happen? What drove you to such an act?" I asked.

"My life there was unbearable," he admitted. "I did everything right—I followed orders, worked hard, didn't drink or borrow from anyone—but nothing was ever good enough. Everyone was cruel to me for no reason. One night, while I was on guard duty, I reached my breaking point. The wind was howling, and it was pitch dark. I was so overcome with despair that I decided to end my life. Twice, I tried to shoot myself, but both times the musket misfired. I don't know why, but I gave up on the idea and continued my watch. Half an hour later, the captain approached. He barked at me angrily, and without thinking, I lunged at him with my bayonet. After that, they marched me forty-six versts to this place. And here I am."

Listening to his story, I felt a mix of disbelief and sympathy. It was hard to reconcile this soft-spoken, childlike man with the crime he had described. It seemed an injustice that such an act, however severe, had condemned him to the same fate as the most irredeemable criminals.

Sirotkin was, in many ways, an anomaly in the special section. His companions in that group, numbering fifteen, were a horrifying contrast to him. Many of them had gray hair, their faces marked with years of brutality and cruelty. Their appearances were grotesque and repulsive, reflecting the monstrous acts they had committed. Among them was Gazin, a figure so fearsome and disturbing that he inspired revulsion in everyone who crossed his path.

Gazin was a Tartar and possessed an intimidating physical presence. Though his tall, muscular frame was imposing, it was his enormous, misshapen head that left the strongest impression. His appearance was enough to conjure nightmares, and the stories surrounding him only deepened the horror. Some claimed he had been a soldier; others said he had escaped from Nertchinsk multiple times, only to be recaptured. Most chilling were the rumors that he had lured children to isolated places, terrorized them, and then killed them for his own twisted pleasure. These tales, though possibly exaggerated, seemed to fit with the eerie aura that surrounded him.

Despite his monstrous reputation, Gazin behaved well enough when he was sober. Yet, there was always a sense of unease about him, as though his darkness lay just beneath the surface, waiting for an opportunity to emerge. It was almost incomprehensible that someone as gentle as Sirotkin could ever have had any kind of connection with a creature like Gazin. Yet, in the strange, surreal world of the prison, even the most unlikely associations seemed to form.

He rarely spoke, and when he did, his words were measured and deliberate, as if he chose each one with care. He avoided disputes, not out of fear or timidity, but with an air of quiet contempt, as if his companions were beneath him. His movements were slow and calculated, his demeanor calm yet resolute, and his gaze, though intelligent, held a cruel, mocking quality. His smile was equally derisive, a sharp weapon he wielded to unsettle those around him. Among all the convicts who dealt in vodka, Gazin was the wealthiest. His illicit trade made him a figure of both resentment and warped admiration. Twice a year, however, his disciplined exterior gave way to a ferocious drunkenness that revealed the full extent of his brutality.

During these binges, his behavior followed a predictable pattern. At first, he would grow increasingly agitated, his sarcasm turning into venomous jabs aimed at the other prisoners. These barbs were not impulsive; they seemed carefully crafted in advance, each word sharpened to wound. As his intoxication deepened, he would lose control entirely, succumbing to fits of violent rage. Seizing a knife, he would lunge at anyone within reach, his towering strength and berserk fury making him a terrifying opponent. The other convicts, well aware of his unstoppable force, would scatter and shield themselves from his wrath.

When it became clear that his frenzy was beyond containment, a group of about a dozen men would intervene. They had devised a brutal but effective method to subdue him: a coordinated assault aimed at his stomach, ribs, and chest, with blows delivered so violently that any ordinary man would have died. But Gazin was no ordinary man. After being beaten into unconsciousness, he would be wrapped in his coat and left on his plank bed to recover. By morning, he would rise as though nothing had happened, silent and brooding, and return to his work. This cycle of self-destruction repeated itself for years. Everyone, including Gazin himself, knew exactly how his drunken episodes would end, yet he continued to drink, driven by some compulsion even he might not have understood.

As the years passed, Gazin's once-formidable strength began to wane. His towering presence diminished, and he became prone to frequent complaints about mysterious ailments. His visits to the infirmary grew more regular, and whispers circulated among the convicts that the mighty Gazin was finally wearing down. "He's giving in," they would murmur, their voices tinged with a mixture of relief and disbelief.

One incident in particular stands out in my memory. Gazin had stumbled into the kitchen, visibly drunk and trailed by the wiry convict who scraped tunes from a battered violin during the prison's rare festivities. The room fell silent as Gazin surveyed the other convicts with a malevolent gleam in his eye. When his gaze landed on our table, where I sat with a few companions, his lips twisted into a grotesque smile. Tottering slightly, he approached us, exuding a sense of menace.

"Where do you get the money for tea?" he sneered, his voice dripping with mockery. "Hard labor must be lucrative if you can afford such luxuries."

I exchanged a glance with my neighbor, silently agreeing that the best course of action was to remain silent. Engaging with him would only escalate the situation. But Gazin was not deterred by our lack of response.

"Answer me!" he demanded, his voice rising in pitch and anger. "Did you come here to drink tea? Is that what hard labor is for?" His sarcasm cut through the tense air, but we held our silence. Frustrated, he became visibly enraged. His face turned livid, and his hands trembled as he scanned the room for something to vent his fury on. His eyes landed on a heavy wooden box used to store bread. Empty at the time, it was large enough to cause serious harm if wielded as a weapon. Without hesitation, he hoisted the box above his head, his muscles bulging with the effort.

The other convicts watched without a word, their expressions a mixture of grim amusement and indifference. Not one voice rose in our defense. Their hatred for men of noble birth like myself outweighed any sense of solidarity. It was clear they found some satisfaction in our predicament. Just as it seemed Gazin would hurl the box at us, a convict burst into the kitchen, shouting, "Gazin, they've stolen your vodka!"

The announcement was like a lightning strike. Gazin froze, the box still poised above him. Then, with a guttural curse, he dropped it to the floor and bolted out of the kitchen. Relief swept over me, but the silence among the other convicts was telling. "God has saved them," someone muttered, repeating the phrase as though it were a chant.

I never discovered whether the theft of his vodka was real or simply a clever ruse to defuse the situation. Either way, it had worked.

Later that evening, as the barracks grew quiet and darkness settled in, I walked to the edge of the palisade, weighed down by a deep, unshakable sadness. Despite the many hardships I endured during my years in the convict prison, that evening stands out as one of the most miserable. The relentless cruelty of my surroundings and the oppressive atmosphere of the place seemed particularly unbearable. A single question haunted me, one that seemed impossible to answer: why was the punishment for crimes so unequal?

Two men might commit murder, yet their actions could be worlds apart. One might kill for a mere onion, a desperate act of robbery gone horribly wrong. Another might kill in defense of a loved one from abuse or dishonor. Yet both are sentenced to the same fate, treated as though their crimes were equal. How could such a system ever be just?

As I stood there in the cold, I realized that this question—like so many others—had no answer. The inequalities of punishment, the absurdities of human suffering, the paradoxes of life in the convict prison—they were as unsolvable as the riddles of existence itself. And so, when the drumbeat signaled the end of the day, I turned away from the palisade and walked back to the barracks, heavy with thoughts I could not escape.

Chapter 5

First Impressions (Continued)

We were once again confined within the oppressive walls of the barracks. The doors were locked with heavy padlocks, each distinct and securely fastened, sealing us in until morning. Inside, the sense of enclosure was suffocating, the dimly lit room filled with the hum of muted voices and the creak of the wooden structure.

The evening routine began with verification. A non-commissioned officer, accompanied by two soldiers, would inspect the barracks. On rare occasions, an officer might oversee this process, in which case the convicts were lined up in the courtyard under the watchful eyes of the guards. But typically, the soldiers performed the headcount within the barracks, often making errors. Their mistakes necessitated multiple recounts, forcing them to shuffle in and out of the room until the numbers matched their records. Only then were the doors bolted shut for the night. Each barrack housed about thirty prisoners, crammed together on narrow camp bedsteads. Personal space was a luxury we could only dream of.

As it was too early to sleep, many prisoners turned to various tasks. In the dim light, some busied themselves with repairs or crafting small items, their hands moving deftly over coarse materials. Conversations ebbed and flowed, punctuated by occasional bursts of laughter or muttered curses. Among us were two old soldiers, each with distinct roles. One, marked by his medal for good conduct, represented the prison administration within our barrack. Yet, despite his medal, he had a harsh demeanor, frequently barking at the convicts, who responded with a mix of sarcasm and jokes. His authority, while acknowledged, was met with a subtle resistance through humor.

The second soldier, more prudent and quiet, rarely involved himself with the others. He remained seated on his modest bedstead, often absorbed in mending his boots. His silence was a shield, and he performed his duties mechanically, avoiding unnecessary interactions. His presence was a stark contrast to the brash demeanor of the medal-wearing soldier, whose roughness seemed incongruous with his supposed good conduct.

That evening, a thought struck me, one that would prove to be true over time: those who dealt with convicts, whether soldiers, guards, or even officers, often viewed us through a distorted lens. They expected violence at the slightest provocation, imagining that at any moment, we might lash out with knives or fists. This exaggerated fear was palpable, and the prisoners, fully aware of it, carried themselves with an air of defiance. It was a curious dynamic, one where fear bred arrogance. Yet, beneath this veneer, I noticed that the convicts responded better to trust and respect than to suspicion and hostility.

Officials who showed courage and calmness in their interactions with us earned an unspoken respect. I had witnessed the surprise and admiration of prisoners when an official entered the barracks alone, without an escort. Such displays of confidence diffused tension and commanded a unique form of authority. Conversely, those who approached with fear or aggression only deepened the chasm between the guards and the convicts.

Despite the widespread fear of convicts, I saw little reason for such trepidation. Yes, many bore the hardened expressions of brigands, their faces scarred by life's cruelties. But appearances could be deceiving. Most were resigned to their fate, content to live quietly within the routine of the prison. The few who displayed arrogance or rebelliousness were often kept in check by the collective will of the other prisoners. The true danger, I realized, lay not with the sentenced convicts, who had made peace with their lot, but with those still awaiting judgment. These men, caught in the limbo of uncertainty, were unpredictable and capable of violence, not out of malice, but as a desperate means of altering their fate.

I recall one such case vividly—a former soldier named Dutoff, a man of bluster and cowardice. Unlike most soldiers, who bore their hardships with stoic endurance, Dutoff was a braggart and a rogue. His punishment had initially been a two-year sentence of hard labor, but like many who passed through the convict prison, he emerged from his sentence more corrupt than reformed. The term "return horse" was apt for men like him, as they invariably found their way back to the prison after brief stints of freedom, often for far longer sentences. Dutoff's freedom lasted only three weeks before he committed theft and mutiny, crimes that brought him back to the convict prison under far graver circumstances.

Faced with the prospect of a severe corporal punishment for his latest offenses, Dutoff's cowardice reached its peak. On the eve of his flogging, consumed by fear, he attacked the officer of the guard with a knife. His act was not one of rage or hatred but a desperate ploy to postpone the inevitable. He hoped that by committing a new crime, his punishment would be delayed. Yet even in this act of rebellion, his cowardice showed—he failed to harm the officer, his attack half-hearted and ineffectual.

The consequences were swift. Dutoff's assault added to his sentence, but it achieved his immediate goal of delaying the flogging. It was a futile rebellion, a small and temporary victory that only prolonged his suffering. In his fear and desperation, Dutoff exemplified the grim reality of life in the convict prison: a cycle of punishment and despair, where acts of defiance were often born not of strength, but of weakness.

As I lay on my narrow bed that night, these thoughts weighed heavily on me. The barracks were silent now, save for the occasional cough or the creak of wood as someone shifted in their sleep. Outside, the wind howled against the walls, a reminder of the world beyond these confines—a world that felt impossibly distant. In this place, fear and survival were intertwined, shaping the lives of guards and prisoners alike in ways that neither side fully understood.

The moments leading up to a punishment by the rods are unbearable for the condemned. I have seen many of these men on the eve of their suffering, often when I encountered them in the hospital during my own frequent illnesses. The hospital, in its peculiar way, became a sanctuary where their dread and anguish were laid bare. Among all those who interacted with prisoners, the doctors stood out as uniquely compassionate. Unlike others, they did not distinguish between prisoners based on their crimes. Their impartial kindness mirrored the attitude of the Russian common people, who, rather than reproaching a criminal, often referred to crime as a "misfortune" and the criminal as "an unfortunate." This instinctive, almost unconscious, empathy for those who had fallen afoul of the law added a rare depth to their humanity.

The convicts often turned to the doctors as a last refuge, especially before enduring corporal punishment. A prisoner sentenced by court-martial typically knew when his punishment would be carried out, though the exact timing could vary. Desperate to delay the inevitable, many sought to feign illness and be admitted to the hospital. Even if their health improved and they were discharged, the act of postponing their punishment offered a fleeting solace. However, the day they left the hospital marked the moment of reckoning. On that day, the air around them grew heavy with an unspoken tension. Some prisoners, driven by pride or bravado, attempted to mask their fear. They laughed, joked, or feigned indifference, but no one was deceived. The silent understanding of the terror that loomed ensured that their companions remained respectfully quiet, sparing them unnecessary words.

One convict in particular left a lasting impression on me. He was a young ex-soldier, condemned for murder and sentenced to receive the maximum number of lashes. On the eve of his flogging, he decided to drink a bottle of vodka, infused with an extraordinary quantity of snuff, in an attempt to dull his senses and lessen his suffering. This ritual of drinking before punishment was a common practice among convicts. The belief that intoxication could dull the pain of the whip was so deeply ingrained that they would go to great lengths to secure alcohol. A prisoner might save for months, depriving himself of necessities, just to afford half a pint of vodka. The desperation to escape even a fraction of the pain spoke volumes about the torment they anticipated.

The young man, however, miscalculated. Moments after consuming the mixture, he became violently ill, coughing up blood until he lost consciousness. He was rushed back to the hospital, but the damage was done. The vodka and snuff had irreparably harmed his lungs, leading to the onset of tuberculosis. Within a few months, he succumbed to the disease. The doctors who treated him were unaware of the true cause of his illness, and his tragic end passed quietly, another life extinguished by the brutal conditions of the convict prison.

While acts of desperation like his were not uncommon, there were also prisoners who displayed an astonishing degree of courage, even defiance, in the face of punishment. One such man, whose story remains vivid in my memory, was Orloff, a notorious bandit whose crimes had earned him a fearsome reputation. News of his impending punishment spread through the infirmary like wildfire one summer day. Whispers filled the air, recounting tales of his unspeakable deeds. It was said he had murdered old men and children with a chilling detachment. Despite—or perhaps because of—his horrifying past, a sense of grim fascination gripped us all. Even I could not suppress my curiosity about this man of extraordinary infamy, who seemed to embody both relentless willpower and cold-blooded brutality.

Orloff was sentenced to be flogged through the ranks, a particularly excruciating punishment reserved for the most heinous crimes. As the sun set, and darkness enveloped the infirmary, he was brought in—or rather, carried in. His body was limp, his face drained of all color. Thick black curls, dull and lifeless, framed his pale, sweat-soaked face. His back was a grotesque sight—raw and swollen, a patchwork of blue bruises and streaks of blood. He seemed barely alive, his breath shallow and labored.

That night, the other prisoners tended to him with a care that was startling in its tenderness. They prepared his poultices, changed them diligently, and positioned him gently on his side to ease his pain. They followed the doctor's instructions to the letter, mixing lotions and applying them to his wounded flesh. It was as if he were a revered elder or a cherished benefactor rather than a reviled criminal. Their actions were devoid of judgment, filled only with the shared understanding of suffering.

To everyone's astonishment, Orloff regained some strength the very next day. He managed to stand, even taking a few unsteady steps around the room. The transformation seemed almost miraculous, given the state in which he had been brought to us. We later learned that the doctor overseeing his punishment had intervened, halting the flogging halfway through. He was convinced that continuing would have killed Orloff outright.

Though Orloff had recovered enough to walk, his ordeal lingered in the minds of all who had witnessed it. The punishment, as brutal as it was, seemed both a grim necessity and a futile exercise—a testament to the cruelty embedded in the system. For Orloff, it was just another chapter in his life of violence and defiance. For the rest of us, it was a reminder of the thin line between survival and annihilation in the unforgiving world of the convict prison. This criminal, weakened by long years of confinement, was a fascinating study in human resilience. Those who have seen prisoners after they've endured flogging will remember their haggard faces, the gaunt lines of their features, and the feverish glow in their eyes—a look that speaks of suffering beyond words. Orloff was no exception at first, his body battered and drained. Yet, unlike many others, he soon summoned a seemingly limitless reserve of strength. His energy and willpower overshadowed his physical frailty, transforming him into a figure of unwavering resolve. He was not an ordinary man, and it was impossible to ignore his presence.

From the moment I encountered him, Orloff intrigued me. I made it a point to observe him closely, using my time in the infirmary to study his character. Over the course of a week, I learned more about him than I had ever expected. His was a personality forged in extremes—a man of implacable determination, driven by an unquenchable thirst for vengeance and an unshakable will. Never before had I encountered someone so firmly in command of himself, a figure of raw power and intensity.

Orloff's demeanor contrasted sharply with another infamous criminal I had once encountered at Tobolsk—a brigand leader named Kareneff. Kareneff was a brute in the most primal sense. His dull gaze and hulking figure exuded danger, yet it was his animalistic simplicity that struck terror into those around him. He was a creature entirely ruled by his basest instincts, caring for nothing beyond his immediate desires. Standing near him was like being in the presence of a predator, unpredictable and lethal. I was convinced that Kareneff, despite his fearsome reputation, would have crumbled under the kind of punishment Orloff endured. He lacked the mental fortitude to face such suffering without breaking or lashing out in blind rage.

Orloff, however, was different—he represented the triumph of mind over body, spirit over matter. He endured pain with a quiet dignity that defied comprehension, his every movement a testament to his inner strength. His pride was not the kind born of arrogance or vanity; it was intrinsic, woven into his very being. He carried himself with a calm authority, as though nothing in the world could unsettle him. He seemed utterly indifferent to the opinions of others, even as he commanded their respect. Though the prisoners admired him, he never sought to exploit their regard for personal gain.

Vanity and conceit, traits that plagued even the most hardened convicts, seemed to have no hold over Orloff. He spoke sparingly, but when he did, his words were marked by a startling frankness. He answered my questions directly, sometimes even with an air of amusement, as though indulging a child's curiosity. When I pressed him about his plans or attempted to detect a hint of remorse in him, he would meet my gaze with an expression of mild disdain, as though humoring someone far beneath his understanding. Yet, there was no malice in his disdain—only a quiet confidence in his own superiority.

One moment that remains vivid in my memory was when Orloff confided in me about his future. His recovery from the first half of his punishment was slow but steady, and he was already looking forward to completing the remainder of his sentence. "Once it's done," he said with a glint in his eye, "I'll be sent to Nertchinsk with the convoy. That's where I'll escape. I'll make it, without a doubt. If only my back would heal faster!" His impatience to move forward, even in the face of such daunting odds, was both unsettling and awe-inspiring.

Over the next few days, Orloff's moods fluctuated between restless energy and moments of unexpected humor. When he was in good spirits, I took the opportunity to ask him about his past exploits. He answered with candor, though his tone often carried a hint of amusement, as if he found my curiosity amusingly naive. He would laugh heartily at my questions, not with derision, but as if genuinely entertained by my attempts to understand him.

Eventually, he declared himself fit to leave the hospital, even though his back was still far from fully healed. We left together, returning to the prison, where he was immediately confined to the guardroom in preparation for his next punishment. Before parting, he shook my hand—a gesture that, in his eyes, was a mark of considerable respect. Yet I couldn't shake the feeling that, beneath his affable exterior, he viewed me with a certain disdain, seeing in me a weakness that he found contemptible.

The day following his release, Orloff faced the remainder of his punishment. By then, the barracks had reverted to their usual atmosphere of uneasy routine. Once the gates were locked and the padlocks secured, the barracks transformed. The prisoners, relieved of the looming threat of sudden inspections, settled into a semblance of domesticity. The air grew thick with the mingled smells of sweat, wax, and smoke as candles were lit, and the convicts busied themselves with various tasks. Some stitched boots or mended garments, while others gathered in corners for games of cards, their grimy hands shuffling well-worn decks.

The barracks came alive in these moments, resembling less a prison and more a strange, makeshift household. Yet beneath this veneer of normalcy lay the stark realities of their existence—gamblers betting their meager savings, workers laboring under the dim light of candles, and the ever-present tension of life behind locked doors. As I observed it all, I couldn't help but reflect on the stark contrast between the quiet, resolute strength of men like Orloff and the chaotic, restless energy of the barracks that housed them. Their stories, their struggles, and their resilience formed a mosaic of human endurance, a testament to the unyielding spirit of those confined within the prison walls.

But I must continue to describe the individuals with whom I was to share the coming years of my life—men who, for better or worse, would become my constant companions. They surrounded me day and night, and I could not help but study them with anxious curiosity, trying to decipher their characters and understand what fate had brought us together.

To my left slept a group of mountaineers from the Caucasus, most of them exiled for brigandage but serving various sentences. Among them were two Lesghians, a Circassian, and three Tartars from Daghestan. Each had a distinct personality. The Circassian was a brooding figure, perpetually silent and distant, with a sideways glare that gave him a sly, almost predatory air. His demeanor was cold and unapproachable, and his rare, fleeting expressions carried the wild intensity of a cornered animal.

One of the Lesghians, an older man with sharp features and a hooked nose, struck me as the epitome of a hardened brigand. He was tall, wiry, and his every movement carried a certain predatory grace. But it was the other Lesghian, named Nourra, who stood out and captured my attention. Nourra was unlike anyone else in the prison—a man of immense physical strength and an unshakable dignity. He was of medium height, powerfully built, with fair hair and striking violet eyes. His features had a slightly Finnish cast, and his body bore the scars of countless battles—bayonet wounds and bullet holes, remnants of a life lived on the edge.

Although Nourra came from a conquered part of the Caucasus, he had thrown his lot in with the rebels, joining them in their raids against Russian territories. Yet, despite his rebellious past, there was nothing bitter or malevolent about him. He was cheerful, affable, and universally liked by the other prisoners. His disdain for dishonesty, theft, drunkenness, or cheating was evident; he would not quarrel or confront others but would turn away in quiet indignation, his face betraying his disgust. In every way, Nourra embodied a sense of moral clarity that was rare among the prisoners. He adhered strictly to his faith, praying fervently each night and observing every fast with the dedication of a true believer.

The other convicts admired him deeply, calling him "Lion" for his strength and character. This nickname stuck, and Nourra seemed to wear it with pride. He clung to the hope that, once his sentence was served, he would be allowed to return to the Caucasus. That hope kept him alive, a light that shone in his otherwise harsh existence. The very first day I arrived, I noticed his calm and honest face amid the sea of grim, sardonic, and twisted expressions that surrounded us. It was impossible not to.

As if sensing my unease, Nourra approached me shortly after I arrived. He touched my shoulder gently and gave me a warm, innocent smile. At first, I didn't understand his gesture—he spoke Russian poorly—but he repeated this small act of kindness for three days in a row. Eventually, I realized he was trying to comfort me, to show me that he understood how painful and disorienting those first days in the prison could be. It was his way of offering sympathy and encouragement, assuring me of his goodwill. I could not help but feel a deep sense of gratitude for his kindness.

Next to Nourra were the three Tartars from Daghestan, all brothers. The two elder brothers were strong, serious men, while the youngest, Ali, slept beside me. Ali was only twenty-two but looked even younger, with a bright, intelligent face that radiated warmth and honesty. From the moment I saw him, I felt fortunate to have him as my neighbor instead of someone less agreeable. His open, childlike smile and large, expressive black eyes exuded friendliness and sincerity. There was something inherently uplifting about his presence, and simply watching him go about his day often eased my own sadness.

Ali's story was a tragic one. He had been drawn into a life of crime by his brothers, who, following the traditions of their people, had ordered him to join them in an armed raid on a wealthy Armenian merchant's caravan. Out of a sense of duty and respect for his elders, Ali obeyed without question, unaware of the full nature of their intentions. The raid ended in violence; the merchant was killed, and the brothers were caught. They were flogged and sentenced to hard labor, with Ali receiving the lightest punishment—four years in the prison. His brothers, hardened by their crimes, treated him with a kind of paternal affection that stood out against their usual cold demeanor. To them, he was not a co-conspirator but a child to be protected and cherished.

Despite the hardships of prison life, Ali retained his innocence and moral integrity. He was uncorrupted by the cynicism and depravity that surrounded him, an astonishing feat given the conditions. His sense of dignity and gentleness never wavered. Even when insulted or provoked, he remained composed, avoiding quarrels without ever appearing weak. His innate goodness seemed to shield him, making it impossible for anyone to harbor ill will against him.

Over time, Ali and I grew close. He was initially polite and reserved, but as we spent more evenings talking, he became more open and expressive. Within a few months, he had mastered Russian, a skill his brothers never managed to acquire. Ali's intelligence, combined with his modesty and sensitivity, made him an exceptional individual— someone who stood apart in every way from the grim reality of our surroundings. To this day, I count my friendship with him as one of the few bright spots in an otherwise dark period of my life.

One evening, long after I had settled into the rhythms of prison life, I noticed Ali lying on his cot, lost in thought. His brothers, typically silent and brooding, were unusually cheerful, celebrating a Muslim festival in their quiet way. Ali, however, seemed preoccupied.

"You look very sad," he said to me suddenly, his voice soft but full of concern.

His observation caught me off guard, coming as it did from someone usually so tactful and reserved. I looked at him closely and saw in his eyes a depth of sorrow I hadn't noticed before. It was clear that he, too, was struggling with memories and emotions he rarely shared. I mentioned this to him, and he sighed deeply, his face softening into a wistful, melancholic smile.

"You must be thinking about home," I said gently. "About how this festival would be celebrated in Daghestan. Life must have been so much better for you there."

His eyes lit up momentarily, and he replied with quiet enthusiasm, "Yes. How did you know?"

"How could I not?" I said. "Your homeland must have been beautiful—a true paradise compared to this place."

Ali's expression shifted, and he looked away, his voice trembling with emotion. "Please, don't speak of it."

His words were simple, but they carried the weight of an exile's longing, a pain so profound that even recalling his homeland was unbearable. It was a moment that deepened my understanding of Ali's inner world, and my respect for him grew even stronger. In his silence and resilience, he exemplified a quiet strength that few others possessed—a strength that, even now, I can only admire from afar.

Ali seemed unusually restless as he responded to my questions, his emotions barely concealed.

"Ali," I said, trying to draw him out further, "did you have a sister?"

"Yes," he replied cautiously, his voice softening. "But why do you ask?"

"I was just wondering," I continued. "If she looks anything like you, she must be very beautiful."

"Oh, no, there is no comparison," Ali said, his face lighting up for a moment with pride. "In all of Daghestan, there is no one as beautiful as she is. My sister is truly extraordinary, unmatched in grace. My mother, too, is very beautiful."

"And your mother? She must have loved you dearly?"

Ali's expression turned tender and reflective. "Of course. What are you saying? My mother adored me. I was her favorite child, even more so than my sister or my brothers. I know she loved me with all her heart. But she must have died of grief after I was taken away. She could not have borne my absence."

He hesitated, his eyes misting over. "Just last night, she appeared to me in a dream. She was weeping for me," he said, his voice barely audible.

After that, Ali fell silent, retreating into his thoughts. He didn't speak again for the rest of the night, but from that moment on, he sought my company with quiet determination. Though always respectful, he never initiated conversation himself. Yet whenever I spoke to him, his face brightened, and he eagerly engaged in our exchanges.

Ali often reminisced about his homeland, sharing vivid tales of life in Daghestan and the customs he missed. His brothers, who at first kept their distance from me, began to soften when they saw the bond growing between us. They even seemed to encourage Ali to spend time with me, perhaps appreciating the positive influence I had on him. Over time, their demeanor toward me became noticeably friendlier.

Ali's kindness was boundless. He was always eager to help with my tasks, whether in the barracks or at work. His attentiveness was never tainted by servility or self-interest; instead, it was a reflection of his pure and heartfelt goodwill. He found joy in easing my burdens and making life just a little less difficult for me.

One day, as we worked side by side, I turned to him with an idea. "Ali," I said, "why don't you learn to read and write in Russian? It could be very useful for you, especially here in Siberia."

Ali looked at me with wide eyes, his curiosity piqued. "I would like that very much," he said earnestly. "But who would teach me?"

"I'll teach you," I offered.

His face lit up, and he straightened in his seat, his hands clasped together in a gesture of earnest gratitude. "Oh, please, teach me," he said, his voice trembling with enthusiasm.

We began our lessons the very next evening, using the only book permitted in the prison—a Russian translation of the New Testament. Without even the aid of an alphabet, Ali showed remarkable dedication, and within weeks, he was reading fluently. His brothers watched his progress with awe, their pride and affection for him growing even deeper.

One evening, as we read together, Ali's voice took on a distinct tone of reverence. We were going through the Sermon on the Mount, and certain passages seemed to move him deeply.

"Do you like this?" I asked, curious about his reaction.

"Yes," he replied with heartfelt conviction. "Jesus is a holy prophet. His words are the language of God. It is beautiful, so beautiful."

"What is it that touches you the most?" I inquired.

He paused for a moment, then said, "The part where He says, 'Forgive those that hate you.' That is divine wisdom. Such words can only come from the Almighty."

Ali shared this insight with his brothers, who listened intently and nodded in agreement. They spoke in their native tongue, their expressions serious but kind. Turning back to me, they offered praise for Jesus, whom they called "Isu," emphasizing His miracles and holiness. They told me of a story from their own traditions, where Jesus fashioned a bird from clay and breathed life into it. Their sincerity was touching, and I could see how much it pleased Ali that his brothers approved of our friendship.

Ali's progress in learning to write was just as swift and impressive as his reading. He insisted on buying his own supplies—paper, pens, and ink—refusing to let me cover the cost. In less than two months, he had mastered the basics of writing. His brothers could hardly contain their pride, often competing to assist me with tasks at the workshop to express their gratitude.

Ali's affection for me surpassed even the bonds he shared with his brothers. I will never forget the day he was finally liberated. As we walked together outside the barracks, he turned to me, his face filled with emotion. He threw his arms around me and sobbed openly, something he had never done before.

"You have done so much for me," he said through his tears. "Neither my father nor my mother ever cared for me as you have. You have made me into a man. I will never forget you. Never!"

Where is Ali now, my kind and generous friend? I often wonder about him, hoping that life has treated him gently.

Beyond Ali and his brothers, our prison housed other groups, including a small contingent of Poles who kept mostly to themselves. Their aloofness and disdain for the Russian convicts made them unpopular among the rest. Among their number were men of education, and they lived as a distinct unit within the prison. But that is a story for another time. For now, my thoughts remain with Ali and the profound impact he had on my life.

Chapter 6
The First Month

Three days after my arrival, I was assigned to work for the first time. The experience left an indelible mark on me, even though, by outward appearances, it was not particularly remarkable. Yet, for me, it represented a profound shift. The stark novelty of my situation heightened every sensation, and I viewed the entire scene with a curiosity that was both intense and pained. Those initial three days proved to be the most difficult of my imprisonment, filled with the raw agony of transition.

My thoughts constantly returned to a single, piercing truth: My wandering was at an end. The restless uncertainty that had carried me this far had ceased. Now, I was firmly entrenched in the grim reality of the convict prison—my home for years to come. I repeated to myself, almost masochistically, This is where I must live now. My thoughts turned darker: Who knows? When I leave this place, perhaps I will do so with regret. The notion was unbearable, yet I could not escape it. Even then, I was beginning to understand how profoundly habit shapes us, molding even the most dreadful circumstances into something strangely familiar. But that understanding lay in the future; for the present, there was only pain.

What compounded my suffering was the attitude of my fellow convicts. Their curiosity was relentless, their gazes piercing as they scrutinized me—a former nobleman, now reduced to their rank. That curiosity often turned hostile, manifesting in overt disdain and even hatred. Their animosity tormented me deeply, pushing me to confront the harshness of my new reality head-on. It was as though I felt compelled to leap straight into the abyss of despair, to measure its depths fully, and to begin, without hesitation, the process of acclimating to life within its confines.

Yet not all the hostility was uniform or absolute. Amid the general indifference and scorn, I began to notice faint glimmers of goodwill from certain individuals. These small gestures of kindness, though rare, were significant, and they buoyed my spirits in unexpected ways. One of the first to show me friendliness was Akim Akimitch, whose steady demeanor became a source of quiet reassurance. Gradually, I learned to discern kind, even good-natured faces in the sea of harsh and sardonic expressions. This realization gave me hope, albeit faint, that even here, among the convicted and condemned, humanity could still flourish.

One prisoner in particular stood out as an example of this. His name was Suchiloff. Though our interactions remained sparse for a long time, I came to see him as the embodiment of simple, unassuming kindness. For reasons I could not initially understand, he began to assist me in small but meaningful ways. He washed my clothes at the central basin in the courtyard, which was crowded daily with convicts scrubbing their garments in buckets. He took on tasks without being asked, boiling my tea-urn, running errands, mending my clothes, and even greasing my boots on a regular schedule.

Suchiloff carried out these duties with an air of quiet diligence, treating them as if they were sacred obligations. What struck me most was his sense of solidarity. He referred to my belongings as though they were shared between us. "We have so many shirts," he would say, or "Our waistcoat is torn." I began to sense that I had become a central focus of his life. It was not servility, but a kind of genuine admiration, paired with the practical reality that my meager payments provided him with his only stable source of income.

His demeanor was devoid of calculation. He accepted whatever little I could give him with gratitude, never once complaining or asking for more. Yet I knew he lived in perpetual hardship. When not working for me, he would earn small sums by acting as a lookout for the gamblers who played cards illicitly in the barracks. This dangerous task required him to sit in the freezing ante-chamber for hours, listening intently for the faintest sound that might signal the arrival of the Major or other authorities. Payment for such vigilance was pitiful, and failure carried the heavy price of punishment.

It struck me that Suchiloff, like so many others I encountered, lacked a clear sense of self. He had no particular trade, no personal ambitions, and seemed content to lose himself in service to others. His individuality appeared entirely subsumed by the roles he performed. And yet, within that obscurity, there existed a quiet dignity, a resilience that allowed him to navigate the harsh realities of prison life with an uncomplaining spirit.

Another figure in my early days was Osip, who had been recommended to me by Akim Akimitch as a cook. For thirty kopecks a month, Osip prepared my meals separately from the communal prison fare, in case I found it intolerable. His official title was "cook-maid," a term used in jest but without derision. The cooks, chosen by the prisoners themselves, were exempt from hard labor and tasked with preparing meals for the barracks. Osip had been selected for this role many times over the years, owing to his affable nature and skill, though he often stepped down when unwell or when presented with an opportunity to smuggle contraband spirits into the barracks.

Osip was a paradox—a convicted smuggler who was remarkably honest in his dealings and thoroughly good-natured. Despite his peaceful disposition, he harbored a chronic fear of punishment, particularly corporal punishment. This fear, however, did not deter his occasional ventures into smuggling, driven less by profit and more by a love for the thrill of the act.

Over time, I grew accustomed to the prison routines, including the humble meals Osip prepared for me. The cabbage soup, initially repulsive, became tolerable with time, and I learned to appreciate the small comforts that helped ease the monotony of life in confinement. Through the efforts of people like Osip and Suchiloff, I began to navigate the complexities of prison society, finding solace in small acts of kindness and the quiet resilience of those around me. Though these early days were fraught with anguish, they also marked the beginning of a journey toward understanding and adaptation—a journey that would shape my perception of humanity in ways I had never anticipated.

Suchiloff was a man whose very existence seemed to evoke pity. There was a quiet meekness about him that appeared to be both a product of his nature and the result of his circumstances. Though life in prison could be harsh and brutal, Suchiloff had clearly never been a man of violence or confrontation. He seemed incapable of lifting his hand against another person, even if provoked. His demeanor was so unassuming, so devoid of malice, that one could not help but feel a deep, inexplicable compassion for him. He inspired pity not because of anything he explicitly said or did, but simply because of the quiet, resigned way he carried himself.

His figure was unremarkable—neither tall nor short, neither particularly old nor notably young. His face, pockmarked by smallpox and framed by fair hair, lacked any distinguishing feature that might have drawn attention. It would be difficult to describe him to someone else, for there was nothing vivid about his appearance or personality. Yet, despite his apparent blandness, Suchiloff was somehow unforgettable, as if his very ordinariness held a quiet tragedy that was impossible to ignore.

I tried many times to engage him in conversation, to draw out something of his inner life, but my efforts were fruitless. He would respond with brief answers, often accompanied by a faint, almost apologetic smile, before lapsing back into silence. The only time he seemed to show any energy or animation was when I gave him a task to do. Whether it was running an errand, mending something, or simply helping with some small chore, Suchiloff would spring into action with a kind of eager determination. It became clear to me that he found solace in being ordered about, as though having something to do gave him a sense of purpose that he could not find on his own.

The other prisoners, though often indifferent to Suchiloff, sometimes found amusement in his simplicity. They would laugh at him, not cruelly, but with a sort of condescending humor, particularly when they spoke of the "exchange" he had made during his march to Siberia. It was a story that seemed to embody his naïveté.

During the grueling journey, Suchiloff had traded his own lighter sentence for the much harsher punishment of another convict named Mikhailoff, a man sentenced to hard labor for a capital crime. In exchange, Suchiloff received a red shirt and a single silver rouble—a paltry price for such a monumental trade. To the other prisoners, this act of "selling himself" was both comical and baffling, a testament to his gullibility.

The practice of exchanging identities among prisoners was not unheard of, though I initially found it difficult to believe. It seemed so absurd, so inherently reckless, that I thought it must be a myth. But the more I learned, the more I realized how real it was. The process was deceptively simple, born of desperation and cunning.

The exchanges usually took place at some waystation along the endless march to Siberia. Among the ranks of prisoners, there were always those with lighter sentences, destined for roles as colonists or workers in the mines. At the same time, there were men like Mikhailoff—hardened criminals with heavy sentences, eager to escape the brutal conditions that awaited them. Mikhailoff, shrewd and manipulative, would bide his time, scanning the group for someone like Suchiloff: meek, simple, and desperate.

Once he identified his target, Mikhailoff would strike up a friendship, ingratiating himself with kind words and offers of small favors. At the right moment, he would make his pitch, often after getting his companion drunk on whatever spirits he could procure.

"My name is Mikhailoff," he would explain. "I've been sentenced to hard labor, but not the ordinary kind. I'm being sent to a special section where the work is much easier. It's hardly different from being a colonist."

The so-called "special section" was a mysterious designation, known only to a few and poorly understood even by those it affected. To the average convict, it sounded vague and almost benign—certainly less ominous than the mines or other brutal forms of hard labor. The ambiguity worked in Mikhailoff's favor, allowing him to paint it as an opportunity rather than a punishment.

For a man like Suchiloff, who was already broken by the journey and had nothing to his name, the offer might have seemed like a stroke of luck. The promise of a red shirt, a silver rouble, and perhaps a less arduous fate would have been hard to resist, even if it meant taking on Mikhailoff's name and sentence.

The truth, of course, was far darker. Mikhailoff, aware of the true severity of his punishment, was eager to rid himself of it. The special section, as I would later come to understand, was reserved for the most dangerous and irredeemable criminals, and the conditions there were anything but lenient. But Suchiloff, trusting and naive, likely had no real grasp of what he was agreeing to.

The exchange, once completed, was nearly impossible to reverse. The authorities, burdened with thousands of prisoners to process, rarely verified identities beyond superficial checks. As long as the names matched the records, the deception went unnoticed.

And so, with a red shirt and a silver rouble in his possession, Suchiloff unknowingly sealed his fate. He took on a sentence that was not his own, trading a future of relative freedom for one of unrelenting hardship. It was a decision that seemed to encapsulate his entire existence—a life defined by meekness, passivity, and an almost tragic inability to assert himself.

The proposition to exchange identities, as it had been presented to Suchiloff, was both cunning and calculated. "Won't you change?" Mikhailoff asked, with a tone that implied it was the most natural thing in the world. Suchiloff, slightly drunk and hopelessly naïve, found it difficult to refuse. Gratitude, mixed with a dim understanding of prison lore, kept him from questioning the offer. He had heard whispers among the prisoners that such exchanges were not uncommon, and the idea seemed less shocking in the dim, warped reality of their world.

For a simple man like Suchiloff, the prospect of a red shirt and a silver rouble seemed like an extraordinary windfall. Mikhailoff, exploiting his comrade's simplicity, ensured the deal was sealed with witnesses. The very next day, Suchiloff awoke, the haze of intoxication replaced by a creeping realization of what he had agreed to. But before

80

regret could fully take hold, another drink was pressed into his hand, and then another. By the time the red shirt and silver rouble were gone—squandered on drink—the transaction had gained the weight of inevitability.

"If you don't like the bargain we made, give me back my money," Mikhailoff would say, feigning fairness. But where could Suchiloff find a rouble? He had no means, no allies, and now no voice to object. If he dared to back out, the "artel"—the convict brotherhood—would intervene. Among the prisoners, the sanctity of one's word was paramount, and an agreement, once made, could not be undone. The "artel" enforced such rules with ruthless efficiency. To defy it was unthinkable; Suchiloff's life would be forfeit if he tried.

Under this crushing weight of expectation, Suchiloff resigned himself to his fate. The agreement was announced openly, and the entire convoy of prisoners accepted it with a collective shrug. What did it matter to them whether Mikhailoff or Suchiloff faced the harshest punishment? The real concern was the free drinks Mikhailoff had provided to secure their silence. By the time the convoy reached its next station, the exchange had become an unspoken fact. When the names were called, Suchiloff answered to "Mikhailoff," and Mikhailoff did the same for "Suchiloff." The deception was seamless, and the journey continued without a ripple.

At Tobolsk, the consequences of the exchange came into sharp focus. Mikhailoff was reassigned as a colonist, a relatively lighter fate, while Suchiloff, now bearing the weight of Mikhailoff's crimes, was dispatched to the dreaded special section under heavy guard. Protests would have been useless. Who would listen to a convict's claim of mistaken identity? The witnesses—those same prisoners who had enjoyed Mikhailoff's liquor—would deny everything if questioned. The exchange was now an immutable fact, sealed by the collective indifference of the system.

Suchiloff's story became a grim joke among the prisoners. They laughed not at the act of exchanging—it was, after all, an accepted part of their strange world—but at the paltry price he had received: a rouble and a red shirt. Most exchanges were settled for much larger sums, often involving several ten-rouble notes. That Suchiloff had traded his freedom for such meager compensation only solidified his reputation as a figure of ridicule. Yet, even in their mockery, there was an undercurrent of disdain for the system that allowed such exchanges to occur.

Despite this, Suchiloff remained a pitiable, almost ghostly presence in the prison. He carried out his menial tasks with quiet efficiency, attaching himself to me as if seeking refuge in the steadiness of service. Over time, I grew accustomed to his unobtrusive companionship, and he seemed to find solace in his small acts of assistance. Yet his existence was so muted, so devoid of individuality, that even the other prisoners found little reason to mock him further.

One day, however, I made a mistake I would later deeply regret. After he failed to complete a task I had given him, he came to me hesitantly, asking for his payment. Irritated, I said something cruel: "You never forget to ask for your money, but you can't even do what you're told." My words were sharp, and I could see immediately that they had struck him deeply. He said nothing in response, but his shoulders slumped, and he turned away to carry out the task.

For the next two days, I noticed a profound sadness in him. He moved more slowly, his usual meekness now tinged with an air of defeat. I suspected that a small debt he owed to another prisoner, Vassilieff, was weighing on him, but he lacked the courage to ask me for help.

Eventually, I approached him with a coin in hand. "Suchiloff," I said, "do you need money to pay Vassilieff? Here, take this."

He stood before me, silent and bewildered. His expression was one of disbelief, as if he could not comprehend that I was offering help without being asked. Then, without a word, he turned abruptly and walked away. Concerned, I followed him outside and found him leaning against the wooden palisade, his face hidden in his arms.

"What's the matter, Suchiloff?" I asked gently.

He did not answer. To my astonishment, I saw his shoulders trembling, and I realized he was on the verge of tears. The sight of this meek, broken man, so overwhelmed by a simple gesture of kindness, struck me deeply. In that moment, I understood the full weight of his suffering—the quiet, relentless accumulation of indignities and disappointments that had crushed his spirit.

"You think, Alexander Petrovitch," Suchiloff began in a trembling voice, his eyes refusing to meet mine, "that I care only for your money, but I—" His words faltered, his voice choked with emotion. He turned abruptly, resting his forehead against the rough wooden palisade, and let out a strangled sob. It was the first time in my years at the convict prison that I had seen a man break down in tears.

The sight stunned me. In this grim, oppressive world, where emotions were rarely displayed and kindness was often interpreted as weakness, Suchiloff's weeping seemed almost surreal. Yet it was undeniably real—a raw, unfiltered expression of pain and humiliation that pierced the stoic facade of prison life. I found it difficult to console him, but eventually, through soft words and reassurances, I managed to calm him. Even so, something had shifted between us. While he resumed serving me with undiminished zeal—if not more—there was a lingering shadow in his demeanor, a quiet hurt that he could not entirely conceal. His heart, I realized, would never fully forgive the reproach I had carelessly uttered.

Meanwhile, the other convicts continued to ridicule and insult him whenever the opportunity arose. His meekness made him an easy target, and his refusal to retaliate only emboldened them further. Remarkably, he remained on good terms with his tormentors, accepting their barbs with a resigned smile that hinted at an inner strength—or perhaps an inner resignation—that I could not fully comprehend. It became clear to me that knowing a man, truly understanding him, is an infinitely complex task, even after years of shared experience.

In those early days, the convict prison felt like a chaotic, incomprehensible world. The intricate dynamics of this strange society eluded me, and I found myself overwhelmed by the sheer weight of my new reality. Much of what I observed confused and disheartened me. The harshness of my fellow inmates, especially toward a former nobleman like myself, compounded my misery. Their suspicion and hostility were palpable, and it seemed as though every interaction was tinged with animosity.

Among the many unsettling figures I encountered, none disturbed me more than A——f, a man whose character seemed to embody the very nadir of human degradation. He was a young man of noble birth, intelligent and cunning, yet utterly devoid of moral integrity. His reputation for treachery preceded him: he was known to be an informer, feeding the Major with reports about the activities in the barracks through the Major's servant, Fedka. This vile habit made him despised yet oddly tolerated by the other convicts, who seemed to regard his treachery as an unavoidable nuisance rather than a genuine threat.

The details of A——f's history were as repugnant as his behavior. Estranged from his family and consumed by a life of debauchery in St. Petersburg, he had sunk so low as to sell out others for money to fund his vices. His descent into depravity culminated in a senseless crime that earned him a sentence of exile and ten years of hard labor in Siberia. Instead of being chastened by his punishment, he embraced his new status as a convict with a perverse sense of liberation. "I am now a convict," he seemed to think, "and can crawl at ease, without shame."

A——f's presence was a blight on the prison. His eternal smirk, his sly demeanor, and his shameless duplicity marked him as a creature utterly devoid of redeeming qualities. His interactions with the other convicts, far from earning him their scorn, seemed to win him a certain grudging acceptance, largely because of his proximity to the Major. This connection, coupled with his unrelenting cynicism, gave him a twisted sort of influence that only deepened my revulsion.

The first days of my imprisonment were thus shadowed by the weight of my circumstances and the appalling characters that surrounded me. My spirit was heavy with despair, and I struggled to reconcile myself to this new existence. I wandered aimlessly through the barracks, stretched out on my camp-bedstead, or busied myself with trivial tasks to pass the time. Among these, I entrusted a reliable prisoner with the task of sewing me some shirts, purchased a meager felt mattress, and assembled a makeshift blanket from scraps of cloth—a process that, though mundane, seemed almost surreal in its stark practicality.

Yet, as I adapted to the rhythms of convict life, I began to discern the complex humanity of those around me. There were good men among the convicts, men like Akim Akimitch, whose quiet reliability offered a glimmer of solace in an otherwise bleak landscape. There were also men like Suchiloff, whose unwavering loyalty and quiet dignity in the face of adversity revealed a depth of character that defied the harsh judgments of others.

In this world, money was a source of both power and illusion. It provided a semblance of liberty, a fleeting sense of agency in a life otherwise bound by chains and rules. Convicts would spend their hard-earned kopecks on trivial luxuries or illicit pleasures, not out of ignorance of its value, but because it allowed them, if only briefly, to feel like masters of their fate. The small rebellions—the clandestine drinks, the defiance of minor rules, the exaggerated boasting—were not acts of recklessness but expressions of a deeply rooted yearning for freedom and individuality.

The convict prison was, in many ways, a microcosm of the human condition, stripped to its rawest form. It was a place where despair coexisted with resilience, where degradation revealed unexpected glimpses of nobility. And as I began to navigate this strange and brutal world, I found myself grappling not only with the realities of my imprisonment but also with the profound and often contradictory truths about the nature of humanity itself.

Chapter 7
The First Month (Continued)

I had a small amount of money, but I kept most of it hidden to avoid it being taken away. I glued some banknotes into the binding of my New Testament—the only book allowed in the prison. That New Testament had been given to me at Tobolsk by someone who had been living in exile for decades. This person, having seen so many others in misery, came to regard them as brothers.

In Siberia, there are people who dedicate their lives to helping those who suffer. Their kindness is like that of a parent toward their child—pure and selfless. I cannot help but share a memory of someone I met during that time.

In the town where we were imprisoned lived a widow named Nastasia Ivanovna. Although none of us had direct contact with her, she devoted her life to helping exiles, especially those of us in the convict prison. Perhaps she had suffered a personal tragedy or lost someone dear who had gone through a punishment like ours. Whatever her reasons, she did everything she could for us. She had little to give because she was poor, but we knew we had a true friend outside those prison walls. She often brought us news, which was a rare and welcome gift, as we were usually cut off from the world.

When I was transferred to another town, I had the chance to visit her and meet her in person. She lived in a suburb, staying with a close relative.

Nastasia Ivanovna was neither young nor old, neither beautiful nor plain. It was hard, even impossible, to tell if she was well-educated or clever. Yet her actions showed immense kindness, an overwhelming desire to help, and a sincere effort to comfort others. Her gentle smile revealed all of this.

I spent an entire evening at her home with some of my fellow prisoners. She met our gaze directly, laughed when we laughed, and joined in our conversation. She agreed with everything we said and tried her best to entertain us. She served tea and small treats. It was clear that if she had been wealthy, she would have done even more to comfort us and make us feel better.

When it was time to leave, she gave each of us a small gift—a simple cigar case made of cardboard. She had made them herself from brightly colored paper, like the kind used for school notebooks. Around the edges, she had glued a thin strip of shiny gold paper as decoration.

"As you smoke, these cases might come in handy," she said apologetically, as if embarrassed by the simplicity of her gift.

Some people claim, as I've read and heard, that kindness is just a hidden form of selfishness. But what selfishness could there possibly be in this? I could never understand that kind of thinking.

Although I didn't have much money when I first arrived at the convict prison, I wasn't really upset with the prisoners who, after tricking me once, came back to borrow money a second, third, and even fourth time. What did bother me, though, was the idea that they might see me as a fool and laugh at me for lending them money again and again. It irritated me to think they might believe I was naïve enough to fall for their tricks. Yet, even knowing this, I couldn't bring myself to refuse them.

During those early days, I was constantly wondering what my place would be in the convict prison and how I should act around my companions. I knew I was stepping into an unfamiliar world, one where I couldn't see clearly what lay ahead. But I also understood that I couldn't live for ten years in a constant state of confusion. I decided to be honest and act according to my conscience and feelings. However, I knew that theory and practice were often very different, and my actions would likely be shaped by the unexpected events I encountered. On top of all the small irritations of prison life, I had one overwhelming fear that grew stronger each day.

"The dead-house!" I thought to myself whenever I looked out from the barracks in the evenings. I saw the prisoners who had just returned from work, wandering the yard between the kitchen and the barracks. Watching their movements and trying to read their expressions, I wondered what kind of men they were and what kind of lives they had lived.

They lingered in front of me, some with their heads downcast, others lively and full of chatter. Every convict's face carried one of these two expressions. They either hurled insults at one another or spoke casually about meaningless things. Some strolled alone, lost in thought, with expressions that were either pitifully tired or smug with pride. And yes, even here—some of them carried themselves with a swagger, their caps tilted jauntily on their heads, their sheepskin coats draped carelessly over one shoulder, their eyes filled with defiance, and their lips curled in mockery.

"This is the world I've been sentenced to," I told myself. "This is where, whether I like it or not, I'll have to exist."

I decided to ask Akim Akimitch, who often drank tea with me, about the convicts, as I was eager to learn more about the people I was surrounded by. At that time, tea was nearly the only food I consumed, especially during those early days in the prison. Akim Akimitch never turned down an invitation to have tea with me. He would help heat our tin tea-urns, which were made in the prison and rented to me by another convict.

After calmly drinking a single glass of tea from his own cup, Akim Akimitch would always thank me politely and go right back to his task of sewing my blanket. Unfortunately, he couldn't provide the answers I was looking for. He didn't understand why I wanted to know about the personalities of the men around us and would just smile at me with a knowing, almost amused look that I can still remember clearly. I soon realized that if I wanted answers, I would have to figure things out for myself. Asking others wasn't going to help.

On the fourth morning, the convicts were gathered in two lines in the courtyard near the guardhouse, just in front of the prison gates. Soldiers armed with loaded rifles and fixed bayonets stood in front and behind us. If a convict tried to escape, a soldier was allowed to shoot, but only if it was absolutely necessary. The soldier would be held accountable for the shot if there was no clear reason for firing. The same rule applied in cases of revolt. But who would risk openly trying to run away?

Soon, the Engineer officer arrived, accompanied by the "conductor," a few non-commissioned officers from the Line, and a group of sappers and soldiers tasked with overseeing the convicts' work. After roll call, the convicts assigned to the tailor's workshop were sent off first. These men worked within the prison, making clothes for the inmates. Next, other groups were sent to the external workshops. Finally, it was the turn of those assigned to field labor, which included me. In total, there were about twenty of us. Our task was to dismantle two old, government-owned barges on the frozen river behind the fortress. The wood from the barges was practically worthless, especially since firewood in the town could be bought for almost nothing. The region was covered with vast forests, making wood an abundant resource.

This assignment wasn't really about the work itself but about keeping us occupied. Everyone understood this. So we approached the task without much enthusiasm. But it was a different story when we were given work with a clear goal, especially when a specific quota had to be met. Even though the prisoners didn't benefit directly from such tasks, they often worked with surprising energy and pride, eager to finish quickly and efficiently. When it came to pointless assignments like dismantling the barges, there was no urgency. We worked until the drumbeat at eleven o'clock signaled it was time to return to the prison.

The day was warm and foggy, with the snow beginning to melt. Our group walked toward the riverbank behind the fortress, the sound of chains jingling faintly beneath our clothes. It was a crisp, ringing sound. A few men broke off from the group to retrieve tools from the storage depot.

I stayed with the others, curious about this new kind of labor. I wanted to see what fieldwork entailed and figure out how I would handle it for the first time in my life. Every detail of that morning remains vivid in my memory. Along the way, we passed a townsman with a long beard. He stopped, reached into his pocket, and handed a convict five kopecks. The prisoner removed his cap to accept the alms, then hurried back to rejoin our group. The townsman made the sign of the cross and went on his way. Later that morning, the five kopecks were used to buy small white bread cakes, which were divided equally among us.

In our group, some men were quiet and withdrawn, while others seemed indifferent and lazy. A few chatted idly, but one man in particular stood out. He was unusually cheerful for no apparent reason, singing and dancing as he walked, his chains clinking and jangling with each step. This man, heavyset and full of energy, was the same convict who, on my first day during the general washing, had argued with another prisoner over the water and had mockingly compared him to some kind of bird. His name was Scuratoff. That morning, he ended up singing a lively tune, the chorus of which I still remember:

"They married me without my consent,

When I was at the mill."

All that was missing was the sound of a balalaika to complete the scene.

Scuratoff's over-the-top good mood didn't sit well with some of the other prisoners, who found it annoying.

"Listen to him shouting like that," said one convict. "It's really not fitting."

"That Tuliak is stealing the wolf's howl," added another, his Little Russian accent giving him away.

"Of course I'm from Tula," Scuratoff replied. "But at least we don't stuff ourselves like you people in Pultava."

"Liar! What did you eat in Tula? Bark shoes and cabbage soup?" the other shot back.

"And you act like the devil fed you sweet almonds," another prisoner chimed in.

"I admit it, my friend," Scuratoff said with a mock sigh, as if he were truly scolding himself. "I'm a delicate, pampered man. I grew up in luxury, raised on plums and fine cakes. Even now, my brothers in Moscow have a huge business. They're big-time dealers—in selling the wind! Filthy rich, as you can imagine."

"And what exactly did you sell?" asked another convict.

"I had a lot of success. When I got my first two hundred—" Scuratoff began.

"Two hundred roubles? No way!" one prisoner interrupted, amazed by the thought of such a large amount.

"No, not two hundred roubles," Scuratoff corrected, laughing. "Two hundred blows of the stick. Luka! Hey, Luka!"

"Some people can call me Luka, but for you, it's Luka Kouzmitch," replied a small, weak-looking convict with a pointed nose, clearly irritated.

"Ah, forget it. You're not even worth talking to," Scuratoff said dismissively. "But back to my story—this is how I ended up leaving Moscow. After my last fifteen strokes, they shipped me off, and I ended up—"

"But why were you sent away?" another convict asked, clearly interested in the tale.

"Don't ask dumb questions," Scuratoff replied. "I was explaining why I didn't make my fortune in Moscow. You have no idea how badly I wanted to be rich."

Several of the prisoners started laughing. Scuratoff was the kind of person who loved to entertain his more serious companions, even though the only reward he got for his efforts was their teasing and insults. He was one of those lively, spirited types whose traits I'll probably describe more fully later.

"And just look at him now," Luka Kouzmitch said. "His clothes alone must be worth a hundred roubles."

Scuratoff's sheepskin coat was one of the oldest, greasiest, and most patched-up things anyone had ever seen. It barely held together. He looked Luka over carefully, from head to toe.

"It's my head, my friend," Scuratoff said. "My head is what's worth something. When I left Moscow, I was almost comforted because, at least, I got to keep my head. Farewell, Moscow! I'll never forget your free air—or that brutal flogging I got there. As for my coat, no one's forcing you to look at it."

"Oh, so we're supposed to admire your head now?" Luka retorted.

"Not even his real property," Luka Kouzmitch sneered. "That head of his was a charity gift! Someone gave it to him at Tumen when the convoy passed through."

"Scuratoff, did you even have a workshop?" another prisoner asked.

"What kind of workshop could he possibly have? He was just a cobbler," one of the convicts scoffed.

"That's true," Scuratoff replied, completely unfazed by the tone. "I did try my hand at mending boots once, but I didn't get past fixing just one pair."

"And did you get paid for that pair?" another convict asked.

"Well, I found someone who must have had no fear of God and no respect for his parents. As a result, Providence punished him by making him buy my handiwork," Scuratoff said with a grin.

The men around him burst out laughing.

"I even worked once here in the convict prison," Scuratoff continued, as calm as ever. "I patched up the boots of Lieutenant Stepan Fedoritch."

"And was he satisfied with your work?" someone asked.

"No, my dear fellows, he certainly was not. He gave me a scolding that I'll remember for the rest of my life. He even shoved me from behind with his knee. Oh, what a fury he was in! My life has deceived me, my friends. I don't see any fun in this convict prison, not one bit."

With that, he broke into song again.

"Akolina's husband is in the courtyard.

There he waits."

He sang, danced, and leapt about, seeming to enjoy himself immensely.

"How improper!" muttered the Little Russian, who was walking beside me.

"What a frivolous man!" said another convict in a serious,

disapproving tone.

I couldn't understand why they were insulting Scuratoff or why they seemed to hold lighthearted convicts like him in such contempt. At first, I thought their irritation stemmed from personal hostility, but I was mistaken. Their annoyance came from the fact that Scuratoff didn't carry himself with the false dignity that permeated the entire convict prison.

However, they didn't direct this annoyance toward every joker or cheerful man. Some convicts had an air of authority that demanded respect, and no one dared to insult them, either jokingly or seriously. Among us was one such man, a lively and good-natured fellow I didn't fully understand until later. He was tall, had a pleasant demeanor, and his face carried a comical expression that made him stand out.

They called him "the Sapper" because he had served in the Engineers, and he was part of the special section.

Not all the serious-minded convicts were as rigid as the Little Russian, who seemed to detest seeing anyone in a good mood.

In our prison, there were several men who sought to achieve a kind of superiority—whether through their skills, cleverness, character, or wit. Many of them were intelligent and driven, and they often succeeded in earning the respect and moral authority they craved. Yet, they also frequently harbored a deep hatred for one another and stirred up envy among their peers. These men carried themselves with an air of dignity and condescension, avoided petty quarrels, and rarely fought without a legitimate reason. Because they were often well-regarded by the administration, they wielded some influence over the work and daily life in the prison. None of them would lower themselves to argue with someone over songs. Throughout my imprisonment, these men were always polite to me, though they were far from open or communicative.

Finally, we arrived at the riverbank, where an old barge lay frozen in the ice a short distance away. That was the vessel we were tasked with dismantling. Across the river stretched the blue expanse of the steppe, meeting a somber horizon. I had expected everyone to immediately get to work, but nothing of the sort happened. Instead, several convicts lazily sat down on wooden beams scattered near the shore. Most pulled out small pouches of tobacco, sold in leaf form at the market for three kopecks a pound, along with short wooden pipes. They lit their pipes, puffing away as the soldiers formed a loose circle around us, watching with weary, uninterested expressions.

"Who on earth decided to sink this barge here?" one convict asked loudly, not addressing anyone in particular.

"Were they really that eager to have it torn apart?" replied another.

"They sure didn't hesitate to give us busywork," a third convict added with a shrug.

After a brief silence, the first man spoke again.

"And where are all those peasants going to work?"

He didn't even seem to notice his companion's response. Instead, he pointed toward the distance where a group of peasants was trudging across the untouched snow in a single file.

All the convicts turned their heads lazily to watch, not out of interest but sheer idleness, and they soon began to mock the peasants as they drew closer. One of the peasants, trailing at the back, walked in an odd, exaggerated manner, with his arms flung outward and his head tilted to one side. He wore a tall, pointed cap, and his shadow stretched clearly on the snow, creating a comical image.

"Look at Petrovitch all dressed up," one of the convicts remarked, mimicking the local peasant dialect. The irony was apparent—most of the convicts had come from peasant backgrounds themselves, yet they looked down on the peasants.

"That last guy looks like he's planting radishes," joked another.

"An important man, no doubt," a third chimed in sarcastically. "He's probably rolling in money."

They all laughed, though their laughter lacked any real amusement.

At that moment, a woman selling cakes approached. She was brisk and cheerful, and the five kopecks the townsman had given earlier were quickly spent on her wares.

A young man who regularly sold white bread in the convict prison bought two dozen of her cakes. He haggled with her for a long time, trying to get her to lower the price, but she stood firm and wouldn't budge.

Finally, the non-commissioned officer in charge of supervising the work arrived, carrying a cane. "What are you all sitting around for? Get to work already."

"Set us some tasks, Ivan Matveitch," said one of the convicts, who acted as a sort of informal leader, standing up sluggishly.

"What more do you want? The task is obvious—take apart the barque," the officer retorted.

Reluctantly, the convicts rose to their feet and shuffled slowly toward the riverbank. A few self-appointed "leaders" among them began barking out instructions. It seemed the barque wasn't to be dismantled carelessly; they were supposed to save the longitudinal and latitudinal beams, which added complexity to the task.

"Pull out this beam first," one of the convicts suggested, though he wasn't a foreman or in charge in any official capacity. This man, quiet and slightly dull, hadn't said much before. He bent down, grabbed hold of a heavy beam with both hands, and waited for someone to help him. But no one moved.

"You won't manage it," muttered someone sarcastically. "Not even your grandfather, the bear, could."

"Well, is anyone going to help, or am I supposed to do this alone?" the man said gruffly, letting go of the beam and standing upright.

"What's the rush?" another convict snapped. "You planning to do all the work yourself?"

"I was just saying," the first man muttered, backing down sheepishly as if apologizing for speaking up.

"Do you all need blankets to keep warm or a fire lit for the winter?" the non-commissioned officer shouted, exasperated at the group's lack of enthusiasm. "Get to work already!"

"There's no point in rushing, Ivan Matveitch," grumbled one of the convicts.

"But you're not doing anything at all, Savelieff. What are you looking around for? Are your eyes for sale? Get moving!"

"What can I do by myself?" Savelieff replied sullenly.

"Give us proper tasks, Ivan Matveitch," someone else chimed in.

"I told you already—I don't have any specific tasks for you. Just dismantle the barque. When it's done, we'll go back. Now get to it!"

The prisoners finally began working, but their movements were sluggish, filled with reluctance. It was clear that the officer's frustration stemmed from seeing these strong men intentionally dragging their feet. When they started removing the first rivet, it snapped immediately.

"It broke!" the convict working on it said defensively, as though excusing himself. The group quickly began murmuring that the tools weren't suited to the job. What could they do? This led to a long and fruitless argument among the convicts, escalating into insults.

The officer shouted at them again, waving his cane irritably, but when the second rivet snapped just like the first, it was agreed that hatchets wouldn't do the trick. They needed better tools. Two prisoners were sent under guard back to the fortress to fetch the proper equipment. In the meantime, the rest of the convicts calmly sat back down on the riverbank, pulled out their pipes, and lit up once again.

The officer, clearly disgusted, spat on the ground. "Well," he grumbled, "this kind of work won't kill you, that's for sure. Oh, what a bunch of people, what a bunch of people!"

Shaking his head in irritation, he gestured dismissively and stalked off toward the fortress, twirling his cane as he went.

After about an hour, the "conductor" finally arrived. He calmly listened to the complaints and explanations of the convicts before laying out the task ahead. The goal, he said, was to remove four rivets intact and demolish a significant portion of the barque. Once that was accomplished, they could return to the prison. Though the task seemed daunting, the reaction of the convicts was remarkable. Suddenly, the laziness and lack of enthusiasm disappeared. Where before there had been clumsiness and reluctance, now there was precision and energy. The hatchets sprang into action, moving swiftly and effectively, and soon the rivets began to come loose.

Those without hatchets made do with thick sticks, leveraging them cleverly to push the rivets out. It wasn't long before the beams were dislodged with a skill that seemed almost professional. The atmosphere transformed completely—gone were the insults and grumbles. Instead, the men worked together with purpose, offering advice and solutions in an organized and efficient manner. Just half an hour before the drum signaled the end of the workday, the entire task had been completed. The convicts returned to the barracks, exhausted but satisfied with having gained a little extra time for themselves.

As for me, my experience during the work was far less positive. Whenever I tried to join in or offer assistance, I was met with irritation and hostility. It didn't matter where I went or what I did—someone would always drive me away, often with an insult. Even the least skilled and least respected convict felt entitled to reprimand me if I came too close to their work area, claiming I was in the way.

At last, one of the more experienced workers bluntly told me, "What are you even doing here? Go on, get lost! No one called for you."

Another chimed in, "Exactly. Why don't you pick up a pitcher and carry water for the construction crew or head to the tobacco factory? You're no use here."

I had no choice but to step aside. Standing idly while everyone else worked felt humiliating, but every attempt to contribute only made things worse. When I moved to the other end of the barque to try my luck, the ridicule started all over again.

"Look at the kind of workers we have here!" someone sneered. "What can you do with a guy like that?"

It was clear they took pleasure in mocking me, delighted at the chance to humiliate a "gentleman" among them.

From that moment, it became evident to me how difficult it would be to coexist with these men. I knew such incidents would happen again and again, but I resolved not to let them change the way I carried myself. I decided to live simply, to act honestly, and to remain indifferent to the scorn or hostility of my companions. I wouldn't push for their approval, but neither would I shun anyone who approached me with genuine intent. Above all, I wouldn't let their threats or hatred frighten me. I understood that any other approach would only lead them to despise me further.

That evening, as I returned to the prison after the day's exhausting work, I was overwhelmed by a deep and heavy sadness. The same thought haunted me as I walked aimlessly, pondering my situation: "How many thousands of days like this will I have to endure?" The monotony of it all seemed unbearable.

As dusk settled, I wandered near the palisade behind the barracks, lost in thought. There, unexpectedly, I saw Bull—the prison dog—bounding toward me.

Bull was a fixture of the prison, much like the mascots often found in military units. He belonged to no one in particular but treated everyone as his master, surviving on scraps from the kitchen. He was a medium-sized black-and-white dog with bright, intelligent eyes and a bushy tail. Though he had been there for years, no one paid him much attention or showed him any affection.

From the moment I arrived, however, I'd made a point to befriend him. I'd offered him a piece of bread, and when I patted his back, he stood perfectly still, his tail wagging gently, as if savoring the rare kindness. That evening, not having seen me all day—the first person in years to show him affection—he ran to me, barking and leaping with joy. The sight touched me deeply. I couldn't help but embrace him, pressing his head against my chest. He placed his front paws on my shoulders and gazed into my face.

"Here is a friend sent to me by fate," I thought to myself. In those first painful weeks of imprisonment, Bull became my one solace. Every evening, as soon as I returned from work, I would seek him out behind the barracks. He would greet me with uncontainable excitement, and I would kneel to hold his head in my hands, sometimes even kissing him. Yet, even in those tender moments, a bitter sadness gripped my heart.

I often thought—and took strange comfort in the thought—that Bull was my only true friend in the world. In those bleak days, this loyal dog became my faithful companion, and I clung to his simple, unconditional affection as if it were the one bright spot in an otherwise dark and desolate existence.

Chapter 8
New Acquaintances—Petroff

Time moved forward, and gradually, I began to adapt to the rhythm of my new existence. The sights and sounds that had once disturbed me no longer had the same sharp sting. In time, the prison, its routines, and its people became a backdrop to my daily life, one that I observed without the intense feelings I had first experienced. It wasn't that I had come to accept this existence as normal—such a thing would have been impossible—but I began to see it as an unchangeable reality. With that realization, the anxious thoughts that had plagued me during my initial days began to recede. I no longer wandered the prison grounds feeling out of place, as though I were lost in some unending nightmare. The convicts' initial curiosity about me, which had been marked by mocking or disdainful glances, had waned as well. They now treated me with indifference, a shift I welcomed with quiet relief.

Over time, I found my place in the barracks. I knew where to go when the day's work ended and where I could lay my head at night. Tasks that had once seemed utterly repugnant became routine. I even started going every week, without fail, to the guardhouse to have my head shaved. This ritual took place every Saturday, as one convict after another was summoned. The regimental barbers would lather our heads with cold water and soap, then scrape at our scalps with razors that seemed more like saws than proper tools.

The mere thought of this process still sends a shiver down my spine. However, I soon found an alternative, thanks to a suggestion from Akim Akimitch. There was a prisoner in the military section who shaved convicts for a kopeck apiece using his personal razor. Many prisoners, even those not particularly sensitive, became his customers simply to avoid the crude treatment of the military barbers.

This man, known to all as "the major," earned his nickname for reasons no one could explain. He bore no resemblance to any real major, but the name stuck. Even now, I can vividly picture his gaunt face. He was a tall, quiet man, not particularly bright, and wholly consumed by his trade. Day and night, he could be seen sharpening his razor on a strop, ensuring it was always in perfect condition. For him, this craft wasn't just a livelihood—it seemed to be the very essence of his life. When his razor was sharp, and his services were sought after, he exuded a kind of contentment. His soap was always warm, and his touch was so light it felt almost like velvet. He took pride in his skill, accepting payment with an air of detached professionalism, as though he worked out of pure passion for his craft rather than the small earnings it brought him.

Once, A——f had the misfortune of referring to this barber as "the major" in front of the real Major, a mistake that did not go unpunished. The Major erupted in fury.

"You scoundrel!" he roared. "Do you even know what a major is? And you dare to call a convict by that title in my presence?"

True to his nature, he grabbed A——f and shook him violently to emphasize his point.

From the very beginning of my imprisonment, I had one persistent thought that consumed me: freedom. I became obsessed with counting the days until my release, endlessly calculating and recalculating them in every possible way. This preoccupation became my constant companion. I'm certain that anyone imprisoned for a set term experiences the same fixation. While not all the convicts shared my level of hopefulness, I was often amazed by how optimistic they could be.

Hope for a convict is a strange thing. For a free man, hope is often tied to achieving goals or improving his circumstances, but life itself continues around him as he works toward those ends. For a convict, particularly one serving a life sentence, hope takes on a much hazier quality. It becomes less about tangible outcomes and more about clinging to the faintest possibilities.

Prisoners with fixed terms tended to view their sentences as temporary, as if they were merely visitors in a foreign land. Even a man serving twenty years might tell himself, "By the time I'm free, I'll still be young and full of life." This mindset allowed him to stave off despair. Even those sentenced to life would dream of improbable scenarios, such as receiving an order from St. Petersburg to transfer to Nertchinsk with a defined sentence.

Such a transfer, though grueling, offered a glimmer of hope. The journey itself would take six months, and life on the road, despite its hardships, was a welcome break from the oppressive monotony of the prison. At Nertchinsk, the prisoner might serve out his term and then—well, who knows? Even gray-haired men, worn down by years of confinement, entertained such thoughts. These fragile dreams, however unlikely, were often the only things keeping the spirit alive amidst the crushing weight of prison life.

At Tobolsk, I saw men chained to the wall with a short length of chain, only about two yards long. Beside them was a small bed, their only comfort in a punishment that could last five or ten years. These prisoners were typically hardened brigands who had committed grave crimes even after being sent to Siberia. However, among them, I once noticed a man who seemed to have a more refined background. He had been part of the Civil Service, spoke in a soft, slightly lisping manner, and carried himself with an air that was both gentle and unsettling. He even smiled faintly, though it was a sickly kind of smile, and he eagerly demonstrated the best way to lie down while bound by the chain. Despite his demeanor, it was clear he was no better than the rest.

All of these men appeared remarkably calm, even content, on the surface. Yet their overwhelming desire to be free of their chains consumed them. Why? The answer was simple yet profound: once freed from their chains, they could move from the damp, suffocating cells to the relative openness of the prison courtyard. They clung to this hope, even though they knew they would never be released from the prison itself and would likely die in their irons. This faint glimmer of freedom, however small, sustained them. Without it, how could they endure years chained to a wall without succumbing to madness or death?

I quickly realized that physical labor would be my salvation. Work would strengthen my body and fortify my spirit, shielding me from the mental turmoil and the stifling atmosphere of the barracks. I resolved to leave this place as strong and healthy as I could.

I remember one of my fellow inmates—a man who arrived strong and full of life. To my horror, I watched him wither away, his health eroded by the harsh conditions. When he finally left the prison, he was a broken man, unable to walk unaided, his chest ravaged by asthma.

"No," I vowed to myself as I observed his decline. "I will live. I must live."

My enthusiasm for work, however, was met with ridicule and derision from my fellow prisoners. They mocked me, but I paid them no mind. I approached every task with a light heart, whether it was breaking and pounding alabaster or something else. My first assignment, working with alabaster, was relatively easy. The engineers overseeing the labor made an effort to assign less demanding tasks to the "gentlemen" prisoners. This wasn't generosity, but fairness—they understood it would be unreasonable to expect the same level of labor from men unaccustomed to physical work. However, this leniency was neither permanent nor overt; we were watched closely, and when the work was truly grueling, we suffered more than the others due to our lack of strength.

Typically, three or four men were assigned to work with the alabaster, often older or weaker prisoners. I was among them. An experienced worker named Almazoff was always sent with us. He was a lean, sunburnt, and severe man of few words who carried himself with a quiet disdain for us. Though he never openly insulted us, his attitude made it clear he thought little of our efforts. He seemed to silently accuse us of injustice, as though our inability to contribute equally was a moral failing.

Our work involved heating alabaster in an oven to calcine it. The next day, once it had cooled, we would break it into fine, powdery dust. This part of the task was surprisingly satisfying. The alabaster shattered easily under the blows of our hammers, and the physical exertion left our cheeks flushed and our blood coursing through our veins. At those moments, we felt lighter, almost invigorated. Almazoff would observe us with a grudgingly amused air, puffing on his pipe and muttering under his breath. Though he often grumbled, I suspected that, deep down, he was not an unkind man.

Later, I was assigned to a different task—working the heavy turning wheel. This wheel required significant effort to operate, especially when large wooden pieces, like balustrades or table legs, were being shaped. No one could manage it alone, so I was paired with B——, another convict of noble birth. This became our regular assignment for years whenever turning work was needed.

B—— was frail but still relatively young. There was something sympathetic about him. He had been imprisoned a year before me, along with two companions of similar background. One of these was an older man who spent his days and nights in prayer, earning the respect of all the prisoners. Unfortunately, he passed away in the prison. The other companion was a robust and courageous young man. During their grueling journey to Siberia, he had carried B—— for hundreds of miles when he collapsed from exhaustion. Their friendship was a remarkable and inspiring bond that I never forgot.

B—— was a man of noble upbringing and generous temperament, but his spirit had been worn down by illness and hardship. Despite his frailty, he remained well-mannered and dignified. We worked together at the turning wheel, and while the labor was exhausting, we developed a rhythm that made the task bearable. For me, the physical exertion proved to be unexpectedly invigorating, a form of exercise that strengthened my body and distracted my mind.

I also developed a peculiar fondness for shoveling snow, a task we often undertook after fierce winter storms. When a blizzard raged for an entire day, it was not uncommon for houses to be buried up to their windows or even completely submerged under snowdrifts. Once the storm subsided and the sun reappeared, we were tasked with clearing these mounds of snow. Armed with shovels, we were sent out in large groups—sometimes the entire prison population—to dig out the homes and streets. Each of us was assigned a specific area to clear, and although the work seemed overwhelming at first, we approached it with surprising enthusiasm.

The snow, light and powdery, had only a thin frozen crust on its surface. As we plunged our shovels into the gleaming white drifts, the snow sparkled like diamonds in the sunlight. We heaved it away in great piles, and the sheer physicality of the work was invigorating. The cold air was bracing, and the rhythmic motion of shoveling lifted our spirits. Laughter and jokes filled the air, and even snowball fights broke out among the convicts. However, these moments of levity often provoked the ire of the more serious-minded prisoners, who viewed such displays of merriment as undignified. Inevitably, the playful atmosphere gave way to arguments and insults.

Despite my initial reluctance, my circle of acquaintances gradually expanded. I was not actively seeking out new connections, as I remained guarded and mistrustful, but some relationships seemed to form naturally. One of the first individuals to approach me was a convict named Petroff. I use the term "visit" deliberately because he lived in a separate section of the barracks, far from mine, and his visits were deliberate and persistent. At first, his attention irritated me; I couldn't fathom what we might have in common. Yet, over time, his visits became a source of comfort, even though he was not particularly talkative.

Petroff was a stocky, agile man with high cheekbones, a confident demeanor, and a voice that carried a certain charm. He always had a quid of tobacco tucked between his lip and gum, a habit shared by many of the convicts. Despite being in his forties, his energetic movements and lively expression made him appear younger. He treated me with an easy civility, speaking plainly but respectfully. If he sensed that I wanted to be alone, he would only linger for a moment before leaving. Each time he departed, he thanked me for my time—a courtesy he extended to no one else.

Though we interacted daily, our relationship remained curiously superficial. Petroff was undoubtedly my friend, but there was a certain distance that never quite disappeared. I could never pinpoint what drew him to me. He never asked for money or favors, nor did he seem to have any ulterior motive. Occasionally, he would pocket something of mine, almost absentmindedly, but he never begged or demanded anything. Whatever his reasons for seeking my company, they remained a mystery.

Petroff often gave the impression that he didn't truly belong in the prison. It felt as though he came from another part of town, dropping by the convict barracks as if by coincidence, simply to check in on me. He always seemed in a hurry, as though someone was waiting for him elsewhere, yet he never appeared rushed or flustered. He had a peculiar habit of gazing past the person he was speaking to, as though searching for something in the distance. His absent-mindedness made me wonder where he went after our conversations. Did he have a secret life beyond the prison walls?

In truth, he went nowhere. He would casually wander into one of the barracks or the kitchen, sit down, and listen to the idle chatter. Sometimes he joined in animatedly; other times, he fell silent, his attention drifting elsewhere. No matter what he was doing, his demeanor always suggested that he had unfinished business somewhere far away, even though he had no real responsibilities beyond the labor assigned to him.

His conversations with me were as enigmatic as his behavior. When he spotted me walking alone behind the barracks, he would suddenly stop, pivot sharply on his heel, and stride towards me with quick, purposeful steps that bordered on a run.

Once he reached me, Petroff would slow his pace, as though he were casually strolling, despite the urgency of his initial approach. His presence was both puzzling and oddly reassuring. His conversations often started abruptly, with no clear beginning or end, and were filled with a peculiar mixture of curiosity and detachment. He would speak to me as though I were the only person worth talking to, yet his gaze seemed to wander past me, as though he were distracted by something just out of sight.

When Petroff spoke, his words were simple but not without thought. He rarely shared anything personal or significant, yet there was an unspoken connection that kept him coming back. His tone carried a hint of irony, and his bold gaze seemed to challenge me to decipher his true intentions. I often wondered why he sought me out and what he hoped to gain from our interactions, but I could never arrive at a definitive answer. He seemed to appear out of nowhere, driven by some internal compass that pointed him in my direction.

Even his departures were abrupt and curious. He would finish speaking, nod politely, and stride away as quickly as he had come. I sometimes watched him as he disappeared into the barracks or joined a group in the kitchen. Despite his seemingly restless nature, he never stayed long in one place and rarely seemed to be fully engaged in anything. It was as if his true purpose lay elsewhere, beyond the prison, in a world only he could see.

Petroff's peculiar demeanor and his persistent, inexplicable visits left me both intrigued and unsettled. While he never expressed any explicit affection or shared deep confidences, I grew accustomed to his presence. His brief, sporadic visits became a small but consistent part of my daily life in the prison. I often found myself wondering about the enigma that was Petroff—a man who, despite being physically confined like the rest of us, seemed to carry an air of freedom, as though his spirit remained unbound by the prison walls. In this strange environment, he was a puzzle I could never quite solve.

"Good morning."

"Good morning."

"I hope I'm not disturbing you?"

"Not at all."

"I wanted to ask you something about Napoleon. Is he related to the one who came to us in 1812?"

Petroff, being the son of a soldier and someone who could read and write, replied quickly.

"Of course he is."

"They say he's a president. What kind of president—and of what?"

His questions came fast and abrupt, as though he couldn't wait to hear the answers. I explained to him what Napoleon was president of and added that he might even become an emperor.

"How could that happen?" he asked.

I did my best to explain the situation, and Petroff listened carefully. When I finished, he leaned closer and said:

"Hem! Well, I wanted to ask you, Alexander Petrovitch, is it true there are monkeys with hands instead of feet, as tall as a man?"

"Yes," I replied.

"What are they like?"

I described them as best I could, sharing what little I knew about them.

"And where do they live?" he asked, his curiosity undeterred.

"In warm climates, like the island of Sumatra."

"Is that in America? I've heard that people there walk with their heads down."

"No, no, you're thinking of the Antipodes," I corrected, explaining what America and the Antipodes were. He listened intently, as though the question about the Antipodes was his sole reason for seeking me out.

"Ah, I see. Last year I read a book about the Countess de la Vallière. Arevieff bought it from the adjutant. Is it true, or just a story? The book was by Dumas."

"It's likely a work of fiction," I told him.

"Ah, I understand. Well, thank you. Goodbye."

And with that, Petroff left as suddenly as he had arrived. Conversations like this were typical between us.

Curious about him, I began asking others for information. M——, upon hearing of my interest, decided to share his thoughts unprompted. He told me that Petroff had left a horrifying impression on him, far worse than any other convict, even the infamous Gazin.

"He's the most dangerous, most unpredictable man in the prison," M—— said. "He's capable of anything. If he gets an idea in his head, he'll act on it without hesitation or remorse. Honestly, I sometimes think he's not entirely sane."

This declaration fascinated me. Yet, despite M——'s strong conviction, he couldn't provide concrete examples to support his opinion. Strangely, I spent years seeing and speaking with Petroff almost daily. He always remained a true friend to me, though I could never fully understand why. Throughout that time, he lived quietly and never did anything outrageous or extreme. Still, I felt that M—— was right—Petroff was probably one of the most fearless and unrestrained men in the prison. What made him so? That was harder to discern.

Petroff was the same convict who once, called up for punishment, nearly killed the Major. As I've recounted before, the Major narrowly escaped, leaving the scene mere moments before the incident could occur.

Years earlier, when Petroff was still a soldier, his Colonel struck him during a parade. It's likely he had endured beatings before, but on that day, something inside him refused to tolerate the insult—especially in front of the entire battalion. Petroff killed his Colonel.

I never learned the full details of the incident, as Petroff himself never spoke about it. What I did understand was that such violent outbursts only occurred when his inner nature overwhelmed him. These moments were rare, but they revealed his underlying intensity. Most of the time, he was composed, even serious. His fiery passions were not extinguished but lay smoldering, like embers glowing beneath a layer of ash.

I never noticed that Petroff showed any signs of vanity or the boastful nature common among so many of the other convicts. He rarely got into quarrels and seemed to have no close friendships, except perhaps a loose association with Sirotkin, and only when he needed something from him. However, I did witness him become genuinely angry on one occasion. Someone had refused him something trivial that he wanted, and this led to a heated argument with Vassili Antonoff, a tall, athletic convict known for his nagging and spiteful personality. Antonoff, though prone to irritating others, was not a coward and came from the class of civil convicts.

At first, it seemed like their shouting match would end as most quarrels did—with a flurry of insults and no real action. But this time was different. Petroff's demeanor suddenly changed. His face turned pale, his lips trembled and turned a bluish hue, and his breathing became labored. Without a word, he rose to his feet and began moving towards Antonoff, slowly and deliberately, his bare feet making no sound as they shuffled across the floor.

The moment was electrifying. The noisy shouting gave way to a tense silence, so profound that the buzz of a fly might have been heard. Everyone watched with bated breath. Antonoff, visibly rattled, pointed at Petroff, his face contorted with fear. Petroff's expression, too, was unsettling; it had become almost inhuman. The scene was too much for me to bear, and I hurriedly left the barracks, fully expecting to hear the screams of a man being killed before I even reached the stairs. But no such sound came.

Before Petroff could close the distance between them, Antonoff threw the object of their dispute at him—a worthless scrap of fabric, barely fit to be called a piece of lining.

Antonoff later hurled insults at Petroff, as if to prove to the crowd—and perhaps to himself—that he hadn't been too frightened to stand his ground. But Petroff didn't so much as acknowledge the taunts. He simply picked up the rag and walked away, satisfied.

Within fifteen minutes, he was casually wandering the barracks again, seemingly aimless but quietly observant, pausing occasionally to join groups in conversation if something caught his interest. Despite this apparent curiosity, he maintained an air of detachment, as though nothing truly mattered to him. He reminded me of a powerful laborer, capable of immense strength but idling for lack of meaningful work, entertaining himself with trivial diversions like a father playing with children.

What puzzled me most about Petroff was why he never tried to escape. He seemed like the kind of man who, if he truly wished to flee, would succeed without difficulty. A man like Petroff could have evaded capture, hiding in forests or river reeds, surviving on next to nothing. But the idea of escape appeared never to have occurred to him. His actions were driven not by logic or planning but by instinct and the sheer force of his will. When he wanted something, he pursued it without regard for obstacles.

I often wondered how a man who had murdered his Colonel for striking him could endure being flogged without resistance, as Petroff frequently was when caught smuggling vodka into the prison. Like many who had no regular occupation, Petroff engaged in smuggling, knowing the risks. Yet, when he was punished, he submitted without protest, almost as if he accepted the justice of his punishment. Had he resisted, the guards would have killed him rather than force him to comply. His behavior seemed a contradiction, but Petroff operated on his own peculiar logic.

He even stole from me, despite his apparent affection for me. On one occasion, I asked him to return my Bible to its place. Instead, he sold it to a fellow prisoner and used the money to buy vodka. That evening, he confessed the theft to me without the slightest hint of regret, as if recounting an ordinary event. I scolded him, upset over the loss of the Bible, and he listened calmly, nodding in agreement that it was indeed a valuable book and a shame that it was gone. Yet, he showed no remorse.

He bore my reproaches with the detached patience of someone indulging a child's tantrum. To him, my anger and disappointment were just the natural reactions of someone inexperienced in the ways of the world. He likely thought me foolish for leaving my belongings vulnerable. Once, he even remarked to me, almost apologetically:

"You are too good-natured, too simple. It makes a person pity you. Don't take offense, Alexander Petrovitch; I don't mean it unkindly."

People like Petroff come alive in moments of chaos or danger. They don't plot revolts or lead others; they act decisively, fearlessly charging into obstacles without hesitation or regard for consequences. Petroff was the kind of man others instinctively followed into peril, drawn by his sheer willpower. Yet, I couldn't help but feel that his life was destined to end violently. If not yet dead, it would only be because the opportunity had not arisen. Still, there was always the faint possibility that Petroff might defy expectations, wandering aimlessly through life until quietly dying of old age.

I remain convinced, however, that M—— was right. Petroff was the most resolute, fearless man in the entire convict prison.

Chapter 9
Men of Determination—Luka

It is not easy to describe men of unshakable resolve, especially in the convict prison, where such individuals are rare. They are recognized by the fear they inspire; others tread cautiously around them. At first, I felt an instinctive urge to avoid them entirely, but over time, my perspective shifted, even toward the most terrifying criminals. There are men who, despite having never taken a life, are more monstrous than those who have killed multiple people. Some crimes are so strange and incomprehensible that one cannot begin to fathom their motives.

One common type of murderer is the ordinary man who lives a quiet and uneventful life. He might be a peasant tied to the land, a domestic servant, a shopkeeper, or a soldier. His circumstances may be harsh, but he endures them, until one day something inside him snaps. Unable to bear his suffering any longer, he takes up a knife and kills his oppressor or enemy. Up to this point, his actions might be understandable—his crime has a clear motive. But after crossing that line, he spirals out of control. He no longer targets just his enemies; he kills indiscriminately, striking down strangers for the sheer thrill of it, for a minor insult, a glance, or no reason at all. He behaves like a man in a frenzy, as if drunk on his own fury.

Once he has breached the boundaries of morality, he becomes a stranger to himself. Suddenly, nothing is sacred to him. He flouts every law, challenges every authority, and revels in his newfound freedom to act without restraint. The chaos within his heart excites him, and the fear he provokes in others gives him a grim satisfaction. Yet he is fully aware that a dreadful punishment awaits him. His state of mind is akin to that of a man standing on the edge of a high tower, staring into the abyss below and feeling an irresistible urge to leap, just to end everything.

Even the most unassuming, timid individuals can descend into such madness. Some revel in their newfound ferocity, adopting an exaggerated swagger. The more subdued and invisible they were before, the more brazen and theatrical they become now. These desperate men delight in shocking others, relishing the disgust they provoke. They act out of despair, often performing acts of senseless destruction, with no concern for the consequences. In fact, they seem eager to hasten their downfall.

Their heightened state of agitation and recklessness persists until they face the pillory. At that moment, the thread of their rage and defiance snaps. All their bravado vanishes, leaving them hollow and subdued. In the pillory, they crumble, pleading for forgiveness from the crowd. By the time they arrive at the convict prison, they are unrecognizable—a shadow of their former selves. No one would ever guess that this meek, subdued creature had once taken multiple lives.

However, not all murderers lose their defiance so quickly. Some retain a semblance of arrogance and bravado even within the prison walls.

"You think I'm ordinary?" they might boast. "I've sent six men to their graves."

These men thrive on recounting their crimes to anyone willing to listen, usually targeting gullible or impressionable listeners. They recount their bloody exploits with a calculated nonchalance, pretending not to care whether their audience is impressed.

"That's the kind of man I am," they say, watching their audience closely for any sign of awe or fear. Their entire demeanor reeks of practiced artifice. It's as though they've honed their craft over time, mastering the art of appearing both dangerous and aloof.

One evening, not long after my arrival, I witnessed one of these storytellers at work. Thanks to my naivety, I mistook him for a hardened criminal, a figure even more fearsome than Petroff. The narrator, Luka Kouzmitch, claimed to have killed a Major for no reason other than sheer impulse. Luka was a small, wiry man, the slightest and weakest in our barracks. He hailed from the South and had once been a domestic serf, unattached to the land. Despite his diminutive stature, his demeanor was sharp and haughty. He had the air of a small bird, quick and feisty, with a sharp beak and claws.

The other convicts, however, had sized him up instinctively. They saw through his pretensions and thought little of him. His excessive pride and prickly nature made him an object of mild amusement rather than fear.

That evening, Luka sat cross-legged on his camp bed, stitching a shirt with deliberate precision. Nearby was Kobylin, a large, good-natured but simple-minded convict who seemed impervious to Luka's frequent displays of arrogance. Kobylin, who was knitting a stocking, listened to Luka with an air of detached indifference. Luka spoke loudly and clearly, ensuring that everyone in the barracks could hear him, though he pretended to address only Kobylin.

"I was exiled as a brigand," Luka began, his needle moving deftly through the fabric.

"How long ago was that?" asked Kobylin, knitting away as if the answer barely mattered.

"When the peas are ripe, it will be just a year," Luka replied with a dramatic pause, clearly relishing the attention. "We reached K——v, and I was thrown into the convict prison. Around me were a dozen men from Little Russia—big, solid, ox-like fellows, all as quiet as lambs. The food was awful, and the Major did whatever he pleased. Day after day passed, and I realized quickly what cowards they all were."

"'You're afraid of that fool?' I asked them."

"'Why don't you go and speak to him yourself?' they said, laughing like the brutes they were. I held my tongue."

Luka paused for effect, glancing at the convicts around him to ensure they were listening. Then, with a sly grin, he added, "There was one fellow—so droll, I tell you. He couldn't stop talking about his trial. He told us how he cried, how he begged, and how a clerk wrote down every word he said. 'I lost my head completely,' he admitted. 'The clerk annoyed me so much, I wanted to send him straight to the devil!'"

"Hand me that thread, Vasili. The stuff we get from the house is useless—rotten," Luka said, breaking his story momentarily.

"There's some from the tailor's shop," Vasili replied, tossing it to him.

"And the Major?" Kobylin asked, bringing the story back on track.

Luka smiled as if he had been waiting for this question. He threaded his needle slowly, as though considering whether Kobylin even deserved an answer. Finally, with exaggerated leisure, he resumed his tale.

"I worked them up so much that they all started grumbling about the Major. That morning, I borrowed the 'rascal'—you know, the knife—from my neighbor and hid it, just in case. When the Major showed up, he was already half-drunk, raging like a lunatic."

"'Come on, you Little Russians,' I whispered to them. 'Now's not the time to lose your nerve.' But oh, their courage had run straight to

117

their boots. They just trembled."

Luka mimicked the Major's furious tone. "'What's this? How dare you? I'm your Tsar, your God!' That's what he screamed."

Luka's voice dropped into a mocking drawl as he continued. "So I walked up to him, the knife hidden in my sleeve, and said, 'No, your high nobility. That's not quite right. You're not our Tsar or our God.'"

"'Ah, it's you!' the Major roared, pointing at me. 'You're their ringleader!'"

"'No, your high nobility,' I replied, stepping closer, 'as everyone knows, there's only one God in heaven, and He's all-powerful. And we have one Tsar placed above us by God Himself. You, your high nobility, are just a Major. Our leader, sure, but only by the grace of the Tsar and your merits.'"

Luka leaned forward, lowering his voice for dramatic effect. "The Major was speechless, his jaw practically hitting the floor. And that's when I did it. Quick as a flash, I plunged the knife into his belly, right up to the hilt."

The barracks fell silent. Luka let the moment stretch before adding, "And that was it. I threw my life away in that instant."

"'Now, pick him up, you fools!' I shouted at the Little Russians."

He paused, surveying his audience, clearly enjoying their rapt attention. Then, with a casual air, he added, "And that's how it happened."

Luka's story sparked murmurs among the listeners, but he seemed indifferent to their reactions. Instead, he turned to Kobylin and asked, "Well, what do you think of that?"

"You must have paid dearly for it," Kobylin said.

"Of course. They gave me five hundred strokes. They nearly killed me," Luka replied, addressing the group now, not just Kobylin. "It was

118

quite the event! The whole town turned out to watch me get flogged. Timoshka, the executioner, undressed me, laid me out, and said, 'Get ready, I'm going to roast you!' I couldn't even scream. By the second stroke, my voice was gone. I didn't hear them count until they reached seventeen. They took me down four times to let me breathe and splash me with water. I thought I was going to die right there."

"But you didn't die," Kobylin said, genuinely puzzled.

The room erupted in laughter. Luka shot him a withering look. "What an idiot! Is he all there?" he muttered disdainfully.

"He's a bit off, I think," Vasili added, smirking.

Though Luka had killed six men, no one in the barracks feared him. His attempts to project an aura of menace were met with mockery rather than awe. It was clear that while Luka craved a reputation as a fearsome figure, he failed to inspire the terror he so desperately sought.

Chapter 10

Isaiah Fomitch—The Bath—Baklouchin

As the Christmas holidays approached, a palpable sense of anticipation filled the air. The convicts, who rarely had cause for celebration, seemed transformed by the promise of something out of the ordinary. Even their movements and conversations hinted that these days would be different. Four days before the holidays, the announcement came that they would be taken to the bathhouse—a rare and eagerly awaited occasion. The news was met with visible excitement, and preparations began in earnest. There was no work scheduled for the afternoon, adding to the festive mood. Among the convicts, none showed more enthusiasm than Isaiah Fomitch Bumstein, a peculiar character who seemed to thrive on these occasions. The bathhouse, it turned out, was his sanctuary, a place where he could indulge in his odd habit of staying in the steam until he nearly lost consciousness.

The bathhouse experience was unforgettable, and whenever I think of it, my thoughts invariably turn to Isaiah Fomitch. This man was a walking enigma, a blend of absurdity and resilience. He was about fifty, his body frail and birdlike, with a face deeply etched with wrinkles and scars from punishments endured. Yet, his demeanor was one of unwavering confidence and contentment. There was an air of inexplicable joy about him, as though he found happiness even in the bleakness of the convict prison. Remarkably, he seemed untroubled by his sentence of hard labor.

A jeweler by trade, Isaiah had no shortage of work. There was no other jeweler in the town, so he earned a decent living even within the confines of the prison. His modest luxuries—a tea-urn, a mattress, a teacup, and a blanket—set him apart from most of the convicts. He saved diligently, even lending money to others at interest. Despite his peculiarities and the teasing he endured, Isaiah was never truly mocked or despised. On the contrary, the other convicts treated him as a source of amusement, a kind of mascot who brightened their otherwise grim existence.

"We've only got one Isaiah Fomitch, so we'll take care of him," the convicts seemed to agree, and Isaiah, in turn, relished his role. He was proud of his unique place in the community. He also looked forward to his eventual release, when he hoped to marry and start a new life. His demeanor was a curious mix of timidity, shyness, and cunning. Yet, his innocence and eccentricity endeared him to everyone.

I heard an account of how Isaiah entered the convict prison, and the story alone was enough to make me laugh. It was a scene straight out of a comedy. The news that a Jew was being brought to the prison spread like wildfire. At that time, there were no Jews among the inmates, so his arrival was a novelty. As Isaiah stepped through the gates, burdened with a small bag of belongings, he was met by a crowd of convicts eager to see him.

He was taken to the civil barracks and shown his place—a plank bedstead. Setting his bag down, he sat cross-legged on the bed, his eyes downcast, radiating nervous energy. The convicts, many with mutilated faces and hardened expressions, surrounded him, chuckling and exchanging amused glances.

Suddenly, a young convict broke from the group, holding up a ragged pair of summer trousers patched with scraps of cloth. Sitting beside Isaiah, he clapped him on the shoulder and declared, "Well, my friend, I've been waiting six years for this moment. Tell me, how much will you give for these fine trousers?"

Isaiah, thoroughly bewildered and terrified, hesitated before lifting his gaze to examine the proffered garment. The crowd watched with bated breath, waiting for his reaction.

"Well, can't you give me a silver rouble? Surely they're worth that," the convict said with a sly grin, winking at the others.

Isaiah, still trembling, managed to stammer his first words in the prison: "A silver rouble? No, but I'll give you seven kopecks."

Laughter erupted from every corner of the barracks. The convicts roared with amusement, their toughened faces softened momentarily by genuine mirth.

"Seven kopecks! Done!" the convict exclaimed, handing over the trousers. "Take care of the pledge, my friend. You're responsible for it with your head!"

From that moment on, Isaiah's reputation was sealed. His timid yet shrewd response made him a figure of fascination and a source of endless entertainment. The convicts' laughter echoed long after the deal was struck, marking the beginning of Isaiah's unique and oddly cherished place within the prison walls.

"With three kopecks added as interest, that makes ten kopecks you owe me," said Isaiah Fomitch as he fished out the agreed-upon amount from his pocket with a deliberate motion.

"Three kopecks interest—for a whole year?" asked the convict incredulously.

"No, not for a year, for a single month," Isaiah replied, with a tone of authority.

"You're a real miser, aren't you? What's your name?"

"Isaiah Fomitch," he answered with a touch of pride.

"Well, Isaiah Fomitch, you'll go far. Good-bye."

As the convict walked off, Isaiah carefully inspected the rags he had just accepted as collateral for the seven kopecks. Satisfied with his assessment, he folded them meticulously and tucked them into his bag. Around him, the other convicts burst into laughter at the absurdity of the transaction, but there was no malice in their amusement.

Though everyone laughed at Isaiah's peculiarities and many owed him money, not one convict truly insulted him. In fact, their lighthearted mockery carried a tone of affection, as though they recognized him as a unique and harmless figure among them. This unspoken camaraderie emboldened Isaiah, who sometimes adopted an air of superiority so comical that it was easily forgiven.

Luka, who had known many Jews during his life as a free man, often teased Isaiah. It wasn't out of cruelty but rather the kind of playful teasing one might direct at a pet or a younger sibling. Isaiah seemed to understand this and rarely took offense.

"You'll see, Jew, I'll flog you one of these days," Luka would say with mock seriousness.

"If you hit me once, I'll hit you back ten times," Isaiah retorted, puffing himself up in mock bravado.

"You scurvy Jew."

"Call me scurvy if you like, but I've got plenty of money," Isaiah shot back with a sly grin.

"Bravo, Isaiah Fomitch," another convict chimed in. "We have to take good care of you. You're our only Jew. But they'll send you deeper into Siberia one of these days."

"I'm already in Siberia," Isaiah replied dryly.

"They'll send you even farther."

"And isn't the Lord God there as well?"

"Of course, He's everywhere."

"Well then! With the Lord God and money, I've got everything I need."

The convicts roared with laughter. Despite knowing they were laughing at him, Isaiah took it in stride, basking in the attention. His eyes sparkled with satisfaction as he began to hum in his peculiar falsetto, "La, la, la, la," repeating the nonsensical tune that would become his trademark. The song was ridiculous and childlike, yet Isaiah sang it with a solemnity that left everyone either chuckling or shaking their heads in disbelief.

When Isaiah became acquainted with me, he solemnly assured me that his song and its tune were of profound historical significance. According to him, it was the very melody sung by 600,000 Israelites as they crossed the Red Sea. He even claimed it was commanded by law to be sung after every Jewish victory. His earnestness made it impossible not to smile.

Every Friday evening, convicts from other barracks gathered in ours to witness Isaiah's Sabbath rituals. He relished their attention and went about his preparations with exaggerated dignity. In his corner, he would spread out a cloth on the table with painstaking care, light two candles, and open a worn book with an air of reverence. Then, with great ceremony, he donned his striped, sleeved chasuble, which he kept at the bottom of his trunk, and strapped leather bracelets to his wrists. The final touch was a small box affixed to his forehead with a ribbon, making it appear as though a tiny horn sprouted from his head.

Isaiah would then begin to pray. His voice droned as he read aloud, occasionally punctuating his prayers with theatrical cries, spits, and wild gestures. The ritual, while deeply rooted in his faith, took on an absurdly dramatic flair in his execution. At one moment, he would clasp his head with both hands, sobbing uncontrollably. His tears would grow louder and more mournful until he nearly collapsed over his book. Then, without warning, he would burst into joyous laughter, chanting a hymn of victory in a triumphant nasal tone. The abrupt transition from despair to elation was so exaggerated that it left the convicts alternately baffled and amused.

"Impossible to understand him," some of the convicts would mutter, shaking their heads.

Curious about the meaning behind these dramatic shifts in emotion, I once asked Isaiah why his prayers veered so sharply between sorrow and joy. He was thrilled by my question and eagerly launched into an explanation. The tears and sobs, he told me, were an expression of mourning for the loss of Jerusalem, a grief mandated by Jewish law. At the height of this sorrow, however, the faithful were instructed to remember the prophecy of their eventual return to Jerusalem. At that moment, their sadness was to give way to unrestrained joy—a celebration of the hope and triumph foretold.

Isaiah explained this with such pride and delight that it was clear he found immense satisfaction in both the practice and its deeper meaning. His theatrical performances were not just acts of faith but also an expression of his eccentric and indefatigable spirit.

One evening, in the middle of his fervent prayers, Isaiah Fomitch continued his ritualistic shouting and gesturing, undeterred by the sudden entry of the Major, flanked by the officer of the guard and a group of soldiers. As was customary, the convicts immediately lined up beside their camp-beds in strict order. Isaiah, however, paid no attention. Confident that his prayers were officially sanctioned and that no one had the authority to interrupt him, he carried on with exaggerated zeal, seemingly relishing the opportunity to perform under the Major's watchful eye.

The Major, curious and slightly taken aback, approached a few steps closer. Isaiah, with theatrical precision, turned his back to the table and faced the officer. He launched into the jubilant section of his hymn, waving his arms and drawing out the syllables in an over-the-top, almost operatic tone. When the moment came to express supreme joy, he squinted his eyes, beamed widely, and nodded directly at the Major, as if to personally include him in his exaltation. The Major, initially bewildered, burst out laughing, exclaiming, "Idiot!" before retreating with his entourage. Isaiah, unfazed, carried on with his exuberant display as though nothing had happened.

Later, when his prayers were complete, I asked him what he would have done if the Major had lost his temper and punished him.

"What Major?" he responded with genuine confusion.

"What Major? He was right there, barely two steps from you, staring at you the whole time," I explained.

Isaiah solemnly assured me that during his prayers, he was so immersed in spiritual ecstasy that he neither saw nor heard anything happening around him. His conviction was unshakable, and I found myself marveling at the peculiar world he inhabited.

On Saturdays, Isaiah would wander aimlessly about the prison, adhering strictly to the Jewish law that forbade work on the Sabbath. Each time he returned from the synagogue, he would bring back absurd rumors and fantastical news from St. Petersburg, gathered from his fellow Jews in the town. The stories were often so ridiculous that I could only shake my head in amusement. Yet Isaiah recounted them with such earnestness that it was hard not to be entertained. His peculiarities made him an unforgettable figure among the prisoners.

There were only two public baths in the entire town. One, run by a Jew, was reserved for the wealthy. It had private compartments, and patrons paid fifty kopecks for the privilege of bathing in relative comfort. The other bath, decrepit and crowded, was for the common people. This was where the convicts were taken. The mere thought of leaving the fortress and walking through the town on the way to the bath brought a ripple of excitement among the prisoners. The anticipation was palpable. Their laughter and banter echoed through the streets as a platoon of armed soldiers accompanied us, muskets loaded, to prevent any escape. The sight of the procession drew curious glances from the townspeople.

Upon arriving at the bathhouse, we found it too cramped to accommodate all of us at once. The convicts were divided into two groups, with one waiting in the cold outer room while the other entered the steaming hot chamber. Even then, the space inside was so limited that it was hard to imagine how half of us could fit at a time.

Petroff, ever attentive, stayed by my side without being asked. He offered to help me undress and even volunteered to rub me down once we entered the bath. Another convict, Baklouchin—nicknamed "the Sapper"—also extended his services. Known for his cheerfulness and wit, Baklouchin had become one of my closest companions in the prison.

Petroff insisted on helping me remove my chains, as I was still inexperienced with the process. Unfastening the leather straps that secured the iron rings around our legs required some skill. These straps, which cost sixty kopecks a pair, were essential for preventing the rings from chafing the skin raw during daily wear. Removing clothing was a feat in itself, especially for novices like me. The process was so cumbersome that it often felt like a small victory when successfully completed. Koreneff, a former brigand chief with years of experience, was the one who had first taught us the art of managing this tiresome task.

I handed Petroff a few kopecks to buy soap and a bundle of birch twigs for scrubbing. Though each convict received a small piece of soap as part of their ration, it was barely enough to be useful. Additional soap, along with cakes, mead, and hot water, could be purchased in the dressing room through a small window in the wall. Those who wanted to wash thoroughly often paid for extra pails of water, as the single bucket provided by the prison was insufficient for a proper bath.

Inside the bathhouse, the scene was chaotic. Imagine a room scarcely twelve feet square packed with nearly a hundred men, with steam so thick it obscured vision. The suffocating heat, combined with the grime and sweat of so many bodies, created an atmosphere that was nearly unbearable. I felt overwhelmed and wanted to leave, but Petroff reassured me, guiding me carefully through the throng.

Space was so limited that even the benches were overcrowded. Petroff negotiated with another convict to secure a spot for me. For a single kopeck, the man surrendered his place near the window and squeezed himself into a filthy corner on the floor. I climbed onto the bench, trying to ignore the filth around me. Everywhere I looked, convicts were either scrubbing themselves, pouring water over their heads, or whipping themselves with birch twigs in a frenzy of activity. The air grew hotter with every passing moment, and the sound of splashing water, clanging chains, and shouted curses created a deafening din.

On the floor below, bundles of birch twigs rose and fell rhythmically as men lashed their bodies into a state of euphoric exhaustion. Convicts crowded around the window where boiling water was handed out, often spilling it over the heads of those seated nearby. Despite the oppressive conditions, there was an almost palpable sense of exhilaration in the air, as though the bath offered a fleeting taste of freedom amid the constraints of prison life.

Through the haze of steam and chaos, the occasional sight of a soldier's face at the door reminded us that we were still under watch. The muskets slung over their shoulders served as a quiet but constant reminder that, despite the temporary illusion of liberty, we remained prisoners.

The shaved heads of the convicts glistened under the thick steam, their red, raw-looking bodies appearing even more grotesque and unnatural in the oppressive heat of the bath. The intense vapors gave their skin a hue like blood, highlighting the scars that streaked across their backs—marks of old punishments inflicted with whips and rods. These scars, long healed but still vividly etched in their flesh, seemed so fresh and raw under the haze of steam that it sent shivers through me. The room was an oppressive mixture of heat, moisture, and sound, a churning cauldron of humanity. In the dense, scorching cloud of steam, heads and bodies moved like phantoms, blending into a surreal scene of chaos, all punctuated by the shrill, triumphant howls of Isaiah Fomitch, perched on the highest bench as though he were reigning over this pandemonium.

Isaiah Fomitch seemed utterly impervious to the heat that overwhelmed others. He reveled in it, his frail body absorbing the intensity of the steam that would have felled most men. He gleefully hired one rubber after another to scrub and beat his back with birch twigs, paying a kopeck to each as they took their turns. When one rubber was too exhausted to continue, he waved him off and summoned another. The spectacle was met with jeers and cheers from the convicts below.

"Isaiah Fomitch is boiling himself well today!" one of them shouted with a mix of amusement and awe.

Isaiah reveled in the attention, his chest puffed with pride as if this endurance made him a conqueror of the bathhouse. Over the din of laughter, cries, and splashing water, his nasal falsetto rose defiantly, belting out his absurdly jubilant tune. The sheer absurdity of the scene struck me as nightmarish, and I whispered to Petroff, wondering aloud

128

if hell might look and sound like this. Petroff glanced around but made no reply, his expression unreadable.

Feeling compelled to show Petroff some gratitude for his attentiveness, I offered to purchase a spot for him on the bench beside me. He refused with a shake of his head, insisting that he was perfectly comfortable sitting at my feet. Meanwhile, Baklouchin, always the entertainer, secured us some extra hot water, ready to assist whenever we needed it.

Petroff busied himself with scrubbing me thoroughly with soap, showing a care that was almost maternal. I tried to assure him I could manage on my own, but he waved away my protests, continuing with methodical precision. When he was finished, he guided me back to the dressing room as though I were made of delicate glass, holding my arm and cautioning me at every step. He even helped me dress, ensuring that my chains were fastened properly. Only then did he return to the bathhouse for his turn to bask in the heat.

Once we were back in the barracks, I offered Petroff a glass of tea as a small token of thanks, which he accepted gratefully. His quiet demeanor lit up with visible pleasure when I surprised him by purchasing a glass of vodka for him. He sipped it with audible satisfaction, exclaiming that it revived him completely. Then, true to his nature, he abruptly excused himself and dashed off to the kitchen, seemingly unable to resist joining whatever conversation might be taking place there.

No sooner had Petroff left than Baklouchin approached, cheerfully taking his place. I poured him tea, and he sat down with his usual lively energy. Of all the convicts I had come to know, Baklouchin was undoubtedly the most engaging. His quick wit and easy laughter made him popular with everyone, though he had a fiery temperament that sometimes led to short-lived quarrels. He never tolerated interference in his affairs, but these spats rarely caused lasting enmity. Most of the prisoners liked him, and his charisma made him welcome wherever he went, even in the town.

Tall and broad-shouldered, Baklouchin had a striking presence. His bright, open face carried a mischievous spark, and he had a knack for twisting his features into hilarious expressions, mimicking others with uncanny accuracy. His antics brought laughter wherever he went, and even those who didn't share his sense of humor knew better than to slight him. Beneath his jovial surface lay a sharp sense of self-respect and an unyielding spirit.

As we sipped our tea, he began recounting a spirited tale of the day's events, particularly how Lieutenant K—— had humiliated the Major during a heated exchange. His narration was so animated that it felt like we were witnessing the scene ourselves. He also revealed an exciting bit of news: the convicts were planning a theatrical performance for the upcoming Christmas holidays. With growing enthusiasm, he described how they had already found actors and begun preparing the scenery. Townsfolk had even promised to lend women's clothing for the production. There was a buzz of anticipation, though everything hinged on whether the Major would allow it. Baklouchin's eyes gleamed with excitement as he declared that he would play a leading role in the preparations. His infectious enthusiasm made it impossible not to share his hope.

The conversation turned more personal as I inquired about his past. Baklouchin had served as a sapper in the Engineers and later been transferred to a garrison battalion in R——. When I asked why he had been sent to the convict prison, he smiled wryly and replied, "Because I was in love."

I laughed. "Surely, love isn't a crime worthy of hard labor."

He chuckled, then added with a touch of theatrical drama, "Ah, but it was love that drove me to shoot a German dead. Tell me, was it worth being exiled to hard labor for killing a German?"

Intrigued, I pressed him to tell the story. "It must be quite the tale,"

I said.

"It is," he replied, leaning in with a conspiratorial grin. "And if you'd like, I'll tell you the whole thing."

And with that, he began his account—a tale that, while not exactly amusing, was every bit as strange and captivating as he had promised.

"This is how it happened," began Baklouchin. "I was sent to Riga—a beautiful city, truly. Its only fault was the overwhelming number of Germans. I was young then, with a good reputation among the officers. I cocked my cap to the side, full of confidence, and spent my time as cheerfully as you can imagine. The German girls were charming, and I was particularly drawn to one named Luisa. She lived with her aunt, and together they worked as fine linen washers and ironers. The aunt was an odd-looking old woman, practically a caricature, but she had money.

"At first, I only passed by their window, stealing glances, but soon enough, Luisa and I became acquainted. She spoke Russian tolerably well, though with a slight accent. Luisa—ah, she was something special, one of the neatest, most affectionate girls I've ever met. She had a way about her, always smiling but maintaining an air of innocence. She was adamant about preserving her virtue until marriage. It was her idea, you see, that we should wed, and how could I refuse her? She was irresistible. But then, everything changed.

"One day, Luisa missed our meeting. Then it happened again, and a third time. I wrote her a letter, but she didn't reply. 'What's going on?' I wondered. If she wanted to deceive me, she could have easily answered my letter and continued meeting me. But no, she cut things off completely. It wasn't like her. 'This must be her aunt's doing,' I decided. Yet I hesitated to go to their house—though the aunt knew of our engagement, we had acted as if she were ignorant of it.

"Finally, I wrote Luisa a sharp letter. I told her, 'If you don't come to see me, I'll come to your aunt's myself.' That frightened her enough to make her come. When we met, she broke down in tears, telling me everything. It seemed a distant relative of theirs, a German clockmaker named Schultz, had proposed to her. He was older, wealthy, and determined to make her his wife. She explained that he wanted to secure her happiness—and, of course, ensure he wasn't alone in his old age. She told me he'd loved her quietly for years and only now gathered the courage to speak.

"'Sasha,' she said, looking at me with tear-filled eyes, 'you want me to be happy, don't you? He's rich, and his proposal is good. Should I give it up?'

"I stared at her, speechless, as she wept and embraced me. For a moment, I thought, 'She's right. What future could I offer her? A soldier's life?' Reluctantly, I resolved to let her go.

"'Is he at least handsome?' I asked bitterly.

"'No,' she replied, laughing through her tears. 'He's old, with a long nose.'

"She burst into laughter, but I couldn't share in her mirth. I left her, my heart heavy. 'It's destiny,' I thought. The next day, I passed by Schultz's shop. She'd told me where it was, and curiosity got the better of me. Through the window, I saw him—an unimpressive man of about forty-five, with an aquiline nose and puffy eyes, hunched over a watch with his high-collared coat. My stomach churned with contempt. I wanted to break his windows, but instead, I spat on the ground and walked away. 'What's the use?' I told myself. 'It's over.'

"Back at the barracks, I threw myself onto my bed and—believe it or not, Alexander Petrovitch—I sobbed like a child. Days passed, but I couldn't forget her. Then, an old washerwoman, who occasionally saw Luisa, informed me that Schultz had rushed the engagement upon learning about me. The old miser refused to spend money or make plans until Luisa swore never to see me again. The washerwoman also mentioned that Schultz had invited Luisa, her aunt, and a poor relative to his house for coffee on Sunday. Apparently, it was during this gathering that the engagement would be finalized.

"When Sunday came, I was consumed by rage. I couldn't sit still. After morning service, I grabbed my coat and—without any real plan—headed to Schultz's house. Before leaving, I slipped a pistol into my pocket. It was a useless old thing, barely functional, but I thought it might come in handy if I needed to scare them.

"I arrived and found the shop deserted. Everyone was inside the workshop. I kicked the door open, my heart racing. Inside, the table was laid out with coffee, brandy, herrings, sausages, and wine. Luisa and her aunt sat on a sofa, dressed in their Sunday best. Schultz, in his ridiculous high-collared coat, looked smug as he played the host. An older, gray-haired German sat silently nearby.

"When I entered, Luisa turned pale, and her aunt jumped in her seat. Schultz, however, rose angrily and marched toward me. 'What do you want?' he demanded.

"'What do I want?' I shot back, pretending to be calm. 'Is this how you welcome a guest? Why not offer me a drink?'

"Schultz hesitated, then said stiffly, 'Sit down.'

"I sat, gritting my teeth as he poured me a glass of vodka. 'Let's hope this is good,' I said, my voice rising with anger. My heart was pounding, and my hand rested on the pistol in my pocket. What happened next, well... let me continue."

Baklouchin paused, a glint in his eye as he leaned closer, ready to unfold the rest of his tale.

"This is how it went," Baklouchin began again, his tone tinged with both regret and a peculiar pride. "When I drank the vodka, I said to the German, 'It's good.' But his smug glance, sizing me up from head to toe, infuriated me, especially with Luisa watching the entire exchange. The anger surged up in me, uncontrollable. I put the glass down and said:

"'Listen here, German, what right have you to speak to me with such disrespect? Let's be friends instead.'

"His response was calm, cutting, and full of disdain: 'I cannot be your friend. You are a private soldier.'

"That broke me. Whatever composure I had left vanished.

"'Oh, you German sausage-maker!' I shouted, the rage spilling over. 'You think you're untouchable? Do you realize how much power I hold over you right now? Do you want me to smash your head open with this pistol?'

"I pulled the old pistol from my pocket and waved it before him. The women froze in terror, wide-eyed and unable to even scream. The older man sitting nearby turned pale as death, trembling like a leaf in a storm. The German, however, had the nerve to act unshaken.

"'I am not afraid of you,' he said firmly, though his voice betrayed a flicker of hesitation. 'And I ask you, as a well-bred man, to stop this nonsense.'

"'You're not afraid, huh?' I shot back, taking a step closer and pointing the pistol at his forehead.

"'I am not afraid,' he repeated, his voice steadier this time. 'And you wouldn't dare to do anything!'

"'Wouldn't dare?' I said, my fury boiling over.

"'No, you wouldn't dare,' he replied confidently. 'You'd be punished severely.'

"That did it. His arrogance was the spark that ignited the fire. 'So, you think I wouldn't dare?' I hissed.

"He barely finished his reply—'No, you wouldn't'—when I pulled the trigger. The room erupted in chaos. Schultz collapsed into his chair, a shocked look frozen on his face. The women screamed, one covering

134

her face while the other fainted on the spot. The older man fled without a word, clutching his hat as though it were his lifeline.

"I tucked the pistol back into my coat and calmly left the house. I walked straight back to the barracks, heart pounding but outwardly composed. On the way, I tossed the pistol into the weeds near the fortress entrance, thinking, 'That's the end of it. They'll come for me soon.'

"Back in the barracks, I lay on my bed, waiting for the inevitable knock at the door. An hour passed, then two. Nothing. I couldn't understand it. By nightfall, my restlessness grew unbearable, and I ventured out again, taking the risk to see Luisa.

"When I reached her, she threw herself into my arms, sobbing uncontrollably. 'It's all my fault,' she cried. 'I should never have listened to my aunt. I should have stayed true to you.'

"Through her tears, she explained everything. The aunt had been so terrified by the incident that she had locked herself away, refusing to speak to anyone. She'd even sworn Luisa to secrecy. As for the older man, the one who fled? He was apparently notorious for his silence and fear of conflict. 'He won't say a word,' Luisa assured me.

"For two weeks, nothing happened. No arrests, no accusations. Those fourteen days were the happiest of my life. Luisa and I saw each other every day, and her devotion to me only deepened. 'If you are sent away,' she said one night, tears streaming down her face, 'I'll follow you. I'll leave everything behind to be with you.'

"I couldn't handle it. Her love was too much—it tore at my heart. But then, as I'd feared, everything fell apart. The aunt and the old man finally broke their silence and reported me. Two weeks of bliss ended with my arrest.

"But that's not the whole story," Baklouchin continued, his voice hardening. "After they took me in, there was another incident—a trial.

During my hearing, the captain in charge began hurling insults at me, calling me every vile name you can imagine. I'd had enough. I shot back, 'Why do you insult me, you fool? Don't you see you're just talking to your own reflection?'

"That, of course, sealed my fate. They tacked on a second charge, and instead of ten to twelve years in the civil section, I was sentenced to four thousand strokes and hard labor in the special section.

"When I was taken out to Green Street to face my punishment, the captain himself was there, but it was also the last time he held any rank. The authorities stripped him of his title and sent him to the Caucasus as a private soldier. Poetic justice, don't you think?

"So, here I am, Alexander Petrovitch, telling you this story. But enough of my past. Don't forget to come to our play during the holidays. We'll give you something to smile about."

With that, Baklouchin laughed—a deep, hearty sound—and clapped me on the shoulder before walking away, leaving me with much to reflect on.

Chapter 11
The Christmas Holidays

The holidays were drawing near, and the air within the convict prison was thick with anticipation. On the eve of the great day, the usual routines began to shift. While some of the convicts still went to their assigned tasks in the sewing workshops or carried out minor errands, they returned quickly to the prison, often in groups, but with an air of quiet excitement. By mid-afternoon, work had come to a standstill for nearly everyone. The administration seemed to understand that the day belonged to the convicts, and the prisoners, in turn, took full advantage of this unspoken truce.

From the early morning hours, the barracks were alive with activity, though it was not the sort mandated by the authorities. Groups of men huddled in corners, whispering and conspiring to smuggle in spirits. Others roamed the grounds under the pretense of running errands, seeking permission to meet friends or retrieve debts owed for previous handiwork. The air was filled with purpose, even among those who had no real business to attend to—they joined the hustle simply to feel part of the unfolding drama. Baklouchin, ever the entertainer, flitted between his theater troupe and other convicts, negotiating with officers' servants to procure costumes and props for their performance. Everyone seemed to be in motion, whether they had an actual task or simply pretended to.

As the day wore on, the atmosphere became more festive. By evening, old soldiers who served as intermediaries between the convicts and the outside world began delivering an array of foodstuffs to the prison. Roasted geese, cuts of meat, and even the occasional delicacy like sucking-pigs made their way into the barracks. The convicts, even the thriftiest among them who had hoarded their meager earnings all year, were suddenly eager to spend their saved kopecks to mark the occasion. It was as though the magnitude of the holiday demanded extravagance, a fleeting moment of indulgence amidst their otherwise bleak existence.

The following day promised even greater significance. Christmas was not just a holiday but a legally recognized day of rest, and no one— neither the administration nor the guards—could force the convicts to work. It was one of only three such days in the entire year, and the prisoners cherished it deeply. The reverence they showed for the occasion was palpable, even touching. Drunken revelry, though not absent, was rare. Instead, the barracks were dominated by a heavy, solemn respect for the day. Laughter was subdued, almost as though it were forbidden. Even those who feasted with the most enthusiasm maintained a serious demeanor, their joy muted by an awareness of the day's deeper significance. An unspoken code of conduct emerged, and any prisoner who disrupted the peace, even unintentionally, was swiftly reprimanded with a chorus of curses and threats. It was as if offending the sanctity of the holiday was an affront to the very fabric of their collective humanity.

This quiet reverence stemmed from more than religious observance; it was a profound expression of the convicts' yearning to remain connected to the world beyond the prison walls. For one day, they could imagine themselves as part of a broader human experience, sharing in the same traditions as families across the country. The memories of past Christmases—spent with loved ones, free and unburdened—flooded their minds, bittersweet but grounding. For a brief moment, they were not merely convicts but human beings with ties to something larger than their confinement.

Among those who approached the holiday with meticulous care was Akim Akimitch. A man of routine and unshakable adherence to duty, he approached the celebration with the same precision he applied to every aspect of his life. He had no sentimental memories of Christmas past, no family gatherings to long for, being an orphan raised in a stranger's house and thrust into the army at the tender age of fifteen. His life had been one of unyielding structure, devoid of personal joys or passions. Yet, even Akim Akimitch felt compelled to mark the occasion with ceremonial rigor.

Days before the holiday, he began his preparations, carefully roasting a sucking-pig stuffed with millet. It was a task he approached with almost religious devotion, treating the animal as if it were a sacred offering rather than an ordinary piece of meat. To him, the pig symbolized the proper observance of Christmas—a tradition so deeply ingrained in him that failing to include it would have felt like a moral failure. Perhaps, in some long-forgotten corner of his childhood, he had seen such a dish served on this day, and the memory had solidified into an unspoken law.

Akim Akimitch's preparations extended beyond food. For months, he had safeguarded a set of new clothes, issued to him by the administration, reserving them for the holiday. On Christmas Eve, he meticulously removed the garments from his trunk, inspecting them for dust, brushing them clean, and trying them on to ensure a perfect fit. When he finally donned them, the transformation was remarkable. The stiff collar of his waistcoat straightened his posture, giving him an almost military bearing. He examined himself in a small mirror with a gilded frame, turning this way and that, a faint smile of satisfaction playing on his lips. For Akim Akimitch, the act of dressing for Christmas was as much a ritual as the roasting of the pig—a small victory of order and dignity in a life otherwise stripped of both.

As the barracks settled into an expectant hush, the solemnity of the approaching day was tangible. Even in the dim, overcrowded confines of the prison, the spirit of the holiday managed to shine through, uniting the convicts in a shared sense of humanity and hope. For a brief, fleeting moment, the walls of the fortress seemed less oppressive, and the weight of their chains a little lighter.

One of the waistcoat buttons seemed slightly loose, and Akim Akimitch immediately noticed it. Without hesitation, he set to work fixing it with a precision that suggested he was handling a matter of grave importance. Once the button was securely in place, he tried on the vest again. This time, it met his meticulous standards. Satisfied, he folded it neatly, along with the other garments, and placed them back in his trunk, locking it with care. His preparations were not yet complete, however. A glance in the small mirror revealed to him that his skull, though adequately shaved, bore the faintest hint of regrowth. This would not do. Concluding that his appearance needed further refinement, he made his way to the "Major," the prison barber, to have his head shaved again.

In truth, no one would have cared to examine him closely the next day, but Akim Akimitch's commitment to fulfilling his duties was unwavering. His sense of order and discipline was deeply ingrained, a principle he carried into every aspect of his life. To him, even the smallest details—a button, a thread, a perfectly shaved head—represented an ideal state of harmony that he was determined to achieve. As one of the senior convicts in the barracks, he took it upon himself to oversee additional preparations, ensuring that hay was brought in and strewn across the floors. This peculiar tradition was observed every Christmas, though no one seemed to know its origin.

Once everything was in place, Akim Akimitch knelt for his evening prayers, as he did every day, and then lay down on his bed with the serene sleep of a man who had fulfilled every obligation. His rest was purposeful; he wanted to rise early to greet the holiday with the same exactitude he brought to his preparations. His example seemed to influence the other convicts, who also retired earlier than usual that evening. The barracks were quiet, devoid of the usual chatter and activity. Even card games, a common pastime, were set aside. There was a collective anticipation, a reverence for the morning to come.

At last, Christmas morning arrived. Long before the sun rose, the drum sounded through the prison, rousing the convicts from their slumber. The under-officer tasked with counting them entered the barracks, greeting the men with a cheerful, "Happy Christmas!" The convicts responded in kind, their voices unusually warm and amiable. There was a rare sense of camaraderie in the air. After a brief round of prayers, many of the convicts—Akim Akimitch among them—hurried to the kitchens to check on their special dishes.

From the small, frost-covered windows of the barracks, the glow of the kitchen fires was visible, their warmth contrasting sharply with the biting cold outside. Smoke curled lazily from the chimneys, mingling with the pale mist rising from the snow-covered ground. Outside, the courtyard was a flurry of activity. Convicts, wrapped in half-fastened pelisses or fully dressed in their ragged garments, bustled towards the kitchens. A few had already visited the drink-sellers and were slightly flushed, though they carried themselves with a surprising degree of restraint. The usual raucousness was absent; instead, there was an unspoken agreement to maintain a sense of decorum.

A remarkable air of goodwill pervaded the prison. Convicts from different barracks visited one another, exchanging cheerful Christmas greetings. For a day, their usual guardedness and animosities seemed to dissolve. Even strangers addressed one another with unexpected warmth. I stepped outside and found myself in the midst of this unusual atmosphere. The icy mist softened the outlines of the buildings, and the faint glow of the rising sun hinted at the promise of the day. Convicts who had never spoken to me before wished me a happy Christmas, their gestures sincere and almost touching.

Near the kitchen, a young convict from the military barracks approached me, calling out my name. His face, round and youthful, bore a shy but genuine smile. He had never spoken to me before, and I did not know his name. He stood before me, grinning awkwardly, his eyes filled with an unspoken joy.

"What do you want?" I asked, perplexed.

He hesitated for a moment, then muttered softly, "It's Christmas Day," as if that simple statement explained everything. Without waiting for a reply, he turned and hurried into the kitchen, leaving me standing there, both amused and bewildered. We never spoke again after that brief encounter.

The kitchen was a hive of activity. Convicts crowded around the stoves, jostling for space, each man keeping a watchful eye on his contribution to the communal feast. The cooks worked furiously, preparing the meal that would be served earlier than usual that day. Though many were eager to begin eating, they refrained out of respect for the collective celebration. The fast would only end once the priest arrived to bless the food, and no one dared break that tradition.

Through the commotion, the voice of the corporal rang out, clear and commanding: "The kitchen! The kitchen!" It was a signal that the preparations were nearing completion. The anticipation in the air was almost tangible, a blend of solemnity and restrained excitement that seemed to unite us all in a shared moment of humanity.

The calls for the cooks to assemble at the kitchens continued without pause for nearly two hours. The cooks were summoned to receive a steady stream of gifts, brought from every corner of the town, a touching display of generosity from the townspeople. The donations included loaves of fine white bread, golden scones, delicate rusks, pancakes, and an array of pastries, all in extraordinary variety. No shopkeeper in town, it seemed, had failed to contribute something to the "unfortunates." Among the gifts were some that were truly splendid—elaborate cakes made of the finest flour and adorned with intricate designs. Yet, there were also modest offerings: humble rolls, each worth only a couple of kopecks, and small, coarse brown loaves barely glazed with sour cream. These meager gifts, often given at great personal cost, carried their own profound weight. They were the offerings of the poor to the poor—an act of solidarity and shared humanity that left no one unmoved.

Every offering was accepted with equal respect and gratitude. It mattered little whether the gift was extravagant or simple. The convicts, upon receiving the items, would remove their caps and bow deeply to the donors, wishing them a heartfelt "Happy Christmas." These gestures, humble yet genuine, carried the weight of a bond that transcended the barriers between the prisoners and the free townsfolk. After expressing their thanks, the convicts carried the gifts carefully into the kitchens.

As the bounty accumulated, the elders of each barrack were called forth to oversee its distribution. It was their task to divide the provisions into equal portions for all the sections of the prison. Despite the potential for disputes, the process unfolded with surprising harmony. The division was carried out honestly and equitably, without complaint or discord. Even among men so accustomed to deprivation and harshness, there was no sign of envy, no attempt to deceive or claim an unfair share.

In our barrack, Akim Akimitch, with the help of another convict, managed the distribution. He worked methodically, ensuring that each man received his due share. The atmosphere remained calm, almost solemn, as each convict accepted his portion without objection. This display of fairness and mutual respect seemed to underscore the collective sense of reverence for the day.

When the task was done, Akim Akimitch returned to his bed to prepare for the festivities. He approached the process of dressing himself with the same solemnity he brought to every task. Button by button, he fastened his waistcoat, his movements deliberate and meticulous. Once fully dressed in his carefully preserved new clothes, he knelt for a long session of prayer, a practice shared by many of the older convicts. The younger men, however, mostly abstained from such displays of piety, limiting their observances to a brief sign of the cross before meals on festival days.

When his prayers were complete, Akim Akimitch sought me out to exchange the customary holiday greetings. His formality was unshaken even in his goodwill. I invited him to join me for tea, and he reciprocated by offering me a piece of his well-roasted sucking pig. As the morning progressed, Petroff arrived to pay his respects. He seemed slightly inebriated, his words few and disjointed. After a brief moment of awkward silence, he wandered off towards the kitchen once more.

Anticipation mounted as the convicts awaited the arrival of the priest. The military section of the barracks, arranged differently from the others with its camp bedsteads lining the walls, had been prepared for the ceremony. A small table stood in the center of the room, adorned with a holy image and a burning lamp. This arrangement created an open space where the convicts could gather.

At last, the priest arrived, carrying the cross and a vessel of holy water. He began the service with prayers and chants before the image, his voice solemn and resonant. Each convict approached in turn to kiss the cross, an act that even the most hardened among them performed with an air of reverence. The priest then moved through the barracks, sprinkling holy water and offering blessings. When he reached the kitchen, he took a moment to praise the bread, which was renowned in the town for its quality. The convicts, delighted by his words, decided to send him two loaves of the freshly baked bread as a token of gratitude, which an old soldier promptly delivered to his house.

The priest's visit marked the culmination of the morning's rituals, and soon after, the Major and the Commandant made their appearance. The Commandant, a figure both liked and respected by the convicts, toured the barracks alongside the Major. He wished the prisoners a happy Christmas, visited the kitchen, and sampled the cabbage soup, which had been prepared with extra care for the occasion. Each convict was entitled to a generous portion of meat that day, along with millet and butter, making the soup unusually rich. The Major, ever watchful and stern behind his spectacles, escorted the Commandant out and then gave the order for dinner to commence.

As soon as the Major departed, the atmosphere shifted. The convicts, who had maintained a composed and orderly demeanor in his presence, began to relax. Within minutes, the signs of revelry became evident. Faces flushed with drink, the sound of balalaiki—the traditional Russian string instruments—filled the air, and the lively strains of a violin soon followed. Baklouchin, the "Sapper," had hired the little Pole to play cheerful dance tunes throughout the day. Though the noise grew louder and the conversations more animated, the dinner passed without major incident.

After the meal, the barracks became a tapestry of contrasting scenes. Some of the older and more serious-minded convicts retired to their beds, preferring rest to revelry. Akim Akimitch, ever dutiful, followed their example. Meanwhile, the Old Believer climbed onto the stove, opened his prayer book, and spent the rest of the day in devout meditation, untouched by the surrounding chaos.

Not everyone found solace in the celebrations. The Circassians, dignified and reserved, watched the drunken revelry with thinly veiled disdain. "Aman, aman," murmured Nourra, shaking his head in disapproval. Isaiah Fomitch, ever the contrarian, lit a candle in his corner and set to work, determined to show his indifference to the holiday.

As the day wore on, card games began in earnest, despite the watchful eyes of the old soldiers. The officer of the guard made several rounds, but his tolerance for minor transgressions ensured that no serious trouble arose. However, the drunkenness soon reached fever pitch. Singing gave way to tears, and groups of convicts wandered about, their movements unsteady, their voices rising and falling in a cacophony of celebration. Gazin, the cunning hoarder of spirits, presided over his makeshift bar with a knowing smile, his stash of liquor hidden safely beneath his bed.

Despite the chaos, the day retained its festive spirit. Amid the wild singing and clashing melodies of balalaiki and guitars, a sense of unity and shared humanity lingered, reminding all that even in the harshest of circumstances, the warmth of Christmas could not be extinguished.

Songs that could truly be called "popular" were uncommon. I recall one that was beautifully sung:

Yesterday, I, a young girl,

Went to the feast.

A variation was added, one I had never heard before. These new lines came at the end of the song:

At my house, the house of a young girl,

Everything is in order.

I have washed the spoons,

I have served the cabbage soup,

I have wiped down the door panels,

I have made the patties.

Most of the songs sung were prison songs. One of them, called "As It Happened," was particularly amusing. It told the story of a man who had once enjoyed a luxurious life, living like a prince, but everything changed when he ended up in the convict prison, where life was much harsher. Another popular song described how its hero had once been wealthy, but now only had his imprisonment to show for it. This is an example of a true convict's song:

The day breaks in the heavens,

We are woken by the drum.

The old man opens the door,

The warder comes and calls us.

No one sees us behind the prison walls,

Or knows how we live in this place.

But God, the Heavenly Creator, is with us;

He will not let us perish.

Another song, even sadder but with a hauntingly beautiful melody, was often sung with words that were simple and imperfect. I remember a few of the lines:

My eyes will never see again

The land where I was born.

Undeserved suffering will be

My punishment to bear.

The owl will screech upon the roof

And echo through the forest.

My heart is broken from my grief.

No, I will never return.

This song was often performed, but not as part of a group. It was always sung as a solo. After the day's work was done, a prisoner might leave the barracks, sit down on the doorstep, rest his chin in his hand, and begin to sing in a high falsetto voice. His song would drift out, slow and reflective. Those who heard him could not help but feel the deep sorrow in his voice.

Some of the prisoners had truly remarkable singing voices. Their songs, though often sad, resonated deeply, filling the air with a sense of longing and pain.

By the time evening came, the mood in the barracks had shifted. The drunken laughter and excitement from earlier in the day gave way to a heavy atmosphere of weariness and sadness. One prisoner, who had been laughing uncontrollably not long before, was now sitting in a corner, crying bitterly in his drunken stupor. Others were either fighting or stumbling around aimlessly, pale-faced and clearly looking for someone to argue with. These men had set out to celebrate the holiday joyfully, but, heaven help them, the day had turned out to be painful and disheartening. They had clung to a vague hope of finding happiness, but it never came.

Petroff approached me twice during the evening. He had only had a little to drink and remained calm, but it was obvious that he was waiting for something extraordinary to happen, something exciting that would lift everyone's spirits. He didn't say this out loud, but it was written all over his face. He moved tirelessly from one barrack to another, searching, but nothing out of the ordinary occurred—just widespread drunkenness, foolish insults from those who'd had too much to drink, and the dizzy chaos of overheated tempers.

Sirotkin was also wandering about. He wore a brand-new red shirt and looked as handsome as ever, moving between the barracks with the same expectation in his eyes as Petroff. But the scene was becoming unbearable—repulsive, even. There were moments of humor, but I was far too saddened by the whole spectacle to laugh. Instead, I felt an overwhelming sense of pity for these men and a deep discomfort being among them.

Nearby, two convicts were arguing over which of them should treat the other to a drink. The quarrel dragged on, growing louder and more heated. One of them had been holding a grudge for a long time, going back to an incident where the other man had sold a coat but kept the money for himself. The one complaining was a tall, muscular young man, not unintelligent, but when drunk, he became overly friendly and eager to unburden himself to others. He was insulting his opponent, but it was clear he hoped to make peace afterward. The other man, a big, heavyset convict with a round face and a sly, fox-like demeanor, seemed much less affected by the alcohol. Known for his wealth among the prisoners, he had little to gain by escalating the argument and instead led his companion to one of the drink-sellers.

The argumentative convict declared that his companion owed him money and should buy him a drink as proof of his honesty. The drink-seller, showing some respect for the wealthier convict but a hint of disdain for the other man drinking on borrowed generosity, poured a glass of vodka.

"No, Stepka, you need to pay because you owe me money," insisted the young man.

"I've had enough of this talk," replied Stepka.

"No, you're lying, Stepka," the first man said, grabbing the glass handed to him by the drink-seller. "You owe me money, and you have no conscience. Everything you have, you've borrowed, and I wouldn't be surprised if even your eyes weren't your own. Stepka, you're nothing but a scoundrel."

"What are you whining about? You're spilling your vodka," Stepka shot back.

"If someone's buying you a drink, you should at least drink it," the drink-seller snapped impatiently. "I can't stand here waiting all day."

"I'll drink it, don't worry," the young man replied. "What's the rush? Here's to you, Stepka Doroveitch," he said with a mockingly polite bow, raising the glass to the man he had just insulted. "To your health, and may you live another hundred years." He drained the vodka, let out a satisfied grunt, and wiped his mouth. Then, in a serious tone, he added, "I've drunk so much brandy in my time, but that's enough for now. You should be thanking me, Stepka Doroveitch."

"There's nothing to thank you for," Stepka replied curtly.

"Oh, so you won't thank me?" The young man's tone turned bitter. "Then I'll let everyone know how you've treated me, and that you're nothing but a blackguard."

"Well, if you're going to talk, I'll have something to say about you, you drunkard," Stepka snapped, finally losing his temper. "Let's divide the world in two—you take one half, and I'll take the other. Then maybe I'll have some peace."

"So, you're not giving me my money back?" the young man demanded.

"What money are you talking about, you drunk fool?" Stepka retorted.

"My money! The money I earned with my own sweat, through my hard work. You'll pay for it in the next life—you'll be roasted for those five kopecks."

"Get lost."

"Why are you trying to drive me off? Am I a horse?"

"Go away, already."

"Blackguard!"

"Convict!"

The insults escalated, becoming more vicious than before, even after their visit to the drink-seller.

Two friends were sitting separately on two camp beds. One was tall, broad-shouldered, and muscular, with a red, fleshy face that made him look like a butcher. He was on the verge of tears, deeply moved by something. The other was slim, lanky, and self-assured, with a large, perpetually stuffy-looking nose and small, pale blue eyes that were fixed on the ground. This second man was intelligent and cultured; he had once worked as a secretary. He treated his friend with an air of superiority that the bigger man couldn't tolerate. They had been drinking together all day.

"You hit me!" shouted the larger man, shaking the head of his companion with his left hand. Among convicts, to "take a liberty" meant to strike someone. This man, who had once been a non-commissioned officer, secretly envied the refined manners of his friend and tried to compensate for his own roughness by attempting to sound sophisticated.

"I'm telling you, you're wrong," replied the secretary in a calm, authoritative tone, still staring at the ground and refusing to look at his companion.

"You hit me! Do you hear me?" the bigger man repeated, shaking his friend even harder. "You're the only person in the world I care about, but I won't let you hit me!"

"Admit it, my dear fellow," said the secretary dryly, "all of this is just because you've had too much to drink."

The larger man staggered backward, blinking stupidly with his drunken eyes at his friend. Then, without warning, he punched the secretary in the face with all his strength. And with that, their friendship for the day came to an abrupt end.

The secretary collapsed unconscious under the bed.

Just then, one of my acquaintances walked into the barracks. He was a convict from the special section—cheerful, good-natured, and quick-witted, always ready with a harmless joke. This was the same man who had been looking for a rich peasant when I first arrived and who had ended up drinking my tea. He was around forty, with thick, oversized lips and a large, red, fleshy nose. In his hand, he held a balalaika, lazily strumming its strings as he walked. Following him was a small convict with a big head, someone I barely knew and who seemed to be ignored by everyone else. Now drunk, the little convict had latched onto my acquaintance and followed him everywhere, waving his arms and banging his fists against walls and bed frames. He looked as if he was about to cry. My acquaintance, however, acted as though the smaller man didn't exist. It was comical since they had nothing in common—not their personalities, habits, or even the barracks they lived in. The smaller man's name was Bulkin.

When my acquaintance, Vermaloff, noticed me sitting by the stove, he smiled and stopped a few steps away, pausing as though deep in thought. Then, with an exaggerated swagger, he stumbled toward me and plucked the strings of his balalaika. He began to sing or recite a tune, tapping his boot on the ground to keep rhythm:

"My sweetheart,

With her full, fair face,

Sings like a nightingale;

In her satin dress,

With its shining trim,

She's a beauty beyond compare."

This song seemed to drive Bulkin into a frenzy. He threw up his arms and shouted to everyone, "He's lying, friends! He's lying like a snake oil seller! There's not a single bit of truth in what he's singing!"

"Greetings, most honorable Alexander Petrovitch," said Vermaloff with a sly grin, addressing me directly. For a moment, it seemed like he might try to embrace me. He was clearly drunk. The phrase "most honorable" was a common expression used by Siberian peasants, even when speaking to a young man. Calling someone old was considered a sign of respect, even flattery.

"Well, Vermaloff, how are things?" I replied.

"Not great, not terrible," he mumbled. "The real party animals have been drinking since the crack of dawn."

Vermaloff's words were slurred, and his voice was unsteady.

"He's lying! He's lying again!" yelled Bulkin, punching the bed frame in frustration.

It was clear that Vermaloff had decided to completely ignore Bulkin. That was perhaps the funniest part of the whole scene because Bulkin hadn't left Vermaloff's side since morning. He trailed behind him constantly, arguing with him about every little thing, wringing his hands, and smashing his fists against the walls and beds until his knuckles were bloody. It was as though Bulkin had made it his personal responsibility to call out every exaggeration or falsehood Vermaloff uttered. He seemed genuinely distressed by it, as if Vermaloff's words were a burden on his own conscience. If Bulkin had had hair, he probably would have torn it out in frustration. Yet Vermaloff carried on undeterred, as though Bulkin wasn't even there.

"He's lying! He's lying! He's lying!" Bulkin shouted.

"Why does it even matter to you?" the convicts asked, laughing at his outburst.

"I must tell you, Alexander Petrovitch," Vermaloff said suddenly, "when I was younger, I was quite handsome, and the young girls adored me."

"He's lying! He's lying!" Bulkin groaned again, and the convicts burst into laughter.

"I used to dress up just to impress them. I had a bright red shirt and wide trousers made of cotton velvet. Back then, I was truly happy. I got up when I wanted and did whatever I pleased. Life was good."

"He's lying," Bulkin interrupted once more.

"I inherited a two-story stone house from my father. Within two years, I squandered it all—both stories gone. All that was left was the front door. But what does it matter? Money comes and goes like a bird."

"He's lying!" Bulkin declared again, this time even more emphatically.

"And when everything was gone, I wrote to my relatives asking for money. They said I had ignored their wishes and disrespected them. It's been seven years since I sent that letter."

"Did they ever reply?" I asked with a smile.

"No," Vermaloff replied, laughing as well and leaning so close that his nose almost touched mine.

Then, as if sharing a grand secret, he told me he had a sweetheart.

"You? A sweetheart?" I asked, surprised.

"Onufriel told me recently, 'My girl has pockmarks and isn't much to look at, but she's got plenty of dresses. Yours may be pretty, but she's a beggar.'"

"Is that true?" I asked.

"Yes, it's true. She's a beggar," he answered, laughing loudly. The other convicts joined in, amused. Everyone knew he was involved with a beggar woman to whom he gave ten kopecks twice a year.

"Well, what do you want from me?" I finally asked, hoping to get rid of him.

He paused for a moment, then looked at me with a sly, ingratiating smile and said, "Could you spare me enough for half a pint? I've only had tea all day," he added while taking the money I offered him. "And tea does strange things to me. I'm afraid it'll give me asthma—it's making me feel bloated."

When Vermaloff took the money, Bulkin's frustration boiled over. He began flailing his arms like a man possessed.

"Good people, listen to me!" he cried. "Everything he says— everything—is a lie!"

"What does it matter to you?" the convicts asked, bewildered by his behavior. "You're acting like a lunatic."

"I won't let him lie!" Bulkin declared, rolling his eyes and slamming his fist on the wooden boards. "I won't let him!"

The convicts laughed even harder. Vermaloff gave me an exaggerated bow after pocketing the money and hurried off toward the drink-seller, making ridiculous faces as he went. It was only then that he seemed to notice Bulkin.

"Come along!" Vermaloff said to him, as if Bulkin's presence was crucial to some grand plan. "Idiot," he added with disdain as Bulkin shuffled ahead of him.

But that was the end of the uproarious scene. The chaos eventually settled, and the convicts sank into heavy sleep on their camp beds. Even in their sleep, they muttered and groaned more than usual. A few die-hards still played cards here and there, but the much-anticipated holiday had come to an end. Tomorrow, the usual grind of hard labor would begin again.

Chapter 12
The Performance

On the evening of the third day of the holidays, we finally had our first theatrical performance. Organizing it had been no small effort. The actors had taken full responsibility for the preparations, while the rest of the convicts only knew that there would be a show. No one even knew what would be performed. The actors, even while working their daily tasks, were constantly thinking about how to gather enough costumes for the event. Whenever I crossed paths with Baklouchin, he would snap his fingers in excitement but wouldn't reveal anything.

I suspected that the Major might have been in a good mood. However, it wasn't clear whether he officially knew about the play, whether he had approved it, or whether he simply decided to turn a blind eye as long as it stayed under control. I imagined he had probably heard whispers about the planned performance but chose to stay quiet to avoid ruining it. Perhaps he reasoned that allowing it would keep the soldiers and convicts entertained and prevent trouble. That would have been a practical decision. After all, if the convicts hadn't organized something like this, the administration might have had to arrange some form of entertainment themselves. However, since our Major had a reputation for being contrary, I can only assume he silently allowed it. He was the sort of person who seemed to thrive on making things difficult for others, enforcing rules rigidly, and taking pride in his strictness. His approach earned him notoriety across the town.

It didn't matter to him if his heavy-handed ways caused resentment. He believed that any resulting disobedience could be met with the appropriate punishment. People like him often think that strictly following the law is enough and see no need for fairness or understanding. They are surprised when people expect them to apply the law with good sense. To them, that expectation is unnecessary and even irritating.

Whatever the case, the Sergeant-Major made no attempt to stop the performance, and that was all the convicts needed. To be honest, I believe that allowing the play was the reason why the holidays passed without serious incidents in the prison. There were no bloody fights, no robberies, and no major disturbances. I saw for myself how some convicts avoided provoking their drunk companions and worked to prevent quarrels, all to ensure that the performance wasn't canceled. The non-commissioned officer had even made the convicts promise to behave themselves, and they gave their word willingly, keeping it with surprising dedication. They took great pride in having their word of honor trusted.

What's more, the performance didn't cost the authorities a single kopeck. The theater could be set up and dismantled within fifteen minutes, and if an order to stop the play came suddenly, the entire setup could be hidden in moments. Costumes were stashed in the convicts' boxes, ready to disappear at a moment's notice. But before describing the performance itself, let me explain how the theater was constructed, what the costumes were like, and what the program included. For the first show, there wasn't even a written program. It was only prepared later for the second and third performances. Baklouchin had written it for any officers or notable guests who might attend, including the officer of the guard, the officer of the watch, and an Engineer officer. The program was their way of honoring these potential visitors.

The convicts believed that word about their theater would spread, possibly reaching the fortress and even the town. After all, N—— had no professional theater, only the occasional amateur production. The convicts reveled in even the smallest success, boasting like children.

"Who knows?" they said to one another. "Maybe the officers will hear about it and come to see it. Then they'll understand what convicts are capable of. This isn't some soldier's play—it's real acting! Nothing like it exists in the town. General Abrosimoff might have performances at his house, and they say he plans another. Maybe they have better costumes, but our dialogue is something else entirely. Maybe even the Governor will hear of it, and—who knows?—he might come himself."

The town had no theater, and this made the convicts' ambitions soar even higher after their first success. Their imaginations ran wild, dreaming that their performance might even lead to rewards or a reduction in their sentences. These thoughts brought laughter among themselves as they realized how far-fetched their fantasies were. In truth, they were like children—true children—even at forty years of age.

I had some idea of the plays to be performed, though no official program existed. The first piece was titled Philatka and Miroshka, Rivals. Baklouchin, who had taken on the role of Philatka, had been boasting for over a week that his performance would surpass anything ever seen, even on the grand stages of St. Petersburg. He strutted through the barracks with an air of immense self-importance. Occasionally, he would recite a line in an exaggerated theatrical style, causing everyone to laugh—not necessarily because the line was funny, but because his enthusiasm was so over the top.

The convicts, as a whole, were reserved and dignified. It was mostly the younger men, unburdened by self-consciousness, or the more respected figures with unshakable authority, who openly enjoyed Baklouchin's theatrics. The rest would listen in silence, neither criticizing nor joining in, making a show of indifference toward the upcoming performance.

It wasn't until the very day of the play that everyone's genuine interest emerged. Questions buzzed around the prison: "What will the Major say? Will this play be as good as the one from two years ago?" Baklouchin assured me that everything was perfectly planned. There would even be a curtain. Sirotkin, playing a woman's role, had eagerly boasted, "You'll see how great I look in women's clothes." The Lady Bountiful was to wear a dress complete with trimmings and carry a parasol, while her husband, the Lord of the Manor, would appear in an officer's uniform, complete with epaulettes and a cane.

The second play, Kedril, the Glutton, intrigued me with its title, but I couldn't find anyone willing to explain it. I only discovered that it wasn't a published play but a manuscript passed down by a retired non-commissioned officer who had likely seen it performed on a military stage. Plays like these were common in remote parts of Russia, developing independently and rarely making it into print. They seemed to emerge naturally, tied to local traditions and preserved through the years by soldiers, laborers, and small-town shopkeepers. In some cases, they were even handed down by the servants of old landed estates, where private theaters once flourished. These small, amateur productions formed the foundation of what we might call the "popular theater."

I doubted that the convicts themselves had created everything I saw on stage. Much of it seemed rooted in old traditions passed from generation to generation. Such traditions might have survived in quiet villages or small provincial towns, carried by the descendants of noble families' servants who had acted in private estate theaters. In these early days of Russian theater, noble households often had their own performers, and their influence still lingered.

As for Kedril, the Glutton, I could learn little more about it, except that demons appeared in the play to drag Kedril to hell. What did the name "Kedril" mean? Why wasn't it "Cyril"? Was it Russian or foreign? I couldn't solve the mystery.

The final performance of the evening would be a musical pantomime. With such a varied lineup, the night promised to be truly fascinating. The cast included fifteen energetic and lively convicts, who threw themselves into rehearsals with great enthusiasm. They often practiced behind the barracks, away from the rest of us, keeping their work shrouded in secrecy. They clearly wanted to surprise us with something remarkable and unexpected.

Normally, the barracks were locked early in the evening on workdays. However, during the Christmas holidays, the gates weren't secured until after the evening retreat at nine o'clock. This special exception had been granted to accommodate the play. Every evening, a small group of convicts would humbly approach the officer on guard to request permission for the performance to continue. They assured him that similar events in the past had gone off without any trouble.

The officer of the guard must have thought carefully before allowing the performance. He likely reasoned that since the previous play had caused no trouble and the convicts had promised to maintain order, they would be their own strict enforcers of discipline. He also knew that if he refused permission, the convicts might cause problems that would leave him in an uncomfortable position. Another compelling reason for his consent was the sheer monotony of guard duty. Authorizing the play meant he could watch something highly unusual—a performance by convicts, a group of people unlike any he had likely seen on stage. The prospect of such a unique entertainment was surely tempting, and he had every right to be there.

If a superior officer happened to inquire about his whereabouts, the guard could easily respond that he was counting the convicts and securing the barracks. Such an answer was simple, believable, and hard to dispute. This practical reasoning is why the authorities allowed the performances to proceed throughout the holidays, and each evening, the barracks remained unlocked until the retreat at nine o'clock. The convicts seemed confident from the beginning that the officer of the guard would not stand in their way, so they felt no anxiety about his approval.

Around six o'clock, Petroff came to fetch me, and we headed to the theater together. Almost all the prisoners from our barracks were present, except for the "old believer" from Tchernigoff and the Poles. The Poles, always aloof, only decided to attend on the final evening of the performances, January 4th, after confirming that everything would

159

be conducted respectfully. Their haughty demeanor annoyed the other convicts, but when they finally showed up, they were received with exaggerated politeness and escorted to the best seats. The Circassians and Isaiah Fomitch, however, were delighted by the play. Isaiah, in particular, seemed overjoyed, contributing three kopecks each evening, except for the final night when he generously placed ten kopecks on the collection plate. His happiness was plain to see.

The actors had agreed that each spectator would pay whatever amount they felt was fair. The funds collected would cover the production costs, and any surplus would be distributed among the performers. Petroff assured me that I would have one of the best seats, regardless of how crowded the theater became. He reasoned that, as someone with more means, I would likely contribute a larger amount and, as a knowledgeable observer, appreciate the acting more than others. His prediction was accurate, but first, let me describe the theater itself.

The military barracks that had been transformed into a theater measured about fifteen feet in length. Visitors entered through a small antechamber before stepping into the main area. This particular barrack was uniquely arranged, with the beds placed along the walls, leaving an open central space. Half of this area was designated for the audience, while the other half, which connected to the adjoining building, served as the stage. What caught my attention immediately upon entering was the curtain—a ten-foot-wide marvel that divided the barrack in two. It was painted with images of trees, tunnels, ponds, and stars, and its presence was nothing short of miraculous.

The curtain was a patchwork creation, made from various scraps of linen contributed by the convicts. These included old shirts and the cloth bandages peasants used in place of socks, all stitched together into a massive sheet. Where linen was lacking, writing paper—sheet by sheet taken from office supplies—was used as a substitute. Our prison painters, including one convict with real artistic talent, had decorated it with oil paints, creating an effect that was both crude and impressive.

This lavish curtain thrilled even the grimmest and most cynical of the convicts. When the play began, every man, regardless of his usual demeanor, transformed into a wide-eyed child. The pride and satisfaction in their expressions were unmistakable, reflecting a shared sense of accomplishment. The theater was illuminated with candle stubs scattered around the room. In front of the curtain were two benches borrowed from the kitchen and three or four large chairs taken from the non-commissioned officers' room. These chairs were reserved for officers, should they choose to attend, while the benches were intended for non-commissioned officers, engineers, clerks, and other supervisors who lacked officer rank but might come to see the performance.

There was no shortage of visitors. On some nights, the audience was larger than others, but for the final performance, every seat on the benches was occupied. It was clear that the enthusiasm for the convict theater had grown with each passing night.

At the back of the theater, the convicts stood packed tightly together. Despite the stifling heat, they remained standing out of respect for the visitors, dressed in their vests or short pelisses. The space was, as expected, far too small to accommodate everyone comfortably. Many prisoners crowded together, particularly in the rear rows, while every camp-bedstead was occupied. Some men who lingered behind the stage in the other barrack tried to catch glimpses of the performance from afar, engaging in quiet disputes over their vantage points.

Petroff and I were directed to move closer to the front, near the benches where the view was better. The convicts regarded me as someone with refined taste, a man who had seen many theaters and could offer informed opinions. Baklouchin's frequent consultations with me about the play had not gone unnoticed, and they interpreted his deference as a sign of my expertise. For this reason, they felt I

161

deserved one of the best seats. Although these men could be vain and superficial at times, they knew how to acknowledge skill and knowledge in a specific domain.

They laughed at me often while I worked, ridiculing my lack of practical skills. Almazoff, for instance, took pride in his superior ability to pound alabaster, mocking my background and the class I represented—a class he likely resented from his past dealings with former masters. Yet, in this setting, their perspective shifted. At the theater, those same men moved aside for me, respecting what they believed was my greater understanding of the arts. Even the convicts who were generally unfriendly toward me seemed pleased to hear my praise of the play and gave way without any sense of servility. They did so not as an act of submission but as a recognition of dignity, both theirs and mine.

The most striking trait of the common people, as I observed it here, is their deep sense of fairness and justice. They are free from false pride or the sly ambition of seeking undeserved status. Such behaviors, common elsewhere, seemed entirely foreign to them. Stripped of their rough exteriors, these individuals revealed qualities that would surprise anyone who studied them closely and without prejudice. Our intellectuals could learn from them; indeed, I would go so far as to say they should.

When Petroff brought me to the theater, he casually mentioned that I would be placed at the front because they expected me to contribute more money. Seats were not assigned or sold at fixed prices; instead, each person gave whatever they could afford when the collection plate was passed around. Even if their decision to seat me near the front was motivated by financial expectations, I could not help but see a certain dignity in their reasoning.

"You have more money than I do, so you should sit in the front row. True, we are all equals here, but your contribution is likely to be greater, and the actors will prefer a spectator like you. Take the better seat, since we have nothing else to offer and must make do with what we have."

There was a noble pride in this approach. It wasn't greed or love of money that guided their actions but rather a deep sense of fairness and self-respect. Among us, money was not overly esteemed. I cannot recall a single instance where anyone demeaned themselves for its sake. Some would engage with me playfully, more out of a love for mischief than any expectation of gain. I hope I've explained myself clearly, though I fear I may have wandered too far from the main subject—the performance itself. Let me return to it.

Before the curtain rose, the room buzzed with an almost chaotic energy. The crowd pressed in from all sides, packed so tightly that movement was nearly impossible. Yet, despite the discomfort, the atmosphere was electric with anticipation. Faces glowed with excitement, their expressions a mix of joy and impatience.

In the back rows, where the throng was most tightly packed, some convicts had brought wooden logs to stand on, placing them against the walls for better views. Balancing precariously, they leaned on the shoulders of others to rest, while their companions stood patiently, seemingly unbothered. A few climbed onto their toes, bracing themselves against the stove for support, and managed to remain in this exhausting position throughout the performance.

The camp-bedsteads offered prime seating, and those lucky enough to secure spots there guarded them jealously. Five convicts had even clambered to the top of the stove, where they enjoyed an uninterrupted view of the stage. Their expressions radiated smug satisfaction, their fortunate position the envy of latecomers who wandered aimlessly, searching for a good place to stand.

Despite the cramped quarters, everyone behaved with remarkable decorum. No one made unnecessary noise, each man eager to present himself well before the distinguished visitors who had come to watch.

The convicts' red faces, damp with perspiration, bore expressions of pure, childlike delight as they waited for the curtain to rise. What a strange transformation! These were the same faces—scarred and hardened, branded with the marks of their crimes—that usually exuded menace and hostility. Yet, in this moment, they glowed with innocent pleasure, stripped of their usual bitterness.

Every head was uncovered in respect, and as I glanced back at the crowd from my place near the front, it seemed as though the entire room was filled with cleanly shaved heads. The contrast between their usual demeanor and the hopeful eagerness now shining in their eyes was astonishing, even touching.

Suddenly, the signal was given, and the orchestra began to play, drawing everyone's attention. This orchestra was unique and deserves special mention. It consisted of eight musicians: two violins, one owned by a convict and the other borrowed from outside; three balalaikas, skillfully crafted by the convicts themselves; two guitars, and a tambourine. While the violins produced uneven tones and the guitars were of poor quality, the balalaikas stood out as exceptional instruments, and the dexterity of their players was remarkable—worthy of praise from even the most skilled musicians.

The orchestra performed mostly lively dance tunes. At particularly exciting moments, the players struck the bodies of their instruments with their fingers, adding rhythm and energy. The tone and interpretation of the melodies were distinct and original. Among the guitarists, one man stood out—a convict who had killed his father. His command over the instrument was evident. As for the tambourine player, his performance was nothing short of extraordinary. He spun the tambourine on a single finger, rubbed the drumhead with his thumb to produce a variety of sounds, and transitioned seamlessly between dull and bright tones.

Eventually, two harmonica players joined the group. I had no idea until then just how expressive these simple, common instruments could be. Their harmony and emotive interpretations surprised me. For the first time, I fully grasped the bold, passionate energy that characterizes Russian folk dance tunes and village songs.

At last, the curtain rose. A ripple of movement swept through the audience. Those standing at the back rose on tiptoes, straining to see, while one person lost their balance and tumbled from their makeshift perch on a log. Immediately, others motioned for silence. The performance had begun.

I was seated near Ali, who was surrounded by his brothers and other Circassians. Their love for the theater was unmistakable—they never missed a single performance. I've noticed that Mohammedans, including Circassians, have a strong appreciation for all forms of entertainment. Close to them sat Isaiah Fomitch, his face glowing with anticipation. As soon as the curtain rose, he was utterly captivated, his expression one of awe. It would have saddened me if he had been disappointed. Ali's radiant face, alight with childlike joy, was a sight to behold. His happiness seemed so pure that it made me smile. Whenever the audience broke into laughter at a witty line, I couldn't help but glance at him to see his reaction. He didn't notice me; he was too engrossed in the performance.

To Ali's left was a grumpy, older convict who always seemed dissatisfied. Even he couldn't help but glance furtively at Ali's charming demeanor, as though the young Circassian's joy was contagious. Among the prisoners, Ali was affectionately nicknamed Ali Simeonitch, though I never learned why.

In the first play, Philatka and Miroshka, Baklouchin's performance as Philatka was truly extraordinary. He brought the character to life, carefully considering every word and gesture. Each movement and line perfectly suited his role. His natural charm, humor, and simplicity made him irresistible. Watching him, it was clear he was born to act. I had seen this same play performed by professionals on stages in St. Petersburg and Moscow, but none of the celebrated actors I'd seen could compare to Baklouchin's portrayal. Those actors seemed like caricatures of peasants, whereas Baklouchin embodied a true Russian moujik. Their attempts to imitate rural life came across as forced, while Baklouchin's performance felt genuine and unpretentious.

Baklouchin's passion for acting was fueled by rivalry. It was widely anticipated that another convict, Potsiakin, would deliver an even more impressive performance as Kedril in the second play. This assumption irritated Baklouchin deeply. Like a child, he came to me repeatedly in the days leading up to the performance to express his frustration. On the day of the play, he was so nervous that he developed a fever. But when the audience erupted into laughter and shouted, "Bravo, Baklouchin! You're incredible!" his face lit up with pure joy. His eyes sparkled with inspiration. The comedic scene where Philatka calls out to his wife, "Wife, your mouth!" and then wipes his own, was particularly hilarious. The entire audience roared with laughter.

What fascinated me even more than the performance was the audience itself. They were completely immersed in the play, laughing freely and with genuine delight. Cries of approval grew louder and more frequent. A convict nudged his neighbor to share his thoughts, seemingly oblivious to who stood beside him. When a comic song began, one man waved his arms enthusiastically, urging others to join in the laughter, before quickly turning back to the stage. Another convict, too restless to stand still, shifted his weight from one foot to the other, smacking his tongue against his palate in delight. By the end of the play, the audience's joy had reached its peak.

The scene was nothing short of extraordinary. Imagine a prison filled with chains, monotony, and years of hard labor—a place of unending hardship. Then, for just an hour, the walls seemed to dissolve, and the prisoners were allowed to forget their grim reality. They organized a play that brought them genuine joy, one so well executed that it could rival performances in any town theater.

"Can you believe it?" people outside the prison would say.

"Convicts putting on such a performance!"

The transformation was astonishing. Seeing men like Nietsvitaeff or Baklouchin dressed in costumes, rather than the worn uniforms they had worn for years, was a strange and almost magical sight. It was a moment of rare freedom and humanity in a place where such things were seldom found.

He is a convict, a genuine prisoner whose chains clink as he moves, and yet there he is, striding onto the stage in a frock coat, a round hat, and a cloak—looking every bit the civilian. He's donned a wig and moustache, producing a handkerchief of vibrant red from his pocket and shaking it about like a true nobleman. The crowd erupts with excitement. Then, the "good landlord" enters, dressed in an aide-de-camp uniform—though visibly aged—with epaulettes and a cocked hat. The audience's reaction is beyond description. This costume had been the source of a heated dispute. Two convicts had argued like children over who would play the role. Both were eager to appear in the military uniform adorned with epaulettes. Finally, the others stepped in to mediate, and by majority vote, the part was given to Nietsvitaeff—not because he was more suited to it or bore a closer resemblance to a nobleman, but because he had assured everyone he would carry a cane and twirl it grandly like a dandy of the highest fashion, something Vanka and Ospiety, who had never met a nobleman, could not convincingly do.

As Nietsvitaeff walked onto the stage with his "wife," his entire focus was on his cane. He made endless loops and circles on the floor, completely absorbed in the performance. This action seemed to him the pinnacle of sophistication and elegance. It was likely a memory from his childhood, when, as a barefoot boy, he had watched some landowner skillfully twirl a cane, and that image had stayed with him for decades. So engrossed was he in this display of refinement that he gave his lines almost absentmindedly, without once lifting his eyes to the audience.

The "Lady Bountiful" also made a striking impression. She wore a tattered old muslin dress that hung on her like rags, with her arms and neck fully exposed. A small calico cap tied beneath her chin completed the ensemble, along with a fan made of colorful paper and an umbrella she held with theatrical flair. Her appearance provoked uproarious laughter, and she herself couldn't help joining in. The convict playing her, Ivanoff, found it nearly impossible to keep a straight face.

As for Sirotkin, who was dressed as a young woman, he looked quite convincing and sang the songs of his part beautifully. The first play ended to resounding applause and laughter, with no one daring to criticize the performance—after all, who among them could claim to judge? The orchestra struck up the lively tune of "Sieni moi Sieni" as an overture, and soon the curtain rose again.

Now it was time for Kedril, the Glutton. Kedril, a comedic character reminiscent of Don Juan, shares with his more famous counterpart the fate of being carried off to hell by devils at the play's end. The piece, as performed, seemed incomplete, with its beginning and conclusion likely lost over time. Still, the convicts presented it faithfully as they knew it. The setting was a Russian inn. The innkeeper ushered a nobleman, wearing a shabby cloak and a battered round hat, into a room. Behind him came Kedril, his valet, carrying a valise and a fowl wrapped in blue paper. Kedril wore a short pelisse and a servant's cap, immediately establishing himself as both gluttonous and cowardly.

The part of Kedril was played by Potsiakin, Baklouchin's rival, while the nobleman was once again portrayed by Ivanoff, who had just played the "Lady Bountiful." The innkeeper, played by Nietsvitaeff, warned the nobleman that the room was haunted by demons before making a hasty exit. The nobleman seemed unbothered, muttering that he was already aware of this, and instructed Kedril to unpack their belongings and prepare supper.

Kedril's character was a fascinating mix of cowardice, greed, and sly humor. Hearing the warning about devils, he visibly paled and began trembling, yet his hunger and curiosity kept him rooted to the spot. He feared his master deeply but still managed to cheat him at every opportunity. Potsiakin's performance was nothing short of brilliant, surpassing even Baklouchin's earlier portrayal. However, knowing how sensitive Baklouchin was, I chose not to share this opinion with him when we spoke the next day.

Ivanoff, in the role of the nobleman, performed with an odd but captivating blend of seriousness and absurdity. Though much of what he said seemed nonsensical, his clear diction and deliberate gestures lent an air of gravitas to his character. While Kedril fussed over the valise, the nobleman paced the room, declaring his intention to live a quiet, virtuous life from now on. Meanwhile, Kedril's asides, filled with grimaces and sarcastic remarks, had the audience in stitches.

The nobleman eventually revealed a dark secret. Some time ago, he had been in mortal danger and had called upon the devils for help. They had saved him, but the time had now come for them to claim his soul as payment. Kedril, hearing this, began trembling uncontrollably. However, when his master ordered him to prepare supper, the mention of food momentarily revived his spirits. Unpacking a bottle of wine, Kedril couldn't resist taking a swig for himself, a scene that sent the audience into peals of laughter.

The tension built as the room filled with eerie sounds. The wind howled, shutters rattled, and the door creaked ominously. Kedril, now utterly terrified, stuffed a massive piece of fowl into his mouth in a panic, too frightened to chew or swallow. Another gust of wind swept through, heightening the suspense.

"Is supper ready yet?" called the nobleman, still pacing the room, oblivious to the chaos unfolding behind him.

"Right away, sir. I'm getting it ready," Kedril replies nervously, seating himself and sneakily devouring the supper meant for his master. He takes great care to eat without being caught, darting glances at the nobleman. Each time the nobleman turns, Kedril ducks under the table, clutching the fowl in his hands. The audience roars with laughter at Kedril's antics, marveling at the cleverness with which he tricks his master. Poseikin, who played Kedril, earned his laughs and applause with an impeccable delivery of the line, "Right away, sir. I—am—getting—it—ready."

As Kedril satisfies his hunger, his panic slowly ebbs. However, when the nobleman calls out, "Kedril, is it ready yet?" he jolts back into action. "Ready, sir!" Kedril boldly replies, only to realize with horror that there's barely anything left—just a single leg of the fowl. Despite this, the nobleman, distracted and preoccupied, sits down without noticing. Kedril takes his place behind him, assuming the role of a proper servant with a napkin draped over his arm. Each word, gesture, and sly grimace directed at the audience makes the convicts laugh even harder. They are utterly charmed by his cheeky confidence.

Just as the nobleman begins to eat, the devils make their grand entrance. The side door creaks open, and ghostly figures step in. One is draped entirely in white, holding a glowing lantern in place of a head and wielding a scythe. The convicts accept these bizarre details without question, certain this was the proper way things should be. The nobleman confronts the apparitions with surprising bravery, announcing he is ready for them to take him. Kedril, on the other hand, reacts like a frightened rabbit. He scurries under the table with a bottle in hand, seeking refuge.

As the devils retreat, Kedril emerges, cautiously surveying his surroundings. Seeing his master is gone, his face lights up with delight. He whispers conspiratorially to the audience, "No more master! I'm my own man now!" The room erupts in laughter at Kedril's mischievous triumph as he pours himself a drink and indulges in the remaining food. "The devils have taken him," he adds, grinning broadly. The convicts cheer his cunning.

But Kedril's victory is short-lived. Just as he raises his glass to his lips, the devils return. Silent and swift, they creep up behind him and seize him. Kedril lets out a piercing scream, frozen with terror, unable to move as he clutches both the glass and bottle. His bulging eyes and gaping mouth, paired with his comic expression of cowardice, send the audience into fits of laughter. The devils hoist him up, kicking and flailing, as he desperately clings to the bottle. His shrieks echo through the barracks as he is dragged offstage.

The curtain falls amidst raucous laughter and applause. The spectators are utterly delighted, and the mood remains lively as the orchestra begins playing the famous dance tune, Kamarinskaia. The musicians start softly, letting the melody gradually build. The balalaiki players strike their strings with vigor, their enthusiasm infecting the crowd. By the time the piece reaches its peak, the rhythm is so intense it feels like the instruments themselves are dancing.

The final act is a pantomime accompanied by music. The stage represents a humble hut. In the scene, a miller and his wife sit inside— the miller patching clothes, the wife spinning flax. Sirotkin plays the wife with charm, while Nietsvitaeff takes on the role of the husband. The scenery is simple and sparse. A blanket substitutes for a back wall, with worn-out screens to the right and visible camp-bedsteads on the left. Yet, the convicts' imagination fills in the gaps effortlessly. For them, the blanket is a solid wall, and the stage becomes a perfect rustic setting.

The miller finishes his work, grabs his cap and whip, and gives his wife a stern warning. Through a series of gestures, he makes it clear that if she entertains anyone in his absence, she'll face his wrath. His wife nods dutifully, clearly familiar with the whip. But as soon as he leaves, she shakes her fist at his back in defiance. There's a knock at the door. The neighbor, another miller, steps in, bearing a gift—a red handkerchief. The wife smiles coyly at his arrival. Suddenly, another knock sounds. Alarmed, she quickly hides the neighbor under the table and resumes spinning her flax as though nothing has happened.

A second admirer now arrives—a farrier dressed in the uniform of a non-commissioned officer.

The pantomime continued flawlessly, with the actors delivering their gestures and expressions so naturally that it seemed as though they had rehearsed for months. It was remarkable to see these prisoners transform into convincing performers, and one couldn't help but marvel at the untapped talent wasting away in exile and captivity across Russia. The convict playing the farrier, for instance, seemed to have experience from amateur or provincial theatre performances. His exaggerated entry—taking long, deliberate strides, throwing back his head, and casting proud glances around—mimicked the grandiose style of classical stage heroes. Though absurd for a comedic character, the audience embraced it as entirely fitting, their laughter and cheers showing no inclination toward criticism.

Soon after the farrier's dramatic arrival, another knock sounded on the door. Panic overtook the miller's wife. She hurriedly stuffed the farrier into a large chest, slamming the lid just in time. The next visitor entered—a Brahmin, fully dressed in a costume that drew immediate laughter from the audience. The convict playing this role, Cutchin, portrayed the character to perfection, his expressive face adding authenticity to his silent pleas for the wife's affection. He gestured dramatically, first raising his hands to heaven, then clasping them on his chest, conveying a deep and comic adoration.

Another, louder knock shattered the scene. It was the husband returning home. The wife froze in terror, unsure of how to manage her hidden admirers. As she fumbled with her spinning wheel, dropping the spindle in her agitation, Sirotkin's portrayal of her panic was so vivid that the audience roared with laughter. The miller kicked the door open and stormed inside, whip in hand. His suspicious glare and accusatory gestures made it clear—he knew everything. The wife's lovers were discovered one by one.

The neighbor, first to be found, was sent fleeing with a powerful

172

punch. The farrier, hiding in the chest, betrayed himself by accidentally lifting the lid with his head. He received a swift thrashing from the whip before making his escape, no longer able to maintain his heroic swagger. The final search for the Brahmin took longer. Hidden behind a cupboard, he was eventually dragged out by his beard. With mock courtesy, the miller bowed before yanking him forward. The Brahmin tried to defend himself, crying out, "Accursed, accursed!"—the only spoken words in the entire pantomime. But his protests were futile, and after dealing with him, the enraged husband turned his attention to his wife.

Realizing her time had come, she bolted, knocking over a pot in her frantic exit, leaving the audience in fits of laughter. Ali, seated beside me, was laughing so hard he could barely stay upright. Grabbing my hand, he exclaimed, "Look at the Brahmin!" His pure joy was infectious. As the curtain fell, the convicts erupted into applause, their cheers echoing through the barracks.

The show wasn't over yet. Two or three more short sketches followed, each one broad, humorous, and improvisational. The actors added new flourishes each evening, keeping the performances fresh and spontaneous. The pantomime concluded with a lively ballet that featured an unexpected scene—a burial. The Brahmin performed incantations over the corpse, and, to the audience's delight, the dead man sprang back to life. Overcome with joy, everyone on stage began to dance, including the revived man and the Brahmin himself. It was a triumphant finale.

As the convicts filed out of the makeshift theater, their spirits were high. They heaped praise on the actors and thanked the non-commissioned officers for allowing the performance. There was no fighting, no bickering, only a shared sense of happiness. That night, the men went to bed with rare contentment, their sleep undisturbed by the usual nightmares or despair.

This was no fantasy, but a vivid moment of truth. For one evening, these outcasts had been allowed to laugh, to feel human, to forget their grim existence as prisoners. The change in their spirits was almost miraculous, if only temporary.

The night deepened, and I stirred from sleep, jolted by a faint unease. In the dim light of the single candle provided by the authorities, I saw the "old believer" still perched atop the tall porcelain stove, praying steadfastly. His murmured words blended with the faint sounds of chains clinking and restless murmurs from other prisoners. Beside me, Ali slept peacefully, his face still alight with the joy of the evening. Earlier, he had fallen asleep chatting with his brothers, reliving the highlights of the play.

As my mind wandered, I reflected on the holiday, the month gone by, and the peculiar mixture of misery and fleeting joy in our lives. I raised my head and scanned the room. The ragged bedding, the exhausted faces, the oppressive air of the barracks—it all grounded me in a harsh reality. This wasn't a nightmare but life itself, stripped bare. A soft groan interrupted my thoughts as someone shifted, their chains jangling faintly. Another muttered in their sleep while the old man's prayer filled the silence: "Lord Jesus Christ, have mercy upon us."

A sense of calm washed over me. "I am not here forever," I reminded myself quietly. "Only for a few years." With that, I laid my head back down on the thin pillow, letting sleep take me once more.

PART 2

Chapter 1
The Hospital

Not long after the Christmas holidays, I fell ill and was sent to the military hospital located about half a verst, or a third of a mile, from the fortress. The hospital was a long, low building painted in a dull yellow color, refreshed every summer with copious amounts of ochre to maintain its brightness. Surrounding the main building was a vast courtyard dotted with smaller structures, including residences for the chief physicians. The primary hospital building housed only patient wards, divided by category. There were many wards, but just two were allocated to convicts, and these were almost always overcrowded, especially in the summer months. During such times, beds had to be pushed closer together to accommodate the influx of patients.

These wards served a mix of "unfortunates." Alongside our own group of convicts, there were military prisoners transferred from guardhouses, detainees awaiting trial, and even those passing through to other destinations. Adding to the grim population were invalids from the Disciplinary Company—a harrowing institution for reforming wayward soldiers. In reality, most men emerged from it even more hardened and corrupt than when they entered, as though it were a training ground for the most irredeemable scoundrels.

When a convict felt ill, he had to report to the non-commissioned officer, who recorded his name on a small card. The convict would then be escorted to the hospital by a soldier. Upon arrival, the convict underwent a medical examination, and only if deemed genuinely unwell would he be admitted to the hospital. My name was duly recorded, and around one o'clock, when my companions had left for their afternoon labor, I made my way to the hospital. Every prisoner heading to the hospital took along whatever bread and money he could manage, knowing that food would not be provided on the first day. Tobacco, a pipe, and flint with match paper were also hidden in boots, as these small comforts were unofficially permitted.

The day I entered the hospital was overcast and oppressive—a humid, gray atmosphere that made the place seem even more dreary and uninviting. The building's somber air, combined with the promise of encountering illness and suffering, weighed heavily on me as I and my escort entered the reception hall. There, two large copper baths gleamed dully, and two other convicts, each with their warders, waited silently. An assistant surgeon appeared, glanced at us with a mix of boredom and superiority, and walked off to inform the physician on duty of our arrival.

Before long, the physician arrived and examined me. He was affable, even polite, as he asked about my condition and wrote my name on an admission paper. The doctor who oversaw the convict wards would later make a proper diagnosis, prescribe my treatment, and set my diet. I had already heard from other prisoners that the hospital doctors were well-regarded, often described with admiration. "They are like fathers to us," the convicts would say, speaking of their attentiveness and fairness.

After my examination, I was instructed to change into hospital attire. My clothes and personal belongings were taken away, replaced with standard-issue items: a set of clean but coarse linen, long stockings, slippers, a cotton nightcap, and a thick brown dressing gown. This dressing gown, lined not with proper fabric but with a layer of accumulated filth, was particularly repellent at first glance. However, I quickly came to appreciate its practicality in the cold, regardless of its condition.

Once dressed, I was led down a long, spotless corridor to the convict wards, located at the far end. The corridor was high-ceilinged, brightly lit, and remarkably clean—a stark contrast to the filth and squalor of the convict barracks. The polished floors and tidy surroundings made an impression on me, though it was likely the sharp contrast with my usual environment that exaggerated their appeal.

The two prisoners who had arrived before me were directed to the left wing of the corridor, while I was shown to my designated room. A sentinel with a musket paced before the padlocked door, and a second soldier stood nearby, ready to relieve him. At the sergeant's order, the sentinel stepped aside, allowing me to enter.

I found myself in a long, narrow ward with rows of green-painted wooden beds lining both walls. There were twenty-two beds in total, a few of which were still unoccupied. The beds, like most hospital furnishings in Russia, were likely infested with bugs, though this was hardly worth complaining about given the conditions we lived with daily. I was assigned a spot in a corner near the windows, which I appreciated.

Despite the number of beds, only a few patients were truly bedridden with serious illnesses. Most of the occupants appeared to be in varying stages of recovery, sitting up or moving about with caution. Their expressions, marked by weariness and resignation, were a grim reflection of the shared hardships that had brought us all to this place. For me, however, this hospital ward represented not only a chance to recover but also a rare glimpse into yet another facet of the convict's life—one I was both curious and reluctant to explore further.

The majority of the hospital's inmates were either recovering from illnesses or suffering from minor ailments. My new companions spent their time lounging on their beds or pacing back and forth between the narrow rows. The space allowed just enough room for them to walk, though not without occasionally brushing past one another. The ward's atmosphere was thick and suffocating, filled with the distinct odor common to hospitals. It was an unpleasant blend of human perspiration, stale air, and the sharp, medicinal scent of drugs. Despite the stove being heated throughout the day, the room retained an oppressive warmth that made the environment even less bearable.

My assigned bed, like the others, was covered with a heavy counterpane, which I promptly removed. Beneath it lay a coarse cloth blanket, lined with linen, and sheets whose cleanliness left much to be desired. Beside the bed was a small wooden table equipped with a pitcher, a pewter mug, and a modest napkin, provided to me upon arrival. The table also served as a stand for a tea-urn, a luxury enjoyed by the wealthier patients who could afford tea. Such men, however, were a rarity in the convict ward. Beneath the mattresses, pipes and pouches of tobacco were concealed, as smoking was a universal habit among the patients—even those suffering from consumption. The hospital staff, including the doctors and attendants, rarely conducted searches. When a patient was caught smoking openly, the staff typically pretended not to notice, provided the behavior was discreet.

The patients, aware of the leniency, took care to smoke only behind the stove, where the activity was less likely to be detected. Smoking in bed was reserved for the nighttime hours, when the officers in charge of the hospital ceased their rounds. This cautious approach underscored the prisoners' ability to adapt to their restrictive surroundings while preserving some semblance of personal freedom.

Until this point, I had never experienced life as a patient in any hospital, so the entire situation felt foreign and curious to me. My arrival seemed to intrigue the other prisoners, who regarded me with a subtle air of superiority. This was the type of quiet dominance often displayed by those already assimilated into a group toward someone newly introduced. I was the outsider entering their established world, and they assessed me accordingly.

To my right lay a man who was awaiting trial. He was a former secretary and the illegitimate son of a retired captain, accused of counterfeiting currency. Despite being in the hospital for nearly a year, he showed no visible signs of illness. He had managed to convince the medical staff that he suffered from an aneurism, an ailment severe enough to exempt him from both hard labor and the corporal punishment to which he had been sentenced. His ploy was so effective that, a year later, he was transferred to T——k and assigned to work at an asylum.

This man, about twenty-eight years old, was robust and sharp-witted, but also cunning and openly self-serving. He possessed the air of a practiced lawyer, capable of spinning words to suit his needs. Though intelligent and articulate, he was deeply arrogant and consumed by a sense of exaggerated self-worth. He carried himself with the conviction that no one was as just or honest as he, and he made no effort to conceal this belief. To him, his alleged crimes were mere misunderstandings, and he felt entirely justified in dismissing any accusations against him.

This individual was the first to strike up a conversation with me. His curiosity about my background was evident as he peppered me with questions, eager to learn more about the newest arrival. With apparent satisfaction, he began explaining the workings of the hospital, offering a guided initiation into this microcosm of convict life. Predictably, he introduced himself by emphasizing his lineage, boasting of his status as the son of a captain. His primary goal, it seemed, was to ensure I viewed him as a nobleman or, at the very least, someone with ties to the aristocracy. His manner was polished but transparently self-important, as though he needed my acknowledgment of his superior social standing to validate his own inflated sense of identity.

Shortly after, an invalid from the Disciplinary Company approached me. He began boasting about how he knew many nobles who had been exiled and, to make his claims convincing, rattled off their first names and patronymics. However, it took only one glance at the man's face to discern that he was lying through his teeth. His name was Tchekounoff, and it became clear that his purpose in befriending me was less about camaraderie and more about suspecting I had money.

His eyes lingered on the small packet of tea and sugar I had brought with me, and immediately, he offered his services. He insisted on boiling water for me and even promised to procure a tea-urn. Although M. D. S. K—— had already assured me that my own tea-urn would be sent through a prisoner working in the hospital, Tchekounoff would not be dissuaded. He sprang into action, bringing me a tin vessel to boil water, eagerly demonstrating his willingness to help. His extraordinary enthusiasm was so transparent that it drew scornful laughter from one of the other patients, a consumptive man named Usteantseff, who occupied the bed opposite mine.

Usteantseff, as I later learned, had been a soldier who endured a horrifying punishment. In a desperate bid to avoid the rods, he had consumed a bottle of vodka infused with tobacco, an act that had severely damaged his lungs and left him gravely ill. I have mentioned him before, but now he lay stretched out on his bed, wheezing and struggling for breath. Until that moment, he had remained silent, his serious gaze fixed on me. However, Tchekounoff's excessive obsequiousness seemed to strike a nerve with him. His gravity, combined with his irritation, gave his outburst a strangely comical edge. Finally, unable to contain himself, he spoke.

"Look at this fellow!" he exclaimed, his voice strained and choked from weakness. "He's found his master!"

Tchekounoff turned around, visibly irritated by the remark. "Who's this talking?" he asked, his tone dripping with contempt as he glared at Usteantseff.

"You're a flunkey," Usteantseff shot back, his frailty doing little to dampen the confidence in his voice. It was as though he had every right to call out Tchekounoff's behavior.

"I'm a flunkey?" Tchekounoff replied, incredulously.

"Yes, you're a flunkey. A true flunkey," Usteantseff retorted, nodding as if confirming an irrefutable fact. "Listen, my good friends!

180

He doesn't believe me. He's in shock, the brave fellow!"

"And why does it matter to you?" Tchekounoff countered angrily. "Can't you see that when some people don't know how to use their hands, they're not used to being without servants? Why shouldn't I serve him, you hairy-snouted buffoon?"

"Who has a hairy snout?" demanded Usteantseff, his indignation evident.

"You!" Tchekounoff snapped back.

"I have a hairy snout?" Usteantseff said, incredulity etched across his gaunt face.

"Yes, you certainly do."

"Well, you're one to talk," Usteantseff fired back, with a weak but pointed tone. "If I've got a hairy snout, then you've got a face like a crow's egg."

The exchange, while biting, had an odd humor to it that lightened the otherwise tense and somber atmosphere of the ward. Despite their barbs, it was clear that these verbal sparring matches were part of the dynamic among the men, a way of asserting themselves even within the confines of their shared suffering.

"Hairy snout! The merciful Lord has already settled your account. You'd be better off staying quiet and waiting to die," Usteantseff rasped, his weak voice laced with biting sarcasm.

"Why should I?" retorted Tchekounoff. "I'd rather bow down before a boot than before a slipper. My father never bowed, and he never taught me to do it either."

He might have gone on further, but his voice was abruptly cut off by a violent coughing fit. His thin frame convulsed painfully as the attack shook him, leaving him gasping for air. After a few moments, he spat out blood into a rag, his forehead breaking out in a cold sweat.

Even though the coughing rendered him unable to speak, the expression on his face made it clear he had plenty more to say. He tried feebly to raise his hand, as if to gesture his defiance, but it was clear his strength was spent. For his part, Tchekounoff didn't push the argument any further and fell silent.

It didn't take much to understand that Usteantseff's anger was directed more at me than at Tchekounoff. Despite his contemptuous remarks toward the latter, everyone in the ward understood that Tchekounoff's servility was driven by his desire for a few kopecks, not by any inherent weakness of character. No one judged him harshly for trying to earn some money in whatever way he could.

The Russian people, I had come to realize, are rarely bothered by such matters. They know how to accept them for what they are. But I had clearly irritated Usteantseff, and the sight of my tea seemed to enrage him further. It wasn't about the tea itself—it was what it represented. What truly annoyed him was that, no matter how much I tried to blend in, I was still a gentleman in his eyes, even with my chains. The mere fact that I appeared to rely on the help of others, even if I neither asked for nor desired it, seemed to offend him deeply.

The irony was that I had gone out of my way to avoid appearing dependent. I tried to manage everything on my own, refusing help wherever I could, hoping to shed the image of an effeminate, high-handed noble. In fact, I took some pride in doing things for myself. Yet, no matter what I did, I couldn't seem to escape the attentions of those eager to assist me. Officious and eager to please, they attached themselves to me without any prompting on my part, often taking over my affairs to such an extent that I felt as if I were the one serving them rather than the other way around. Against my will, I became the picture of a nobleman who couldn't do without servants—a role I neither embraced nor wanted. The misunderstanding frustrated me deeply, but I was powerless to change how others saw me.

For Usteantseff, already irritable and bitter due to his illness, my mere presence seemed to amplify his anger. The other patients, however, regarded me with an indifferent air, though tinged with faint contempt. They were far more preoccupied with an event they eagerly anticipated later that evening.

As I listened to their hushed conversations, I learned that a convict was to be brought into the hospital that evening. At that very moment, he was undergoing a flogging. The prospect of this new arrival intrigued the patients, and their curiosity was palpable. They talked in low tones about the punishment, describing it as relatively minor— only five hundred strokes. Despite the grim nature of the topic, their voices carried an air of anticipation.

I glanced around the ward, taking note of the patients. Most of them were genuinely ill, suffering from scurvy and various eye diseases, ailments common in this region. Others battled fevers, lung diseases, or other illnesses. There was no effort to separate the patients based on their conditions; everyone, regardless of their ailment, shared the same crowded space.

That said, not all of the patients were genuinely sick. Some convicts had managed to gain admission simply to escape the harsh conditions of the prison or the guardhouse. The doctors, aware of this, admitted them out of pity, especially if there were empty beds available. For many, the hospital, despite its suffocating atmosphere and strict rules, offered a welcome reprieve from the grueling life of hard labor and confinement. It was a small haven, however imperfect, where they could find some semblance of relief.

Some men seemed to find a peculiar comfort in the hospital, even taking pleasure in its grim routines. These individuals were often from the Disciplinary Company, a group of soldiers notorious for their severe punishments and corrections. I observed my new companions with a mix of curiosity and unease, and one of them left me particularly baffled. He was a consumptive man, clearly in the final stages of his illness, and his bed was just a few feet away from mine, slightly beyond

Usteantseff's.

His name was Mikhailoff, and I remembered seeing him in the Convict Prison a couple of weeks earlier, even then gravely ill. It struck me as tragic that he had resisted treatment for so long, enduring his worsening condition with astonishing fortitude. By the time he came to the hospital around the Christmas holidays, it was far too late—he succumbed to his illness just three weeks later, consumed by galloping consumption. He seemed to have burned out like a flickering candle in its final moments. What left an even deeper impression on me, though, was the horrifying transformation in his face. I had taken note of him on my very first day in the prison; now, he was a shadow of the man I remembered.

In the bed next to his was an old soldier from the Disciplinary Company. This man had a repellent appearance that was difficult to ignore—his whole demeanor radiated something unpleasant. He was coarse and unkempt, with an expression that seemed permanently etched with bad intentions. His presence was one of the first things to initiate me into the strange and unsavory peculiarities of the hospital ward.

The old soldier suffered from a severe cold that made him sneeze incessantly, even in his sleep. Each fit of sneezing was like a string of salutes—five or six violent sneezes in a row, punctuated by his raspy exclamation: "My God, what torture!" Between these outbursts, he would sit upright on his bed, eagerly stuffing his nose with snuff from a crumpled paper bag as if he were preparing for the next round. The sneezing seemed to bring him some peculiar satisfaction, as if the strength and regularity of it were achievements to be admired.

His sneezing routine was grotesque to watch. After each fit, he would unfold his faded, threadbare cotton handkerchief—its original pattern long lost to endless washing—and blow his nose loudly, his face twisting into a maze of wrinkles. His gums, bright red and slick with saliva, peeked through a mouth lined with decayed, blackened teeth. When he finished, he would wipe the handkerchief on the lining of his dressing gown with a casual indifference that turned my stomach.

I couldn't help but inspect the dressing gown I had been issued with a new sense of dread. Its condition left little to the imagination. The fabric reeked of a nauseating cocktail of medicaments and old bodily odors, smells that intensified when warmed by body heat. It was as though the garment had absorbed every ailment and treatment it had ever encountered. Stained with patches that hinted at old poultices and salves, its lining was an archive of the hospital's grim history. Perhaps it had been washed at some point in its long existence, but the evidence suggested otherwise.

The worst offenders were the gowns worn by those who had just endured the rods. After their punishment, men were brought straight to the hospital, their backs raw and bleeding. Compresses and poultices were hastily applied to their open wounds, but the blood and other fluids soaked through their wet shirts and seeped into their gowns. These garments, already steeped in filth, now bore fresh stains from the gruesome aftermath of the flogging, further adding to the unbearable stench that clung to the hospital.

Throughout my time in hard labor, whenever I had to go to the hospital—which happened more often than I would have liked—I always regarded the issued dressing-gown with a mix of mistrust and revulsion. It was something I could never grow used to. After Tchekounoff had brewed my tea (I must add that the water, brought in during the morning and left to stand all day, became stale and almost toxic from the oppressive air of the room), the door swung open, and a soldier who had just undergone flogging with the rods was brought in, flanked by a double escort. This was the first time I had witnessed someone immediately after receiving such a punishment, though it would not be the last. Every time a whipped man was admitted, it cast a heavy shadow over the ward.

These unfortunate men were received with solemn quiet. Their

185

reception, however, often depended on the severity of their punishment and the gravity of the crime for which it was administered. Men infamous for heinous crimes or celebrated as bold brigands might command a kind of grim respect or awe. In contrast, those punished for simpler, less dramatic offenses—like the young recruit brought in that day—were met with a colder indifference. Still, there was never mockery or undue curiosity. The men in the ward knew better than to pester or interrogate the newly arrived.

Care for these beaten men was conducted in a matter-of-fact way, especially if they were too incapacitated to help themselves. The assistant surgeons entrusted the nursing of these patients to those in the ward, confident that their wounds would be tended by experienced hands. The treatment was straightforward but far from gentle: compresses of cold water were applied regularly to their raw backs. Additionally, pieces of broken rods embedded in the flesh had to be meticulously removed—a process agonizing to endure. Yet what struck me most was the extraordinary stoicism these men displayed.

I saw many convicts who had endured brutal floggings—some who had suffered hundreds of lashes. Yet, not once did I hear a single groan or scream escape their lips. Their silence was not born of indifference to pain but from sheer force of will. Even so, the aftermath was clear in their pale, ashen faces, the trembling of their lips, and the wild, unfocused glitter of their eyes. Some even bit their lips until they bled, desperate to suppress any sound of suffering.

The soldier brought in that day was in his early twenties, tall and muscular, with the bronzed skin of a man accustomed to hard labor. His back, bare to the waist, was a canvas of crimson welts and open wounds. He trembled visibly under the damp sheet covering his injuries, his body racked with fever. For over an hour, he paced the ward in silence, unable to sit or lie down. His expression was a haunting mix of wildness and vulnerability, his eyes darting from object to object without focus, as if searching for an anchor in his disoriented state.

I noticed his gaze lingering on my steaming cup of tea. Though he said nothing, I could sense his need. I offered the cup to him. He hesitated for a moment, then turned toward me without a word. Taking the cup, he drained its contents in one gulp, not even bothering with sugar. Without looking back at me, he placed the cup back in silence and resumed his pacing. He was too engulfed in pain to muster words of gratitude—or even the energy for conversation.

The other patients didn't bother him either. Once his wounds had been dressed with compresses, they left him alone, respecting his need for solitude. They seemed to understand instinctively that questions or expressions of pity would only burden him further. He appeared content with this unspoken agreement.

As night fell, the room's single lamp was lit, casting a dim, flickering glow over the ward. A few of the wealthier patients had their own candlesticks, but they were the exception. The doctor came by for his evening rounds, offering a few kind words to the patients—an act of humanity that was deeply appreciated, even by the most hardened criminals. Afterward, a non-commissioned officer arrived to count the patients, ensuring all were accounted for before locking the room for the night.

The prisoners held their doctors in the highest regard, often describing them as "fathers" for their compassion and dedication. These physicians treated their patients with a sincerity that went beyond mere duty. Their kindness wasn't a performance but an expression of genuine humanity. They understood that even a convict deserved clean air to breathe and the basic dignity of humane treatment. Convalescents were allowed to stretch their legs in the corridors to escape the stifling, pestilential air of the ward. However, once the doors were locked for the night, there was no leaving under any pretext.

One detail of prison life had always puzzled me deeply, a question that lingered in my mind for years: Why were convicts forced to wear their chains even in the hospital? I had seen men dying of consumption, gasping their final breaths, still shackled with heavy irons. The image haunted me, an insoluble riddle that seemed to epitomize the cold, unrelenting cruelty of the system.Everyone had long become accustomed to the sight of convicts shackled in chains, even those who were severely ill or on the verge of death. It was accepted as an inevitable fact of life in the penal system, unquestioned and unchallenged. Not even the doctors, whose role was ostensibly to alleviate suffering, seemed to consider requesting the removal of irons from the sickest inmates. The thought of sparing the dying or the severely ill this burden never appeared to cross anyone's mind, as if such an idea were unthinkable or irrelevant within the established order.

The chains themselves were not exceptionally heavy by design, weighing no more than eight to ten pounds on average. For a healthy, robust man, this weight was manageable, even if it became a constant source of irritation. Yet, over time, I had heard claims that these chains caused the legs of convicts to gradually waste away, becoming emaciated and weak after years of bearing the unrelenting weight. Although I never confirmed this scientifically, I found the notion plausible. Even a seemingly modest burden, when perpetually attached to the body, imposes an abnormal and unyielding strain. Over time, this must surely take its toll, weakening the muscles and bones, diminishing the natural vitality of the limbs.

For a healthy prisoner, the physical toll of wearing chains might be tolerable, if grueling. However, for the sick and the frail—those weakened by disease or years of deprivation—the weight became an insupportable cruelty. Imagine the plight of the consumptive, whose body already wastes away from within, their limbs frail and shrunken, forced to endure the added agony of iron shackles. For these souls, it is not just a physical burden but an unbearable weight upon their very existence.

Even a small concession, such as exempting consumptive prisoners from wearing irons, would have been an act of immense compassion and humanity. Such a measure could have made an enormous difference in the last days or weeks of a convict's life. Yet, when one raises the idea of such leniency, the argument against it is swift and unyielding: "They are criminals, undeserving of compassion." But should society deliberately add to the suffering of those already marked by the hand of death? Should the punishment inflicted by human justice be compounded when divine justice has already made its verdict clear?

No one could seriously argue that these measures serve any purpose of reform or correction, especially when applied to the dying. Consumptive convicts, for instance, are often exempted from corporal punishment because of their frailty. Why, then, should they not be spared the humiliation and physical agony of wearing chains? Surely, no one believes that a consumptive prisoner—a man whose every breath is labored and whose strength is almost gone—poses a flight risk. The very idea is absurd. Once the disease has reached a certain stage, escape becomes an impossibility, not because of the chains but because the body itself is no longer capable of such an effort.

It is impossible to mistake a consumptive for a healthy man. The disease leaves unmistakable signs that any doctor can recognize at a glance. So, what purpose do the chains serve for such individuals? They do not prevent escape; they cannot, in any practical sense, secure the prisoner. Chains are easily defeated by the resourceful convict, who can file through them or break the rivets with a stone if he is determined enough. The irons, then, are not a means of security but a form of symbolic punishment—a physical reminder of degradation and shame. Yet what purpose does this symbolism serve for a man already at death's door?

It is difficult, if not impossible, to discern any rational justification for this practice. The only conclusion one can draw is that it continues out of sheer inertia, a relic of a system that prioritizes punishment over any consideration of humanity or sense. Shouldn't even the smallest measure of mercy be extended to those whose lives are ending? Shouldn't the burden of chains be lifted, at least for the dying, as a final acknowledgment of their shared humanity? Such questions are rarely asked, and even more rarely answered. The silence surrounding this issue speaks volumes about the priorities and values of the system.

As I reflect and put these thoughts into words, the image of a man who died in the hospital resurfaces vividly in my mind. His face, hollowed and haunted, lingers in my memory, tied indelibly to the scene of his slow, agonizing death from consumption. This man, Mikhailoff, whose bed was only a short distance from mine, passed away just four days after my arrival at the hospital. His death and the events surrounding it left a profound impression on me, coloring my thoughts and feelings about all the consumptive patients I encountered during my time in confinement.

Mikhailoff was young, not older than twenty-five, with a thin, frail frame and a strikingly fine face. He belonged to the "special section," a detail that marked him as different, though in what way, I never fully knew. What set him apart more than anything was his quietness, his strange, subdued demeanor. His silence was soft, almost sorrowful, and deeply unsettling. The other convicts, who seemed to remember him from earlier days, described him in their own way, saying that he had "dried up" in the prison—a grim, haunting phrase that perfectly captured his desiccated appearance and spirit. What remains most vivid to me were his eyes—large, expressive, and full of something I could never fully define. I cannot say why this detail comes back to me with such clarity, but it does.

He died on an unusually clear and bright afternoon, around three o'clock. It was one of those winter days when the sunlight cuts sharply through the frozen air, refracting in golden beams through the icy, greenish panes of our hospital ward. The light poured across the room and fell over his gaunt body, illuminating him in a way that seemed cruelly indifferent to the suffering he endured in his final hours. His decline had been rapid. By morning, his vision had blurred, and he no longer recognized those who came near him. The convicts, despite their hardened lives, showed an unexpected tenderness. They tried in whatever ways they could to ease his suffering, though there was little they could do.

His breathing was labored, each breath a struggle that shook his entire chest. He gasped for air like a man drowning, his thin body rising and falling with a desperate rhythm. He clawed at his blanket and the few clothes he wore, tossing them aside as though they were suffocating him. When they removed his shirt, I saw the true extent of his frailty. His body was impossibly long and emaciated, with limbs like twigs and ribs so prominent they seemed to push against his skin, ready to break through. It was a body reduced to its barest elements, little more than a skeleton adorned with the iron chains on his wasted legs and the cross that hung over his chest.

The room had grown silent, the usual murmurs and noises replaced by an air of solemnity. Even the other patients, often indifferent to the suffering around them, seemed to sense the gravity of the moment. They walked on tiptoe, speaking in whispers or not at all, casting the occasional glance at the dying man. The sound of his labored breathing, that horrible death rattle, filled the room and grew louder, more unbearable, as time passed.

In his final moments, his trembling hand reached for the cross on his chest. It seemed to him as though even that small object, meant to comfort, was now a burden too great to bear. He tried to pull it off but lacked the strength. Someone finally removed it for him, and he relaxed momentarily. Ten minutes later, he died.

A soft knock on the door broke the oppressive stillness as someone summoned the sentinel. The warder entered, glanced briefly at the lifeless body, and walked off to fetch the assistant surgeon. The surgeon arrived quickly, a man whose demeanor was pleasant enough but who seemed perpetually more preoccupied with his appearance than his duties. He strode into the room with long, purposeful steps that clattered loudly on the floor, breaking the fragile quiet. Without hesitation, he went to the body and, almost perfunctorily, felt for a pulse. His face betrayed no emotion, no recognition of the tragedy before him. After a moment, he made a vague gesture with his hand, indicating the obvious—that life had left the young man—and turned on his heel to leave.

The noise of his departure echoed in the room, leaving behind an even deeper silence, one heavy with the weight of death and the inevitability of suffering in a place like this. Mikhailoff's frail, lifeless form remained where it was, bathed in the cold, indifferent sunlight. It was over for him, and yet it was not. For those of us who had witnessed his passing, the scene stayed with us, a stark reminder of how fragile life was within those walls, and how little dignity was left for those who met their end there.

Word of Mikhailoff's death was quickly passed on to the guard-house, as he was a significant prisoner due to his status in the special section. Proper documentation of his death required adherence to a series of formalities, and so we waited for the hospital guard to arrive. The room was heavy with silence, broken only by the occasional murmur. One of the convicts whispered softly, "Someone should close the dead man's eyes." This suggestion prompted another prisoner to step forward quietly. Without a word, he approached Mikhailoff's still form, gently pressing the eyelids shut. His gaze then fell on the small cross lying on the pillow beside the deceased, taken from his neck in his final moments. Picking it up, he examined it briefly, placed it back down, and made the sign of the cross over himself.

The lifeless body, now at peace, began to take on the rigid stillness of death. A pale shaft of sunlight illuminated his face, accentuating the two rows of perfectly white teeth visible between his thin, drawn lips. The flesh had tightened over the gums, leaving his mouth slightly open in a frozen grimace. The sight was unsettling, yet oddly serene, as though the light itself sought to soften the harshness of his end.

At last, the non-commissioned officer arrived, his musket slung over his shoulder and his helmet securely strapped beneath his chin. Two soldiers accompanied him, their faces as impassive as ever. The officer slowed his pace as he approached, his movements hesitant, as if something unseen held him back. His gaze flickered briefly toward the gathered prisoners, who stood silently watching him with dark, unreadable expressions. He seemed uneasy, perhaps unnerved by their solemn stillness.

He stopped abruptly, just a step away from the body, as if rooted to the spot. The sight before him—the gaunt, skeletal figure of Mikhailoff, his thin frame still bound by the heavy iron chains—seemed to strike him deeply. Slowly, almost ceremoniously, the officer reached up to unfasten his chin strap and removed his helmet, though this was not a required protocol. He stood bareheaded for a moment, his weathered face reflecting years of hard service. Then, with deliberate care, he made the sign of the cross, his lips moving in a silent prayer. The man's hair, streaked with gray, caught the same pale sunlight that had shone on Mikhailoff moments earlier.

Nearby, another gray-haired figure stood watching—Tchekounoff. His eyes were fixed intently on the officer, his expression unreadable but intense. There was something almost visceral in the way he observed every gesture, every slight movement. Their eyes met briefly, and something unspoken seemed to pass between them. Tchekounoff's lips twitched, his teeth clenched tightly, and he exhaled sharply as if trying to suppress some overwhelming emotion. Finally, as though compelled by an invisible force, he spoke.

"He had a mother, too," he said, his voice low but clear, and his head nodded slightly toward the lifeless form of Mikhailoff.

The words struck me deeply, piercing through the room's silence with the weight of an unexpected truth. Why had he said it? What had prompted this simple, heartbreaking remark? It hung in the air, raw and poignant, as if it encapsulated every unspoken grief and unacknowledged humanity that filled the prison walls. The reminder that even this skeletal figure, stripped of all dignity, had once been someone's beloved son resonated with a power that I could not ignore.

The somber mood lingered as the corpse was prepared for removal. The body, still draped in the mattress, was carefully lifted. The straw beneath creaked under the shifting weight, and the chains, heavy and unyielding, clattered against the floor with a sharp, metallic sound. One of the soldiers bent down to gather the chains, their cold weight rattling in his hands as the body was carried out of the room. As they passed through the door, conversation among the prisoners resumed almost instantly, the quiet vigil breaking like a spell.

From the corridor came the commanding voice of the non-commissioned officer, barking orders for someone to fetch the blacksmith. The chains had to be removed, even in death—a grim reminder of the relentless grip of the system. The words echoed down the hallway, mingling with the muffled footsteps of the men carrying the body.

And so the moment ended, life resuming its harsh, unrelenting pace. Yet the image of Mikhailoff, the weight of those simple words, and the solemnity of the scene remained etched in my mind. It was a fleeting glimpse of something profound—humanity glimpsed through the smallest of actions and the quietest of voices.

Chapter 2
The Hospital (Continued)

The doctors made their rounds in the wards each morning around eleven o'clock, moving in a procession led by the chief physician. This visit was always preceded by the earlier round of the regular physician, who would begin his inspections about an hour and a half before the larger group arrived. The regular physician was a quiet and reserved young man, unfailingly polite and gentle in his demeanor. He was well-regarded by the prisoners, who appreciated his medical expertise and his considerate nature. However, they often remarked that he was "too soft." This wasn't a critique of his skill but rather of his overly accommodating attitude. He seemed uncomfortable in the presence of the prisoners, occasionally blushing or appearing flustered, especially when making decisions about their treatment or diet. At times, he seemed ready to agree to whatever the patient requested, though this did not diminish the genuine affection and respect he commanded.

Doctors in Russia often inspire similar feelings of respect and even affection among the general populace, and this admiration is well-deserved, based on my observations. This might seem paradoxical when one considers the widespread mistrust among the people for modern medicine, foreign treatments, and hospital care. Many individuals, even when seriously ill, still prefer to rely on the remedies offered by local witches or old women versed in traditional cures. These folk remedies, while not without merit, often take precedence over seeking help from trained physicians or hospitals.

This mistrust stems less from doubts about medicine itself and more from deeper-rooted fears and prejudices. The people are skeptical of anything associated with officialdom or government administration, and hospitals often embody those very qualities they distrust. Tales of horrors—sometimes exaggerated, but occasionally rooted in truth—circulate among the common folk, further discouraging them from seeking medical care. These stories speak of terrifying experiences within hospital walls, painting the institutions as places of alienation and fear.

Above all, the concept of "Germanism" in hospitals repels many. The idea of being attended to by foreigners, subjected to strict diets, or treated by seemingly cold and detached surgeons makes them uneasy. The specter of autopsies and dissection also looms large in their imagination, reinforcing the perception of hospitals as impersonal and dehumanizing places. Compounding these fears is the belief that doctors, being educated and part of the professional class, are essentially nobles. This perception widens the gulf of understanding between the physicians and the people they aim to serve.

However, once the people get to know their doctors personally— a process that often begins with hesitation but ends in trust—their initial fears tend to dissipate. In most cases, especially with younger doctors, their humanity and compassion win over even the most skeptical patients. This transformation is not an exception but a common occurrence, reflecting the dedication of many doctors to their craft and their commitment to caring for others. My own experiences and observations in various regions affirm this.

Certainly, there are exceptions. In some remote areas, instances of corruption and neglect exist. Some doctors accept bribes, exploit their positions for personal gain, or neglect their duties altogether, even forgetting the essence of their medical practice. Yet these cases are, thankfully, rare. The majority of doctors are guided by a spirit of generosity and compassion, which breathes new life into the medical profession and gives it a sense of moral purpose.

The rare "wolves in the sheepfold," as one might call the less scrupulous practitioners, often excuse their failings by pointing to the challenging circumstances of their work. They claim that difficult environments justify their actions, especially when writing or speaking with eloquence to shift blame. But such excuses are hollow. These individuals fail not because of their circumstances but because they abandon the very humanity that makes a doctor effective. It is the kindness, empathy, and genuine care of a physician that often serve as the most powerful remedies for a patient.

It is time to move past these tired complaints about adverse conditions. Yes, the challenges are real, but they are not insurmountable. Those who fall short of their responsibilities cannot hide behind their circumstances. True dedication shines through regardless of external difficulties, and the example set by compassionate doctors should remind us of what is possible. In this way, the profession continues to be a source of hope and healing for many, even amid skepticism and adversity.

Once again, I have strayed from my topic. My intention is simply to highlight that the mistrust and aversion the common people feel are directed more toward the broader system of officialdom and government-employed physicians than the doctors themselves. However, when people come to know these doctors personally, many of their deeply rooted prejudices and fears begin to dissipate.

Our hospital doctor, for example, would carefully visit every bed, engaging seriously and attentively with each patient. He would question them about their symptoms, examining them closely before prescribing remedies, potions, or treatments. Occasionally, though, it became evident that some of these supposed invalids were not sick at all. Their illness was a fabrication, their presence in the hospital an attempt to escape the relentless grind of labor or to enjoy a rare respite in a warm room with a mattress—luxuries compared to the damp, plank floors of the guard-house, crammed with other pale, frail detainees awaiting their trials.

In fact, it is worth noting that prisoners in Houses of Detention, often awaiting trial, appeared far more broken in both body and spirit than those who were already convicted. Their situation, both materially and emotionally, was undeniably worse.

When the doctor detected such cases of feigned illness, he would often write down a diagnosis of febris catharalis. This term, which loosely suggested a vague, mild fever, had become an unspoken agreement between the doctor and the patient. Everyone knew it meant the individual wasn't sick at all. Despite recognizing the charade, the doctor often indulged these patients, allowing them to remain in the hospital for up to a week before firmly asking them to leave. This arrangement elicited laughter among the other patients, who appreciated the humor and subtle mercy in this made-up diagnosis.

There were some, however, who stretched the doctor's kindness too far, staying as long as possible and only leaving when forcibly turned out. On these occasions, the doctor's discomfort was palpable. Confronted by the patient's stubbornness, he seemed reluctant to plainly tell them they were fit to leave. Even though he had the authority to simply write sanat. est.—meaning "cured"—and send them away without further explanation, he would instead drop gentle hints.

"You know it's time to go," he would say, "You're well now, and we're running out of space here."

When such appeals failed, he would resort to outright pleading, hoping to appeal to the patient's sense of decency. More often than not, the patient would eventually feel ashamed of their prolonged stay and agree to leave.

The chief physician, on the other hand, struck a very different figure. While compassionate and fair, he was far more decisive and unyielding than the regular doctor. The patients respected him greatly, even when he showed a merciless severity that could be unnerving. Accompanied by a retinue of hospital doctors, he would make his rounds with a commanding presence, pausing longest at the bedsides of those who were gravely ill. His tone was encouraging, and his words carried weight, offering a rare sense of care and justice.

Yet, even the chief physician was no pushover. He never sent away convicts diagnosed with febris catharalis immediately, but he was firm when it came time for them to leave. "You've had your rest," he would say firmly. "It's time to go now. You can't take advantage of the system."

This resolve was often tested during the summer months, when the intense heat and grueling labor drove many convicts to seek sanctuary in the hospital. Others, especially those who had been sentenced to corporal punishment, tried to prolong their stays to avoid returning to their harsh reality. I remember one case in particular where the doctors had to adopt an unusually firm stance to rid the hospital of a particularly persistent patient.

This man, who suffered from a chronic and painful inflammation of the eyes, had arrived seeking relief. His condition seemed genuine at first—his eyes were alarmingly red, and he complained of constant, sharp pain in his eyelids. The medical team tried everything: plasters, leeches, blisters. Yet, no treatment seemed to help. His condition stubbornly refused to improve, and his complaints persisted. It eventually became clear that while he might have had a legitimate ailment, his insistence on staying in the hospital stemmed less from his condition and more from a desire to escape his harsh prison environment.

Ultimately, even the chief physician had to intervene to send him back to the convict barracks. It was a harsh reminder that even in a system built on compassion, limits had to be drawn.

This memory encapsulates the delicate balance doctors had to maintain: offering compassion and care while remaining vigilant against exploitation of their kindness. It was a constant dance between humanity and discipline, especially in an environment where many saw the hospital as a temporary refuge from the grinding hardships of convict life. The story of this persistent patient, with his painfully inflamed eyes and relentless determination to stay, highlighted the challenges faced not only by the prisoners but also by those charged with their care.

The regular doctor, with his gentle demeanor and reluctance to enforce rules harshly, often bore the brunt of these cases. His approach was a reflection of his empathy, though it sometimes left him at a disadvantage with more obstinate patients. The chief physician, by contrast, operated with a different ethos. His authority and decisiveness allowed him to enforce boundaries, even when doing so required an unwavering firmness. Together, these two figures represented the duality of the medical profession in such a setting: one rooted in compassion, the other in pragmatic necessity.

These interactions were not just about treating ailments but navigating the intricate dynamics of life in the prison hospital. Every patient, every diagnosis, and every dismissal reflected the broader reality of the convict system—a reality shaped by suffering, resilience, and, at times, quiet acts of resistance. Through it all, the doctors remained a symbol of hope and humanity, offering a glimpse of dignity in an otherwise dehumanizing world.

The doctors soon began to suspect that the man's illness was entirely fabricated. The inflammation of his eyes neither worsened nor improved despite their treatments, which raised doubts. They quickly came to understand that this was a deliberate deception, although the man stubbornly refused to admit it. He was a robust and youthful-looking individual, with a certain physical appeal, yet he managed to create an uneasy atmosphere among his fellow patients. His demeanor was secretive, brooding, and filled with mistrust. He avoided eye contact and preferred to keep to himself, which only deepened the unease surrounding him. Many of the convicts found his presence unsettling, fearing he might one day commit an act of violence in his growing despair.

This suspicion wasn't unfounded. Before arriving at the hospital, this man had been a soldier who had been caught committing a petty theft. For this crime, he was arrested, tried, and sentenced to a thousand strokes of the rods. Following his punishment, he was to be transferred to a disciplinary company. Such punishments were dreaded to the point of madness, and prisoners would go to extraordinary lengths to delay or avoid them, even temporarily. The desperate might stab a fellow inmate or even one of their guards on the eve of their scheduled punishment, knowing this new crime would necessitate another trial. Though it meant an eventual doubling or even tripling of their punishment, it also provided them with a temporary reprieve from the immediate horror.

In this man's case, his desperation led him to fake an illness, hoping to prolong his time in the relative safety of the hospital. Some of the patients believed he should be closely monitored, fearing that he might harm someone during the night in a moment of panic or despair. Yet, despite these concerns, no special precautions were taken. Even those who slept in the beds nearest to him remained passive, their own survival instincts dulled by the oppressive monotony of convict life.

It was observed, however, that the man was rubbing his eyes with bits of plaster scraped from the walls and other substances to maintain the appearance of redness. His goal was clear—to convince the doctor during daily rounds that his condition was real. But the chief physician, growing impatient with this charade, eventually resorted to a stern ultimatum. He threatened to treat the supposed inflammation with a seton—a harsh and invasive medical procedure used as a last resort for resistant illnesses.

The seton procedure involved pulling up a fold of skin at the back of the neck and making a deep incision through which a thick skein of cotton was threaded. This skein had to be moved back and forth daily to keep the wound from healing, ensuring a constant flow of suppuration. The process was excruciatingly painful, designed to force the body to react and heal. The man was presented with a choice: endure the seton or admit his deceit.

Faced with no alternative, the man submitted to the procedure. He endured the agony for several days, his suffering evident in every wince and moan. Despite his initial resolve, the unrelenting pain eventually broke his will. He finally agreed to leave the hospital. Remarkably, his inflamed eyes healed almost overnight, as if they had never been afflicted. The transformation was so sudden and complete that it left no doubt about the deception.

With his "recovery" complete, the man's brief sanctuary came to an end. Once his neck had sufficiently healed from the seton, he was discharged from the hospital and sent back to the guardhouse. His reprieve had run its course. The very next day, he was led out to receive the first of the thousand strokes he had worked so hard to avoid. Despite his efforts to escape the inevitable, the punishment awaited him, a grim reminder of the relentless justice of the convict system.

The moments before a punishment like flogging must be unimaginably dreadful, so much so that perhaps I have been too harsh in labeling as cowardly those who are consumed with fear at the thought of it. It is difficult to truly comprehend the intensity of such terror unless one has stood in those shoes, knowing that an unbearable ordeal lies just ahead. This fear becomes even more striking when we consider how some convicts willingly risk a doubling or tripling of their punishment simply to delay the inevitable for even a short time. That speaks volumes about the psychological torment they endure.

Yet, strangely, there are those who, having endured part of the flogging, choose to return for the remainder before their wounds have even healed, preferring to finish the ordeal rather than prolong their suffering in a guardhouse. This is revealing, for life in a guardhouse is so harsh and degrading that it is considered worse than the punishment itself. Such decisions, born of desperation or sheer resolve, highlight the unfathomable depths of human endurance.

Repeated exposure to floggings seems to create a grim resilience in some convicts. Those who have been whipped multiple times often develop a hardened demeanor, both physically and emotionally. Over time, they come to see this brutal punishment as nothing more than a grim inconvenience, something to be endured rather than feared. Their bodies grow calloused, their minds almost numb to the pain and humiliation.

One convict in particular stands out in my memory. He was a Tartar who had converted to Christianity, and in the prison, he was mockingly called Alexandrina by the others. His real name was Alexander. He had once told me, with surprising amusement, about the time he endured 4,000 strokes. He would laugh and joke about it as though recounting a mildly unpleasant episode, but when he spoke seriously, he credited his ability to survive such a horrific punishment to his upbringing. His back was a patchwork of scars, unhealed reminders of a childhood steeped in brutality. He believed that the beatings he received in his youth had prepared him for the torment he later faced as a convict.

"They beat me for anything and everything, Alexander Petrovitch," he said one evening, sitting with me by the fire. "For fifteen years—ever since I can remember—I was beaten for no reason, many times a day. It didn't matter who it was; anyone who felt like it could beat me. At some point, I stopped feeling it. It made no difference to me anymore."

His tone was almost casual, as though describing a mundane part of his life. I often wondered about his past and how he ended up in the army. Perhaps he wasn't entirely truthful in his tales, for there were hints that he might have been a deserter or a vagabond before becoming a soldier. But one story he told me seemed genuine, and it left a deep impression on me. He once recounted the sheer terror he experienced when he was condemned to 4,000 strokes for killing one of his officers.

As he described that moment, his usual nonchalance gave way to something raw and unguarded. For all his bravado, there was no masking the fear that had gripped him then. It was a fear so profound that it lingered, even in the retelling, as though he could still feel the echoes of that fateful day. That he could survive such an ordeal, let alone speak of it later with laughter, is a testament to the human capacity for resilience—a resilience forged, in his case, through years of unrelenting hardship.

Alexander's story was unique in its details, but the essence of it was all too common in the convict prison. It underscored the brutal reality that many of these men had lived lives of unimaginable suffering long before they ever arrived there. In a sense, the punishments they endured as prisoners were merely a continuation of the pain and injustice that had defined their existence from the start.

"I knew they would punish me harshly," he began, his voice calm but laced with a bitter undertone, as though he were recounting a story etched deeply into his bones. "Even though I had grown accustomed to being whipped, I couldn't shake the thought that I might die this time. The devil take it—4,000 strokes is no joke. And then there was the matter of my officers. They were absolutely livid with me after what happened. I had no doubt they wouldn't spare me. This wasn't going to be anything like 'rose-water,' I could tell. Honestly, I was convinced I'd meet my end under those rods."

He paused, his expression momentarily darkening as though reliving the grim anticipation of that day. Then he continued, his tone shifting slightly. "So I decided to get baptized. I thought, maybe, just maybe, they'd show some mercy. My comrades told me it wouldn't change a thing, that it was pointless. But I thought, who knows? Maybe they'd pity a Christian more than a Mohammedan. So, I went through with it. They baptized me and gave me the name Alexander. But guess what? It didn't make the slightest difference. They flogged me just the same, didn't spare a single stroke."

He chuckled dryly at this, shaking his head. "I was furious. I thought, 'Wait, just wait. I'll outsmart them yet.' And you know what? I did. I managed to fool them all. I figured out how to look like a dead man—not completely lifeless, mind you, but close enough to convince them that I was taking my last breaths. They lined me up before the battalion to deliver the first thousand strokes. The pain was unbearable, my skin felt like it was on fire, and I screamed with all my might. When they got to the second thousand, I thought, 'That's it. I'm done.' My mind went blank, and my legs gave out. I collapsed to the ground, my face blue, my mouth frothing, and my breathing stopped. When the doctor came, he declared me near death. They rushed me to the hospital, and as soon as I got there, I came back to life."

He laughed at this, but it was the laugh of a man who had long since numbed himself to the absurd cruelty of his circumstances. "They flogged me twice more after that. Oh, they were furious when I 'died' again after the third thousand strokes. They were determined to finish me off during the last round. And, by God, did they beat me! Each stroke of that cursed fourth thousand felt like three of the first. I thought they'd finish me for good if I tried playing dead too soon. But I held out, gritted my teeth, and endured it. By the time there were only 200 strokes left, they could have hit me with all their might—I didn't care anymore. Compared to what I'd already endured, those last 200 were nothing."

He smirked, his expression a mix of defiance and pride. "You know why I could stand it? Because I grew up under the whip. When I was a kid, anyone who felt like it could beat me, for no reason at all. Day after day, year after year, they whipped me until I stopped feeling it. That's what saved me."

He leaned back, staring into the distance, his tone softening. "Well, I'm alive now, aren't I? But I've been beaten more times than I can count. No one could count them—not even me. There aren't enough numbers for it."

He glanced at me then, his eyes crinkling as a simple, natural laugh escaped him. I couldn't help but smile in return. "Do you know something, Alexander Petrovitch?" he asked, leaning closer as though sharing a secret. "Every time I dream at night, I'm always being flogged. Nothing else. Just the whip. It wakes the others up sometimes. They yell at me—'What are you howling about, you devil?'"

Despite the grim humor, there was something almost childlike in his laughter. This man, short and stocky, no more than forty-four years old, with a surprisingly robust and active demeanor, was both a figure of camaraderie and mischief among the prisoners. Though he often stole from others—an act that inevitably got him flogged—he managed to live on good terms with most of them. His ability to take what wasn't his, knowing full well it would lead to punishment, seemed more like a reflex than malice.

What struck me most about him, and about so many of the others, was their astonishing ability to recount their suffering without a trace of bitterness or hatred. These were stories of unimaginable pain, stories that could make my heart pound with dread as I listened. And yet, they laughed as they told them, like children recalling some harmless mischief from their past. It wasn't just resilience—it was something deeper, something unshakable in their spirit, despite the horrors they had endured.

It was quite different with M——tçki when he told me about his punishment. Unlike others who might recount their suffering with a detached or even lighthearted air, his response revealed a profound and enduring pain. As he was not a nobleman, he had been sentenced to flogging—a punishment he bore without outward complaint but with an unmistakable sense of humiliation. He never spoke to me about it unless prompted. When I asked if the rumors were true, he answered with just two terse words: "It's true." But his voice was strained, and his expression betrayed him. He did not meet my eyes, turning red as if the mere acknowledgment of it brought back the indignity. When he finally did look up, his eyes burned with an intense, smoldering anger, and his lips quivered with suppressed rage. It was clear to me that this episode in his life was one he would never, and could never, forget.

Unlike many of the other convicts, who often recounted their ordeals with a peculiar mixture of humor and resignation, M——tçki's memory of his punishment was seared into him like a brand. His silence on the subject spoke volumes, and I could tell that the humiliation weighed on him far more than the physical pain. For others,

206

these events were often turned into stories of defiance or survival, recounted with a certain bravado or laughed off as just another chapter of their lives. They rarely showed signs of guilt or remorse, even when their crimes had been committed against their fellow convicts. As for offenses against superiors or authorities, they rarely mentioned those at all. It seemed to me they regarded such acts as fated events, dictated by an uncontrollable impulse or by circumstances beyond their control. In their eyes, these were not personal failings but inevitable clashes with authority, and their punishments were accepted with a kind of stoic resignation.

For many of them, this acceptance came from a deep-seated belief that the communities they came from—the common people—would not condemn them for their actions. They trusted that their peers would not consider them truly dishonorable unless their crime had been directed against someone of their own class. This conviction gave them an odd sense of peace. Their conscience remained untroubled, and they retained an inner composure that even the harshest punishments could not shake. They seemed to view the knout or the rod as simply an unavoidable consequence, a part of the natural order of things. For them, receiving punishment was neither an exceptional disgrace nor something that set them apart. It was just another trial in a life filled with hardships, one endured by countless others before them.

This perspective reminded me of soldiers who fight in wars. Does a soldier harbor personal hatred for the enemy he is ordered to kill? Not usually. He fights because he must, not out of malice, and he accepts that the same may be done to him. Similarly, the convict bore his punishment without dwelling on hatred for those who delivered it. Once the ordeal was over, it was simply another story to tell.

Still, not all these stories were told with indifference. There were instances where deep emotions surfaced, especially when certain individuals were mentioned. One name, in particular, always drew an angry reaction: Jerebiatnikof. I first learned of him during my initial stay in the hospital, hearing of him only through the convicts' whispered accounts. Later, I saw him for myself when he came to command the guard at the prison. He was a man in his early thirties, with a large, heavyset frame, ruddy cheeks that sagged slightly, white teeth, and an unsettling, booming laugh. There was a crudeness about him, a lack of reflection or humanity that was immediately apparent.

The convicts hated him, and for good reason. He seemed to derive genuine pleasure from supervising punishments. When it was his duty to oversee a flogging, he did so with what could only be described as enthusiasm. Other officers despised him for it, considering him a monstrosity even by the grim standards of the prison. The convicts shared this view. They saw him as the embodiment of cruelty, a man who found joy in the suffering of others.

It was a relic of a time not so distant from our own, yet already hard to believe—a time when some executioners seemed to revel in their work. Most officers carried out their duties with a grim sense of necessity, administering strokes with neither passion nor pleasure. But Jerebiatnikof was different. He represented a level of brutality that stood out even in this brutal world, and his name became a byword for the kind of cruelty that left scars far deeper than the physical ones inflicted by the lash.

This lieutenant was a rare and appalling exception, a man who derived genuine pleasure and satisfaction from administering punishment. For him, the act of flogging was not merely a duty but a source of unnatural excitement that fed the darkest corners of his base soul. It wasn't enough to simply oversee justice; he turned punishment into a cruel performance, one he orchestrated with a sinister glee.

Picture the scene: a prisoner is brought to the designated place of punishment, trembling with dread. Jerebiatnikof, the officer in charge, is already there, setting the stage for his grim spectacle. Soldiers armed with heavy rods stand in a long, ominous line, their faces hardened by the roles they are compelled to play. Jerebiatnikof walks along the line with a self-satisfied air, his eyes scanning the soldiers, ensuring they are ready to carry out their grim task. His words of encouragement are laced with unspoken threats—he doesn't need to spell out the consequences of slacking in their "duty." The soldiers know precisely what "otherwise" means in his vocabulary.

The condemned man, stripped to the waist, is tied to the butt end of a musket in preparation for his harrowing march down the "Green Street." This infamous corridor of punishment is named for the green rods that will be used to flay the flesh from his back as he is dragged along. If the prisoner is unfamiliar with Jerebiatnikof's cruel games, he might cling to a desperate hope, unaware of the torment that awaits.

Begging for mercy is part of the ritual Jerebiatnikof relishes most. The prisoner, his voice trembling with despair, pleads with the officer in charge.

"Your nobility," he cries, his tone desperate and tearful, "have pity on me! Treat me like a human being. Be merciful, and I will pray to God for you every day of my life. Do not destroy me. Show mercy!"

This is the moment Jerebiatnikof has been waiting for. He halts the proceedings, as if moved by the plea, and begins to engage the prisoner in a mockingly sympathetic conversation. His voice takes on an almost paternal tone, dripping with false compassion.

"But, my good man," he says, shaking his head as though burdened by the weight of his responsibility, "what can I do? It is the law that punishes you, not me."

The prisoner, seeing a glimmer of hope, latches onto the lieutenant's words. "Your nobility! You have the power to show mercy. Have pity on me, I beg you!"

Jerebiatnikof, feigning sorrow, responds with a theatrical sigh. "Do you think I take any pleasure in this? Do you believe I enjoy seeing you whipped? I am a man, just like you. Answer me—am I not a man?"

"Of course, your nobility," the prisoner replies, seizing on what he believes is a chance for reprieve. "We know the officers are like fathers to us, and we are their children. Please, be a compassionate father to me!"

The lieutenant nods solemnly, as though deeply moved by the man's words. "Yes, my friend, you are right. Officers are like fathers, and I ought to be merciful. I should take pity on you, sinner though you may be."

The prisoner, encouraged by this show of sympathy, agrees eagerly. "Your nobility speaks the absolute truth!"

Jerebiatnikof pauses, his voice turning grave. "And yet, I must serve God and my country. I would be committing a grave sin if I interfered with the punishment decreed by the law. Do you understand that? It is not I who punish you—it is the law."

The prisoner's hope begins to falter, but he clings to his desperate plea. "Your nobility, please…"

And so, the conversation drags on, Jerebiatnikof savoring every moment of the prisoner's anguish, wringing every last drop of desperation from him before finally allowing the flogging to proceed. The entire exchange is a cruel charade, designed not to ease the prisoner's suffering but to prolong it, to break his spirit even before the first blow falls.

Jerebiatnikof's methods were infamous among the convicts, and his name was spoken with bitterness and hatred. Yet, for all his posturing, he was not admired even among his peers. Other officers regarded him with disdain, recognizing in him a cruelty that went beyond the harshness of their duty. To the convicts, he was not just an officer enforcing the law; he was a symbol of the very worst excesses of power—one who reveled in the pain of others and turned punishment into a perverse form of entertainment.

"Well, what am I to do?" Jerebiatnikof would begin, his voice dripping with mock sincerity. "Think about it. I know that I'm in the wrong if I don't punish you as the law demands, but, fine, let it be as you wish. I'll show mercy. I'll punish you lightly. But consider this—if I go easy on you this one time, won't you think you can act foolishly again and expect the same mercy? What would you say to that?"

The prisoner, desperate and clutching at any hope of escape, would reply in a tearful, pleading voice, "Your nobility, have mercy! Before the throne of the heavenly Creator, I swear—"

"No, no!" Jerebiatnikof would interrupt, wagging his finger theatrically. "Don't swear in such a way; it's a sin. I'll believe you if you simply give me your word."

The prisoner would stammer out his agreement, his voice shaking. "Your nobility, I swear, I will never offend again."

Jerebiatnikof, assuming the tone of a benevolent patriarch, would add, "Well then, listen. On account of your tears—your orphan's tears, because you're an orphan, aren't you?"

"Yes, your nobility," the prisoner would sob. "An orphan on both sides. I'm alone in the world."

"Well, on account of those orphan's tears, I will have pity on you," Jerebiatnikof would declare, his voice feigning emotion so convincingly that the prisoner, now overwhelmed with gratitude, would thank God for sending such a compassionate officer.

But the charade ended there. As soon as the procession moved out, the drum rolled, and the soldiers readied their rods, Jerebiatnikof's true colors showed.

"Flog him!" he would bellow, his voice booming like a clap of thunder. "Harder! Skin him alive! Beat him harder, this rogue, this orphan!" His words, dripping with cruelty, were accompanied by his peals of laughter, loud and guttural, as though the entire ordeal was the height of entertainment for him.

The soldiers, knowing they dared not slacken their blows, struck with all their might, each rod landing with brutal force on the prisoner's back. The convict screamed, his body writhing in agony, while Jerebiatnikof, clutching his sides, staggered about, laughing so hard he could scarcely stand upright. "Flog him harder!" he howled between fits of laughter. "Show no mercy to this brigand, this orphan!"

Sometimes, Jerebiatnikof would invent variations to make the punishment more grotesque. In one of his games, the prisoner, having no knowledge of the horrors awaiting him, would beg for mercy. This time, Jerebiatnikof would dispense with the false sympathy and propose a "favor" directly.

"Look here," he would say with a sly smile. "I'll punish you as the law dictates, but I'll grant you one mercy. I won't tie you to the musket. Instead, you'll run down the line. Just run as fast as you can, and the rods will catch you naturally. It'll be over sooner that way. What do you say? Want to try?"

The prisoner, torn between hope and suspicion, would hesitate before agreeing. "Well, your nobility, I consent."

"Good, I consent too," Jerebiatnikof would declare, his voice laced with mock encouragement. Then he would turn to the soldiers, barking his orders. "Come on now, do your duty!"

The prisoner, believing this method might spare him some pain, would begin to run. But before he had gone more than a dozen paces, the soldiers, eager to avoid reprimand, struck him with their full strength. The rods came down like a relentless storm, and the man's screams pierced the air as he stumbled and fell, unable to withstand the brutal onslaught.

"No, your nobility," the prisoner would cry out, barely able to lift himself from the ground. "I'd rather be flogged the usual way!"

Jerebiatnikof, who had anticipated this outcome all along, would double over with laughter, his cruel mirth echoing down the "Green Street."

"Ah, what fun!" he would exclaim. "You see, I always know best."

But Jerebiatnikof's sadism extended far beyond these instances. Countless stories circulated among the convicts, tales of his inventive cruelties and twisted amusements. Yet to recount every one of his vile "diversions" would be impossible, not to mention deeply unsettling. Suffice it to say, his reign of terror left scars—both physical and emotional—that lingered long after the beatings were over.

My companions also spoke of Lieutenant Smekaloff, a man who once acted as Commandant before the arrival of our current Major. Unlike the contempt with which they regarded Jerebiatnikof, there was an air of nostalgia and genuine affection whenever Smekaloff's name came up. Jerebiatnikof, with his sadistic tendencies, was dismissed with indifference; there was no hatred, just disdain. Smekaloff, however, was remembered with surprising warmth, even when the subject was the punishments he had overseen, many of which were severe. How could it be that a man who ordered such chastisements was recalled not with bitterness, but with a kind of fondness? What secret had he possessed that allowed him to win the admiration of the convicts?

The explanation lay, perhaps, in the peculiar disposition of my companions and, indeed, of the Russian people as a whole. They have an astonishing capacity to forgive pain and humiliation if it is accompanied by even the smallest kindness. A gentle word, a moment of understanding—these were enough to transform the memory of a punishment into something almost bearable, even sentimental. This curious tendency requires no intricate analysis; it is simply an observable fact, a testament to the resilience and forgiving nature of the people.

Lieutenant Smekaloff embodied this principle perfectly. He had a way of commanding respect and affection despite his role as an enforcer of punishment. He was not particularly merciful, nor could he be called lenient, but he possessed a natural quality that endeared him to those under his authority. It was as though he radiated an air of camaraderie, a sense of shared humanity that bridged the gap between his position and theirs. Smekaloff was simple-minded, straightforward, and free of pretension. Unlike some officers who reveled in their power and lorded over the convicts with an air of superiority, Smekaloff lacked any sense of caste. He treated the prisoners not as lesser beings, but as people, flawed perhaps, but deserving of dignity.

This, I believe, was the key to his popularity. He did not despise the men under his charge, and they, in turn, did not despise him. It wasn't that he went out of his way to be kind—kindness, as an overt act, can sometimes breed suspicion. Rather, his natural demeanor had an earthy, approachable quality. The convicts sensed that he was one of them in spirit, if not in station. There was no artifice in his interactions, no trace of the aloofness or condescension that so often poisoned relationships between superiors and subordinates. He was, as they often said with a sigh, "as kind as a father."

And yet, Smekaloff was no stranger to punishment. He did not hesitate to order severe chastisements when he deemed them necessary, but even in these moments, he managed to strip the act of its usual cruelty. The men did not harbor resentment against him, even after enduring the rod at his command. Remarkably, they would often recall these episodes with laughter. It was not that he inflicted less pain, but rather that he had a way of disarming bitterness with his approach. He made the punishment feel less like a vendetta and more like an unfortunate duty that had to be fulfilled.

Smekaloff's unique sense of humor played a role in this dynamic. He had only one practical joke—a single, curious routine that he employed during punishments—but it was enough to endear him to the convicts. It wasn't a cruel jest; rather, it was a simple piece of theater that amused both him and the prisoners, softening the edge of the proceedings.

When a punishment was about to take place, a chair and a long pipe were brought to him. Smekaloff would sit down casually, light his pipe, and engage the convict in conversation. It wasn't mockery; he seemed genuinely interested in the man before him, as though the punishment were merely an excuse to have a chat.

"No, comrade," he would say gently, waving off the convict's pleading. "Lie down. What's troubling you?"

The convict, resigned to his fate, would stretch himself out on the ground with a sigh.

"Can you read fluently?" Smekaloff might ask, puffing thoughtfully on his pipe.

"Of course, your nobility," the convict would reply, trying to maintain some dignity. "I am baptized, and I learned to read as a child."

"Then read this," Smekaloff would say, handing the convict some random piece of paper, often a scrap with meaningless scribbles.

The convict, confused but eager to comply, would squint at the paper and begin to mumble a response, only for Smekaloff to cut him off with a hearty laugh.

The punishment would proceed, but Smekaloff's odd blend of humor and humanity lingered in the air, leaving the convicts with a strange sense of having been treated fairly, even respectfully. It was this rare ability—to uphold discipline without alienating those he disciplined—that made Smekaloff an enduring figure in their memories. Unlike Jerebiatnikof, who inspired only fear and contempt, Smekaloff left behind a legacy of warmth, even amid the harsh realities of the prison.

The prisoner knows exactly what is going to happen and how it will

215

end because this same trick has been played more than thirty times. But Smekaloff also knows the prisoner isn't fooled, just like the soldier holding the rods above the poor man's back isn't fooled. The prisoner begins reading aloud, and the soldiers with the rods stand completely still, waiting. Smekaloff stops smoking, raises his hand, and listens for a specific word they've agreed on ahead of time. When the word is spoken—chosen because it could also mean to start—the Lieutenant raises his hand, and the whipping begins.

The officer bursts out laughing, and the soldiers around him laugh as well. The man swinging the rods laughs, and even the man being whipped joins in the laughter.

Chapter 3
The Hospital (Continued)

I have written here about punishments and the people who carry them out because I got a very clear understanding of the subject during my time in the hospital. Before that, I had only heard general stories about it. In our room, there were prisoners from the battalion who were waiting to be punished with rods, as well as others from the military base in our town and the surrounding district.

During my first few days, I observed everything around me with intense curiosity. The strange behavior of the men—some who had just been whipped and others who were about to be—made a deep and horrifying impression on me. I felt shaken and scared.

As I listened to the conversations and stories shared by the other prisoners about these punishments, I asked myself questions I couldn't answer. I wanted to understand the levels of punishment, the different types, and what the prisoners themselves thought about them. I tried to imagine what was going on in the minds of the men who had been whipped.

As I have mentioned before, it was rare for a prisoner to face his punishment calmly, even if he had been beaten several times before. The condemned man felt a fear that was overwhelming—purely physical and unconscious—something that completely disturbed his emotional state.

During the years I spent in the convict prison, I had plenty of time to observe the prisoners who stayed in the hospital to recover from their injured backs before going through the second half of their punishment. This break in the punishment was always ordered by the doctor, who was present at the flogging to ensure the man could physically handle the next round.

If the number of strokes is too many to be given all at once, the punishment is divided based on the doctor's recommendation at the scene. The doctor decides whether the prisoner can handle the entire punishment or if it puts their life at risk.

Sometimes, five hundred, one thousand, or even one thousand five hundred strokes are given at once. But if the punishment involves two or three thousand strokes, it is split into two or three separate sessions.

Prisoners who had recovered after the first round of punishment and were about to face the second became gloomy and silent the day before they were sent out. They appeared numb and detached, speaking to no one and remaining in complete silence.

It's notable that other prisoners avoid speaking to those about to be punished. They never offer consolation or unnecessary comments, and the topic is never mentioned. Ignoring the prisoner entirely seems to be the best approach for them.

There are, however, exceptions.

One prisoner, Orloff, whom I've mentioned before, wished his wounds would heal faster. He was eager to finish his punishment so he could join a group of prisoners being transported, planning to escape during the journey. Orloff had a fiery, determined personality, and this was his only focus.

A clever man, Orloff appeared happy when he first arrived, though he was unusually tense despite trying to hide it. He had feared that he might collapse or die before completing even half of his punishment. While awaiting trial, he had heard of steps being taken by the authorities regarding his case, and he believed he wouldn't survive the ordeal. However, after enduring the first round of strokes, his courage returned.

When Orloff was brought to the hospital, I had never seen injuries as severe as his. Yet, he was in high spirits, hopeful about surviving. He realized the stories he'd heard weren't true, or else the punishment would not have been stopped midway.

Now he began dreaming of the long journey to Siberia and the possibility of escaping to freedom, to open fields and forests.

But just two days after leaving the hospital, Orloff was brought back, only to die on the same bed he had used during his earlier stay.

He couldn't survive the second round of punishment, as I have already described.

All the prisoners, without a single exception—even the most timid and fearful, even those who were consumed with anxiety and dread for days or nights before their punishment—faced it with remarkable courage when the moment arrived. It was a display of resilience that seemed almost unreal. Despite the severity of their ordeal, I hardly ever heard cries or groans in the barracks during the night that followed an execution. It was as if they had trained themselves to endure pain in silence, to suffer without complaint. These men, hardened by their circumstances, seemed to carry an unspoken understanding of pain as an inevitable part of their existence.

I often questioned those around me about the nature of this pain, trying to grasp the depth of their suffering and compare it to something familiar. My curiosity wasn't idle or detached; I was deeply affected by what I saw, both frightened and unsettled by the harshness of the punishment. Yet, no matter how persistently I asked, the answers I received never seemed to fully satisfy my need to understand.

"It burns like fire," they would say, almost in unison. The description was always the same, no matter whom I asked.

I remember speaking to M—tski about it, hoping for a more detailed explanation. "It burns like fire!" he repeated, his voice trembling with the memory of it. "Like hellfire! It feels as if your back is being roasted in a furnace." His words struck me, painting a vivid and horrifying image of what they endured.

One day, I made an observation that I found both strange and disturbing. It seemed to me—and the opinion of the convicts themselves confirmed this—that among all the punishments in use, the rods were the most excruciating. At first, the idea seemed absurd, even impossible. Yet the evidence was undeniable. While five hundred strokes with the rods, or even four hundred, could be enough to kill a man, a similar number of strokes with sticks was far less likely to cause death. Beyond five hundred strokes with the rods, survival became nearly impossible. Even the strongest, most robust men would succumb before reaching a thousand strokes. In contrast, a thousand strokes with sticks, or even two thousand, could often be endured by a man of average strength without the same risk of death.

The convicts themselves insisted that the rods inflicted a far greater degree of suffering than sticks or ramrods. "Rods hurt more and torture more," they would say with grim certainty. Their unanimous agreement left no room for doubt. The rods inflicted a uniquely agonizing pain, one that seemed to target the nervous system, pushing it to its limits. They didn't just hurt; they shattered the body's defenses, leaving a torment that lingered long after the punishment had ended.

I cannot help but think that this level of suffering, this ability to cause pain so precise and so overwhelming, might have had an allure for certain twisted individuals. There are people who, like predators thirsting for blood, derive a perverse pleasure from the torment of others. In such people, the act of punishment becomes a grotesque spectacle, a thrill derived from the breaking of another's will and spirit. This kind of cruelty recalls the darkest figures of history—people like the Marquis de Sade or the Marchioness Brinvilliers—whose delight in suffering was as incomprehensible as it was horrifying.

Such individuals, in their intoxication with power and cruelty, often lose all traces of their humanity. Those who have absolute control over the bodies, blood, and souls of others—fellow human beings who, by the laws of morality and faith, should be their equals—become trapped by their own unrestrained desires. This power to degrade and dehumanize others becomes an addiction, transforming them into something no longer recognizable as human.

Tyranny, I believe, is more than a behavior; it is a habit, one that can grow and fester until it becomes a disease. Even the kindest and most compassionate person can, over time, become hardened and desensitized to such an extent that they are no longer distinguishable from a wild beast. Blood and power intoxicate the mind, feeding a dangerous cycle of callousness and debauchery. Once a person reaches this state, their capacity for cruelty becomes limitless, turning the suffering of others into a source of pleasure.

When this happens, the individual ceases to be a man or a citizen and becomes a tyrant, a creature wholly consumed by their basest instincts. From this point, a return to humanity, a recognition of dignity, or a path to moral redemption becomes almost unthinkable. Repentance and rebirth seem forever out of reach, and what remains is a shell of a person, lost in their own monstrous desires.

That the unchecked power to inflict such punishment has a corrupting and contagious influence on society as a whole is beyond question. A society that witnesses such acts without outrage, that regards them with indifference or apathy, has already succumbed to a deep moral infection. It is no exaggeration to say that allowing one person the authority to physically punish another is one of the gravest flaws in our social structure, a festering wound that threatens to poison the very foundation of civic life. This kind of power erodes any sense of shared community or mutual respect and instead plants the seeds of inevitable decay and disintegration within society.

It is curious how society reserves its disdain for the executioner by trade, yet remains largely indifferent to, or even approving of, the so-called noble executioner. Every employer, every master of a workshop, must feel a faint, almost subconscious pleasure when they realize the worker under their control depends entirely on them—not just individually, but with their entire family as well. This dependency, rooted so deeply in our social fabric, is not something that can be easily eradicated. I am convinced that such deeply ingrained attitudes, passed down through generations and ingrained from birth, cannot be uprooted quickly or easily. It is not enough to simply admit to these failings. Mere acknowledgment is insufficient—paltry, even. True change requires far more effort, far more time. Such deeply seated habits and instincts cannot be undone in a single moment of awareness or confession. They must be methodically uprooted, and this is a long and arduous process.

I have already spoken of executioners, but it bears repeating that the instincts of an executioner—those impulses that drive a person to inflict suffering—exist in latent form in nearly all of us. These tendencies may not always develop to the same degree, but when they overpower all other human qualities, they transform a person into something monstrous. When the balance of one's nature tips toward cruelty, the result is a horrifying distortion of humanity.

There are, as I see it, two distinct types of executioners: those who embrace their role willingly and those who perform it out of obligation, as part of their official duties. The voluntary executioner, who chooses to inflict harm of their own accord, is morally inferior even to the professional, salaried executioner—despite the latter being universally regarded with disgust and fear. People instinctively feel a kind of mystical horror for the professional executioner, a revulsion so deep it borders on superstition, while the voluntary executioner is often met with far less hostility. Why is there such a stark difference in the way these two are perceived? Why is the former met with loathing, while the latter is treated with indulgence or indifference?

I have known instances of seemingly honorable men—kind, respected individuals, admired by their friends—who, when faced with a situation requiring punishment, found it entirely natural, even necessary, to ensure that the culprit was beaten until they cried out for mercy. To them, it was not only justified but indispensable. Yet, if the victim refused to plead for mercy, this so-called honorable man, whom I might otherwise consider good and decent, would take it as a personal insult. Initially, he might have intended the punishment to be mild, but when the expected cries of "Your nobility!" or "Have mercy!" failed to come, he would lose all composure. His frustration would grow, and his sense of being wronged would compel him to demand harsher punishment. Fifty additional blows would be ordered, all in the hope of finally breaking the victim's silence and extracting the cries and supplications that seemed so necessary to him. Eventually, the pleas would come.

"Impossible! He is too insolent!" the man would exclaim, his frustration evident, as though the victim's endurance had been a deliberate act of defiance against his authority. These words, spoken with such seriousness, reveal the disturbing depth of his conviction that punishment must elicit submission—not just physical but emotional—as if anything less undermined his sense of order and control. This mentality, rooted so deeply in those who wield such power, is both terrifying and profoundly revealing of the human capacity for cruelty.

As for the executioner by office, he is typically a convict selected specifically for this grim role. His initiation begins with an apprenticeship under a seasoned practitioner, learning the trade until he becomes proficient. Once trained, he remains in the convict prison, living in isolation. His quarters are separate, shared with no one. Occasionally, he may be given a small establishment of his own, but he is always under strict guard. Despite his role being officially sanctioned, the executioner is not devoid of human emotions. He is no machine. Though his actions are part of his duty, he sometimes succumbs to rage or even derives a twisted pleasure from his work. While he harbors no personal hatred for his victims, the desire to demonstrate his expertise and refine his technique often fuels his vanity. He approaches his task as an artist might, taking pride in his skill, even as he recognizes that he is despised and feared by all. This awareness of his societal rejection inevitably influences his character, exacerbating his base instincts.

Even children whisper strange things about him, claiming he has neither father nor mother, as if his very existence is an enigma. It's a curious phenomenon, revealing the depth of superstition and revulsion surrounding him.

All the executioners I have encountered shared certain characteristics. They were intelligent men, often with a pronounced sense of self-importance. This conceit seemed to grow as a reaction to the universal contempt they faced and was perhaps further bolstered by the fear they inspired in their victims. The power they wielded over those condemned only served to strengthen this arrogance. Their role, surrounded by an air of grim theater, likely cultivated a certain haughtiness, a belief in their own importance.

For a time, I had the opportunity to observe an ordinary executioner closely. He was a man of about forty, with a lean, muscular build and an agreeable, intelligent face framed by long, curly hair. His manner was composed and serious, and his behavior reflected a certain dignity. He responded to questions clearly and thoughtfully, though his tone carried a subtle condescension, as if he believed himself to be superior to anyone addressing him. This sense of superiority was palpable in his demeanor. Even the officers of the guard treated him with a measure of respect, which he keenly noticed and responded to by becoming even more polite and self-assured in their presence.

He was scrupulously courteous, never failing to maintain an air of refined politeness. Yet, it was evident to me that he considered himself far above those who spoke to him. His expression revealed this belief, an unshakable confidence in his own importance. During the summer months, he was sometimes tasked with an additional duty—killing the stray dogs that roamed the town with a long, slender spear. These dogs multiplied rapidly and became especially dangerous during the heat of the dog days, prompting the authorities to assign the executioner this degrading job. Yet, to him, it was not humiliating in the least. He carried out the task with a gravity that bordered on theatrical. Walking through the streets under the watchful eyes of his armed escort, he projected an aura of authority that frightened women and children. His gaze swept over the passersby with an air of detached superiority, as though he were elevated far above them all.

Executioners, despite their grim duties, live in relative comfort. They have money to travel with ease and indulge in luxuries like vodka. A significant portion of their income comes from the bribes offered by prisoners sentenced to flogging. Before an execution, the condemned often slip gifts into the executioner's hands, hoping for leniency. Wealthier convicts may negotiate directly, with the executioner demanding sums as high as thirty roubles or more, depending on the victim's means. While the executioner has no formal right to go easy on his victims, a well-placed bribe ensures he strikes with less force. If no bribe is given, he feels no obligation to hold back and may unleash his full strength, knowing he has the power to do so.

This transactional cruelty extends even to the poorest prisoners. In such cases, the victim's relatives often rally to gather funds, pleading and bargaining with the executioner to lower his demands. However, failing to satisfy him almost always results in brutal consequences. The superstitious fear surrounding the executioner often compels families to comply, knowing the alternative could be devastating. Tales about the executioner's prowess only add to this dread. I was told remarkable, almost mythical stories—that with a single blow, the executioner could kill a man outright.

"Is this your experience?" I once asked him, curious to separate fact from fiction. His response, like the man himself, was enigmatic, leaving me to wonder about the complex and often terrifying nature of his role.

Perhaps so. Who can say for sure? The tone in which these things were told left little room for doubt, as though the matter was self-evident to those who spoke of it. They also claimed that the executioner, if he chose, could strike a criminal in such a precise way that the victim would feel no pain and bear no scar. This mastery over his craft seemed to elevate the executioner's reputation, even in a setting where his presence inspired fear and loathing.

Even when the executioner receives a bribe to go easy, tradition dictates that the first blow must be delivered with all his strength. It is a deeply ingrained custom, upheld without exception. After this initial brutal strike, he may moderate the intensity of the subsequent blows, especially if the payment was generous.

Why this ritual of the first punishing strike is adhered to is not entirely clear. Perhaps it serves to prepare the victim, numbing their body and dulling their senses for the remaining lashes, which might feel less agonizing in comparison. Or perhaps the intent is psychological: to terrify the prisoner and ensure they understand the force and authority of the one delivering the punishment. It may even be a matter of vanity—a performance to showcase the executioner's strength and skill before an audience. Whatever the reason, the executioner often seems slightly exhilarated before an execution, as though the act itself excites him. In that moment, he is not merely a tool of punishment but a performer in a grim theater, aware that the public watches him with a mixture of horror and fascination. The moment becomes a spectacle, heightened by his customary warning to the victim: "Look out! You are going to have it!" These fatal words, spoken with foreboding certainty, invariably precede the first blow.

It is almost incomprehensible to think of a human being reduced to such a level, where cruelty is both an art and a duty.

On the first day of my stay in the hospital, I listened intently to the stories shared by the convicts. These tales broke the monotony of the long, dreary hours and provided a strange sort of entertainment in an otherwise oppressive atmosphere.

Each day followed a predictable routine. In the morning, the doctor's visit was the first event, a brief distraction from the endless hours of confinement. Next came the highlight of the day: dinner. This was no ordinary meal but an event laden with significance for the prisoners, who measured their circumstances by the portions they received. The meals varied depending on the nature of each patient's illness. Some were served only thin broth with groats, while others received nothing more than gruel or semolina—a dish that was surprisingly popular. Over time, the prisoners grew finicky about their meals, their hardships softening them into a strange kind of delicacy.

Those in better condition or further along in recovery received a piece of boiled beef, while the most fortunate—those suffering from scurvy—were given the best food: roast beef served with onions, horseradish, and, on occasion, even a small glass of spirits. The bread provided with the meals also varied, ranging from black to brown, depending on the patient's condition. The meticulous care taken in distributing these rations often provoked laughter among the prisoners, though it was tinged with irony.

Not all patients consumed their allotted portions. Many traded their meals, creating an informal economy within the hospital. Food intended for one patient was often eaten by another. Those on restricted diets, receiving only meager portions, would barter with the scurvy patients, offering money for meat or other richer foods. A single portion of meat could fetch as much as five kopecks, and some wealthier prisoners, eager to satisfy their hunger, would pay to eat two full portions. When there was no meat available in our room, the warder would be sent to another section to procure some, and if none could be found there, he might even venture to the military infirmary, which we mockingly referred to as the "free infirmary."

Despite the general poverty among the prisoners, there were always some who managed to scrounge together a few kopecks to purchase small luxuries. Cakes, white bread, and other delicacies from the market were highly sought after. The warders carried out these errands without complaint, showing an unexpected sense of fairness in fulfilling the prisoners' requests.

The most difficult time of the day was after dinner. With nothing to occupy their minds, many prisoners succumbed to boredom. Some chose to sleep, finding escape in rest, while others filled the silence with loud arguments or boisterous storytelling.

Excitement was rare, but the arrival of a new patient always caused a stir, breaking the monotony of our routine. These arrivals were particularly intriguing if the newcomer was a mystery to the rest of us. Questions about their past would immediately arise, as the other prisoners sought to learn their story.

The most fascinating newcomers were the so-called "birds of passage"—prisoners who moved frequently from one place to another. These individuals always had tales to share, stories of their travels and exploits, which captivated their audience and briefly transported us from the bleak confines of the hospital. These moments of connection, fleeting as they were, became precious glimpses into lives beyond our own suffering.

Of course, they never spoke openly about their own faults or crimes. If a prisoner didn't choose to discuss such matters himself, no one would question him about them. The other convicts seemed to understand instinctively that some topics were better left untouched.

Instead, their inquiries centered on practical details. The new arrivals were asked where they had come from, who had accompanied them on the road, what the conditions of the journey were like, and where they were being taken. These questions were simple but meaningful, offering the convicts a way to connect and compare their shared experiences. Stimulated by the newcomers' tales, the rest of the group would often launch into their own stories, recounting what they had seen, endured, or overheard. Conversations frequently revolved around the convoys, the officers in command, and the men tasked with carrying out sentences. These discussions seemed to offer both distraction and a grim sense of camaraderie.

Occasionally, towards evening, those who had been scourged would return to the hospital. Their arrival never failed to leave an impression, as I've mentioned before. Yet, these occurrences were not daily, and in their absence, life in the hospital fell into a state of unbearable monotony. When nothing of interest happened, the sheer boredom seemed to intensify the tension among the patients. The sick grew irritable, often snapping at one another over the smallest things, their frustrations boiling over into heated arguments and occasional squabbles.

The convicts, however, found a strange sort of amusement when someone feigned madness to avoid punishment. When a supposed lunatic was taken away for medical examination, the others would watch with interest. It was not uncommon for prisoners sentenced to be scourged to pretend insanity in the hope of being excused from their punishment. Sometimes the act was convincing enough to fool even the doctors, while in other cases, the prisoner would simply drop the charade. Those who voluntarily abandoned their ruse did so with a resigned air, their faces dark with a kind of grim acceptance. They would calmly ask to be discharged from the hospital, their earlier antics ignored by both the convicts and the doctors. No one chided them for their deceit or spoke of their outrageous behavior. Their names were quietly added to a list, and they were taken elsewhere to face their punishment. A few days later, they would return, their backs raw and bloody from the ordeal.

The arrival of a genuinely mad prisoner, on the other hand, was an entirely different matter. It cast a shadow over the entire room. If the lunatic was cheerful and lively—singing, shouting, or dancing—he might initially provoke laughter or even enthusiasm from the other convicts. "Here's some entertainment!" they would say, amused by the exaggerated expressions and erratic movements. But this initial reaction of levity quickly faded, replaced by an overwhelming sense of unease. The spectacle of madness, so stark and uncontrolled, was deeply unsettling. For my part, I could never observe such a scene without a profound feeling of misery. The sight of a mind unraveling was too much to bear.

One such lunatic was kept in our room for three weeks. His presence was unbearable. Had there been any place to hide, we would gladly have taken refuge there. Just when we thought the situation couldn't grow worse, another madman was brought in. His arrival affected me deeply, more so than I could have anticipated.

In the early days of my exile, during my first month, I was assigned to work with a gang repairing kilns at the brickworks, about two versts from the prison. On my first morning there, M—tski and B. introduced me to the non-commissioned officer who supervised the work. This man was a Pole, well into his sixties, tall and lean, with a dignified and somewhat imposing presence. Despite his humble origins, he carried himself with the composure of someone accustomed to respect. He had spent many years in Siberia, having served as a soldier during the uprising of 1830. M—tski and B. spoke highly of him, admiring both his character and his intelligence.

The Pole was often seen reading the Vulgate, and when I spoke with him, I found him to be a thoughtful and engaging conversationalist. His stories were fascinating, told with an easy eloquence that held my attention. He was straightforward, good-natured, and remarkably even-tempered. I didn't see him again for two years, during which time I heard troubling rumors that he had become "a case" under investigation. Then, one day, he was brought into our room, completely mad.

He entered shouting and laughing, his voice echoing off the walls. Without hesitation, he began to dance in the center of the room, his movements wild and indecent, reminiscent of the Kamarinskaïa dance. The convicts were delighted, cheering and laughing at his antics. For them, it was a rare moment of diversion. For me, it was unbearable. I cannot explain why, but his madness filled me with a profound sadness.

Three days later, the mood in the room had shifted. The man's behavior grew more erratic and disturbing. He quarreled with everyone, erupted into fits of rage, groaned loudly in the night, and sang incessantly. His aberrations became so extreme, so grotesque, that they turned our stomachs. The room, already oppressive, felt like it was closing in on us. It was an experience I will never forget, one that left me deeply shaken.

He feared no one and nothing. Even when they restrained him in a strait-waistcoat, it did little to resolve the chaos. Bound as he was, he continued his quarreling, shouting, and picking fights with everyone in the room. His madness was undeterred by the physical restrictions placed upon him. After three exhausting weeks of his presence, the entire room collectively pleaded with the head doctor to remove him to another ward, one reserved for convicts. Reluctantly, their request was granted, and he was moved. However, after only two days, the patients in the other ward made their own desperate appeal to have him sent back, unable to tolerate his behavior. And so, he was returned to our infirmary.

This exchange of lunatics between the rooms became a miserable routine. At one point, both wards found themselves with a madman at the same time. The situation escalated into a pitiful game of passing them back and forth, each ward temporarily relieved when one was removed, only to find the chaos returned with the other. Eventually, an agreement was reached to alternate who would house them, taking turns as though the suffering could be shared. Still, a collective sigh of relief was felt by all when the madmen were finally removed altogether and taken far away to some unknown location, far enough that we could at least breathe freely again.

There was another madman who left a lasting impression on me—a peculiar and extraordinary figure. It was during the summer when they brought him to the infirmary. He was a man under sentence, roughly forty-five years old, with a robust and sturdy build. His face was deeply pitted with smallpox scars, his expression somber and forlorn. His small, swollen eyes were red with fatigue or sorrow, and he carried an air of profound sadness. When he entered, he quietly sat beside me, saying nothing. He seemed lost in his thoughts, absorbed in a deep and solitary reflection.

As night fell, he suddenly broke his silence and addressed me. Without any introduction, he began speaking hurriedly, his words charged with excitement, as though revealing a profound secret. He told me that he was sentenced to receive two thousand strokes with the rod, but that he had nothing to fear. Why? Because, as he explained with absolute conviction, the daughter of Colonel G— had taken a personal interest in his case and was working to save him.

I looked at him with surprise, trying to make sense of what he was saying. His tone and demeanor were so earnest that, for a moment, I almost believed him. Still, I replied skeptically, suggesting that the daughter of a Colonel was unlikely to have any influence over such a matter. I had not yet realized what kind of man I was dealing with. He had been sent to the hospital under the pretense of physical illness, and I had no reason to suspect that his mind was unwell. To understand better, I asked what illness had brought him here.

He replied with a shrug, saying he had no idea. He had been sent to us for reasons unknown to him, but he assured me he was in excellent health. Then, with unwavering confidence, he launched into the story of the Colonel's daughter and her supposed love for him. He claimed that two weeks earlier, as he was gazing out from behind the barred window of the guardhouse, she had passed by in a carriage. At the mere sight of him, she had fallen hopelessly in love.

From that moment on, he said, she had made every effort to see him again. He recounted, in vivid detail, how she had visited the guardhouse three times, each time under a different pretext. On the first occasion, she accompanied her father, ostensibly to visit her brother, an officer on duty. On the second visit, she came with her mother, distributing alms to the prisoners. Each time she passed by him, she whispered that she loved him and vowed to secure his release.

He shared these tales with an air of utmost sincerity, describing every encounter as though it were an absolute fact. His manner was calm and assured, as if there was no doubt in his mind that this young woman of noble upbringing had fallen madly in love with him, a nearly fifty-year-old man with a pockmarked face and a somber disposition. He believed wholeheartedly that her affection would lead to his punishment being revoked.

Listening to him, I could only marvel at the intricate delusion he had woven. It was both absurd and deeply tragic. This bizarre and romantic fantasy, involving the love of a young, well-bred girl for a man so far removed from her world, was a testament to the overwhelming fear consuming him. His mind, unable to bear the thought of the brutal punishment awaiting him, had conjured this elaborate tale as a means of escape. It was a pitiful and poignant reflection of the human psyche under extreme duress, a desperate attempt to cling to hope in the face of unimaginable suffering.

It is possible that he had indeed glimpsed someone through the bars of the window, and that this fleeting image, combined with the overwhelming fear of his impending punishment, had taken root in his mind and blossomed into the delusion he so fervently believed. His fear, unchecked and all-consuming, had found an outlet in the form of this desperate fantasy—a romance conjured by a mind teetering on the edge of madness.

This unfortunate soldier, a man who likely had never before entertained thoughts of young ladies, had built an elaborate story within his ailing imagination and clung to it as though it were his last shred of hope. He held onto this delusion with such tenacity that it seemed his very sanity depended on it. I listened to him in silence, moved by the tragic absurdity of his tale. Later, I recounted the story to the other convicts, who were naturally curious and eager to question him themselves. Yet, when approached, he refused to elaborate. He remained silent, his demeanor almost reverent, as if guarding a sacred secret.

The next day, the doctor came to examine him. Despite his evident distress, the man insisted that he was perfectly healthy. Taking his word for it, the doctor marked him down as fit for transfer, writing "Sanat. est" on his record—a notation signifying that he was cured. By the time we learned of this decision, it was too late to intervene or warn him. To complicate matters, none of us were entirely sure of the nature of his condition. Was he truly mad, or was his delusion simply a symptom of extreme fear and stress?

The fault lay with the authorities who had sent him to the hospital without providing any explanation for their decision. Their negligence, leaving us to guess at the reason for his presence, was both inexcusable and tragic.

Two days later, the poor man was taken out to receive his punishment. We soon learned that he had been utterly bewildered to find that, contrary to his expectations, the punishment was indeed to proceed. To the very last moment, he clung to the belief that he would be pardoned. But as he was led before the assembled battalion, reality struck him with full force. Overcome with terror and disbelief, he began to cry out for help, his voice echoing in desperation.

After the flogging, there was no room for him in our apartment, so he was placed in the infirmary. I later heard that for eight days following the ordeal, he spoke not a single word. He seemed trapped in a state of shock, his mind clouded by misery and confusion. His silence was unnerving, as if his spirit had been irreparably broken. When his wounds finally healed, he was taken away. After that, I never heard anything more about him.

As for the general treatment of the sick in the hospital, it was a curious affair. Those who were only slightly unwell often ignored the doctor's instructions entirely. They paid no attention to their prescribed treatments and avoided taking their medicines whenever possible. In contrast, those who were seriously ill followed the doctor's orders with remarkable diligence. They carefully took their powders and mixtures, doing everything in their power to recover. Yet, even among the truly ill, there was a noticeable preference for external remedies over internal ones.

Cupping glasses, leeches, poultices, and bloodletting were viewed with an almost superstitious reverence. These traditional treatments, which caused visible pain or discomfort, were held in high esteem by the patients. There was a peculiar satisfaction in undergoing these procedures, as if their very harshness validated their effectiveness.

What struck me as particularly strange was how these men, who endured the tortures of flogging and rods without so much as a murmur, would howl, groan, and complain over the smallest physical ailment. Whether their reactions were exaggerated for effect or genuine,

I could not say. The contrast was striking, and I often wondered what it revealed about the nature of their suffering and resilience.

One instance stands out vividly in my memory. Cupping treatments were a common occurrence in the hospital, but the device used for making the quick incisions in the skin had fallen into disrepair. As a result, the staff had to resort to using a lancet for the procedure. The process, already unpleasant, became even more painful, yet it was endured with a stoicism that was both impressive and unsettling.

These moments offered a window into the strange and often contradictory world of the convicts—men who could endure unimaginable suffering one moment and crumble under the weight of the mundane the next. It was a world governed by its own rules, where pain and resilience coexisted in ways that defied understanding.

For a cupping procedure, twelve small incisions are required to let the treatment take effect. When done with a proper machine, the cuts are almost painless, as the device works quickly and efficiently, making all the necessary incisions instantaneously. However, when the lancet is used instead, the process becomes far more tedious and painful. The lancet cuts slowly, its sharp edge slicing into the skin one prick at a time. For ten cupping points, about one hundred and twenty pricks are needed, each one sharp and irritating. I underwent this procedure myself and found it not only painful but also deeply unsettling. Beyond the physical pain, the repeated pricks caused considerable nervous irritation. Still, the suffering was not unbearable; one could suppress groans or cries if one made an effort to maintain composure.

What was amusing, though, was the sight of large, strong men wriggling and howling as if they were children being chastised. These were men who could endure the lash of the rod with stoic silence but would lose all dignity at the mere touch of a lancet. Watching them, I couldn't help but think of those men who are calm and steadfast in serious situations but are utterly insufferable in trivial matters, particularly within the safety of their homes. Such men are often quick to anger over the smallest inconveniences—a meal served late or a misplaced object. Their irritability grows in proportion to their comfort, making life difficult for those around them. This type of personality was not uncommon in the prison, where close quarters forced us to endure one another's quirks and tempers on a daily basis.

Sometimes, the other prisoners would mock or jeer at those who complained too loudly, and this often had an immediate silencing effect. It was as though the complainers only needed to be ridiculed to realize how absurd they sounded. The teasing acted as a corrective, bringing a sudden end to their protests.

One man who took great pleasure in addressing such behavior was Oustiantsef. He had little patience for whining or grimacing and was quick to put offenders in their place. Scolding others seemed to be a habit for him, perhaps born out of his own struggles with illness and a natural inclination toward being overbearing. He had a way of staring intently at someone before launching into long-winded admonishments, delivered with an air of calm authority. His tone suggested that he saw himself as a guardian of order and morality, a self-appointed overseer of the prison's social conduct.

"He's got to poke his nose into everything," the prisoners would joke, often laughing behind his back. Despite their amusement, they pitied him and generally tried to avoid direct confrontations with him.

"Has he talked enough yet?" they'd say. "It would take three wagons to haul away all the nonsense he spouts."

Another prisoner might chime in, "Why do you need to stick your oar in? Nobody's going to make a fuss over a little prick from a lancet."

"What harm do you think it'll do you? A mere touch, and you're crying like a baby."

At this point, another voice, laced with dry humor, would interject. "No, comrades, the cuppings are nothing. I've had them myself. But you know what's really awful? When they pull your ears for a long time. That shuts you up completely."

This remark would send the entire room into laughter. "Have you really had your ears pulled?" someone would ask, grinning.

"By Jove, I have," the man would reply, with mock indignation. "Why do you think they stick up like this, as straight as hop poles?"

The convict speaking was Chapkin, a man with notably long and upright ears. His appearance alone was enough to add a layer of hilarity to his stories. Chapkin was young, intelligent, and had lived the life of a vagabond. His humor was dry and delivered with such seriousness that his tales often left the listeners in fits of laughter.

"How in the world was I supposed to know someone had pulled and stretched your ears, you brainless idiot?" Oustiantsef would grumble, his temper flaring yet again. But Chapkin, with his usual composure, ignored the insult entirely, much to the amusement of the others.

"Well, who did pull your ears for you?" someone asked, eager to hear another of Chapkin's absurd tales. The room waited, stifling laughter, as Chapkin prepared to spin his next comical account, his long ears standing tall as though to lend credence to whatever wild story he was about to tell. The lighthearted banter, however fleeting, offered a rare moment of relief from the oppressive atmosphere of the prison."Why, the police superintendent, by Jove, comrades! That's who pulled my ears," Chapkin said, leaning back with a grin. "Our crime? Oh, just the usual—wandering around without any fixed place to stay. Vagrancy, they call it. So, here's the story: me and another tramp, Eptinie—he didn't even have a proper family name—decided to try our luck in the town of K——. On the way, we had stopped for a bit in a hamlet called Tolmina. Yes, there's actually a place with that name—Tolmina. We stayed there just long enough to freshen up a little before moving on to the town.

"When we arrived in K——, we started looking around, trying to spot a good opportunity for a bit of 'tramp business,' if you know what I mean. The plan was simple: make some quick gains and then leave the town before anyone could notice us. In the open countryside, you're free as the wind, but once you step into a town, everything changes. Eyes are always watching, and there's less room for mistakes.

"The first thing we did was head straight for a public-house. As we opened the door, we took a quick look around to see who was inside. The place wasn't much—a dingy sort of establishment, as you'd expect—but what caught our eye was a sunburnt fellow in a ragged German coat that looked ready to fall apart. He wasted no time and walked straight up to us, his steps confident, though his appearance was anything but.

"'Excuse me,' he says, 'but may I ask if you gentlemen happen to have any papers with you?'

"'No, we haven't,' we replied.

"'Well, neither do we,' he said with a grin, gesturing to two companions who were loitering nearby. 'These are my comrades. We're in the service of General Cuckoo, if you catch my meaning.'

"That meant they were forest tramps—men who roamed the wilds, living off whatever they could find. Then he adds, 'We've been enjoying life a bit lately, but right now we're down to nothing—not a penny to our name. Would you be so kind as to order a quart of brandy for us?'

"'With the greatest pleasure,' we told him, and before long we were all drinking together like old friends. As the brandy loosened tongues, they began telling us about a house at the edge of town, a wealthy merchant's place full of good things ripe for the taking. It was exactly the kind of opportunity we'd been looking for, so we decided to give it a go that very night.

"There were five of us altogether, and just as we were about to get started, the police swooped in. They caught us red-handed, marched us to the station-house, and then straight to the head of the police himself.

"He was a sturdy fellow with a thick set of whiskers, and when we were brought before him, he lit his pipe and sipped at a cup of tea as if he had all the time in the world. 'I'll examine them myself,' he said. There were five of us in our group, plus three other tramps who'd just been brought in for unrelated mischief.

"Now, comrades, you must understand that there's nothing funnier in this world than a tramp when he's caught. You could beat him with a cudgel till your arms are tired, and still, the only answer you'd get is that he's forgotten everything—his name, his past, everything.

"The superintendent turned to me first and asked, 'Who might you be?'

"'I've forgotten all about it, your worship,' I replied, just like the others.

"'Just you wait,' he said, fixing me with a long, hard stare. 'I know your face.'

"But the truth was, I'd never seen the man before in my life. Then he moved on to the next tramp.

"'Who are you?' he asked.

"'Mizzle-and-scud, your worship,' the man replied without missing a beat.

"'Mizzle-and-scud? That's your name?'

"'Precisely that, your worship.'

"'Well and good, you're Mizzle-and-scud,' the superintendent muttered before turning to the third tramp. 'And you? What's your name?'

"'Along-of-him, your worship,' the man answered, pointing to Mizzle-and-scud.

"'Along-of-him?'

"'That's what they call me, your worship.'

"'And who gave you that ridiculous name, you hound?'

"'Very worthy people, your worship,' the tramp said, his face as serious as a judge. 'There are lots of worthy people about, as you surely know better than anyone.'

"The superintendent raised an eyebrow. 'And who exactly are these "worthy people"?' he asked, leaning forward with mock interest.

"We all held our breath, waiting to see what kind of nonsense the tramp would come up with next."

"'Oh, Lord, it has slipped my memory, your worship. Do be so kind and gracious as to overlook it,' the tramp said, scratching his head as if the act of thinking might somehow jog his memory.

"'So you've forgotten them, all of them, these "worthy people"?'

"'Every single one of them, your worship,' he replied earnestly, his tone suggesting that forgetting was as natural as breathing.

"'But surely you must have had family—a father, a mother. Do you remember them?'

"'Well, I suppose I must have had, your worship. But I can't say I recall much about them—my memory's not what it used to be. Now that you mention it, though, I'm sure I did have some, your worship.' He scratched his chin thoughtfully, as if trying to pull long-lost memories from the fog of his mind.

"'And where have you been living all this time?' the superintendent asked, leaning forward.

"'In the woods, your worship,' the tramp said without hesitation.

"'Always in the woods?'

"'Always in the woods!' the tramp repeated emphatically.

"'Even during winter?' the superintendent pressed.

"'Never saw any winter, your worship,' the man replied, his face a mask of innocence.

"The superintendent leaned back in his chair, baffled by the absurdity. 'Get along with you!' he exclaimed, turning his attention to the next man. 'And you—what's your name?'

"'Hatchets-and-axes, your worship,' the tramp answered confidently, as though it were the most ordinary name in the world.

"'And yours?' the officer continued, addressing another.

"'Sharp-and-mum, your worship,' came the reply.

"'And you?' he asked the last.

"'Keen-and-spry, your worship.'

"'And not a single one of you remembers anything about your past?'

"'Not a single one of us, your worship,' they all chorused, their faces solemn.

"The superintendent stared at them for a long moment, then burst into laughter. He couldn't help himself, the absurdity was too much. Seeing him laugh, the rest of us couldn't resist and began laughing too. It was contagious, the kind of laughter that builds and rolls until it feels like the walls might shake. For a brief moment, even the grim surroundings of the station-house seemed a little less oppressive.

"But, comrades," Chapkin said, lowering his voice, "it doesn't always go like that. Sometimes, when the officers aren't in the mood for games, they take a different approach. Those same big, burly police can knock your teeth out with their fists if you don't play along the way they want. They're strong, let me tell you—devilish strong. You don't

241

want to be on the receiving end of that."

"'Take them off to the lock-up,' the superintendent finally said, waving his hand dismissively. 'I'll deal with them later. As for you,' he said, pointing at me, 'you stay right here.'

"That's me he was talking about," Chapkin added, leaning forward with a knowing grin. "'You just sit over there,' he says, pointing to a desk where there's paper, a pen, and an inkwell. So I think to myself, 'What's he got in mind now?'

"'Sit down,' he says again. 'Take the pen and write.'

"Before I could protest, he reaches out and grabs my ear, giving it such a yank that I thought he'd tear it clean off. I looked at him then, comrades, in the kind of way the devil must look at a priest—like I was ready to make a deal or burn everything to ashes, depending on how this went.

"'I can't write, your worship,' I told him plainly, because, truth be told, I couldn't."

Chapkin paused, his expression serious for a moment, then broke into a wide grin. "And that's when the real fun began, but I'll save that for another day. Let's just say, comrades, the pen isn't always mightier than the fist—especially in the hands of a police superintendent with a fondness for pulling ears!"

"'Write, write!' he kept shouting, his voice sharp and relentless.

"'Have mercy on me, your worship!' I pleaded, but he wouldn't hear it.

"'Write your best, write!' he barked again, and all the while his hand stayed firmly on my ear, pulling and twisting as though trying to wring the truth out of me. Pals, I swear to you, I'd have taken three hundred lashes with the cat over what he was doing to me. It was pure torment, worse than anything I'd ever imagined.

"'Write, write!' he repeated endlessly, as though the words themselves could force the pen to move.

"Had the man lost his mind? What in heaven's name was this madness about?

"Well, no—he wasn't mad at all, though I certainly thought so at the time. Turned out, not long before this, a secretary over in Tobolsk had pulled off a grand piece of thievery. The fellow had robbed the local treasury, made off with a fortune, and vanished without a trace. The only thing they knew about him—aside from his crime—was that he had unusually large ears. Ears, comrades, just like mine! The news had spread like wildfire across the region, and before I knew it, I was the unlucky sod who matched the description. That's why the superintendent was so intent on getting me to write. He wasn't interested in my ear for its size—he wanted to see my handwriting, to check if I might be the infamous thief.

"'A clever chap, wasn't he? But did it hurt much?' one of the convicts asked.

"'Oh, Lord above, don't even bring it up,' I said, shaking my head. 'You've no idea how bad it was.'

"The room erupted into laughter. They couldn't help themselves.

"'Well, did you write, then?' another chimed in, eager to hear more.

"'What else could I do?' I replied. 'There wasn't anything proper to write, so I just scrawled away over the paper, making enough marks to satisfy him. I must've done a good job, too, because he finally stopped twisting my ear. Gave me a dozen solid thumps instead—standard issue, I guess—and sent me on my way. Off to prison I went, happy to leave with my ear still attached.'

"'So you really do know how to write, then?' someone asked, his tone half curious, half mocking.

"'Of course I know how to write!' I shot back. 'What kind of question is that? Back in the day, I could write just fine. But that was before they started using pens for it—I've forgotten the whole blessed thing now.'

"The story, absurd as it was, had us all laughing until our sides ached. Tales like these, passed around in the hospital, were the only things that made time feel even a little quicker. Without them, the days would have dragged endlessly, suffocating in their monotony. And still, Almighty God, how bored and weary we were. The hours stretched on and on, one indistinguishable from the next. If only I'd had a single book to read.

"I spent much of my time in the infirmary, especially in the early days of my exile. Sometimes it was because I was genuinely unwell, but more often it was for the simple relief of escaping the harsher parts of the prison. Life in the main quarters was unbearable, crushing not just the body but the soul. There, the atmosphere was poisoned with constant tension and hostility. For those of us from the nobility, it was even worse. We were perpetual targets of envy and spite, enduring endless quarrels and accusations. Every moment felt like a trap, every glance directed at us brimming with hatred.

"But here, in the sick-rooms, things were different. The infirmary offered a strange kind of reprieve. Among the patients, there was a sense of equality, a fragile yet real camaraderie. Whatever grudges and divisions existed elsewhere seemed to fade in the shared space of illness. For a while, at least, we were all just men—sick, tired, and longing for some measure of peace."

The most melancholy and oppressive moment of the day was evening, as night began to set in. Darkness brought with it a unique kind of desolation, a weight that seemed to settle on everyone in the room. We went to bed very early, though sleep often eluded us. A single smoky lamp provided the faintest point of light at the far end of the room, near the door. In the corner where I lay, we were plunged into near-total darkness. The air was heavy, suffocating, laden with a pestilential stench that seemed to cling to every breath. It was an atmosphere that made the hours of night stretch unbearably long.

Some of the sick, unable to find rest, would rise from their beds and sit motionless, hunched over, as if lost in deep and troubling thoughts. They would remain like this for an hour or more, their heads bent low, their silhouettes barely visible in the dim glow of the distant lamp. I would watch them, studying their still forms, trying to guess what weighed on their minds. What memories were they dredging up in that darkness? What hopes or regrets held them captive? Watching them, I would lose myself for a time, as if their musings might somehow help me escape the crushing monotony.

And then, inevitably, I would turn inward. The past would rise before me, vivid and detailed, its outlines sharpened by the oppressive stillness of the room. Scenes long forgotten would suddenly spring to life in my imagination, illuminated as though by some inner light. Joyful moments and painful ones alike took on a clarity they never had before. Even the smallest, most inconsequential details seemed magnified, forcing themselves into my consciousness with an intensity that was almost overwhelming. These recollections, emerging unbidden, gripped me completely, dragging me further into myself.

When the past released me, the future loomed in its place, vast and uncertain. My thoughts would shift, and I would find myself asking the same unanswerable questions over and over. When will I leave this prison, this place of endless restraint and suffering? Where will I go when I am finally free? What will become of me? Will I return to the place of my birth, or will life take me somewhere entirely unexpected? As I brooded over these questions, glimmers of hope would sometimes stir in my soul, faint but persistent. For a fleeting moment, I would imagine a future beyond these walls, a life renewed, and I would cling to that vision, however fragile it might be.

But not all nights brought such reveries. At times, in sheer desperation, I would resort to counting: one, two, three, and so on, willing myself to fall asleep. I would count into the hundreds, sometimes even as far as three thousand, only to find that sleep remained as distant as ever. The effort was maddening, a futile exercise that only heightened my awareness of the restless silence around me.

Occasionally, the stillness was broken. Someone would shift or groan in their bed, the sound sudden and jarring in the quiet. There was Oustiantsef, whose persistent coughing echoed through the room—a cough that spoke of his worsening condition, the unmistakable rasp of a consumptive nearing the end. Between fits of coughing, he would groan softly, almost to himself, and stammer in a weak, broken voice, "My God, I've sinned, I've sinned!" The words, so fragile and full of despair, carried an eerie weight in the otherwise complete silence.

In one corner, some of the sick who were still awake would whisper to one another, their voices low and faint, barely carrying across the room. I would catch fragments of their conversation: one man telling the story of his life, recounting events from a world that now seemed infinitely far away. He spoke of his days wandering the earth, of his wife and children, of the small joys and struggles of a life that was now forever lost to him. His tone betrayed the finality of his circumstances—he spoke not as a man reminiscing but as one mourning the severed connection to all that had once been his. Listening to him, one could feel the weight of his isolation, the inescapable truth that he had been cast aside, cut off from the world of the living.

Another man would listen intently, his silence speaking volumes. From somewhere deeper in the room, faint murmurs could be heard, the indistinct sounds of voices blending into a background noise that reminded me of water flowing far away—a soft, ceaseless sound, almost comforting in its constancy.

I remember one particular winter night, a night that seemed as if it would never end. The cold seeped into every corner, and the darkness felt even heavier than usual. That night, I overheard a story—a strange, haunting tale that at first seemed like the incoherent ramblings of someone caught in a nightmare or the fevered delusions of the sick. The story, fragmented and dreamlike, unfolded in the gloom, its details swirling through the stifling air. Even now, I cannot forget it. Here is how it went...

Chapter 4
The Husband of Akoulka

It was late at night, around eleven o'clock. I had been asleep for some time when I suddenly woke with a start. The room was cloaked in a dim, almost ghostly light from the faint and flickering lamp at the far end near the door. Its feeble glow barely reached the corners, leaving much of the room in deep shadow. Nearly everyone was fast asleep, even Oustiantsef, whose labored breathing and the faint, rattling sound in his throat marked his fragile state. The night was otherwise quiet, with only the occasional creak of a bed or the rustle of someone shifting in their sleep.

From the ante-chamber came the distant and deliberate footsteps of the patrol. Their movements were heavy, measured, and steady, punctuated by the dull thud of a gun butt striking the floor. The door to the room opened slowly, and the corporal entered, his steps soft as he made his rounds to count the sick. He moved carefully, taking note of each figure lying in their pallet. After completing his duty, he quietly closed the door behind him, leaving a new sentinel stationed outside. The patrol departed, their steps fading into the distance, and the room fell silent once again.

It was then that I noticed two prisoners near me who were awake and speaking in hushed tones. Their conversation was so subdued that I hadn't initially realized they were talking at all. It was not unusual for this to happen—two men, whose beds were close and who might not have exchanged a word for weeks, suddenly striking up a conversation in the middle of the night. Such moments often carried a peculiar intimacy, the stillness of the late hour loosening tongues that had been silent for days or even months. Often, one would begin recounting his life story, and the other would listen, sometimes out of genuine interest, sometimes merely as a way to pass the endless hours of darkness.

As I lay there, curiosity kept me awake. I hadn't heard the beginning of their conversation and couldn't immediately make out what they were saying. But gradually, as my ears adjusted to their murmurs, I began to piece together their words. Sleep was far from me now, so I turned my attention fully to their dialogue.

One of them was speaking with noticeable energy, half-lying on his bed but leaning forward, his head raised and tilted towards his companion. His tone was animated, almost urgent, as though he had been holding in his thoughts for too long and now couldn't stop himself from speaking. The need to tell his story seemed to consume him, driving every word.

The other man, however, listened with an air of detached indifference. He sat upright on his pallet, his legs stretched out flat on the mattress, and responded only occasionally, muttering short phrases that seemed more a matter of politeness than genuine engagement. He repeatedly took snuff from a horn box, a habitual gesture that made it clear his attention was only partially on the conversation. This listener was Techérévin, a soldier from the company of discipline—a dour and pedantic man, rigid in his reasoning but lacking true depth of character. He carried himself with a certain smugness, an overinflated sense of self-worth that made him insufferable to most. His cold, analytical demeanor contrasted sharply with the narrator's passionate storytelling.

The one speaking was Chichkof, a civilian convict who appeared to be about thirty years old. Until that moment, I had barely noticed him during my time in the prison. He was an unremarkable figure, the kind of man who faded into the background of daily life. Even now, as

I listened to him, I found it difficult to muster much interest in him. There was something about his manner—conceited and self-assured—that repelled rather than invited attention. His voice carried the confidence of someone who believed his words were of great importance, though I doubted whether his story could live up to his own estimation of it.

Yet despite my initial disinterest, there was something compelling in the scene itself: Chichkof's animated gestures and urgent tone set against Techérévin's stoic, almost dismissive attitude. The juxtaposition of their characters—the one driven by a need to connect and the other by a desire to remain detached—created a tension that drew me in. And so, I lay there in the dark, listening as the story unfolded, wondering if it would reveal something unexpected or merely reinforce my impression of the two men.

Sometimes Chichkof would go for weeks without uttering a single word, sitting in sullen silence that made him seem as surly and brutish as a cornered animal. During these stretches of self-imposed muteness, he gave off an air of resentment, as if perpetually at odds with the world around him. But just as suddenly as the silence began, it would shatter. Out of nowhere, he would insert himself into whatever was happening, speaking and behaving in a way that was both insufferable and utterly baffling. He had a habit of working himself into a frenzy over trivial matters, turning minor events into grandiose dramas.

In these moments, he would launch into long-winded stories that were completely pointless—rambling tales about one barrack or another, filled with complaints about everything and everyone. His narratives often spiraled into incoherent rants, full of insults and wild accusations, as if he were a man possessed. Eventually, someone would lose patience with him, put an end to his tirade with a well-placed blow, and Chichkof would retreat into another of his silent spells.

He was not a man who inspired respect. Small and wiry, with a bony frame and restless, darting eyes that rarely stayed focused, he seemed perpetually on edge. Occasionally, his gaze would shift, and his expression would take on a strange, vacant look, as if he were lost in thought. But whatever he was thinking about, it always seemed muddled and unclear. When he spoke, he did so with feverish intensity, waving his arms and gesticulating wildly as though trying to physically drag his audience into his chaotic mind. Yet he could never stick to the point. His stories jumped erratically from one subject to another, bogging down in irrelevant details until he finally lost track of what he was saying altogether.

Chichkof was often embroiled in petty squabbles. During arguments, his tone would shift dramatically—he would pour out insults in a strange, almost tearful voice, as if genuinely heartbroken by whatever slight had provoked him. His voice would quaver, and his eyes would glisten as though he were about to cry. The effect was more pitiful than intimidating. Still, Chichkof had his talents. He was quite skilled at playing the balalaika, and he took great pride in it. On special occasions or holidays, he would sometimes be persuaded to dance, a task he carried out with surprising grace and enthusiasm. Despite his flaws, Chichkof could be easily coaxed into doing what others wanted, not because he was naturally agreeable but because he craved approval and sought to endear himself to those around him.

That night, as I lay listening to him, I found it difficult to follow his story. He rambled incessantly, constantly veering off course to talk about unrelated matters. At times, it seemed as though he was speaking more for his own satisfaction than for that of his listener. Perhaps he had noticed that Techérévin, his audience for the evening, was only half-listening, nodding occasionally but clearly indifferent to the tale being spun. If Chichkof was aware of this, he chose to ignore it, pressing on with his narrative as though determined not to let apathy discourage him.

"When he went out on business," Chichkof said, his voice rising with enthusiasm, "everyone saluted him politely, showed him the greatest respect. A man with money, that's what he was."

Techérévin finally stirred from his lethargy long enough to ask, "You say he was in some trade?"

"Yes, trade indeed!" Chichkof replied, his tone turning almost scornful. "Though the trading class in my country is wretchedly poor—just scraping by, really. Most of them are little better than beggars. The women work themselves to the bone, hauling water from the river over long distances to keep their gardens alive. They sweat and toil all day, and still, when winter comes, there's nothing to show for it—not even enough to make a pot of cabbage soup. It's starvation, plain and simple."

Chichkof paused for dramatic effect before continuing. "But this man was different. He owned a good piece of land, and he had laborers to work it—three of them. He kept hives and sold honey, and he dealt in cattle, too. Everyone respected him in our parts. He was old, well into his seventies, and his years weighed heavy on him. But when he came into the market square wearing his fox-skin pelisse, people treated him like a king. They'd call out to him, 'Good day, daddy Aukoudim Trophimtych!' and tip their hats."

As Chichkof recounted this part of the story, his voice took on a reverent tone, as though he were describing a figure larger than life. Yet for all his animated gestures and vivid descriptions, I couldn't help but wonder if even he believed the tales he was spinning. Chichkof's stories, much like the man himself, were a strange mix of bravado and pathos, filled with both humor and a certain kind of sadness. It was hard to take him seriously, yet equally hard to dismiss him entirely. For better or worse, he was an enduring presence in the prison, his voice one of the many that filled the oppressive silence of the night.

"'Good day,' he'd reply with a nod and a measured tone, always polite but never overbearing.

"'How are you getting along?' someone would ask, showing him the respect he commanded from all in the market.

"'God keep you, Aukoudim Trophimtych!' another would chime in.

"'How goes business with you?' he would ask in return, his voice steady and warm, without a hint of condescension.

"'Business is as good as tallow's white with me; and how's yours, daddy?' they'd reply, eager to keep the conversation flowing with the old man.

"'We've just got enough of a livelihood to pay the price of sin, always sweating over our bit of land,' Aukoudim would say, his tone carrying the weight of years of labor and modest ambition.

"'Lord preserve you, Aukoudim Trophimtych!' they would say, marveling at his humility and the wisdom in his words.

"Despite his standing, Aukoudim never looked down on anyone. He treated everyone with dignity and respect, and his advice was considered invaluable. People said that every word he spoke was worth a rouble. He was a learned man, though his learning was confined to religious books. A great reader, he often called his wife over, saying, 'Listen, woman, take well in what I say,' before explaining the passages he had read. His wife, Marie Stépanovna, was not what you'd imagine as an old crone. She was his second wife, younger than him, married to provide him with children, as his first wife had been unable to.

"He had two young boys, the second of whom was born when Aukoudim was nearly sixty years old. His daughter, Akoulka, was the eldest, an eighteen-year-old girl already of marrying age.

"'Your wife, isn't it?' someone interrupted.

"'Wait a bit, wait,' the storyteller said, clearly irritated at being rushed. 'Now, this Philka Marosof starts causing trouble. He says to Aukoudim, "Let's split the difference. Give me back my four hundred roubles. I'm not your beast of burden, and I don't want to marry your Akoulka. I want to live my life now that my parents are gone. I'll spend my money as I please, drink it away if I feel like it, and then I'll enlist as a soldier. In ten years, I'll come back a field marshal!'"

"Aukoudim, despite his temper, gave Philka back his money—every last kopeck of it. You see, Aukoudim and Philka's father had been business partners for years, pooling their resources for mutual gain.

"'You're a lost man,' Aukoudim told Philka, his voice steady but tinged with disappointment.

"'Lost or not, you old gray-beard, you're the biggest cheat I know!' Philka spat back. 'You'd try to make a fortune out of four farthings, scraping and piling like a miser. I spit on it. While you're digging and hoarding like the devil's accountant, I've got my own plans. And I'll tell you this: I'll never marry your Akoulka. In fact, I've already slept with her!'

"'How dare you insult a respectable father—a respectable girl?' Aukoudim shouted, his voice trembling with fury. 'When did you sleep with her, you dog, you hound, you liar?' Aukoudim's face had turned red with rage, his hands shaking as he demanded an answer.

"But Philka only laughed. 'I'll not only refuse to marry her, but I'll make sure no one else does—not even Mikita Grigoritch. She's disreputable! We had a grand time together all last autumn, she and I. I wouldn't take her if you gave me all the money in the world.'

"After that, Philka went on a spree. For three months, he burned through every last kopeck, living recklessly. The whole town turned against him, disgusted by his behavior. But Philka didn't care. He gathered a group of other wayward fellows around him and indulged in one wild escapade after another.

"'I want to see the bottom of this money,' he declared. 'I'll sell the house, sell everything I own. Then I'll either enlist or take to the road.'

"He was drunk morning to night, parading around in a carriage with a fine pair of horses, living as if he were some grand nobleman. The girls in the town adored him, though—he had a charm about him and played the guitar beautifully.

"'So it's true, then? He really was involved with Akoulka?' someone interrupted again, unable to resist.

"'Wait, wait, can't you?' the storyteller snapped. 'I'd just buried my father around that time. My mother, bless her soul, made a living baking gingerbread. We barely scraped by, working for Aukoudim. It was a tough life, I tell you. We had a small patch of land beyond the woods where we grew a bit of corn, but it wasn't enough. After my father passed, I went on a bit of a spree myself. I forced my mother to give me money, though I'm ashamed to say I had to give her a good hiding first.'

"'You beat your mother?' another voice chimed in, shocked. 'That's a great sin!'"

The room fell silent for a moment, the weight of the confession hanging heavy in the air. But the story, like life itself, moved forward, dragging everyone with it into the next twist of the tale.

"Sometimes I was drunk from morning till night, the whole blessed day, without a thought for anything else. We lived in a house that was falling apart from dry rot, barely standing, but it was ours—or what was left of it. Hunger was a constant companion, gnawing at our bellies. For weeks at a time, we had almost nothing to eat, just scraps and rags to chew on to quiet the pain. Mother was at her wit's end trying to keep things together, but her scolding and tricks only pushed me further away. I didn't care about a thing, not one damn thing.

"My constant companion in those days was Philka Marosof. We were inseparable, day and night. He'd lounge around and call out, 'Play the guitar for me!' while he lay on his bed, as if he were some kind of prince. 'I'll throw money to you,' he'd say, laughing. 'I'm the richest chap in the world!' Of course, everything he said was a lie, but that didn't stop him from talking.

"There was one curious thing about Philka, though—he prided himself on being honest. He wouldn't touch a single thing if he knew it had been stolen. 'I'm no thief,' he'd say, puffing his chest out. 'I'm an honest man.' Yet his idea of honesty didn't stop him from saying, 'Let's go and daub Akoulka's door with pitch. I won't have her marry Mikita Grigoritch, not if I can help it.' And that was that.

"Now, the old man, Aukoudim Trophimtych, had long planned to marry Akoulka off to this Mikita Grigoritch. Mikita was well past his prime, a trader who wore spectacles and carried himself like a man of importance. But when he got wind of the rumors about Akoulka's so-called bad behavior, he came straight to Aukoudim and said, 'This would be a terrible disgrace for me, Aukoudim Trophimtych. I've decided it's best I don't marry after all. It's too late for me anyway.'

"So, with Mikita backing out, Philka and I set about our mischief. One night, we slathered Akoulka's door with pitch. It was a cruel thing to do, but we thought ourselves clever for it. The next morning, her family found it, and all hell broke loose. Her parents were furious. They beat Akoulka so badly that the entire neighborhood could hear her screams. Her mother, Marie Stépanovna, cried, 'I shall die of shame because of this!' And the old man, shaking with anger, said, 'If this were the time of the patriarchs, I'd hack her to pieces on the chopping block. But now everything is rottenness and corruption in this world.'

"The beatings didn't stop there. From one end of the street to the other, neighbors whispered about Akoulka, while her family punished her day after day. Philka, meanwhile, strutted around the marketplace, shouting for all to hear, 'Akoulka's a jolly girl to get drunk with! I've given those people something to remember me by. They won't forget it in a hurry!'

"One day, I happened to meet Akoulka while she was fetching water with her bucket. I couldn't resist taunting her. 'A fine morning to you, pet Akoulka Koudimovna!' I called out. 'You're the girl who knows how to please fellows! Who's living with you now? And where do you get the money for all your finery?'

"She didn't reply, just stared at me with wide eyes. She looked so thin, like she hadn't eaten in weeks, her face gaunt and lifeless. But her mother, standing on the doorstep, saw her looking at me and shouted, 'Impudent hussy! What do you mean by talking to that fellow?' From that moment, the beatings started again. Sometimes they whipped her for an hour at a time. Her mother would scream, 'I give her the whip because she's no daughter of mine anymore!'

"'Was she really as bad as they said?' someone interrupted.

"'Now listen to my story, nunky, will you?' I snapped. 'We used to get drunk all the time, Philka and me. One day, while I was lying in bed, my mother stormed in. She was furious.

"'What d'ye mean by lying in bed, you hound, you thief!' she shouted. She cursed me for what felt like an eternity, then said, 'Marry Akoulka. They'll be glad to give her to you, and they'll throw in three hundred roubles as a dowry.'

"'But, mother,' I said, 'the whole world knows she's a bad girl.'

"'Hush,' she hissed. 'The marriage ceremony cures all that. Besides, she'll always be afraid of you, so you'll have the upper hand. Their money would make us comfortable. I've already spoken to Marie Stépanovna, and we're of one mind about it.'

"I thought about it for a moment, then said, 'All right. Let's see twenty roubles down on the spot, and I'll take her.'"

"Well, believe it or not, I was drunk straight through to the wedding day. I didn't care about anything, just kept drowning myself in vodka. Meanwhile, Philka Marosof wouldn't let up, always taunting me, pushing my temper to the edge.

"'I'll break every bone in your body,' he'd say. 'And you, a nice fellow to be getting married—to Akoulka, no less. If I feel like it, I'll sleep with her every single night after she's your wife. What do you think of that?'

"'You're a hound and a liar,' I told him straight to his face. But he didn't stop. He insulted me in the street, in front of everyone, making a mockery of me. I couldn't take it anymore, so I stormed off to Aukoudim's place and said, 'I won't marry her unless you give me fifty roubles right this moment.'

"'And they really gave her to you?' someone asked.

"'Why wouldn't they?' I replied. 'We were respectable people, after all. Don't let appearances fool you—my family wasn't always down on its luck. My father had been a wealthy man before a fire destroyed everything he owned. He'd been better off than Aukoudim Trophimtych himself.

"But old Aukoudim wasn't having it. 'A fellow without a shirt to his back like you ought to be grateful to marry my daughter,' he said, puffing out his chest like he was doing me a favor.

"'And what about your door?' I shot back. 'And the pitch we plastered all over it?'

"'Stuff and nonsense,' he said, waving me off. 'There's no proof the girl's gone wrong.'

"'Suit yourself,' I told him. 'But if that's how it is, you can keep your daughter—and give back the money you've already taken from me!'

"That's when Philka and I hatched a plan. We sent Mitri Bykoff to Aukoudim to deliver a message: we'd insult him publicly, right to his face, for everyone to hear. That put some fire under him. In the end, we settled things, but let me tell you, I stayed drunk all the way to the wedding day. I only sobered up when I stepped foot in the church.

"After the ceremony, they brought us back to her family's house.

Everyone was tense. Her uncle, Mitrophone Stépanytch, looked at me and said, 'This isn't a nice business, but it's over and done now.'

"And there was old Aukoudim, sitting in the corner, crying like a baby. The tears rolled down his gray beard, and you could see the shame written all over his face. But listen to this, comrade—I'd made up my mind. Before we even left for the church, I had slipped a whip into my pocket. I was determined to show everyone, including Akoulka, that I wasn't to be trifled with. They had swindled me into this marriage, and I wasn't about to let the world think I was some kind of fool."

"You wanted to make sure she knew what was coming to her?" someone interjected.

"Quiet, nunky, let me finish!" I snapped. "Among our people, there's a custom. Right after the wedding ceremony, the couple is taken to a room apart while the rest of the guests stay behind, drinking and making merry until the couple comes back. That's how it was. They left me alone with Akoulka.

"She was pale as a ghost, not a trace of color in her cheeks. She looked terrified, like a lamb being led to slaughter. I'll give her this— she was a strange one. Odd as they come. She had this fine hair, bright and soft like flax, and these enormous eyes that seemed to take up her whole face. But she almost never spoke. You'd think she was mute if you didn't know better. An odd creature, Akoulka, that's for sure.

"Well, you can imagine the scene. The whip was ready, lying there on the bed. I was ready too. I'd made up my mind to settle accounts then and there, to let her know exactly what kind of marriage this was going to be. But then, something stopped me.

"She didn't fight, didn't argue, didn't even flinch. She just stood there, trembling like a leaf, looking at me with those big, haunted eyes. And, comrade, you won't believe this, but I swear on my life—she was as pure a girl as ever was. Not a word of all those rumors was true."

The room fell silent, the weight of the story hanging heavy in the air. Even the usual murmurs and whispers were absent. It wasn't just a tale about a marriage—this was a story about shame, cruelty, and the unexpected revelations that sometimes emerge when you least expect them.

"Impossible!" someone exclaimed, their disbelief echoing through the room.

"It's true, I swear it," I said, my voice steady with conviction. "She was as good a girl as any family might wish for their son."

"Then, brother, why—why had she to endure all that suffering? Why did Philka Marosof slander her so cruelly?" another asked, their voice tinged with anger and confusion.

"Yes, why indeed?" I repeated, shaking my head. The question haunted me even now.

I paused, gathering my thoughts before continuing. "Well, after realizing the truth, I climbed down from the bed and dropped to my knees before her. I clasped my hands together as if in prayer, and I said, 'Little mother, pet, Akoulka Koudimovna, forgive me for being such an idiot, for believing all those vile lies. Forgive me, I beg you. I'm nothing but a hound.'

"She sat on the bed, looking at me with those wide, deep eyes of hers. For a moment, she didn't move, just stared. Then she placed her hands on my shoulders, and suddenly she started laughing. But at the same time, tears poured down her cheeks. She sobbed and laughed all at once, and it was as though the weight of all her suffering was pouring out of her in that moment.

"Afterward, I stormed out of the room into the company of the wedding guests and said, 'Let Philka Marosof watch his back. If I find him, he won't be long for this world.' My anger was burning, and I meant every word.

"The old people were overjoyed, practically beside themselves with relief and happiness. Akoulka's mother was ready to fall at her daughter's feet, crying as if she'd been forgiven for some terrible sin. And the old man, Aukoudim, he looked at Akoulka and said, 'If we had known the truth, my dearest child, we would never have given you to a man like this.'

"Ah, but you should have seen us the first Sunday after our wedding! When we left the church, we were dressed to impress, let me tell you. I had a long coat made of fine cloth, a fur cap, and plush breeches. Akoulka wore a brand-new hareskin pelisse and a silk kerchief on her head. We were a sight, both of us. One was as fine as the other, and everybody admired us. I have to admit, I looked good, and so did pet Akoulka. I'm not one to brag, but people like us aren't turned out by the dozen."

"Not a doubt about it," someone muttered in agreement, their voice tinged with amusement.

"Just listen to the rest of it," I said, holding up a hand to silence them. "The day after the wedding, drunk as I was, I ran out of the house and into the streets, yelling at the top of my lungs, 'Where's that scoundrel Philka Marosof? Just let him come near me, the hound, that's all!' I went up and down the market, shouting like a madman. I was so drunk I could barely stand, but my rage kept me going.

"It took three men to drag me back home. They finally caught me near Vlassof's place and hauled me back, struggling and cursing the whole way. The entire village was talking about it for days. Everywhere you went, people were saying, 'Well, did you hear? Akoulka was innocent after all!'

"And then, not long after, I ran into Philka Marosof. Right there, in front of everyone—strangers included—he had the audacity to say, 'Sell your wife and spend the money on drink. Jackka the soldier did just that—married for money and didn't even spend a single night with his wife. But he drank himself happy for three years on what he got.'

"I turned to him and spat out, 'Hound!'

"But Philka just laughed. 'You're an idiot,' he said. 'You didn't even know what you were doing when you married her. You were drunk out of your mind! How could you tell whether it was the truth or not?'

"His words stung, and they planted doubt in my mind. I went straight home, still fuming, and burst through the door, shouting, 'You married me when I was drunk!' I was wild with anger, pacing back and forth.

"Akoulka's mother tried to hold me, tried to calm me down, but I wasn't having it. I turned to her and shouted, 'Mother, you don't know anything but money. Bring me Akoulka!' And that, comrades, is how things stood."

"And didn't I beat her! I tell you, I beat her for two solid hours without stopping, until I was so exhausted I collapsed on the floor myself. My arms were trembling, my breath was ragged, but I didn't stop until I physically couldn't continue. She couldn't get out of bed for three weeks after that. Three whole weeks!"

Tchérévine, who had been listening quietly, spoke up with his usual phlegmatic tone, "It's a dead sure thing. If you don't beat them, they— well, you know what happens. But tell me, did you catch her with her lover?"

Chichkoff hesitated, his face clouded with discomfort, and after a long pause, he replied, "No, to tell the truth, I never actually caught her." He spoke slowly, as though the words were difficult to get out. "But I was hurt—a good deal hurt. Everyone was laughing at me behind my back, and that stung worse than anything. And all of it, every bit, was because of Philka."

He paused, his voice trembling with anger as he continued. "'Your wife is just made for everyone to look at,' Philka said to me one day. It was his way of taunting me, of twisting the knife. And he never stopped. One day, he even invited us over to his place. I don't know why I went, but I did. As soon as we were there, he started up again. 'Just look at what a good little wife he has!' he said, his voice dripping with mockery. 'Isn't she tender and fine? Nicely brought up, so affectionate and full of kindness for everyone. Tell me, my lad, have you forgotten how we daubed their door with pitch?'"

Chichkoff's hands clenched into fists, his knuckles white. "I was drunk at the time, so drunk I could barely stand. Before I knew it, he grabbed me by the hair and threw me to the ground. 'Come on, dance!' he shouted. 'Aren't you Akoulka's husband? I'll hold your hair for you while you dance—it'll be good fun!' I spat out at him, 'Dog!' But he just laughed and said, 'I'll bring a pack of jolly fellows to your house, and I'll whip your Akoulka right before your eyes, as long as I please.'

"Would you believe it? For an entire month after that, I didn't dare leave the house. I was terrified he'd show up and drag my wife through the mud—literally and figuratively. And how I beat her for it!" Chichkoff's voice cracked, his anger mingled with a strange, bitter regret.

"What was the use of beating her?" Tchérévine said, shaking his head. "You can tie a woman's hands, but you can't tie her tongue. It's no good to give them a hiding too often. Beat them a bit, scold them well, and then fondle them. That's what a woman's made for."

Chichkoff fell silent for a moment, staring into the distance. Finally, he spoke, his tone softer but no less pained. "I was hurt, deeply hurt. And the hurt didn't go away—it just festered. I started beating her for no reason at all. If she didn't get up from her seat the way I liked, I beat her. If she walked too slowly or too quickly, I beat her. When I wasn't beating her, time hung heavy on my hands, like a weight I couldn't shake off.

"Sometimes, she'd sit by the window, silently crying. And seeing her like that, so broken, it hurt me too. But I beat her anyway. It didn't matter—nothing mattered. Sometimes her mother, Marie Stépanovna, would scold me, calling me a scoundrel, a gallows-bird. I'd shout back at her, 'Don't say a word, or I'll kill you. You made me marry her when I was drunk. You swindled me!'"

He paused, as though the memory itself was tiring. "Old Aukoudim tried to step in at first. 'Look here,' he said to me one day, 'you're not such a tremendous fellow that one can't put you in your place.' But he didn't get far with that talk. Marie Stépanovna, though—she changed. She became meek, sweet as milk. One day, she came to me, her face wet with tears, and said, 'My heart is breaking, Ivan Semionytch. Please, I'm begging you—let her go. Let her leave you. She's my child. Let her live.'

"She threw herself at my feet, sobbing like a broken woman. 'Do give up this anger,' she pleaded. 'Wicked people have slandered her, but you know, deep down, that she was good when you married her.' And then, crying harder than ever, she pressed her face to the floor. But I stood there like a stone. 'I won't hear a word you have to say,' I told her. 'What I choose to do, I'll do—to you, to her, to anyone. I'm crazed with it all.' And then, for reasons I can't even explain now, I added, 'As for Philka Marosof, he's my best and dearest friend.'"

Chichkoff's words trailed off, the room heavy with his confession. He sat there, his face unreadable, as if trying to make sense of the man he had been.

"You and Philka had started your tricks again, had you?" someone interrupted, their tone a mix of curiosity and disbelief.

"No, not this time," Chichkoff replied, shaking his head. "By then, Philka was out of the picture. He was drinking himself into oblivion, killing himself with booze, nothing less. He'd burned through every last kopeck he had and finally enlisted as a substitute soldier for a townsman—a common enough arrangement in our parts."

He paused, his expression hardening. "You see, when a lad agrees to be a substitute, he essentially becomes the master of the house he's serving until the day he's called to the ranks. They give him the agreed-upon sum when he leaves, but until then, he's treated like royalty, no matter how he behaves. Sometimes, they stay for months—six months, even—and, let me tell you, there isn't a horror in the world those fellows don't commit. It's enough to make people take down the holy icons from their walls out of sheer shame. From the moment the bargain is struck, the substitute considers himself a benefactor, the savior of the family, and he makes them pay dearly for his 'generosity.' He's the master, and they have no choice but to dance to his tune—or else he calls off the deal.

"And Philka Marosof, well, he played the devil himself in that townsman's home. He did whatever came into his drunken head. He seduced the daughter, dragged the master of the house around by his beard after meals, and acted as if the entire household existed solely for his amusement. Every day, they had to heat the bath for him, and not just the bath—they had to prepare brandy fumes to mix with the steam. And, if you can believe it, he made the women lead him to the bathhouse by the arms like some kind of king."

Chichkoff paused, shaking his head with a grim chuckle. "And it didn't stop there. When Philka came back from a night of revelry, staggering drunk, he'd stop in the middle of the road outside their house and yell, 'I won't go in by the door—tear down the fence!' And they had to do it. They actually pulled down the fence to let him in, even though the door was right there. He had them wrapped around his finger, and they were too afraid to refuse him anything."

"But it didn't last forever. The day came when they took him off to the regiment. That was the end of his mischief. For once, he sobered up—at least enough to understand what was happening. The whole street turned out to watch. People gathered along the road, murmuring, 'They're taking off Philka Marosof!' He saluted everyone as he passed, bowing right and left like some kind of hero being sent off to war.

"And then, just as they were leading him away, Akoulka came back from the kitchen garden, carrying a bundle of greens. The moment Philka saw her, he jumped down from the cart and threw himself at her feet. Right there, in front of the whole crowd.

"'Stop!' he shouted. And then, kneeling before her, he cried out, 'My soul, my sweet little strawberry, I've loved you for two long years. And now they're taking me off to the regiment, with the band playing and the drums beating. Forgive me, honest girl of an honest father. I'm nothing but a hound, and all you've suffered is my doing.'

"Then, as if the first wasn't enough, he threw himself down before her a second time. At first, Akoulka was terrified, her face pale as a sheet. But then, to everyone's amazement, she bowed deeply, nearly bending herself in two, and said, 'Forgive me too, my good lad. But I am not angry with you—not at all.'

"As she turned to go back into the house, I followed close behind her, boiling with rage. The moment we were inside, I snarled, 'What did you say to him, you she-devil?'

"And, comrades, you may believe it or not, but she turned to me, as bold as you please, and looked me straight in the eye. Then she said, clear as day, 'I love him better than anything or anyone in this world.'

"For a moment, I couldn't even speak. The audacity of it! The gall! And yet, there she stood, unflinching, her words hanging in the air like a challenge I didn't know how to answer."

"'I say!'"

Chichkoff's voice was steady, yet there was a tension in it that hinted at the storm raging inside him. "That day, I didn't say another word—not one. The whole day passed in silence. But as evening came, I finally spoke to her. 'Akoulka,' I said, 'I'm going to kill you now.'

"She didn't reply, and I didn't expect her to. That night, I couldn't

265

close my eyes. Sleep was impossible. My mind was a chaotic swirl of anger, hurt, and despair. I got up and went into the little side room connected to ours. I drank kwass, glass after glass, trying to drown out the thoughts that wouldn't let me be. But nothing worked. As soon as day broke, I went back into the house. 'Akoulka,' I said, 'get ready. We're going to the fields.'

"This wasn't unusual; I had made arrangements to go there beforehand, and she knew it. She didn't seem alarmed. 'You're right,' she said calmly. 'It's time to start reaping. I heard the laborer's been sick and isn't doing any work.'

"I didn't reply. I went out and hitched the horse to the cart, working in silence. The journey was long. There's a forest about fifteen versts outside the town, and at the end of it lies our field. As we entered the woods, the dense trees on either side of the path cast long shadows that seemed to close in around us. When we were about three versts into the forest, I pulled the horse to a stop.

"'Get down, Akoulka,' I said. 'Your end has come.'

"She turned to look at me, her eyes wide with fear, but she didn't argue. She climbed down from the cart without saying a word.

"'You've tormented me enough,' I told her. 'Say your prayers.'

"I grabbed her by the hair—those long, thick tresses that had once been her pride. I wrapped them around my arm and held her between my knees. My other hand reached for the knife at my belt. I threw her head back, exposing her throat, and I drew the blade across her skin. She screamed—a high, piercing sound that seemed to echo through the trees—and the blood spurted out, warm and sticky, splashing my face and hands.

"Then something broke inside me. I threw the knife away and pulled her into my arms, holding her tightly as though I could crush the life out of her with sheer force. I pressed her to the ground and embraced her, yelling at the top of my lungs. She screamed too, struggling with every ounce of strength she had left. The blood kept flowing—so much blood—covering us both, soaking into the ground.

"I don't know how long it went on. It felt like hours but must have been only moments. Then fear took hold of me, a cold, paralyzing fear that I couldn't shake. I let her go, left the horse and cart, and ran. I ran as fast as I could back to the house.

"When I got there, I didn't go inside. Instead, I slipped around to the back and hid in the old bathhouse we never used anymore. It was falling apart, practically a ruin, but it was shelter. I crawled under the seat and lay there, trembling, until the dead of night."

"And Akoulka?" someone asked, their voice low, almost hesitant.

"She got up," Chichkoff said after a long pause. "She managed to get back on her feet and started walking toward the house. They found her later, just a hundred steps from where it happened."

"So you didn't finish her?" another voice interjected.

"No," he admitted, his tone hollow. "I didn't. She was still alive when I left her. But by the time they found her that evening, she was cold. The blood loss had taken her."

"And then?"

"They told the police. They searched for me, and they found me hiding in the old bathhouse. That's how it ended. I've been here four years now," he added, his voice trailing off.

Tchérévine, who had been listening quietly, spoke up again, his tone casual, almost indifferent. "If you don't beat them, you get nowhere. Still, my lad, you behaved like a fool. Look at me—I caught my wife with her lover, plain as day. I didn't go mad; I dealt with it smartly. I made her come into the shed, and I doubled up a halter. Then I said to her, 'To whom did you swear to be faithful? To whom did you swear it in church? Tell me that.'

"She didn't answer, so I gave it to her with the halter. Beat her and beat her, for a good hour and a half. At last, she couldn't take it anymore. She fell to her knees, completely spent, and cried out, 'I'll wash your feet and drink the water afterward!'"

"Her name was Crodotia," he added, almost wistfully, as though recalling a long-lost treasure.

The room fell silent, the weight of their words pressing down on everyone present. Each man seemed lost in his own thoughts, their expressions a mix of pride, regret, and resignation.

Chapter 5
The Summer Season

April has arrived, and with it, the promise of Holy Week not far off. The days grow warmer, the sun brighter, and the air itself seems charged with the spirit of renewal. Everywhere you look, there is a sense of life awakening, a stirring in nature that touches even those behind prison walls. The atmosphere, alive with the freshness of spring, exerts a profound effect on the human spirit. Even the convicts, weighed down by their chains and burdens, feel it. The golden sunlight, the soft breezes—these bring to the surface longings buried deep within them: yearning for home, for freedom, for the simple pleasures of a life lost to them. It's as though the beauty of the season sharpens the edge of their confinement, making their yearning for liberty more acute than during the dark, dreary days of winter.

I've observed this countless times. On clear, sunny days, a convict's mood becomes restless, irritable, even volatile. A flicker of joy might cross his face as he gazes at the endless blue sky, but this is often followed by deeper frustration, even anger. It's as though the beauty of the day mocks him, taunting him with what he cannot have. The prison becomes noisier in spring. Tempers flare more often, fights break out more frequently, and the tension in the air is almost palpable.

During work hours, I would notice prisoners standing still, lost in thought, their gaze fixed on the horizon beyond the Irtych River, where the vast expanse of the free Kirghiz Steppe stretches out, endless and open. For many, this distant view becomes an escape in itself, a place where their minds can wander beyond the confines of their chains. Sometimes, a long, deep sigh escapes from a prisoner's chest, as if the very thought of those wide, untamed plains compels him to breathe more deeply. It seems as though the vastness of that imagined freedom offers a fleeting solace to his crushed and fettered soul.

Then, suddenly, a cry bursts from the prisoner's lips—an anguished, drawn-out sound that pierces the air. Seizing his pickaxe or hefting a load of bricks, he throws himself into his work with a ferocious intensity, as though trying to drown his grief in sheer physical exertion. But the effort is short-lived. Minutes later, he's laughing or shouting insults at his companions, his mood swinging wildly, like a pendulum between despair and defiance. These men are in the prime of life, their bodies strong, their spirits still capable of resistance despite the crushing weight of their circumstances.

In the spring, the chains seem heavier, more oppressive than ever. Every step drags, every movement feels like a fight against the iron that binds them. This isn't sentimentality—it's an observation grounded in reality. The spring, with its radiant energy and the resurrection of nature all around, makes the prison walls feel even more stifling, the surveillance more suffocating, and the domination of another's will more unbearable.

It's in this season, when the first song of the lark fills the air, that across Siberia and Russia, men begin their escapes. The arrival of spring seems to awaken a primal urge for freedom. Prisoners, God's creatures, break loose when they can, fleeing into the woods, into the unknown. They leave behind the chains, the oppressive heat of the ditches where they labor, the boats, the rods, and the whips. Once free, they become vagabonds, wandering wherever their feet take them, living on what they can scavenge or beg. Their days are unpredictable, their nights spent under the open sky. They lie in fields or forests, gazing up at the stars, untroubled by the bars and chains they've left behind, feeling, if only for a moment, like birds in God's vast creation.

But this freedom is far from idyllic. It's a hard, uncertain life. Hunger gnaws at their bellies, exhaustion weighs heavy on their limbs, and they must always stay on guard, hiding from those who would capture them. Often, desperation drives them to theft, robbery, and even murder. Yet, for all its dangers, this life—wandering aimlessly under the watchful eye of the stars—feels like a reprieve. For them, even a fleeting taste of freedom, no matter how fraught with peril, is worth risking everything.

"'Send a man there and he becomes a child, throwing himself at everything he sees.' That's what people say about those sent to Siberia, and it's true in a way. But this saying fits the tramps even better. Most of them are brigands and thieves, not so much by choice but by necessity. It's the only life they know. Some are hardened beyond redemption, their ways too set to ever change. But there are others— men who serve their time, are given a piece of land to call their own, and seem on the brink of a new life. They should be content, their daily bread secured, the promise of stability within reach. Yet, for reasons that defy logic, they cannot stay. Something within them, a pull stronger than reason, drives them to wander again.

"This life in the woods—harsh, lonely, fraught with danger—has an allure, a strange and mysterious seduction for those who have lived it. For many, the freedom it offers, even with all its hardships, is irresistible. Among these fugitives, you'd find men who once seemed destined for a peaceful, settled existence. Men with good hearts, steady hands, and the temperament to build a home. A convict might marry, raise children, and live quietly for years, only to vanish without warning one bright morning. He leaves behind a bewildered wife, children too young to understand, and a community scratching their heads in disbelief. What compels such a man to abandon everything? What calls him back to the wilderness he once fled?

"I remember one such man vividly. He was pointed out to me at the convict establishment—a deserter not just of home and family but of every station in life he'd ever been given. This man had committed no obvious crime; at least, no one could accuse him of one. Yet his life was a series of desertions, one after another. He was a runaway, not just from the prison system but from the very notion of permanence. He'd been everywhere—the southern frontier of the empire, the far side of the Danube, the Kirghiz Steppe, Eastern Siberia, the Caucasus. His life was one long, restless journey.

"Under different circumstances, perhaps, this man might have been a modern-day Robinson Crusoe, driven not by necessity but by an insatiable wanderlust. But here, his urge to roam was a curse rather than an adventure. He didn't talk about himself, and he never spoke unless he absolutely had to. I learned most of what I know about him from other convicts, for he kept his own counsel, wrapping himself in silence.

"He was a small man, a peasant of about fifty years, with a quiet demeanor and a face so expressionless it seemed devoid of meaning. His stillness was almost eerie, as if he were carved from stone. Sometimes, he would sit outside for hours, basking in the sun, humming a low, tuneless song between his teeth—so soft that you couldn't hear him unless you stood right beside him. His features never moved, his gaze never shifted. It was as though he had shut himself off from the world entirely.

"His habits were simple, almost ascetic. He ate little—mostly black bread—and never spent money on luxuries like white bread or spirits. In fact, I doubt he had any money at all, and even if he did, I'm not sure he would have known what to do with it. He seemed entirely indifferent to his surroundings, to life itself. Yet there were glimpses of something deeper beneath his stillness. He was known to feed the prison dogs with his own hand—a rare sight, for Russians generally don't like to hand-feed animals. It was a small act, but one that hinted at some buried softness in his otherwise impenetrable character.

"There were rumors about him, as there always are in places like this. People said he had been married—twice, in fact—and that he had children somewhere, though no one seemed to know where. What crime had brought him here? No one could say for certain. We convicts often speculated that he would escape someday. There was something about him, a quiet watchfulness, that made it seem inevitable. But the moment never came—or perhaps it came and passed, and he let it slip away. He served his time without protest, moving through the days with a calm so deep it was unsettling.

"Despite his apparent passivity, I always felt there was something dangerous about him, something hidden. It wasn't that he seemed violent or threatening—quite the opposite. But there was a quality to his silence, his stillness, that felt like a coiled spring. You couldn't trust it. Yet even if he had escaped, where would he have gone? What would he have done? His life seemed so detached from purpose, so removed from any kind of plan, that freedom might have been as meaningless to him as captivity.

"He was, in every way, an enigma—an alien presence in the prison, neither fully part of it nor entirely separate from it. He drifted through his punishment like a shadow, leaving behind nothing but questions."

Compared to the rigid, soul-crushing existence of the convict prison, the life of a vagabond roaming the forests seems almost like a glimpse of Paradise. It's a wretched existence, no doubt—filled with hunger, cold, and the constant fear of capture—but it is free. And that freedom, however tenuous, is intoxicating. It's little wonder, then, that with the first warm rays of spring, prisoners across Russia begin to stir with restlessness. The very air seems to awaken something within them, a primal urge to escape the suffocating confines of their captivity.

Yet, for most, the desire remains just that—a yearning rather than a plan. Few prisoners dare to form a concrete strategy for flight. The obstacles are immense: the vigilance of guards, the harsh terrain, the risk of starvation, and, most frightening of all, the brutal punishment that awaits those who are caught. Out of a hundred convicts, perhaps one will summon the courage and resolve to make a real attempt. For the other ninety-nine, the idea of escape becomes a constant, nagging presence in their minds—a dream that refuses to die, even as they remain too fearful or resigned to act on it.

Still, even the faintest glimmer of hope can bring a kind of solace. Prisoners spend hours, even days, recounting stories of successful escapes, dissecting every detail, comparing circumstances, and speculating on their own chances. They cling to these tales like lifelines, as if the mere act of discussing them might somehow make their own freedom attainable.

Among those who entertain such thoughts, there is a stark difference between prisoners awaiting trial and those already sentenced. The former are far more likely to attempt an escape; the uncertainty of their fate gives them a sense of urgency. For those already serving their sentences, the calculus is different. In the early days of imprisonment, some may try to flee, driven by desperation and the belief that they have little to lose. But as the years drag on, many abandon the idea. They start to count their time served as a kind of investment—years that could lead to eventual release and the chance to rebuild a life. Why risk forfeiting that hard-earned progress for an escape attempt that might fail?

There are exceptions, of course. Convicts serving extraordinarily long sentences—fifteen, twenty years, or even life—often find the prospect of enduring such endless punishment unbearable. For them, time stretches out like an infinite, unbroken chain. The thought of spending decades in shackles, with no end in sight, drives them to acts of desperation. And yet, even for these men, true freedom is rarely the goal. The branding that marks them as convicts is a near-insurmountable obstacle. No matter how far they run, it follows them, a permanent reminder of their status and a signal to anyone they encounter.

"Changing your lot" is the term convicts use to describe an escape attempt. It's a strange, almost poetic expression, one that captures both the act and the desperation behind it. When an escaped convict is caught, he'll be formally interrogated and asked why he fled. The answer is almost always the same: "I wanted to change my lot." It's an acknowledgment that, for most, escape isn't about achieving true liberty—it's about escaping the unbearable conditions of their current prison. They don't dream of freedom; they dream of something different. Another convict establishment, a place on the land, or even a fresh trial for a new crime—anything that might take them away from their current torment.

For many fugitives, the harsh reality of their situation catches up with them quickly. Without a safe place to hide, without someone willing to shelter them, their chances of surviving the winter are slim. The lucky ones might stumble upon a benefactor, someone willing to conceal them or provide forged papers. The less fortunate are left to fend for themselves, often resorting to robbery—or worse, murder—in a desperate bid to secure the documents that would allow them to move freely.

By autumn, the dream of freedom often fades. The forests grow cold, food becomes scarce, and survival becomes a daily battle. Many fugitives, beaten down by hunger and exhaustion, present themselves at the gates of towns and prisons. They confess to being escaped tramps, willingly returning to captivity to endure another winter behind bars. They do so not out of defeat, but out of hope—a quiet, stubborn belief that come spring, they'll try again. The cycle repeats, year after year, as the fleeting promise of summer calls them back to the woods, to the life of a wanderer, and to the dream of a freedom that remains just out of reach.

Spring, with all its vibrant energy, had a profound effect on me, just as it did on the others. I vividly recall the almost desperate way I would fix my gaze on the horizon, peering through the narrow gaps in the prison's wooden palisades. There I would stand for what felt like hours, my forehead pressed against the rough wood, staring out at the patch of green grass that had begun to sprout in the ditch surrounding the fortress. Beyond that, the vast blue sky stretched out endlessly, its color deepening as my eyes traveled farther. That view—limited though it was—seemed to pull at something deep within me, and I couldn't tear myself away.

But with every glance at that distant sky, my heart grew heavier. The sight of nature awakening to life outside the prison walls only intensified the weight of my confinement. The days seemed to drag endlessly, each one adding to the oppressive hatred I felt from the other convicts. My noble status made me an object of scorn and resentment, and in those early years, their hostility was a constant poison to my soul.

"You nobles have beaks of iron, and you tore us to pieces with your beaks when we were serfs," the convicts would say, their words laced with bitterness and fury. How I envied the commoners who were sent to the prison. For them, there was no barrier of class to overcome. They were accepted, almost embraced, by the other convicts from the moment they arrived, blending seamlessly into the camaraderie of the prison population. I, on the other hand, was a perpetual outsider.

And so, in spring, when freedom seemed to whisper through the air, tantalizing but unreachable, my melancholy deepened. The joy of the season, evident in every blade of grass and every ray of sunshine, only heightened my sense of despair. My irritability grew sharper; my nerves felt frayed, as though they might snap under the strain.

As the sixth week of Lent arrived, I found an unexpected reprieve.

During Lent, the sub-superintendent divided the convicts into seven groups, each corresponding to one of the weeks leading up to Easter. Each group, consisting of about thirty men, was assigned to attend religious services in the nearby church. When my turn came, I welcomed it as a rare solace. It had been so long since I had set foot in a church, and the idea of leaving the prison walls, even briefly, filled me with a strange anticipation.

The Lenten services stirred something deep within me. They brought back memories of my childhood, of the solemn prayers and rituals I had once known so well. In my father's house, Lent had been a sacred time, and the traditions I now revisited seemed to awaken those long-dormant recollections. I felt as though I had been transported back to those innocent days, reliving moments I thought I had forgotten.

I remember the mornings vividly. The ground, frozen overnight, crunched under our boots as we made our way to the church under the watchful eyes of soldiers with loaded guns. The guards stayed outside, leaving us to gather inside the church near the door. We were packed together so tightly that it was difficult to hear much of the service. The deep, resonant voice of the deacon reached us only faintly, and occasional glimpses of a black chasuble or the priest's bare head were all we could see.

Even so, those moments held a strange joy for me. They brought back flashes of the past, of times when I had stood at the back of a church as a child, watching the common folk crowded near the door. I remembered how they would shrink back deferentially to make way for some officer with gleaming epaulettes or a well-dressed noblewoman, eager to secure the best seats at the front. The sight had always left an impression on me. Back then, I had felt that true prayer—the kind offered with genuine humility and fervor—was to be found only near the door, where the ordinary people stood. There, among the simple folk, prayer seemed honest, unadorned by vanity or pretense. When they prostrated themselves on the floor, it was with a full sense of unworthiness, a sincerity that seemed absent from the grand gestures of those who pushed their way to the front.

In those moments, standing among the convicts in the church, I felt a connection to that memory, to that simplicity. Despite the chains, despite the soldiers outside, it was as though I could catch a faint glimpse of freedom—not in the physical sense, but in the stirring of something deeper, something that no prison walls could confine.

And now, I found myself standing among the common people in the church—but not truly among them, for we were marked as different. We were convicts, bound by chains and burdened by our degradation. The townspeople kept their distance from us, their fear and mistrust palpable. When they offered us alms, it was done reluctantly, almost as if tossing coins or bread to beggars they dared not touch. Yet, strange as it may seem, this treatment stirred something unexpected in me—a peculiar, almost refined pleasure. "Let it be so!" I thought to myself. "Even in this, there is a certain dignity."

The convicts, despite their chains, prayed with deep and heartfelt devotion. Each carried a precious coin, no matter how small, to buy a candle or contribute to the church's collection. It was as if each offering was an assertion of humanity, a silent declaration: "I, too, am a man. Before God, we are all equals."

The simplicity and sincerity of their gestures struck me deeply. In that shared moment of prayer, there was a sense of unity, even if it was fleeting and fragile. I could not help but wonder if these acts of faith, however modest, offered them a glimpse of the freedom their bodies had been denied.

When the six o'clock mass concluded, we approached the priest to receive communion. The ritual was solemn, the silence broken only by the murmured prayers of the convicts and the clanking of their chains. As the priest, holding the ciborium, recited the words, "Have mercy on me as Thou hadst on the thief whom Thou didst save," many of the men prostrated themselves. To them, these words were not merely scriptural; they were deeply personal. They saw themselves in the thief, hoping for the same mercy, the same redemption.

Holy Week arrived, bringing with it a rare kind of benevolence. The authorities presented each of us with an Easter egg and a small piece of wheaten bread—a simple gesture that, in its rarity, carried immense significance. The townspeople, too, showed their goodwill, offering small gifts and acts of kindness. It reminded me of Christmas, with the priest's visitation, the solemn inspections by the heads of departments, and the special meal of larded cabbage. There was a noticeable lightness in the air, a temporary reprieve from the usual monotony. We could now walk in the courtyard and warm ourselves in the sun, which felt like a small freedom in itself.

But even in this brighter season, there was an undertone of sorrow. The endless summer days, with their oppressive heat and stark clarity, seemed more unbearable than the dark, confining days of winter. On church holidays, when work ceased, time stretched unbearably. At least on workdays, the labor provided some distraction, the exhaustion shortening the hours in a strange way.

The summer brought with it its own set of challenges. Our tasks became more grueling, primarily involving engineering works. We built, dug, laid bricks, repaired Government buildings, and engaged in locksmithing, carpentry, or painting. Among all these tasks, the work in the brick-fields was considered the hardest. Located about four versts from the fortress, the brick-fields required a daily gang of fifty convicts.

The mornings began early, with the gang departing at six o'clock, each man carrying his day's bread. The distance was too far to return for midday meals, so they worked continuously until evening, only eating when they finally returned to the prison. Each convict was assigned a specific quota of work for the day—an immense and nearly impossible amount. They had to dig clay, transport it, moisten it, mold it, and produce hundreds of bricks—sometimes as many as two hundred and fifty.

I was sent to the brick-fields only twice, but those experiences left an indelible mark on me. The men returned each evening utterly exhausted, their bodies aching from the relentless toil. Yet, as they rested in the barracks, they often argued and complained, each accusing the others of shirking the hardest tasks. Strangely, these reproaches seemed to provide them with a form of solace, as if venting their frustrations made the burden a little easier to bear.

Despite the grueling nature of the work, some convicts found a kind of solace in the brick-fields. The fields were far from the prison, situated along the banks of the Irtych River. The open country, the expansive sky, and the natural beauty of the surroundings offered a stark contrast to the oppressive, gray walls of the fortress and the lifeless Government buildings. There, under the vast sky, they could feel a fleeting connection to the freedom they longed for.

There were other small freedoms, too. In the brick-fields, the guards allowed the convicts to smoke freely and even rest for half an hour during the day—a rare luxury that many cherished deeply. For a moment, lying in the grass with a cigarette in hand, they could forget their chains and taste a semblance of the life they had lost. Even in the harshest circumstances, such small mercies could kindle a flicker of hope, a reminder of the world beyond the prison walls.

During my time in the prison, I was often assigned to one of the workshops, where I would pound alabaster or carry out various mundane tasks. For two consecutive months, however, I was tasked with carrying bricks—a job that, surprisingly, suited me quite well. My task was to transport the bricks from the banks of the Irtych to a construction site about 140 yards away, passing the fortress ditch along the way to reach the barrack under construction. At first, the labor was grueling. The cord used to carry the bricks bit sharply into my shoulders, leaving them raw and sore. But as the days turned into weeks, I found a strange satisfaction in the work. My strength, both physical and moral, began to grow.

When I started, I could barely manage to carry eight bricks at a time, each weighing around twelve pounds. Gradually, however, I pushed myself to handle twelve, then fifteen bricks in one trip. This progress thrilled me; it felt like reclaiming a piece of myself, a strength that prison life sought to strip away. I realized that I needed this strength—not only to endure the torment of the present but also to prepare for the future. When the day of my release finally came, I wanted to emerge alive, not as a broken shell of a man but someone ready to embrace life fully.

The task of carrying bricks had another unexpected reward: it took me daily to the banks of the Irtych. That riverbank was one of the few places where I could escape the suffocating confines of the fortress and catch a glimpse of the world beyond. The sight of the vast desert steppes stretching endlessly on the other side filled me with a bittersweet longing. The barren beauty of the landscape, with its unbroken horizon and its infinite sky, stirred something deep within me. It was freedom's whisper—a haunting reminder of what I had lost but also a fleeting solace amidst the monotony of imprisonment.

The fortress itself, with its gray, oppressive walls and austere buildings, was a symbol of everything I detested. I could never pass the Commandant's house without a surge of visceral hatred. It seemed to embody the very essence of my captivity, a place of cruelty and control. In contrast, the riverbank became a sanctuary. There, I could forget myself for a few precious moments. Gazing across the steppe, I would let my eyes wander over the open expanse, as if trying to touch the distant freedom it represented. Everything in that place—no matter how simple or humble—felt precious to me. The sunlight pouring down from the vast blue sky, the faint song of a Kirghiz herdsman from across the water, even the sight of a smoky cabin on the horizon—all of it seemed imbued with a grace and beauty I could never find within the prison walls.

Sometimes, I would fix my gaze on the curling smoke rising from a Kirghiz hut or watch a woman tending her sheep, absorbed in the rhythm of her life. These scenes were rugged, poor, and unvarnished, but they spoke of freedom. I watched birds in flight, marveling at how they skimmed over the water, disappeared into the sky, and reappeared as tiny specks in the distance. Even a small flower, clinging to life in a crack along the riverbank, could captivate me and bring tears to my eyes. Its fragile existence, defying the harshness around it, felt like a mirror to my own.

The first year of my imprisonment was an unrelenting tide of melancholy. The weight of my new reality bore down on me, smothering my ability to take in anything beyond my own anguish. I was blind to the subtleties of my surroundings, deaf to any voice of kindness that might have reached me. The poisonous talk of the convicts was a constant downpour, corrosive and inescapable. Amid this sea of misery, one simple, heartfelt expression of empathy came my way—spoken by a man who had suffered more than I could imagine. But even now, I struggle to dwell on it. It feels like a fragment of light in a cavern of shadows, too fleeting to grasp fully.

Strangely, the exhaustion from my labor was a source of comfort. It promised me the gift of sleep—something that, during the suffocating summer nights, was often elusive. When the sun finally dipped below the horizon, the prison courtyard would cool, and the air would grow crisp. The nights on the steppe were breathtakingly beautiful in their quiet simplicity. After the day's punishing heat, the cold night air felt like a balm. The convicts, before being herded back to their barracks, would gather in small groups, particularly near the kitchen area, where news and rumors were exchanged with an almost feverish excitement.

It was in these moments that the isolation of our existence seemed to soften slightly. Even the most absurd rumors could ignite animated discussions. I remember one particularly ridiculous story: someone claimed the Major had been abruptly dismissed from his post. Everyone knew the source of the rumor was Kvassoff, a notorious liar whose tales were as unreliable as they were imaginative. Yet the convicts latched onto the story with almost childlike enthusiasm. For a brief moment, they allowed themselves to believe it, taking joy in the idea of the Major's misfortune. When the truth inevitably emerged, and the story was proven false, they felt duped but also strangely satisfied by the diversion it had provided.

Such moments were rare but vital. In the barren emotional landscape of the prison, even a thread of gossip or a fleeting glimpse of the open steppe could provide a lifeline, a reason to keep going amidst the relentless grind of convict life.

"I'd like to see who dares to show him the door," exclaims one convict with a derisive laugh. "That man knows how to cling to power, don't you worry about that."

"But he's got superiors over him," retorts another, his tone confident. This one clearly fancies himself a seasoned debater, someone who's seen enough of life to speak with authority.

"Wolves don't eat one another," murmurs a third, his voice low and bitter, as though speaking to himself. He's an older man, his hair streaked with gray, who habitually takes his sour cabbage soup to a solitary corner to eat alone.

"Do you think his superiors will even consider what you think about showing him the door?" interjects a fourth convict, his tone indifferent as he idly strums a balalaïka.

"Why not?" snaps the second man, his voice rising with irritation. "If someone asks you, speak your mind! But no, with us lot, it's all noise and bluster. When it's time to act, everyone slips away like a coward."

"That's the truth," agrees the balalaïka player lazily. "Hard labour and prison break a man's spirit. You lose the will to fight."

"Just like the other day," continues the second convict, undeterred by the lack of enthusiasm from his companions. "There was some wheat left over—just the sweepings, practically nothing. The idea was to sell the refuse and get a bit of money. But no, they brought it to him, and he confiscated the whole lot. Called it 'economy.' Was that fair? Yes or no?"

"But who can you even complain to about it?" asks someone skeptically from the group.

"To whom? To the Inspector, of course," the second man answers with a touch of defiance.

"What Inspector?" asks another, intrigued but cautious.

"It's true, pals. An Inspector is coming soon," pipes up a younger convict. This one has a bit of education—enough to set him apart. He's read a few books, including The Duchesse de la Vallière, and served as a Quartermaster in his regiment before landing in prison. His reputation as a man of learning gives him a peculiar status among the convicts, who treat him with a grudging respect.

Without waiting for more questions, he strolls over to the cook and casually asks for some liver. The cooks often buy entire livers, slice them up, and sell portions to the other prisoners as a sort of informal trade.

"Two kopecks' worth or four?" the cook asks, already reaching for the knife.

"Give me four kopecks' worth," the younger convict replies with a grin. "I'll eat, and the rest can watch and drool."

Then, turning back to the group, he adds nonchalantly, "Yes, lads, it's true. A real general is coming from Petersburg—a big shot here to inspect all of Siberia. I heard it at the Governor's place myself."

The effect of this announcement is immediate and electric. For a good quarter of an hour, the convicts buzz with speculation. Who is this General? What's his name? What rank does he hold? Is he higher in status than the Generals from our own town? The conversation quickly spirals into an excited debate.

The convicts, like many Russians, have a fascination with ranks and hierarchies. They take great pleasure in discussing who wields power, who must bow to whom, and who holds the ultimate authority. It's a strange pastime, but one that animates them deeply. Voices grow louder as the debate heats up, and soon enough, the men are quarreling, hurling insults back and forth. In their enthusiasm, fists sometimes fly. All of this fervor, all this noise, in honor of a man none of them has ever seen and who likely doesn't know they exist.

What could possibly drive such passion? Why this intense interest in Generals and officials, figures so far removed from the grim reality of their lives? Yet, the conversations reveal something profound. They hint at the lives these men led before the prison—at the world they once inhabited, with its structures, hierarchies, and ambitions. Among ordinary Russians, even those in far higher social circles, such discussions of rank and title are often regarded as the height of serious, intellectual conversation. It's no wonder, then, that the convicts, clinging to fragments of their former lives, find themselves caught up in the same futile but oddly comforting debates.

"Ah, so they've finally sent our dear Major packing, haven't they?" Kvassoff declares with a sly grin. He's a small, rotund man with a ruddy complexion and a fiery temper, known more for his loud mouth than any particular wisdom. He's the same fellow who earlier spread the news about the Major being replaced, though no one trusts the accuracy of his claims.

"Well, let's grease their palms and see what happens," mutters the old, dour convict in the corner, the one who always eats his sour cabbage soup alone. His voice is low and cutting, as if speaking to

284

himself, but loud enough to invite a reaction.

"Grease their palms? Of course, he will," another chimes in with a mocking laugh. "The scoundrel's stolen plenty of cash, hasn't he? That brigand's been feathering his nest ever since he got here. Don't forget, he was just a regimental Major before he landed this cushy post. And look at him now. Why, only last year he was engaged to the head priest's daughter!"

"Engaged? Ha!" someone scoffs from across the room. "He didn't even manage to get married. They dumped him like garbage, and that just proves he's broke. What kind of man gets engaged when he's got nothing but the coat on his back? Did you hear? He lost everything he had at cards last Easter. Fedka told me."

"Bah! Marriage, what's that for a poor man?" Skouratoff, a wiry convict with a cynical smirk, suddenly interjects. "I've been married myself, and let me tell you, taking a wife is quick work, but the fun of it doesn't even last as long as a smoke."

"Do you think anyone cares to hear about your sorry life, Skouratoff?" the ex-quartermaster sneers, leaning back with an air of superiority. "Kvassoff, you're a fool if you think the Major can bribe an Inspector-General. Do you think they send someone all the way from Petersburg just to deal with your precious Major? You're muddled, my friend, absolutely muddled. Take it from me, you don't understand how these things work."

"And you think because he's a General, he doesn't take bribes?" comes a skeptical voice from the crowd, dripping with sarcasm.

"Of course he does! And plenty of them, too," another convict answers confidently. "The higher the rank, the bigger the bribes. That's the way of the world."

"Exactly," Kvassoff declares with a self-satisfied nod. "A General always has his palm greased. It's the natural order of things."

Baklouchin, a sharp-tongued convict known for his disdain of nonsense, suddenly steps into the fray. His tone is dripping with contempt as he turns to Kvassoff. "Oh, really? And tell us, wise man, have you ever given a General money yourself? Or are you just talking out of your hat? Have you even seen a General in your life?"

"Yes, I have!" Kvassoff blurts, though his bravado falters.

"Liar!" Baklouchin snaps.

"Liar yourself!" Kvassoff fires back, though his voice wavers.

"Alright, alright," says another convict, eager to stir the pot further. "If he says he's seen a General, let him name the man. Come on, Kvassoff, don't keep us waiting. I know all their names, so you'd better not try to bluff your way out of this."

Kvassoff hesitates for a moment, clearly flustered, then blurts out, "General Zibert! I've seen General Zibert!"

The room erupts in laughter. Kvassoff's tone lacks conviction, and the others can see right through him. Some jeer, others roll their eyes, and Baklouchin, triumphant, simply shakes his head.

"You're hopeless, Kvassoff," he says with a smirk. "Hopeless."

The conversation drifts into laughter and scattered remarks, but Kvassoff's feeble attempts to bolster his claims linger in the air, adding yet another layer of absurdity to the endless debates that filled the convicts' long, monotonous days. For all their harshness, these moments of banter offered a peculiar reprieve—a chance to mock, to argue, and, in some strange way, to remind each other that they were still human.

"Zibert! There's no General by that name," scoffs a convict, his voice dripping with mockery. "That must've been the General who was 'inspecting' your back when they gave you the cat-o'-nine-tails. Maybe Zibert was a Lieutenant-Colonel at best, but you were shaking so hard with fear you mistook him for a General."

The room erupts in laughter, but Skouratoff jumps in, eager to defend the claim. "Now, just listen to me, because I've got a wife and I know what I'm talking about. There was a General Zibert—a German, but a Russian subject. I swear it on my life! He confessed his sins to the Pope every year—mostly about his wild escapades with loose women—and they say he drank water like a duck. Forty glasses of Moskva water in one sitting to cure himself of some disease. I got it straight from his valet, so don't call me a liar!"

This bizarre detail is met with chuckles and disbelief. "Forty glasses of water? What was he, a fish? Did carp start swimming around in his belly?" asks the convict with the balalaïka, grinning from ear to ear.

"Shut up with your nonsense," growls another, trying to bring the conversation back on track. "Can't a man speak seriously for once without someone turning it into a joke? Who's this Inspector that's supposed to be coming, anyway?"

The question comes from Martinof, an old convict who had once served in the Hussars and carried himself with an air of importance, as though still wearing his uniform. His question silences the room briefly as the men look at one another, searching for answers.

"Set of lying fools," mutters one skeptic, his voice cutting through the pause. "Who knows where you lot get all this nonsense from? It's nothing but empty talk, I swear."

"It's not nonsense," declares Koulikoff, who had been silent until now. He speaks with the weight of authority, his voice calm and deliberate. Koulikoff, a Tsigan with a sharp mind, a knack for fixing horses, and a side business selling wine in the prison, rarely wasted his words. "I heard about it last week, and I'm telling you it's true. The man coming is no ordinary Inspector. He's a General, big and fat, with proud, haughty manners. The kind who looks down on everyone but loves to show off how important he is. A General with epaulettes that sparkle brighter than most."

The room listens intently as Koulikoff continues, choosing his words as if each one were a rare coin. "This General is coming to inspect all of Siberia, no less. Of course, his palms will be greased—Generals like him don't do anything for free. But don't think for a second that our Major will get close enough to slip him anything. Not a chance. There are Generals, and then there are Generals, just like there are fagots and fagots. This one is too high up, too important. Our Major won't dare crawl into his shadow. You can bet on that."

"But the Major's shaking in his boots," someone interjects. "He's been drunk since this morning."

"Fedka says they've already loaded up two carts with his things tonight," adds another, leaning in as though sharing a dark secret.

"A leopard doesn't change its spots," mutters a gray-haired convict in the corner. "You've all seen him drunk before. What's the surprise?"

"Yeah, but it'd be a devil of a shame if the General doesn't do something about him," another convict chimes in, his voice tinged with frustration. The murmurs of agreement ripple through the room, and the convicts begin to grow visibly agitated, the excitement mounting.

The news of the Inspector's impending arrival spreads through the prison like wildfire. Everywhere in the courtyard, convicts are whispering, speculating, and debating the significance of this unexpected visit. Some pace anxiously, their minds racing with possibilities. Others sit casually on the steps, plucking melodies from their balalaïkas, as though to calm themselves or pretend indifference. Yet, the tension in the air is palpable.

Groups of men form and dissolve, gossiping in hushed tones or raising their voices in heated arguments. A few convicts, uninterested or feigning indifference, continue their routines, as though nothing out of the ordinary is happening. Yet even they cannot entirely ignore the restless energy that has taken hold of the courtyard. In one corner, a small group begins to sing a slow, melancholy tune, their voices weaving a haunting counterpoint to the bustling activity around them.

Despite the uncertainty, one thing is clear: the prospect of the Inspector's visit has stirred the convicts into a frenzy of emotion. Hope, fear, resentment, and curiosity swirl together, and the prison, so often steeped in monotony, feels suddenly alive with possibilities. Whether the General will bring change or simply pass through without a second glance, no one can say. But for now, the anticipation alone is enough to ignite the spirits of men long accustomed to despair.

Around nine o'clock, as was the nightly routine, we were counted and sent off to our respective barracks, the heavy doors shutting us in for the short summer night. Though the morning drum would sound at five o'clock sharp, no one managed to find any rest before eleven. Conversations hummed through the stifling air, men shifted restlessly on their wooden bunks, and sometimes card games were hastily organized, just as in the depths of winter. The heat was oppressive, thick and suffocating, and even the open window seemed powerless against it. The coolness of the night air struggled to reach us, but it offered no real relief. Convicts tossed and turned like men in delirium, as if seeking escape from a torment that went beyond the physical.

And the fleas—endless, relentless, maddening. In winter, they were a nuisance; in spring, they became an army; by summer, they were an overwhelming plague. I would never have believed it if I hadn't experienced it myself. The torment they inflicted wasn't just physical; it gnawed at the mind, wore down the spirit. It reached a point where you could almost get used to them, but the price was steep—a kind of fevered exhaustion that left you half-delirious even in moments of shallow, fleeting sleep.

Finally, just as the early hours of morning brought a fragile, delicious slumber, the harsh, unyielding drum-call shattered it. Those rapid, sharp strokes seemed to mock the fragility of sleep. You would huddle in your semi-pelisse, trying to cling to those last moments of rest, but the thought intruded, heavy and relentless: This is how it will be tomorrow, and the day after, and the day after that, until liberty comes. But when? Where? Freedom felt like a phantom—unreachable, hiding in some distant, unseen world.

Grudgingly, you rose. Around you, the barracks came alive with noise and movement. Men dressed, some muttering curses, others hurriedly preparing for the day's work. The usual clamor began, and the rhythm of prison life resumed. True, there was an hour at midday when you could lie down, but even that small mercy did little to ease the exhaustion.

Amid this monotonous misery, a ripple of excitement had begun to spread. The rumors about the Inspector were true—more details emerged every day. It became certain that a high-ranking General from Petersburg was traveling through Siberia, already as far as Tobolsk. Each day brought fresh whispers from the town, carried in by those who had some connection to the outside world. Panic seemed to grip every official and authority figure, each scrambling to present themselves in the best possible light. Receptions, balls, and fêtes were being planned to dazzle the visitor, while convicts were sent in gangs to prepare the fortress. They leveled pathways, smoothed over rough patches, painted fences, plastered walls, and repaired anything that might catch the Inspector's eye.

Among the prisoners, the anticipation and speculation reached a fever pitch. Everyone understood what the flurry of work was really for, and the discussions grew heated and animated. The convicts' imaginations ran wild, soaring far beyond the walls that confined them. They even began discussing demands they might present to the General—a futile but somehow invigorating exercise. Yet, this newfound energy didn't put an end to the usual quarrels and bitter exchanges among them.

Meanwhile, the Major was in a constant state of agitation. He prowled the jail with increased frequency, barking orders and lashing out over the slightest infractions. His fury seemed to grow with each passing day. Men were sent to the guard-room or subjected to punishment for offenses so minor they would usually be ignored. He was especially vigilant about the cleanliness and order of the barracks, sparing no effort to make everything appear flawless in anticipation of the Inspector's arrival.

Then came an incident that might have been expected to unsettle the Major but instead appeared to bring him a grim satisfaction. A convict named Lomof struck another prisoner, Gavrilka, with an awl, the weapon piercing dangerously close to the heart. Gavrilka, one of the hardened tramps who lived for the next escape or scheme, was known only by this name within the prison. Whether he had another, no one seemed to know, and it hardly mattered. His life, like that of so many others, was reduced to the nickname whispered or shouted in the barracks.

The attack threw the jail into uproar. For the Major, it was an opportunity—not a disaster. It allowed him to tighten his grip, to impose more discipline under the guise of order, to flex the authority he clung to so desperately. For the convicts, it was just another episode in the grim, endless drama of their existence—a reminder of the violence that simmered beneath the surface, ready to erupt at any moment. And so, the routines continued, the days dragging on under the shadow of an Inspector's visit and the ever-present weight of captivity.

Lomof had once been a prosperous peasant in the Government of T——, district of K——, living comfortably with his family. There were five of them in the household: two Lomof brothers and three sons. They were known as rich peasants, so wealthy that rumors circulated throughout the district that they had amassed more than 300,000 roubles in paper money. Their main trade was currying and tanning, but their true income came from more dubious ventures— usury, harboring tramps, and receiving stolen goods. These underhanded dealings put half the peasants of their district in debt to them, and thus under their control. Known for their cunning and sharp intelligence, the Lomofs carried themselves with arrogance, as if they were untouchable.

Their influence extended far beyond their hamlet. A notable provincial dignitary once stayed at the elder Lomof's home and took a liking to him, impressed by his bold, unvarnished speech. This encounter only emboldened the Lomofs, who began to believe they were above the law. They became brazen, openly flouting local authorities and district tribunals, knowing full well that their power and wealth offered protection. Resentment simmered among the villagers, who longed to see the Lomofs brought low but could do little against them. For a time, it seemed as if nothing could disrupt their reign.

But fortune has its limits. The Lomofs' downfall didn't come from their numerous illicit activities, but from a false accusation that would unravel their lives. Ten versts from their village, they owned a farm where six Kirghiz laborers toiled under conditions barely better than slavery. One day, all six were discovered murdered. The event shocked the district and led to a prolonged investigation. Though the Lomofs vehemently denied involvement, the inquiry unearthed many of their unsavory dealings. Accusations flew thick and fast, and suspicions grew that they had killed the laborers to avoid paying debts. Despite their wealth, the Lomofs' reputation for avarice made such claims believable.

The trial was catastrophic for the family. Their property was seized or squandered during the proceedings, leaving them penniless. The father died under the weight of the scandal, and the sons were sentenced to transportation. One of them, along with their uncle, was condemned to fifteen years of hard labor. The irony of their fate was bitter, for the Lomofs were innocent of the murders.

The truth emerged in an unexpected way. Gavrilka, a notorious tramp with a reputation for mischief and gaiety, eventually confessed— or was at least widely believed by the convicts—to be the real perpetrator. Gavrilka, known for his roguish charm, had been loosely connected with the Lomofs before their imprisonment. Together with three other drifters, he had killed the Kirghiz laborers in a brazen attempt to loot the farm. Whether Gavrilka openly admitted to the crime or it was inferred by his behavior, the convicts all believed him to be the true culprit.

Despite this revelation, the Lomofs were never absolved. The uncle, a hot-headed and quarrelsome man, often clashed with the other convicts, earning their scorn. His nephew, in contrast, was sociable and intelligent but did little to improve the Lomofs' standing among their fellow prisoners. The two became targets for ridicule and mistreatment. Meanwhile, Gavrilka, with his lively humor and easygoing nature, was widely liked in the prison. Even knowing he had committed the crime that sent them to Siberia, the Lomofs avoided any confrontation with him. For his part, Gavrilka seemed entirely indifferent to their plight.

The fateful quarrel between Uncle Lomof and Gavrilka erupted over a sordid matter—a rivalry involving a girl of questionable reputation. Gavrilka had openly boasted about her favor, taunting Lomof until the latter, consumed with jealousy, attacked him in a blind rage. Grabbing an awl, Lomof drove it into Gavrilka's chest, narrowly missing his heart.

Though the Lomofs had lost everything, whispers persisted among the convicts that they still had hidden wealth. They owned a samovar and drank tea regularly, small luxuries that stood out in the harsh prison environment. Their modest indulgences did not escape the Major's notice. The Major despised the Lomofs and subjected them to relentless harassment, far exceeding his usual cruelty. Most believed he did so in hopes of extracting bribes, but the Lomofs either couldn't or wouldn't comply. Whether out of defiance or sheer desperation, they refused to grease the Major's palm, and his wrath followed them at every turn.

And so, their days passed, marked by loss, resentment, and the bitter irony of punishment for a crime they had not committed. The

Lomofs were a study in contradiction—once feared and envied, now broken and reviled, yet still clinging to the faint vestiges of dignity that their ruined lives allowed.

If Uncle Lomof's awl had gone just a hair's breadth deeper into Gavrilka's chest, it would have been fatal. As it turned out, the wound, though alarming, wasn't serious. The incident was quickly reported to the Major, who wasted no time in arriving on the scene. I can still picture him, slightly out of breath but radiating a peculiar satisfaction, as if this unfortunate event had somehow pleased him.

He approached Gavrilka with what he probably thought was an air of fatherly concern, his tone unnervingly affable. "Tell me, lad," he began, "can you make it to the hospital on your own, or will you need someone to carry you?" Then, as if suddenly struck with a brilliant idea, he bellowed to the sub-officer, "No, no, better fetch a horse immediately! Let them harness it this very moment!"

Gavrilka, always lighthearted and dismissive, tried to wave off the fuss. "I don't feel it much, your worship. It's nothing more than a scratch, a bit of a prick."

But the Major, ignoring him entirely, continued in a tone of exaggerated gravity. "You don't understand, my dear fellow," he insisted. "You'll see. It's not the size of the wound that matters; it's the location. And that scoundrel—he struck you just below the heart! Wait, just you wait!" he growled, turning his attention to Lomof, his voice rising to a howl. "I've got you now! Take him to the guardhouse at once!"

The Major kept his word with a vengeance. Lomof was brought to trial, and although Gavrilka's injury was minor, the charge of malice aforethought was undeniable. The court extended Lomof's sentence by several years and handed down a punishment of a thousand strokes with the rod. The Major could barely contain his glee. His delight over Lomof's misfortune was palpable, as if it were a personal victory.

Finally, the long-anticipated day of the Inspector's visit arrived.

The town had been buzzing with activity for days, and preparations at the convict prison had reached a fever pitch. Everything had been scrubbed to a gleaming finish. The barracks, the yard, even the walls seemed unnaturally clean. The convicts themselves had been given extra attention—freshly shaved, clothed in spotless linen, and drilled relentlessly on how to behave. Their summer uniforms of canvas waistcoats and pantaloons, each with a black circular patch sewn on the back, had never looked so neat. They were rehearsed to the point of exhaustion on what to say and how to say it should the Inspector address them. Every word, every gesture was carefully choreographed.

The Major, in his desperation to make a flawless impression, was visibly unhinged. By the time the Inspector was due, the convicts were already at their posts, lined up like statues, their little fingers rigidly pressed against the seams of their trousers. The tension was so thick it felt as though the very air held its breath.

At precisely one o'clock, the Inspector entered the prison compound. He was a General of imposing stature, his bearing so imperious that it seemed to cast a shadow over everything in his wake. His presence exuded authority, the kind that could unsettle even the most seasoned officials. Behind him trailed a retinue of other Generals and Colonels from the town, their deference to him evident in their every step.

One figure in the procession stood out—a tall, distinguished civilian dressed in a finely tailored frock coat and polished shoes. His demeanor was strikingly self-assured, even nonchalant, and it was clear that he commanded respect. The General himself addressed this man with an almost excessive politeness, turning to him frequently as if seeking his approval. The sight of such a powerful figure deferring to a civilian sparked a storm of curiosity among the convicts. Who could this man be, to command such attention from a General of this stature?

For the rest of the day, the civilian was the subject of endless speculation. His identity and purpose were unknown, but his presence had left an indelible impression. Rumors swirled and theories abounded, some plausible, others outlandish. The convicts couldn't resist discussing him, their imaginations running wild as they tried to piece together the mystery. Later, they would learn the truth about who he was and the role he played, but for now, his identity remained an enigma—a tantalizing puzzle that added yet another layer of intrigue to an already momentous day.

Our Major, decked out in his full uniform with its bright orange collar, seemed to have pinned all his hopes on impressing the visiting General. Unfortunately for him, his overall appearance was less than ideal. His bloodshot eyes, coupled with the unmistakable fiery redness of his face, betrayed habits that no amount of polished brass or crisp attire could hide. Hoping to make a better impression, he had removed his spectacles—perhaps thinking this would lend him a sharper air—but the result was a man squinting slightly, looking ill at ease and anxious.

Standing a little apart from the General's retinue, he held himself ramrod straight, like a schoolboy desperate to be noticed by the headmaster. His every movement radiated the feverish anticipation of a subordinate ready to spring into action at the faintest hint of a command. He was clearly yearning for some opportunity to demonstrate his usefulness, to prove that he was indispensable. But as the minutes dragged on, it became painfully obvious that the General felt no such need.

The General, his demeanor cool and detached, moved through the prison methodically. His steps were measured, his gaze sharp but disinterested. He passed through the barracks without uttering a word, barely acknowledging the rows of convicts lined up at rigid attention. His inspection of the kitchen was similarly perfunctory, a brief glance at the bubbling pots of sour cabbage soup, which he sampled with an indifferent expression. It was clear he was a man accustomed to formality, protocol, and brevity, and that his visit here was just another item on a long list of duties to fulfill.

At one point, someone pointed me out to him, identifying me as a former nobleman, convicted of what they described vaguely as "this, that, and the other." There was a flicker of interest in the General's eyes as he turned his attention to me.

"Ah," he said, his tone neutral, neither curious nor dismissive. "And how does he conduct himself?"

The question, simple as it was, sent a ripple of tension through the officials present. The Major, who had been hovering nervously in the background, seized the opportunity to respond with almost comic eagerness.

"Satisfactorily, your Excellency. Satisfactorily for the time being," he replied, his voice strained with an attempt at firmness, as if overcompensating for his own insecurities.

The General gave a brief nod, acknowledging the response without offering further comment. It was a gesture that seemed to close the matter entirely. Within moments, he had turned on his heel and exited the jail, his retinue trailing behind him like shadows.

The entire inspection had lasted mere minutes, and its abrupt conclusion left the convicts in a state of baffled disappointment. For days leading up to the visit, they had whispered, speculated, and even dreamed of what this moment might bring—justice, reform, or at least some acknowledgment of their grievances. But none of those hopes materialized. The General's departure felt like the end of a story that had never truly begun.

As for the idea of lodging complaints against the Major—any lingering thoughts of that vanished as quickly as the General himself. It was clear to everyone that the Major had anticipated this possibility and prepared accordingly. Whatever steps he had taken, they had ensured that no convict would dare speak out against him. The realization hung heavy in the air, and the men returned to their routines, disillusioned but not surprised.

Chapter 6
The Animals at The Convict Establishment

Gniedko, a sturdy bay horse, was purchased shortly after a significant event in the prison. His arrival was a much more engaging and pleasurable diversion for the convicts than the visit of the high-ranking official, whose brief inspection had left them disheartened. The jail needed a horse for a variety of tasks—hauling water, removing refuse, and other similar duties. Gniedko was placed under the care of a convict specifically assigned to handle and drive him, albeit always under the watchful eye of an escort. The horse worked diligently morning and night, performing his tasks with a patient and dependable nature. Though he had already seen many years of service, he was respected and appreciated by the convicts, who came to view him as an integral part of their grim daily routine.

One bright morning, on the eve of St. Peter's Day, Gniedko collapsed while pulling a water barrel. It happened suddenly, and within moments he was gone. His unexpected death stirred a wave of regret and sorrow among the convicts, who quickly gathered around his lifeless body. Former cavalrymen, Tsigans, veterinary experts, and others with a background in handling horses joined in a lively and heated debate about the cause of his death. They passionately shared their insights, examining the poor beast's lifeless form with a mixture of curiosity and respect, though no amount of argument or speculation could bring him back. There he lay, stretched out on the ground, his belly swollen, while the men continued to crowd around, each feeling compelled to touch or examine him, as if in doing so they might better understand his demise.

The incident was reported to the Major, who decided without delay that a new horse had to be purchased to replace Gniedko. Early the next morning, on St. Peter's Day, the prison yard was abuzz with excitement. After mass, the convicts, now gathered together in full force, prepared for the unusual event: choosing a new horse. It was an extraordinary occurrence, and the men were eager participants. A series of horses, brought in by horse-dealers, were paraded before them. The decision-making was left to the prisoners, many of whom were seasoned experts in horse trading, thanks to their diverse and colorful pasts. With over 250 convicts, including Tsigans, Lesghians, and former cavalrymen, the horse dealers faced an audience that was nearly impossible to deceive.

The convicts, despite their chains and grim circumstances, threw themselves into the process with childlike enthusiasm. Each new horse sparked fresh discussions and evaluations. It was as though, for a brief moment, they were free men again, making decisions about something as if it were their own. They took their task seriously, carefully scrutinizing each horse, debating its merits, and rejecting three before finally settling on the fourth. The air was electric with their spirited debates and animated gestures, a stark contrast to the usual monotony of prison life.

The horse-dealers, in turn, were visibly uneasy. They were accustomed to haggling with peasants and townsfolk, not with a gathering of men marked by their shaven heads, branded skin, and the clinking of chains. The presence of armed soldiers, who kept a close watch over the proceedings, added to their discomfort. Yet, what seemed to unnerve them the most was the sheer number of convicts— over 200 men, all keenly focused and at home in their environment. This was their world, their domain, and the dealers, though ostensibly there to do business, could not help but feel a sense of awe and respect for the unusual setting and its inhabitants.

When the decision was finally made, and the chosen horse became the prison's new Gniedko, the convicts took pride in their choice. For a fleeting moment, the purchase of the horse had allowed them to step out of their harsh reality and into a role that felt almost normal. It was a small reprieve, a brief connection to a life that might have been, and for that, it brought a surprising sense of satisfaction and unity among the men.Our convicts employed a surprising array of tricks and tests to determine the true worth of each horse presented for sale. They approached the process with an air of grave importance, as if the success of the entire prison rested on acquiring the right animal. They examined every detail, from the strength of the hooves to the gleam in the eyes, with a seriousness that seemed almost comical given their circumstances. It was hard to believe that men with no personal stake in the matter could be so invested. Yet even those who were otherwise subdued and resigned to their fate—the silent, downtrodden souls who rarely spoke—suddenly displayed a keen interest. It was as though the simple act of evaluating the horse momentarily lifted them out of their despondency and allowed them to participate in something larger than themselves.

Among the most animated participants were the Circassians. Their energy was infectious as they leapt onto the horses' backs, their sharp, wild eyes scanning every movement. They spoke rapidly in their native tongue, a cascade of unintelligible words accompanied by expressive gestures. Their hooked, copper-toned noses flared as they inspected the animals, their white teeth flashing in eager debate. Though few could understand their words, the Russians and other convicts watched intently, trying to discern their conclusions through body language and facial expressions. It seemed clear to everyone that the Circassians' judgment carried weight.

Not to be outdone, the Tsigans and former horse-traders also claimed a central role in the discussion. Among them was Koulikoff, a seasoned Tsigan and former horse-dealer who had long been regarded as the authority on all matters equine within the prison. His reputation for expertise was well established, though it was also known that he had a tendency to embellish his skills. Still, he had carved out a position of respect, earning substantial fees from townspeople who sought his advice on their ailing horses. He was an enigmatic figure of quiet authority, speaking only when absolutely necessary and doing so with a measured gravitas that commanded attention. His demeanor suggested a life of varied and significant experiences, though his past remained shrouded in mystery. Among the convicts, he was treated with the deference of an aristocrat.

Koulikoff's dominance, however, faced a serious challenge with the arrival of Jolkin, a Siberian peasant and self-taught veterinary practitioner. Jolkin was a man of unassuming appearance but remarkable skill. Within weeks of his arrival, he had usurped much of Koulikoff's town practice by successfully treating horses that others, including certified veterinarians, had declared hopeless cases. Jolkin's expertise earned him swift recognition, and his down-to-earth manner made him popular among the townspeople. It was a blow to Koulikoff, whose carefully cultivated status began to wane.

Jolkin's backstory was as fascinating as his talents. He was one of the "old believers," a sect known for its strict religious practices, and had been sentenced to hard labor for coining counterfeit money. Oddly enough, he took pride in sharing his tale, laughing at the absurdity of needing three genuine gold coins to produce one counterfeit. His easygoing nature and sharp wit endeared him to the convicts, though his rise undoubtedly irked Koulikoff.

The rivalry between Koulikoff and Jolkin added another layer of drama to the horse-buying process. Each man sought to outdo the other, their expert opinions clashing as they inspected the animals. Their exchanges were intense but carried a veneer of professionalism, as if each knew they were being watched and judged by their peers.

Ultimately, the purchase of a new horse became more than a mundane necessity—it was a spectacle, a contest of skill and knowledge that provided the convicts with a rare moment of camaraderie and excitement. Even those who had no direct involvement in the selection process were drawn into the fervor, their spirits momentarily lifted by the shared experience. In the end, the chosen horse was not merely an acquisition for the prison but a symbol of collective effort and the brief illusion of freedom in a life otherwise marked by confinement and monotony.

Koulikoff was visibly unsettled by the rapid ascent of Jolkin, a humble peasant, whose expertise had eclipsed his own carefully cultivated reputation. It was a bitter pill to swallow for someone like Koulikoff, who had once been the unofficial aristocrat among the convicts, a man who not only wielded influence but had even maintained a mistress in the suburbs, donned a plush jacket, and strutted in top-boots. Now reduced to running a tavern within the prison, his standing had diminished considerably. The purchase of the new horse seemed to promise an arena for Koulikoff to reclaim some of his former glory, and anticipation among the convicts ran high. Many were eager for a clash between the two rivals, expecting a dramatic showdown. The tension in the air was palpable as opinions divided; factions formed quickly, and arguments broke out before anything substantial had even occurred.

Jolkin's expression remained unreadable, his sharp, peasant face crinkling into a smile that was more mocking than friendly. Yet the outcome was far from what anyone anticipated. To everyone's surprise, Koulikoff avoided any direct confrontation or open dispute. Instead, he maneuvered with subtlety and tact, a master of strategy. At first, he appeared to yield ground, listening intently and even deferentially to Jolkin's assessments. This seemed to throw Jolkin off balance, giving him the impression of an easy victory. Then, at just the right moment, Koulikoff interjected sharply, seizing upon a flaw in his rival's reasoning. With a tone that was both humble and firm, he systematically dismantled Jolkin's points, exposing errors and asserting his own expertise.

The effect was immediate. Jolkin, despite his skill and cunning, found himself outmaneuvered. Koulikoff's handling of the situation won him admiration from many quarters. Even those who had sided with Jolkin were forced to concede, albeit grudgingly.

"I'll tell you, boys," said one convict, nodding in approval, "you just can't catch him out. He knows his business inside and out."

"Well, Jolkin knows more if you ask me," another retorted, though his tone lacked the venom of real animosity. The rivalry had turned into something resembling mutual respect among the partisans.

"He might know more," came another voice, "but Koulikoff's got a lighter hand, and more brains for sure. When it comes to stock—horses or otherwise—he's the one who'll come out on top."

"Don't sell Jolkin short," someone else added, unwilling to let the peasant's reputation go unnoticed. "He's no slouch either."

As for the new horse, the convicts collectively deemed it a splendid choice. It was a strong, young gelding with a gleaming coat, a testament to good breeding and health. The convicts' enthusiasm turned toward haggling over the price, an activity they threw themselves into with the same vigor as their debates. The seller initially asked for thirty roubles, but the prisoners, determined to strike a bargain, refused to go beyond twenty-five. The negotiations dragged on, punctuated by bursts of laughter and cheeky remarks.

"What's all this fuss about? It's not like the money's coming out of your own pockets," one convict teased.

"Yeah, what's the big idea? Saving for the government treasury, are you?" another chimed in, grinning.

"But it's our money—money that belongs to all of us," someone argued, attempting a more serious tone.

"'Belongs to all of us,' he says!" another convict quipped, rolling his eyes. "You don't need to plant idiots—they sprout up just fine on their own!"

In the end, the horse was purchased to general satisfaction, though the final price was likely a compromise. The convicts dispersed, still buzzing with the energy of the event, their spirits lifted for a time. The acquisition of the new gelding became a small triumph, a bright spot in their otherwise monotonous and oppressive lives. It was a moment of shared purpose and fleeting camaraderie, a rare and cherished thing in the confines of the prison.

The deal was finally struck at twenty-eight roubles, and the convicts eagerly informed the Major, who quickly approved the purchase. Bread and salt were ceremoniously brought out, a traditional gesture of welcome, and the new addition to the prison was led in triumph into the yard. It seemed that every convict took a moment to pat the horse's neck or stroke its head, as though this simple act connected them to something brighter than their grim surroundings.

Once the horse was officially theirs, he was immediately put to work hauling water. The convicts watched him with great interest as he pulled the heavy barrel, his movements measured and steady. There was an odd sense of pride and satisfaction among them, as though the new horse's performance somehow reflected on them all.

Roman, the convict assigned as the horse's caretaker, observed him with quiet, almost solemn, satisfaction. Roman, a former peasant of about fifty, embodied the typical Russian coachman—serious, unhurried, and deeply connected to his charge. His demeanor carried an air of dignity, as if his bond with horses conferred on him a unique wisdom. He was a man of few words, preferring instead to communicate with his horse and his surroundings through subtle gestures and expressions. Always with a snuffbox in hand, he would pause occasionally to take a pinch, his calm gaze unwavering.

Roman's position as the prison's waterman and horse handler was uncontested. No one questioned his authority over the animals, nor his competence. When the bay horse, Gniedko, had collapsed and died, not a single convict suggested that Roman was at fault. Even the Major, not known for his leniency, accepted it as the will of God. Roman, after all, knew his work and had faithfully cared for every horse entrusted to him. Gniedko, the bay, had been no exception.

Gniedko had quickly become a favorite among the convicts, despite their often rough exteriors. The affection they showed him was a testament to the small humanity that still burned within them. Each time Roman returned from the river with the water barrel, the convicts would watch with a peculiar mix of admiration and amusement as Gniedko stopped at the gate and waited for instructions.

"Go on, you know the way," Roman would say, gesturing casually.

Obediently, Gniedko would trot to the kitchen, where the cooks and other workers would fill their buckets with water. The sight of the horse, so calm and cooperative, always drew comments.

"Look at him! Gniedko's a marvel. He knows exactly what he's doing!" one would exclaim.

"He's not just any horse—he's one of us," another would add with a grin.

The horse seemed to understand the praise, often shaking his head and snorting as if in acknowledgment. Someone would inevitably bring him a treat—bread or even a handful of salt. Gniedko would nibble it with an air of quiet gratitude, and then shake his head again, as though to say, "I understand. Thank you."

Even I found joy in feeding Gniedko small pieces of bread. Watching his soft, warm lips gently take the crumbs from my palm was a strangely soothing experience, a moment of simple connection that stood out in stark contrast to the harsh realities of our lives.

The convicts had a deep, almost instinctive affection for living creatures. If regulations had permitted, they would have gladly filled the barracks with birds, dogs, and other animals. Such companionship might have softened their harsh dispositions, brought a touch of solace to their restless souls. But the rules forbade it. Space was scarce, and the prison's authorities saw no value in the idea. Yet, in their hearts, many of the convicts longed for the simple joy that such companionship could bring. Gniedko, for a time, became a surrogate for that yearning, a living presence that reminded them of life beyond their confinement.

During my time in the prison, several animals managed to make their homes within the confines of the jail. Beyond Gniedko, our hardworking horse, we had a small menagerie that included some dogs, a few geese, a he-goat named Vaska, and even an eagle, though the latter stayed only briefly. Each of these animals brought a small measure of life and movement to an otherwise dreary and stagnant environment.

Among the dogs, Bull held a special place in my heart. I believe I have mentioned him before. Bull and I quickly became friends, though his presence was largely ignored by the other convicts. To them, as is common among the lower classes, dogs were considered impure creatures unworthy of affection. Bull lived entirely within the prison grounds, sleeping wherever he could find space in the courtyard and surviving on scraps from the kitchen. Despite his neglect by the others, he recognized every convict as his master, greeting them with unreserved enthusiasm whenever they returned from their assigned labor.

At the cry of "Corporal," which signaled the men's return, Bull would dash eagerly to the gate, wagging his tail with hopeful energy and gazing into the eyes of each man as though expecting a friendly pat on the head. Yet for years, his simple gestures of affection went unnoticed by everyone but me. I was the only one who took the time to stroke his fur or whisper kind words, and so Bull naturally came to favor me above all others.

Somehow, another dog eventually joined us. This one was called Snow, a creature whose appearance was both pitiable and bizarre. Snow's back had been broken by a telega, leaving his spine curved unnaturally. When he moved, his contorted form made it seem as though he were two dogs fused together by some cruel twist of fate. His fur was patchy and mangy, his eyes perpetually bleary, and his tail, devoid of hair, hung limply between his legs as though in perpetual defeat.

Snow's life was marked by misfortune, and he seemed resigned to his lot. His demeanor was one of abject submission, as if he had internalized his unluckiness and sought only to avoid further suffering. He never barked, never growled, and rarely showed any sign of defiance. Most of the time, he could be found lurking near the back of the buildings, keeping out of sight. If anyone approached him, he would immediately roll onto his back in a gesture of total surrender, as if to say, "Do whatever you want to me; I won't resist."

This act of submission did little to endear him to the convicts. On the contrary, they seemed to see it as an invitation to mistreat him. Almost every man who passed Snow felt compelled to deliver a quick, dismissive kick, accompanied by a muttered, "Ugh, filthy beast!" Snow, for his part, accepted these indignities without a sound. If the blow was particularly harsh, he might emit a faint, stifled yelp, but he never fought back, never protested.

Snow's submissiveness extended even to other dogs. When he ventured near the kitchen to scavenge for scraps, he would cower and stretch himself flat if another, more dominant dog approached. The larger dog, often barking and aggressive at first, would usually stop short, puzzled by Snow's utter lack of resistance. After sniffing him over, as if trying to make sense of this strange, abject creature, the intruder would typically lose interest and move on. Snow, trembling from the encounter, would pick himself up and limp away, joining the nearest pack of stray dogs.

Sometimes Snow would trail after a female dog, or yutchka, with a faint glimmer of hope. He knew, of course, that she would never give him a second glance; her pride and station were far above his. Yet even the futile act of following her seemed to offer him a small solace, a brief distraction from his otherwise miserable existence.

Snow had no concept of dignity or propriety; his life was singularly focused on survival. For him, securing a meal was the highest aspiration, and he made no effort to conceal this fact. His cynicism was plain in every action, but it was hard to blame him for it. Snow's existence, stripped of hope or joy, was a grim reflection of the convicts' own struggles—a silent testament to the indomitable instinct to endure, no matter how bleak the circumstances.

Once, I decided to show Snow some affection. The act must have been entirely foreign to him, for as soon as I reached out to pet him, he collapsed onto the ground in a quivering heap, overcome by a strange, whimpering joy. It was as though he could scarcely believe that someone had finally chosen to be kind to him. His delight was so moving, so pitiful, that it deepened my sympathy for him. I made it a habit to caress him whenever I saw him, and soon, he began to recognize me. The moment he spotted me, he would break into plaintive, tearful whining, expressing an almost overwhelming gratitude for the small kindness I showed him.

Despite my care, Snow's miserable life ended abruptly. He was killed at the back of the jail, torn apart by other dogs in a cruel and unceremonious end. He died as he had lived—unnoticed by most, a fleeting presence in the lives of the convicts.

Koultiapka, another dog, was a very different sort of creature. I had brought him into the jail myself when he was just a tiny pup, freshly born in one of the workshops. Perhaps it was the simple pleasure of nurturing something small and vulnerable in such a harsh place that motivated me to take him in. I fed him, watched him grow, and marveled at his antics. Bull, the elder dog, quickly adopted Koultiapka, taking him under his wing—or rather, his paw. The two were inseparable. Bull showed an unusual patience with the puppy, allowing him to tug at his ears and bite at his loose skin without so much as a growl. He even played with Koultiapka in that peculiar way older dogs often humor younger ones, full of gentle indulgence.

Koultiapka was an odd little fellow. He didn't grow in height like most dogs, but rather spread out in length and width. His soft, fluffy coat was mouse-gray, and his ears added to his whimsical appearance— one drooping down while the other stood permanently upright. He was full of youthful energy, bounding and yapping with uncontainable joy whenever he saw me. He would leap to lick my face as if to say, "See how happy I am? Forget decorum, this is all about love!"

The bond between us grew strong. At the mere call of his name, "Koultiapka," he would come charging out of some hidden corner, spinning and tumbling over himself in noisy, joyful abandon. I was deeply attached to him and found solace in his unreserved affection. I fancied that he was destined for a life filled with simple pleasures—a bright spot amid the dreary monotony of the prison. But this illusion was shattered.

One day, a convict named Neustroief, who made women's shoes and tanned hides, noticed Koultiapka. There was something in the way he appraised the dog, running his hands over Koultiapka's soft fur, that made me uneasy. The puppy, ever trusting, wagged his tail and barked in delight. The next day, Koultiapka was gone.

I searched for him, calling his name and looking in every corner of the jail, but he had vanished. Two weeks later, the truth emerged. Neustroief had been unable to resist the allure of Koultiapka's thick, soft fur. He had killed the dog, skinned him, and used the hide to fashion fur-trimmed boots for a young official's wife. When the boots were finished, Neustroief showed them to me with great pride. Their inner lining was beautiful, luxurious—and unmistakably Koultiapka.

This wasn't an isolated incident. Many of the convicts worked with leather and fur, and it wasn't uncommon for dogs with fine coats to mysteriously disappear. Some convicts stole or bought dogs expressly for their pelts. I once saw two men behind the kitchen with a handsome black dog on a leash. It turned out that a footman had stolen the animal from his master and sold it to the shoemakers for thirty kopecks. They planned to hang the dog, skin it, and discard the carcass in a foul-smelling refuse ditch at the far corner of the courtyard.

I remember the dog's eyes as they prepared to kill it. It seemed to sense its fate, looking around at each man with a desperate, pleading gaze. Occasionally, it would wag its bushy tail timidly, as if trying to win over its captors with a display of trust and submission. Unable to bear the sight, I walked away. The convicts carried out their grim task without interference.

As for the geese in the jail, their presence was something of a mystery. Nobody seemed to know who owned them or who cared for them, but they had become a source of delight for the convicts. The birds roamed freely, honking and flapping about, bringing an unusual liveliness to the otherwise oppressive environment. Their antics and occasional squabbles were a topic of endless amusement and even earned them a certain notoriety in the town beyond the prison walls.

The geese of the convict establishment had an oddly naturalized existence, as though they belonged as much to the jail as the inmates themselves. Hatched within its walls, their lives revolved around the rhythms of prison life. The kitchen was their unofficial headquarters, where they lingered until the drumbeat signaled the convicts' departure for work. As the prisoners assembled near the main gate, the geese emerged in formation, flapping their wings noisily and cackling with excitement.

When the convicts began their march, the geese followed closely, bobbing along and sometimes hopping awkwardly over the threshold of the gate as if they too were bound for labor. Once outside, they stayed nearby, foraging and pecking at the ground while the convicts toiled. When the workday ended and the prisoners started their return march, the geese instinctively joined the procession.

Passersby couldn't help but remark on the strange spectacle. "Look at that—prisoners and their loyal geese," some would say, laughing. Others, intrigued by the birds' odd companionship, would ask, "How did you train them to follow you?" Occasionally, a sympathetic onlooker would reach into their pocket and say, "Here, take some money for your geese!" The sight was amusing, almost surreal, a rare moment of levity in the grimness of penal life.

Yet, for all their charm and loyalty, the geese ultimately met a somber end. Despite their place in the convicts' routines, their fate was sealed during one Lenten season when they were slaughtered to prepare a feast. Their devotion and quirky antics were forgotten in favor of a celebratory meal.

Vaska, our goat, was a different story. Unlike the geese, who were primarily an amusing backdrop, Vaska was adored by everyone in the prison. Nobody knew exactly how he came to be there or who brought him in, but he was a white kid when he first appeared, bright-eyed and impossibly endearing. Within days, he captured the hearts of all. His playful antics and friendly demeanor made him a favorite. To justify his presence, someone claimed that a goat was necessary for the stables, but Vaska rarely stayed there. Instead, he roamed freely, spending most of his time in the kitchen or mingling with the convicts.

He was as mischievous as he was lovable. Vaska had a penchant for jumping onto tables, playfully locking horns with the convicts, and darting around the courtyard in bursts of energy. He answered when called, his enthusiasm making him seem almost human. His greatest delight was wrestling matches, a favorite game among the prisoners.

One evening, Babaï, a Lesghian convict, decided to wrestle with Vaska. Sitting on the barracks' stone steps, Babaï butted his forehead against Vaska's, mimicking the goat's playful challenges.

Suddenly, with the precision of a practiced athlete, Vaska sprang onto the top step, balanced on his hind legs, pulled his forelegs in tightly, and struck Babaï square on the back of the neck. The blow sent Babaï tumbling headlong down the steps, much to the raucous delight of everyone watching, including Babaï himself. The goat's playful victory only solidified his legendary status in the prison.

When Vaska reached maturity, his scent became an issue. A general meeting was called, and it was decided that he would undergo a minor operation performed by one of the prison's amateur veterinarians. The procedure was a success, and the prisoners joked, "At least he won't smell like a goat anymore."

With the operation behind him, Vaska's personality remained unchanged, but his physique transformed. He began to gain weight rapidly, becoming a rotund, majestic creature with a splendid coat and imposing horns. His rolling gait, a result of his sheer size, added to his charm. The convicts fed him generously, indulging him with treats and scraps whenever they could.

Vaska became more than just a companion; he was a symbol of pride. When the convicts went to work, he accompanied them, to the amusement of both inmates and onlookers. On the banks of the river, where prisoners often labored, they would gather willow branches and wildflowers to create garlands for Vaska. His horns were adorned with foliage, and his body was festooned with floral decorations. Draped in his makeshift finery, Vaska would lead the gang back to the jail, a vision of rustic beauty that brought a rare sense of joy and camaraderie to the convicts.

The sight of Vaska in his full glory, strutting at the head of the procession, was a moment of collective pride for the prisoners. It was as if, through him, they found a fleeting sense of freedom and dignity—qualities often stripped away in the harsh confines of the prison. Vaska wasn't just a goat; he was a small, radiant beacon of life in a place that otherwise seemed determined to extinguish it.

The affection the prisoners had for Vaska reached such a peak that a truly whimsical idea was proposed—to gild his horns. This suggestion, born perhaps of the convicts' longing for something beautiful and extravagant in their bleak lives, was seriously debated. I even consulted Akim Akimitch, a convict renowned as the best gilder in the jail, to see if such a thing were possible. Akim examined Vaska's horns with the solemnity of a craftsman considering an intricate piece of work. After much contemplation, he declared that while it could be done, the gilding would not last and would ultimately serve no real purpose. The project was abandoned, but the very discussion showed how deeply Vaska was cherished.

Vaska's charm and antics might have made him a lifelong companion to the convicts, had it not been for an unfortunate encounter. One day, as he led the gang of prisoners back from their labor, festooned with the garlands that had become his signature adornment, his path crossed that of the Major, who was passing in his carriage. The sight of a goat, so ornately decorated and marching proudly at the head of the convicts, seemed to offend the Major's sense of order.

"Halt!" the Major roared. "Whose goat is this?"

The convicts, hesitant but honest, told him. The Major's face grew dark with indignation.

"What! A goat in the prison? And no one asked my permission?" His voice was sharp with disbelief. He turned to the sub-officer and barked orders: the goat was to be killed immediately, its skin sold, and the proceeds added to the prisoners' communal account. As for the meat, it was to be cooked and served with the convicts' cabbage soup.

The Major's decree was final, and no one dared to disobey. The convicts mourned the loss of Vaska, but their sorrow was overshadowed by the harsh realities of prison life. Vaska met his end near the ditch where the convicts disposed of waste. One of the prisoners bought the carcass for a rouble and fifty kopecks. With the money, white bread was purchased and shared among the convicts. The goat's roasted meat, sold in pieces by its purchaser, was said to be delicious. Vaska's death became a topic of discussion for weeks, his absence leaving a void in the small joys of their days.

Around the same time, another creature briefly took up residence in the prison—a steppe eagle, a small and fierce species. A convict had found the bird wounded and near death, bringing it back to the jail. The eagle, unable to fly because of a damaged wing and with one leg severely injured, was a pitiful sight. Its fiery spirit, however, was undiminished. When a curious crowd gathered to see it, the bird glared at them with fierce defiance, its crooked beak open in a threat, as though prepared to defend itself to the last breath.

When the initial curiosity wore off, the eagle retreated to a distant corner of the courtyard, as far from the convicts as it could manage. There, it hunched against the palings, a solitary, proud figure. During the three months it lived in the prison, the bird rarely left its chosen refuge. At first, the convicts visited frequently to marvel at the wild creature's stubborn dignity. They even set Bull, the dog, on the eagle, hoping for some entertainment. At first, Bull was cautious, wary of the bird's claws and snapping beak, which thrilled the spectators. "He's a tough one!" they would laugh.

Over time, Bull grew bolder, pulling at the eagle's injured wing, while the bird retaliated with sharp jabs of its beak. Yet even in its suffering, the eagle retained a regal demeanor, its piercing gaze unwavering as it defended itself. The convicts soon tired of the game, and the bird was left alone.

Yet someone—whose identity remained a mystery—took pity on

314

the bird. Each day, a piece of fresh meat and a small vessel of water appeared near the eagle's corner. For days, the eagle refused to eat, its pride or mistrust perhaps too great. Eventually, necessity overcame its defiance, and it began to eat what was left for it. But it would never eat in public or accept food from a hand. It maintained its aloof dignity to the end.

Sometimes, from a distance, I watched it eat, marveling at its strength of spirit. It seemed to embody something larger than itself— a wounded king, proud even in captivity. Its presence in the prison, though brief, left a deep impression, a reminder of freedom and wildness that no cage could fully extinguish.

When he thought no one was watching and believed he was alone, he would cautiously leave his corner and limp along the fence for about a dozen steps before turning back. He repeated this back-and-forth pacing as though he were following a doctor's orders to get some exercise. But the moment he caught sight of me, he would rush back to his corner as fast as he could, hobbling and hopping. Once there, he would throw his head back, open his beak, fluff up his feathers, and look like he was preparing to defend himself.

I tried to approach him gently, but it was useless. He would bite and struggle the instant I got close. He never accepted the meat I offered, and as long as I stayed near him, he fixed his sharp, menacing eyes on me. Alone and filled with resentment, he seemed to be waiting for death, refusing any kindness or reconciliation with the world around him.

For two months, the convicts completely forgot about him, but eventually, they remembered and surprised me by showing unexpected sympathy. They all agreed he should be set free.

"Let him die, but let him die in freedom," one of them said.

"A bird like that could never adapt to prison life," another added.

"He's nothing like us," someone murmured.

"Well, of course not. He's a bird, and we're people," came another response.

"The eagle is the king of the skies," Skouratof began to say, but no one paid attention to him that day.

One afternoon, as the drum signaled the start of work, the prisoners decided to set the eagle free. They tied his beak to keep him from biting—he fought wildly against them—and carried him out to the ramparts of the prison. The twelve convicts in the group watched eagerly, curious to see what he would do once he was free. It was an odd sight—every one of them seemed as thrilled as if they themselves had been given their freedom.

"That ungrateful thing," muttered the man holding him, almost fondly. "You try to help him, and he only tries to tear your hand apart."

"Let him go, Mikitka," someone urged.

"He doesn't belong in prison. Let him have his freedom, the freedom he deserves."

With that, they tossed the eagle from the ramparts onto the steppe below. The day was cold and gray, and the autumn wind howled across the barren steppe, rustling the dry yellow grass. As soon as they let him go, the eagle flapped his injured wing and took off, eager to get as far from them as possible and find a place to hide from their prying eyes. The convicts stood silently, watching him move with his head low, just above the grass.

"Can you still see him?" one of them asked thoughtfully.

"He hasn't looked back even once," another noted.

"Did you really think he'd turn around and thank us?" a third man said with a smirk.

"He's free now. He feels it. That's freedom."

"Yes, freedom," another murmured.

"You won't see him again, pals."

"Move along! Get going!" shouted the escort, breaking their reverie. The convicts began to trudge to their work, leaving the steppe and the eagle behind them.

Chapter 7
Grievances

At the beginning of this section, the editor of the "Recollections" by the late Alexander Petrovitch Goriantchikoff feels it necessary to share the following information with the readers.

"In the first part of the 'Recollections of the House of the Dead,' there was mention of a nobleman convicted of parricide, used as an example of how the convicts often speak indifferently about the crimes they committed. It was also mentioned that this man completely refused to confess his guilt to either the authorities or the court. However, due to evidence provided by people who knew the details of his situation, his guilt was considered beyond question. These individuals informed the author of the 'Recollections' that the man had lived a reckless and immoral life, was burdened with debt, and had murdered his father to inherit the family estate. Moreover, the entire town where this man was imprisoned recounted the same story. The editor of these 'Recollections' personally verified these accounts. It was also noted that, even in prison, the man seemed cheerful, carefree, and somewhat thoughtless, despite being intelligent. The author of the 'Recollections' himself stated that he had never noticed any signs of cruelty in the man, adding, 'For this reason, I could never bring myself to fully believe in his guilt.'

"Recently, the editor of the 'Recollections of the House of the Dead' received news from Siberia confirming the man's innocence.

317

After spending ten years in prison performing hard labor, it was revealed that he had been wrongfully convicted. The real perpetrators were discovered, confessed to the crime, and the innocent man was finally released. These facts have been fully verified and come from credible, authoritative sources."

There is no need to elaborate further. The tragic reality of this case speaks for itself. Words feel powerless in the face of such a devastating mistake, where an innocent life was shattered by false accusations. These kinds of errors are among the most terrifying possibilities of life, and they bring an even deeper and more poignant meaning to the 'Recollections of the House of the Dead,' reminding us that a prison can hold both the guilty and the innocent.

To continue, I have mentioned that I eventually became somewhat used to life as a convict, though I would not say I ever truly accepted it. It was a long and agonizing journey to reach this point. It took nearly a year before I could adapt to prison life, and I will always consider that first year the most dreadful of my entire existence. Every detail of it is etched deeply in my memory. I believe I could recount each event and emotion from that year, hour by hour, as if it had just happened.

I have mentioned that, like me, the other prisoners also struggled to adapt to the life they were forced to lead. Throughout that first dreadful year, I repeatedly asked myself whether they truly felt as calm as they appeared on the surface. These questions constantly pressed on my mind. As I have noted before, every convict seemed trapped in an environment that was entirely alien to them, a place they could never truly accept or call home. It felt as though they were stuck in some cursed inn, an unwelcome stop on a never-ending journey. For these men, who were exiles from life itself, there was a constant undercurrent of agitation, smoldering just beneath the surface, or a deep and impenetrable sadness. Yet despite this, each of them still clung to certain ideas or aspirations, though they seemed more like fragile embers of hope than fully formed thoughts.

This restless energy, which rarely broke the surface but was always palpable, combined with the faint and often irrational hopes they couldn't entirely suppress, created a unique and oppressive atmosphere. These hopes, so faint and implausible that they bordered on madness, gave the prison its strange, haunting character. It was a place like no other, a world where everyone wandered through their days as though caught in a waking dream. There was no escape from the overwhelming impressions the place made on every man who lived there. It created a kind of heightened sensitivity, a neurosis that affected everyone. These dreams of freedom, impossible as they were, cast a dark shadow over the prisoners, leaving most of them brooding and irritable. For many, the word "morbid" would hardly suffice to describe their state of mind.

The majority of the convicts were silent and quick to anger. They kept their innermost thoughts and futile hopes buried deep within themselves, unwilling to share or admit them. Any sign of openness or candor was treated with contempt. Because these hopes were so hopeless, so obviously unattainable, the prisoners seemed ashamed of them, even to themselves. They guarded these private fantasies as if they were precious secrets, while at the same time lacking the strength to abandon them. Perhaps they felt embarrassed by their own imaginations. Who can say for certain? The Russian character, after all, tends to be pragmatic and ruthlessly self-critical in normal circumstances, and this quality was not lost even in the bleakness of prison life.

This inner dissatisfaction, this gnawing discontent with themselves, likely fueled the impatience and hostility the convicts directed toward one another. Their sharp tongues and cruel words seemed born out of their own misery. If one of them, more naive or open-hearted than the rest, dared to voice the same dreams and schemes that every one of them secretly harbored—be it visions of freedom or elaborate escape plans—they would immediately silence him with brutal efficiency.

Their sarcasm and relentless mockery could make life unbearable for the poor soul who had spoken too freely. Ironically, those who were most vicious in shutting others down were often the ones who indulged in the most extravagant fantasies in their own minds.

I have already mentioned that simplicity and candor were considered traits of fools in this strange world. The convicts viewed anyone who exhibited these qualities with scorn, as if they were dim-witted or naive. The bitterness and hypersensitivity that consumed the prisoners made them resent any display of kindness or selflessness. These traits were viewed almost as weaknesses, deserving of ridicule. Broadly speaking, I would divide the prisoners into two groups: those who were inherently good and those who were bad. Within these groups, you could further distinguish the morose from the cheerful, with a separate category for the ingenious fellows who couldn't seem to keep their mouths shut.

The majority of the prisoners were sour-tempered. Some of these were quite talkative, but their chatter was often filled with gossip and envy. They loved to meddle in others' affairs while guarding their own inner thoughts jealously. Sharing their true feelings or aspirations would have been unthinkable—it simply wasn't done in this strange little society. The truly good men, though few in number, were quiet and gentle. They kept their hopes—if they had any—to themselves, and their faith in those hopes seemed stronger and more genuine than that of their gloomier peers.

There was one additional group worth mentioning: those who had completely lost all hope. These were the prisoners who had given up on life entirely, like the old man from Starodoub. They were the ones who had reached the depths of despair, though they were very few.

The old man of Starodoub! He was a quiet and subdued figure, always keeping to himself, but there were small signs of the inner turmoil that consumed him. Though he tried to mask it, I could see that his life was filled with an unbearable sense of horror and despair.

Yet, he found solace in two things: prayer and the belief that he was enduring his suffering as a martyr. His faith seemed to sustain him when nothing else could.

Another prisoner who comes to mind was the man always reading the Bible, whom I mentioned earlier. He was the one who eventually went mad and attacked the Major, throwing a brick at him. This man likely belonged to the same group as the old man of Starodoub—those who had utterly lost all hope. Hope is essential to life, and when it disappears entirely, the emptiness it leaves behind can drive a person to extreme acts. This man claimed that he attacked the Major not out of any personal grievance but simply because he wanted to suffer—to have torment inflicted upon himself. It was as if his misery had become so overwhelming that he sought punishment as a form of release.

What could have been happening in his mind to lead him to such a point? No one can live without some kind of purpose, without striving toward something. When there is no purpose, no hope to cling to, the resulting anguish can transform a person into something unrecognizable. For most of us in the prison, the ultimate goal was freedom—escaping the confines of hard labor and confinement. This longing for liberty, even when it seemed impossible, kept many of us going.

I have tried to classify and categorize the convicts in various ways, but reality resists such neat divisions. Life, in all its complexity, defies rigid definitions and abstract thought. It splinters into infinite subtleties and nuances that cannot be captured by clear-cut classifications. Each convict had his own deeply personal and private inner world, a life that existed beyond the reach of regulations or official supervision. No two of us were alike, even though we were bound by the same chains.

In the early days of my imprisonment, I couldn't fully grasp this inner world. Everything around me was so overwhelmingly bleak that it drowned out my ability to see beyond the surface. The sights and sounds of the prison filled me with a sadness I cannot adequately describe. Sometimes, in my moments of deepest despair, I even felt a kind of hatred for my fellow prisoners. I envied them because I believed they belonged to each other in a way I did not—that they shared an understanding, a commonality, that I lacked. But this belief was an illusion. In truth, their forced companionship, dictated by commands and reinforced with whips and rods, was as detestable to them as it was to me. Each man, in his own way, sought solitude, trying to shield himself from the misery of others.

This irrational envy I felt toward them, this occasional hatred, was not entirely without reason. It stemmed from the deeper complexities of human suffering. There are those who claim that a nobleman or a man of education does not suffer more than a simple peasant in the same conditions. I have often heard and read this assertion, and while it may seem logical in theory, reality tells a different story. Such a notion is rooted in noble sentiment—after all, we are all human and suffer as humans—but the lived experience is far more intricate.

I do not wish to argue definitively that those of higher education or culture feel pain more deeply or acutely than others. However, it is equally wrong to assume that all souls can be measured by the same standard. Neither one's level of education nor any other factor can serve as a universal measure for suffering or punishment. The reality of pain and endurance is far too complex to be reduced to a single principle. Only experience, lived and felt, can truly shed light on the profound differences in how people endure hardship.

It brings me great comfort to say that, even amidst such appalling suffering and in conditions so degraded and cruel, I found undeniable evidence that the potential for moral growth and humanity was still present. In our convict establishment, there were men I had known for several years, men whom I had come to see as little more than wild beasts, and whom I despised as such. Yet, out of nowhere, and often when I least expected it, these same men would reveal a depth of feeling and a capacity for empathy so profound that it was astonishing.

They would show an acute awareness of the pain of others, seen through the lens of their own experiences of suffering, and this sudden transformation felt as though scales had fallen from their eyes. The abruptness of these moments could be almost stupefying, leaving one in disbelief.

At the same time, the reverse could also occur. Educated men, brought up in refined circumstances, sometimes displayed a level of savage, cynical cruelty that was so shocking, so disgusting, that it was almost impossible to excuse, no matter how much one might try to be charitable. This juxtaposition was one of the great paradoxes of life in the prison, constantly challenging any preconceptions about human nature.

I do not wish to dwell too much on the complete upheaval of material circumstances, such as the change in food or living conditions, though these are no small matters. A peasant or laborer might adapt more readily, accustomed as they often are to going hungry or enduring hardships in their daily lives. By comparison, such men found the steady, if meager, rations in the prison almost comforting. For a person of the higher classes, however, the transition was far more jarring. Even for those with great inner strength, the adjustment to these external degradations was no trivial thing. But the physical discomforts—the filth, the unclean and insufficient food, the weight of the irons, and the oppressive confinement—were minor compared to a deeper, more haunting kind of suffering.

The greatest torment of all was not the physical conditions but the profound isolation and alienation felt by certain prisoners, particularly those of noble birth. A peasant or working-class prisoner, no matter how new or unfamiliar with prison life, would quickly find their place among the others. Within a matter of hours, they would be treated as equals, fully integrated into this grim society of convicts. They shared a common language, a shared culture of suffering, and a sense of mutual understanding that bound them together. They became one with this strange city of the enslaved, where each man mirrored the other in outward appearance and habits. They understood one another without needing to explain themselves, and this mutual recognition was immediate.

For a nobleman, however, the experience was entirely different. No matter how just, fair, or intelligent he might be, he was despised and distrusted by the others from the moment he entered the prison. Their hatred and scorn would persist for years, long before he could hope for even a modicum of respect or understanding. To them, he was neither a comrade nor a friend. At best, he might eventually succeed in preventing outright insults, but even that was no guarantee. He was forever an outsider, an alien presence in their tightly knit world, and no amount of effort could bridge the chasm that separated him from the rest.

This isolation was not always due to deliberate malice or ill-will on the part of the other prisoners. Often, it was simply an inevitable result of the nobleman's presence in a world where he did not belong. He was not part of the gang, and that alone was enough to keep him apart. The burden of this endless, unrelenting solitude, this inability to find even a single point of connection with others, was a grief unlike any other. It was a constant reminder that he did not and could never fully belong in this harsh and unforgiving environment.

There is nothing more dreadful than being removed from the social environment to which you naturally belong. A peasant, relocated from Taganrog to Petropavlosk, will easily find other Russian peasants like himself, and between them, mutual understanding will quickly arise. In no time, they will forge a bond, share an izba or a barrack, and live together with ease. For the nobleman, however, the situation is entirely different. An insurmountable chasm separates him from the lower classes, a chasm that becomes most painfully evident when he loses his privileged status and is thrust into the life of the common people.

Even if you spend decades in close contact with the peasant, sharing daily interactions over forty years—perhaps through your work, administrative duties, or acts of charity—you will never truly understand what lies at the core of his thoughts or feelings. You might think you know him, but it is nothing more than an illusion, a mirage that disappears under scrutiny. Many may accuse me of overstating the case, but I am utterly convinced of its truth. My perspective does not come from theoretical speculation or bookish notions; it is grounded in lived experience. Life itself, through long and often painful lessons, has given me ample time to refine and solidify my understanding of this reality. Perhaps one day, everyone will recognize the validity of what I now assert so confidently.

When I first arrived at the convict establishment, these thoughts were merely theoretical, formed in the abstract. However, the events I witnessed and the realities I faced soon turned them into unshakable convictions. These experiences weighed so heavily on me that they affected my physical health as well as my mental state. During the first summer, I wandered through the prison, as much as my restricted movement allowed, feeling completely alone and cut off from everyone around me. My solitude was profound. I was so consumed by my own situation that I failed to recognize the few among the convicts who, over time, would come to show me some measure of care, even though the distance between us could never truly be bridged. There were other former nobles like myself in the prison, but their company offered no solace; instead, I found their presence repugnant.

One particular incident from that period vividly illustrates the depth of my isolation and the strangeness of my position in the convict establishment. It was a warm day in August, around one o'clock in the afternoon—a time when most of the convicts typically took a nap before resuming their work. Suddenly, and without warning, the prisoners rose as one and gathered en masse in the courtyard. Until that moment, I had been utterly unaware that anything unusual was happening. I was so preoccupied with my own thoughts and internal struggles that I paid little attention to the life unfolding around me.

What I later learned was that the convicts had been simmering with agitation for three days, possibly even longer. Looking back, I recalled overhearing fragments of conversations, stray remarks, and noticing a marked increase in tension and irritability among the men. At the time, I dismissed these signs, attributing them to the exhausting summer labor, the seemingly endless days under the blazing sun, and the longing for freedom and the forests, which the season inevitably stirred in them. The nights, too short for proper rest, compounded their frustration. In hindsight, it became clear that all these factors had coalesced into a growing discontent, waiting only for a catalyst to erupt. That catalyst turned out to be the food.

For several days, the convicts had been openly complaining about the food, voicing their dissatisfaction loudly in the barracks and making it clear during meals. One of the cooks had been replaced, but after just a couple of days, the new one was dismissed, and the previous cook was reinstated. Despite this, the mood remained tense, and it was evident that trouble was brewing among them.

"We're working ourselves to death, and all they give us is garbage to eat," one man grumbled in the kitchen, his frustration spilling over.

"If you don't like it, maybe you should order jellies and fancy desserts," another replied mockingly, drawing a few chuckles from the crowd.

"Sour cabbage soup? Now that's a real treat," chimed in a third with heavy sarcasm. "I could eat it all day—it's so... juicy."

"But what if they gave us beef, just beef, every day?" someone else interjected. "Would that satisfy you?"

"Yes, of course," said a fourth. "At least then we'd have some real food. We're practically worked to death in the workshops, and by the time we're done, we're starving. What they give us doesn't even begin to fill the hunger."

"That's the truth," another voice agreed bitterly. "The food's a disgrace—plain and simple."

"And don't think for a second that someone isn't pocketing the money meant for us!" growled one man, his voice dripping with suspicion.

"Who cares? It's not your problem," shot back another dismissively.

"Not my problem? My stomach is my business! If we all stood up together and raised hell, you'd see things change real quick."

"Sure," muttered another, "and haven't we been beaten enough already for complaining, you fool?"

"He's right," said someone else. "Nothing good ever comes from rushing into things without a plan. So, how exactly do you suggest we 'raise hell'? Tell us that."

"I'll tell you," said a bold voice, full of determination. "If everyone's in, I'm in too. I've had enough of starving. Sure, it's easy for those who get better food, eating separately from the rest of us, to stay quiet. But for those of us stuck with this slop—well, we've got nothing to lose."

"That one over there," said another, pointing with a nod, "he's got eyes that never miss a chance. You can see the envy shining in them every time he spots something better than what he's got."

"Well, what are we waiting for, pals?" someone else called out, their voice brimming with agitation. "Have we suffered enough yet? They're robbing us blind—those thieves! Let's do something about it."

"And what good would that do?" countered a calmer voice. "We've got no choice but to swallow what they give us and get on with it. What, you want someone else to chew your food for you too? We're in prison, and that means we've got to endure it."

"That's the reality," added another with a resigned tone. "We're in prison, and this is just how it is."

"That's always how it is. The people starve, and the Government gets fat," one prisoner said with a bitter tone.

"That's for sure. Our eight-eyes—the Major—has gotten plenty plump from it. He just bought himself a pair of gray horses."

"And, of course, he doesn't care for his drink, not at all," added another convict sarcastically.

"Just the other day, he was at cards with the vet," chimed in a third. "Two hours he played without a single kopeck in his pocket. Fedka saw the whole thing."

"And that's why we're stuck with cabbage soup that even the pigs wouldn't touch."

"You're all fools!" snapped another. "None of it matters—nothing we do matters."

"Well, I say if we all stand together and lodge a complaint, let's see what he has to say for himself."

"Say for himself? He'll just slam his fist down on you, and that'll be the end of it."

"I'm telling you, they'll have to investigate him and put him on trial."

The prisoners were restless, their frustration mounting with every word. The truth was, the food had become intolerable. The constant hunger, the bitter resentment, and the long days of suffering seemed to be building toward something inevitable. Convicts, by their nature, are quarrelsome and prone to rebellion, but actual uprisings were rare. They could never agree on the details, and often their fiery words fizzled out before they turned into action.

This time, though, the anger didn't simply fade away. Small groups formed in the barracks, whispering, shouting, and debating. They recounted every one of the Major's supposed offenses, dissecting his actions, and discussing their grievances in heated tones.

In such moments, leaders and agitators always emerge. They are a particular kind of person, and not just in prisons. You see them in work camps, among soldiers, and anywhere large groups of people toil together. These leaders have a thirst for justice, a sense of urgency, and a belief in their cause that borders on childlike naivety. They're simple, earnest, and often remarkably strong-willed. Some of them are even highly intelligent, but they lack the restraint to measure their actions wisely.

True leaders—the kind who can guide a group to success and lasting change—are exceedingly rare in Russia. Most of the time, you find only the more impetuous, fiery type of leader. These individuals are passionate and honest in their indignation, which gives them tremendous influence over others. Their zealous drive and blind faith in the righteousness of their cause inspire the more hesitant and skeptical among the group.

The confidence of these leaders often rests on shaky, even childish reasoning. Yet, despite the obvious flaws in their logic, they manage to ignite something in their followers. They believe so fervently in the possibility of success that even the hardest cynics find themselves drawn into their orbit, caught up in their fiery momentum.

These leaders are rarely victorious. Their reckless enthusiasm tends to lead to failure, and in the end, the prisons and work camps only become more crowded. Still, it is this very recklessness—their refusal to stand down—that makes them so compelling to those desperate for change.

The reason these fiery leaders had such influence lay in their boldness. They placed themselves at the forefront of the movement and charged ahead without hesitation. They moved forward recklessly, often with no real understanding of the larger picture or a clear plan.

They lacked the cunning or calculated practicality that allows some shrewd and opportunistic individuals to rise to the top, even when they have little merit or morality. These leaders didn't try to manipulate their way through situations; instead, they crashed headlong into obstacles, no matter how insurmountable they seemed, often dashing their efforts against figurative stone walls. In daily life, they were usually quick-tempered, irritable, and intolerant of others, often carrying themselves with a certain fervor that was simultaneously their strength and their downfall.

Unfortunately, they rarely focused on the core issues at hand. Instead of targeting the root causes of their grievances, they got bogged down in minor details. This lack of focus was their undoing. Yet, they understood the people they led, and the people understood them, which made them a powerful force, albeit one prone to self-destruction.

I need to explain what is meant here by "grievance."

Some of the convicts had been exiled because they were involved in grievances or disputes against the authorities. These individuals tended to be the most passionate and vocal in moments of unrest. One of them was Martinoff, a former Hussar, an impulsive and hot-headed man, but also truthful and well-meaning. Another was Vassili Antonoff, who had a cold and calculated way of expressing his anger. He carried himself with an air of defiance, his sarcastic smile always present, yet he was also a man of integrity and some education. There were many like them, though I won't list them all here.

Petroff was especially notable during this incident. He moved quickly and purposefully from one group of convicts to another, speaking little but clearly carrying the same intensity as the others. He was the first to rush out of the barracks when the gathering in the courtyard began.

Our sergeant, who also served as the acting sergeant-major, soon arrived at the scene, visibly shaken and alarmed. The convicts had formed ranks and addressed him politely but firmly. They requested that he inform the Major they wished to speak with him and ask some questions. Behind the sergeant came the invalids, who quietly took their places opposite the convicts.

The sergeant was terrified. He clearly did not want to deliver their message but saw no choice in the matter. If the convicts chose to rebel, the consequences could be catastrophic. Even if the convicts dispersed peacefully, he was obligated to report the incident to the higher authorities. His fear rendered him incapable of reasoning with the prisoners, and he quickly ran off to the Major without attempting to calm the situation. It was clear to him that the convicts would not tolerate any argument or dismissal of their concerns.

At the time, I had no idea what was happening. Without understanding the situation, I automatically joined the ranks of prisoners, assuming it was time for a roll call. However, I soon noticed that the soldiers who usually verified the lists were not present, which puzzled me. As I looked around, I began to notice the intense emotions on the convicts' faces. Many were pale, their features taut with tension. They stood in a stern silence, seemingly deep in thought, preparing what they would say to the Major when he arrived.

I noticed some of the convicts glancing at me with confusion and curiosity. It was clear they found my presence among them unexpected. Their looks seemed to question my motives, as if they couldn't believe that someone like me, a former nobleman, would join them in their protests. Some quickly averted their eyes, while others turned back to stare at me again, as though unsure of what to make of my involvement.

"What are you doing here?" Vassili Antonoff demanded, his voice loud and rough. He stood a little apart from the others, and his rudeness caught me off guard, as he had always been unfailingly polite to me before.

I looked at him, puzzled, trying to figure out the meaning behind his question. Something unusual was clearly happening in the prison, but I was still in the dark.

"Yes, what are you doing here? Go back to the barracks," said a young soldier-convict I hadn't noticed before. His tone wasn't hostile, just firm, and he seemed like a decent, quiet sort of fellow. "This isn't your concern."

"Aren't we here for roll call?" I asked, confused. "Haven't we fallen into ranks for that?"

"Look at him, he's here, too!" one of them shouted, a sneer in his voice.

"Iron-nose!" another jeered.

"Fly-killer!" added a third, his tone dripping with disdain. This new nickname sparked loud laughter among the group.

"These kinds of fellows have it easy wherever they are," someone else chimed in, with open contempt. "We're stuck here in hard labor, and they live like princes, with their wheat bread and sucking pig. Don't you have your special meals? What are you doing here?"

"This isn't your place," Koulikoff said brusquely, stepping forward. He grabbed my arm and led me out of the ranks. His usually composed demeanor had vanished. His face was pale, his dark eyes flashed with intensity, and his lower lip was bloodied from where he had bitten it. Unlike the others, however, Koulikoff hadn't lost his composure entirely. His calm authority and sharp clarity set him apart.

I often found Koulikoff fascinating during moments like these, when his true character revealed itself—flawed yet compelling. While he sometimes postured, he was also decisive and courageous. I had no doubt he would face death with a certain dramatic dignity. Despite the open hostility around me, Koulikoff remained extraordinarily polite, though his firm tone left no room for argument.

"This is our business, Alexander Petrovitch," he said, his voice steady but resolved. "You have no place here. Go anywhere else and wait until this is done. Your people are in the kitchens. Go join them."

"They're having their fun down there," someone muttered.

I glanced toward the kitchen and saw the Poles standing by the open window, surrounded by other convicts. Unsure of what to do, I started heading in that direction, my retreat punctuated by mocking laughter, whispered insults, and the low, menacing grumbles that served as the prison's version of catcalls and jeers.

"He doesn't like it! Look at him, chu, chu, chu! Catch him!"

Never since my arrival at the prison had I been so openly and cruelly insulted. The moment stung deeply, though I could understand that it was fueled by the heightened tension and agitation gripping everyone. Still, it was a bitter experience.

In the kitchen's ante-room, I ran into T—vski, a young nobleman. Though not particularly well-read, he had a strong, generous character, and the convicts, surprisingly, had a degree of respect for him. He seemed to be an exception to their usual disdain for men of noble birth; in fact, some of them almost liked him. Everything about him—his movements, his demeanor—exuded courage and energy.

"What are you doing, Goriantchikoff?" he called out, his voice urgent but welcoming. "Come over here, quickly!"

"But what is all this about?" I asked, still bewildered.

"They're planning to lodge a formal complaint—don't you realize that?" said T—vski with a sharp undertone. "It's pointless. Do you think anyone will actually listen to convicts? They'll just figure out who the ringleaders are, and if we're suspected of being involved, we'll bear the brunt of it. Remember why we're here, why we were transported in the first place. They'll get off with a whipping, but for us, it'll mean a full-blown trial. The Major hates us, despises us, and would jump at any opportunity to destroy us. He'll shove all the blame onto us to cover his own tracks."

As we reached the kitchen, M—tski added grimly, "The convicts wouldn't hesitate for a moment to tie us up and sell us out. They'd throw us under the cart if it suits them."

"They'll never show us any mercy," T—vski agreed, his tone bitter.

In the kitchen, there were around thirty other prisoners, a mix of those who didn't join the complaint for various reasons. Some were too scared to get involved, others dismissed the whole thing as a futile endeavor. Among them was Akim Akimitch, who stood there with his usual composed indifference. He opposed anything that even remotely disrupted order or routine and waited calmly to see how the situation would play out. He clearly believed the authorities would squash the disturbance without much effort.

Isaiah Fomitch seemed visibly unsettled. His nose drooped, and he listened to our conversation with a blend of fear and morbid curiosity. The tension rattled him deeply. Alongside the Polish nobles stood a few lower-class Poles and some timid Russian convicts, men who lacked the nerve to join the protest and now stood silently, their expressions heavy with apprehension as they waited for the outcome. There were also several grim, discontented prisoners who had chosen not to participate—not out of fear but because they saw the whole ordeal as absurd and doomed to fail. Yet even they looked uneasy, their faces betraying a flicker of guilt, as though they felt like traitors for staying behind while their comrades marched into conflict.

Jolkin, the cunning Siberian peasant known for his sharp mind and knack for getting the better of Koulikoff's town practice, stood there too. Beside him was the old man of Starodoub, his demeanor as somber as ever. The cooks, meanwhile, had not left their posts, likely considering themselves part of the prison's authority structure and unwilling to join in any act of defiance.

"For all that," I murmured to M—tski, "nearly every convict is out there except these few." My words betrayed a hint of doubt, though I tried to suppress it.

"What does that have to do with us?" B—— grumbled irritably. "We would have risked far more than they ever would by joining them. And for what? Je hais ces brigands! I hate those scoundrels. Do you honestly think they have the guts to go through with it? I don't see why they'd bother sticking their heads into the lion's mouth like this. Fools."

"It's doomed to fail," muttered an old, sour-tempered convict with characteristic stubbornness. Almazoff, who stood near us, nodded in agreement.

"A good fifty of them will get a thrashing, and that'll be the end of it," someone else remarked with a grim chuckle.

"Look out! The Major!" cried a voice suddenly, and in an instant, everyone rushed to the windows.

The Major arrived in full fury, his face as red as a turkey's comb and his temper even fiercer. His greasy cap with its yellow trim sat crooked on his head, and his tarnished silver epaulettes only added to the wicked, almost devilish image he projected in my imagination, which was already heightened by the tension of the moment. His eyes blazed with anger, and his steps were quick and deliberate as he marched straight up to the line of convicts. Whatever else could be said about him, the Major did have an unusual amount of courage and composure during such incidents, though it was no secret that he was usually half-drunk. Behind him trailed the quartermaster, Diatloff, a clever and manipulative figure who had his hands in nearly everything that went on in the prison. Diatloff wielded considerable influence over the Major and was known for his shrewdness. Despite his involvement in many of the prison's harsher policies, he wasn't entirely disliked by the convicts, who generally regarded him with a mix of caution and begrudging acceptance. Following close behind was the sergeant, accompanied by only three or four soldiers. The sergeant had already received a severe dressing-down and likely anticipated more punishment if things escalated.

The convicts, standing in line with their caps off, shifted uneasily from one leg to the other before freezing into stillness. They waited for the storm they knew was coming, their eyes fixed straight ahead, bracing for the Major's first words—or more accurately, his first shouts.

It didn't take long. The Major erupted into a tirade almost immediately, his voice booming with fury. From the windows, we could see him pacing along the line, shouting and gesticulating wildly, stopping every now and then to unleash a torrent of questions at individual convicts. Though we couldn't hear most of the exchanges from where we stood, his shouts carried through the air—a chaotic blend of yelling, growling, and grunting that was as intimidating as it was incomprehensible.

"Scoundrels! Mutineers! You'll feel the cat, every last one of you! Whips and sticks, that's what you deserve!" he roared, jabbing a finger at one of the men. "You—yes, you! You're one of the ringleaders!"

The convict in question stepped out of the line and headed silently toward the guardhouse. Another man followed him, and then a third. It was clear that the Major was intent on rooting out whoever he thought was behind the unrest.

"I'll have every single one of you dragged before the Committee! You'll see what happens then!" he bellowed. Then, spotting us at the kitchen windows, he turned his rage in our direction. "And who's in the kitchen over there? Get them out! All of them, every last one!"

Diatloff strode toward the kitchens, where we were gathered, his expression a mix of frustration and disdain. When we assured him that we had no part in the complaints, he nodded curtly and returned to the Major to relay the message.

"They're not involved," Diatloff said, lowering his voice slightly.

The Major's tone softened a little, but his anger was far from gone.

"Fine, but bring them here anyway!" the Major snapped.

Reluctantly, we stepped out of the kitchen and joined the others. Humiliation washed over me as we walked, heads bowed, under the watchful eyes of the guards and convicts alike. The tension in the air was palpable, and every step felt like a mile.

"Ah, Prokofief! And Jolkin! Almazof, you too! Get over here, all of you!" the Major barked, gasping for breath as he pointed at us. His tone had shifted slightly, almost as though he were trying to sound accommodating. "M—tski, you're here as well? Good, good. Diatloff, write down all their names! Make two lists—one for the grumblers and one for those who aren't complaining. Every name, without exception. I want the lists handed to me personally. We'll see about all this when the Committee gets involved... Brigands!"

That word—"list"—hung heavily in the air, sending a ripple of unease through everyone present. It was clear that this would not end well for anyone involved.

"We have nothing to complain about!" shouted one of the convicts in a voice that seemed to choke with fear and defiance.

"Oh, nothing to complain about, is it?" bellowed the Major, his eyes darting across the ranks. "Who said that? Let anyone who has nothing to complain about step forward. Out of the ranks, I said!"

A few voices echoed hesitantly, "All of us, all of us!"

"Oh, the food is fine then, is it? You've been set up to this— ringleaders, mutineers! You'll see what that gets you," he sneered, his voice dripping with sarcasm.

"But what do you mean by that?" came a bold, yet nervous voice from somewhere in the crowd.

"Who said that?!" the Major roared, charging toward the sound like

337

a bull scenting its target. "Rastorgouïef! You—you're the one! Off to the guard-house with you!"

Rastorgouïef, a towering young man with a round, ruddy face, stepped out reluctantly. He hadn't spoken a word, but once accused, he didn't dare protest. He walked slowly, his steps heavy, toward the guardhouse.

"You're all too well-fed, that's the problem!" the Major yelled after him. "Fat makes you unruly! Just wait, you great oaf—you'll see what I have in store for you!"

Turning back to the line, he barked, "I said, let all who have no complaints come out of the ranks!"

Some convicts muttered, "We've nothing to complain about, Your Excellency," their voices low and sullen. Most of the others stayed silent, their expressions unreadable, their eyes fixed ahead. The Major seized on their compliance.

"Ah, now I see it," he said, his tone shifting to one of forced satisfaction. "Nobody has any complaints. Just as I thought! This is all the work of ringleaders, troublemakers. We'll root them out, every last one of them," he added, speaking pointedly to Diatloff. "Drummer! Drummer, a roll!"

He began breaking the men into work detachments himself, impatient and sharp with his orders. The convicts shuffled away reluctantly, their heads low, relieved to escape his presence but burdened by the tension hanging thick in the air. The groups dispersed with little of the usual chatter, subdued by the events.

Once the work crews left, the Major made his way to the guardhouse, clearly intent on dealing with the so-called ringleaders. Yet, despite his fiery threats, he didn't pursue the matter with much vigor. It became apparent that he wanted to put the incident behind him quickly. One of the accused men later shared that he had pleaded for forgiveness, and the Major had let him go without further punishment.

It seemed the Major had been shaken. Mutiny, or anything resembling it, was always a risky business, and even though this incident wasn't a full-blown rebellion, the mere fact that the prisoners had shown unity was enough to rattle him. The Governor had been informed of the unrest, and the Major likely feared repercussions from higher up. His main priority now was to defuse the situation and restore order.

The ringleaders were released soon after, and the next day, the food improved noticeably. However, the improvement didn't last long; within days, things returned to the usual poor standard. The Major began patrolling the prison more frequently, scrutinizing every detail and doling out punishments for the slightest infractions. His anger seemed to linger, but his fear of another outbreak kept him cautious.

The sergeant, on the other hand, appeared bewildered by the entire ordeal. He moved about the prison in a dazed state, as if still processing the upheaval and its implications. The convicts, too, took some time to settle. Their agitation didn't fade overnight, but its nature shifted.

Some walked with their heads down, silent and brooding, lost in thought. Others grumbled about the events, their voices tinged with frustration and helplessness. Many began criticizing their own actions, speaking bitterly of their failed effort, as though they had lost faith in themselves.

The prison returned to its monotonous rhythm, but an uneasy tension lingered in the air, a reminder of how fragile and combustible the atmosphere could be.

"I say, pal, take and eat!" someone shouted, holding out a piece of bread with a mocking grin.

"Where's the brave soul who was so ready to bell the cat?" sneered another, his voice dripping with sarcasm.

"We should just thank our stars he didn't have us all flogged," added a third, his tone more resigned than angry.

"It'd be better if you thought a bit more and talked a lot less," came a gruff retort from the corner.

"What are you, a schoolmaster now? Who made you boss around here?" snapped another convict, his tone sharp and defensive.

"You need putting in your place," replied the first, glaring.

"Who are you to talk down to me?" came the indignant response.

"I'm a man! What are you?" he shot back defiantly.

"A man? You're—"

"You're—"

"Enough already!" someone yelled. "Shut up, will you? What's the point of all this noise?"

The conversation dissolved into grumbles and muttered insults, but the tension lingered like smoke in the air. The mood in the barracks that evening was heavy, with tempers still simmering from the day's failed mutiny. Conversations came and went, rising to bursts of anger and quickly dying out as exhaustion set in.

Later that evening, after the day's work had ended and the convicts had dispersed, I encountered Petroff behind the barracks. He seemed to have been looking for me, though he approached in an absent-minded, almost mechanical way. His lips moved as if he were muttering something under his breath, but his words were inaudible. As he drew nearer, he fell silent and walked alongside me without a word.

"Petroff," I ventured after a few moments, "your fellows aren't angry with us, are they?"

"Who's angry?" he asked, startled from his thoughts and blinking at me as if he'd forgotten I was there.

"The convicts—are they upset with us nobles for not supporting them?" I clarified, carefully gauging his reaction.

"Why would they be angry with you?" he replied, his voice flat, as though the thought had never occurred to him.

"Well, because we didn't stand with them," I said, hesitating. "We're all in this together, after all."

"Why would you have gotten involved?" Petroff said after a pause, his tone oddly detached, as though he were trying to process the idea. "You nobles have your own table."

"Yes, but there are some among you—those who aren't nobles—who don't eat the regulation food either," I pointed out. "They stood with you. We should have stood with you too. We're in the same place; we should act like comrades."

Petroff stopped walking and turned to face me, his brow furrowed with genuine confusion. "Comrades?" he repeated, as though the word were foreign to him. "You think you're our comrades?"

The question hung between us, heavy and unspoken, until the silence stretched so long that neither of us knew how to break it. Petroff stared at me, his expression a mix of disbelief and something else—something like pity. Then, without another word, he turned and walked away, leaving me alone to ponder what exactly I had hoped to hear.

I looked at him, trying to understand his perspective, but it was painfully clear he had no grasp of what I meant. Meanwhile, I understood his meaning all too well—deeply and with a clarity I wished I could avoid. What had previously been an unsettling, vague suspicion now became a harsh, undeniable truth.

In that moment, it became clear that any meaningful connection, any sense of true camaraderie between the convicts and myself, was impossible. Even if I spent the rest of my life in this place, there would always be an unbridgeable chasm separating us. I was marked as a convict of the "special section," a designation that forever set me apart, making me an outsider no matter how much time passed or how much effort I made.

Petroff's response lingered vividly in my mind: "Comrades? How can that be?" The expression on his face, a mix of innocent surprise and genuine bewilderment, seemed burned into my memory. There was nothing hostile in his tone, no hint of irony or malice, but rather a plain and unvarnished honesty that stung far worse. Still, I couldn't help but wonder for a fleeting moment if there was some hidden derision in his words, some subtle mockery that I had missed. Yet, no—it was completely sincere. His reaction carried no hidden layers. I was not one of them, and I never would be. That simple truth was carved in stone. To them, it was as if to say: "You walk your path, we walk ours. Your world is yours, and ours is ours."

I couldn't shake the thought that, in the wake of the failed mutiny, the convicts might turn on us with all the anger and frustration they could muster, making our lives unbearable. I half-expected taunts, insults, and outright hostility, believing they would blame us for our neutrality or for not supporting their cause. But to my surprise, nothing of the sort happened. There were no harsh words, no biting remarks, no confrontations about what had taken place.

Instead, they treated us exactly as they always had. The occasional teasing continued, as opportunistic and thoughtless as ever, but it carried no extra venom or malice. There wasn't a single reproach directed at us, not even a passing comment laced with resentment. Even those who had been the first to loudly declare that they had "nothing to complain about" were left in peace. Everything about that day's events was simply ignored, as though it had never happened.

I was astonished by this unexpected turn of events. Their silence on the matter puzzled me deeply, but it also brought a strange kind of relief. It was as though they had chosen, collectively and wordlessly, to let the episode fade into oblivion, refusing to let it sow division or disrupt the fragile balance of our shared, grim existence.

Chapter 8
My Companions

As one might expect, in those early days, I felt most drawn to people of my own background—those of "noble" birth. Yet, even among them, I found little solace or companionship. Of the three ex-nobles who were Russians in the prison, I interacted with only one, Akim Akimitch. The others were a notorious spy named A—v and the man believed to be guilty of parricide. Even with Akim, my conversations were rare and limited to moments of extreme desolation—times when my melancholy became so suffocating that I thought I might never connect with another human being again.

In the preceding chapter, I attempted to sort the convicts into distinct categories based on their personalities and behaviors. However, when I think about Akim Akimitch, I find it nearly impossible to place him within any classification. He was entirely unique—a man so unlike anyone else in the prison that he seemed to occupy a category all his own.

Perhaps in other places, there are individuals like Akim, men for whom it seems to make no difference whether they are free or confined in a prison, condemned to hard labor. But in our establishment, he stood alone in this extraordinary detachment. It was as though he had resigned himself entirely to his circumstances without the slightest resistance, accepting the penal colony as his permanent station in life. He settled into the prison as if it were his natural habitat, arranging his few belongings—a mattress, some cushions, and basic utensils—with such order and care that it seemed he had taken up residence in a modestly furnished home of his own. There was nothing makeshift or transient about him—no sense of someone enduring temporary hardships. Everything about him, from his possessions to his habits and demeanor, radiated an air of permanence.

Though he had many years of punishment still ahead of him, I doubted he ever spent a moment reflecting on the future or imagining the day he might be released. His acceptance of his fate was so complete that it seemed less a result of deliberate effort and more an innate quality of his submissive nature. Whether he consciously reconciled himself to his condition or simply lacked the imagination to yearn for something else, the effect was the same—he appeared entirely at ease with his lot.

Akim was not, by any means, a bad man. In fact, during my early days in the prison, he often gave me advice and assistance that proved invaluable. His calm demeanor and practical approach to life in confinement were a stabilizing presence for me when everything around felt unbearable. Yet, at times, I must admit, his peculiarities weighed on me heavily. They heightened my own despair, amplifying the deep, unrelenting melancholy that already pressed down on me.

His indifference to his circumstances, while admirable in its own way, sometimes filled me with an almost physical sense of anguish. Watching someone exist so resignedly, without hope or protest, made me question my own ability to endure. It was as though his acceptance of prison life mirrored my worst fears—that this place, with all its misery and dehumanization, might one day feel "normal" to me as well. And that thought was nearly too much to bear.

When the solitude and silence became unbearable and my soul felt trapped in a cage, I often found myself seeking out Akim Akimitch for conversation. It wasn't because I found his company particularly comforting or engaging, but because I desperately needed to hear the voice of another human being. I yearned for words—any words—that would break the oppressive stillness. I longed for someone to echo the bitterness and despair I felt, to give voice to the gall and hatred that consumed me. Yet, when I turned to him, the response I received was always the same: calm, measured, and devoid of passion. He would sit there quietly, busying himself with the meticulous task of sizing lanterns, and then, in his monotonous, unruffled way, he would launch into some tedious anecdote about a review of troops he had attended in 18—.

He would recount details about the division's general, describe the maneuvers as "very pretty," and explain changes in the skirmisher's system of signaling—all with the detached precision of someone discussing the weather. His voice never rose, never faltered. It was like water dripping steadily, drop by drop, into an unchanging pool. Even when he spoke of having participated in a fierce battle in the Caucasus—a skirmish that had earned him the Riband of St. Anne—his tone barely shifted. The only sign of any feeling was a slight change in his voice, which grew a touch slower and more solemn as he mentioned "St. Anne." It was as though he was revealing some sacred mystery, though the reverence quickly passed, and he would lapse into silence for several minutes, his expression serene, his manner unaltered.

In that first year, I experienced moments of intense and irrational hatred toward Akim Akimitch. These feelings would well up suddenly, like a storm breaking within me. I detested him with a vehemence I could not explain. I cursed my misfortune that had placed him so close to me—his camp bed was beside mine, so near that our heads nearly touched when we lay down at night. It was as though his very presence, his placid demeanor, and his indifferent outlook amplified my misery. In those dark moments, I would rage against the cruelty of fate that had paired me with such a man, whose impenetrable calm seemed to mock my inner turmoil.

But just as quickly as the hatred came, it would subside, leaving me filled with guilt and self-reproach. An hour later, I would find myself ashamed of my outbursts and would scold myself for my unkind thoughts. How could I direct such loathing at Akim Akimitch, who had never wronged me in any way? He was, in his own peculiar way, kind and harmless. Yet his unfaltering steadiness, his complete lack of emotion, was at odds with everything I needed in those moments. I wanted fire, passion, anger—anything but the cold, unyielding neutrality he exuded.

As time passed, however, my feelings toward him began to change. Gradually, I adapted to his peculiar nature, and the intensity of my earlier reactions faded. I came to see him for what he was: a man shaped by his own experiences, with a temperament vastly different from mine. The bitterness and frustration I had once felt gave way to acceptance, even a grudging respect. By the second year of my confinement, I could no longer summon the same violent emotions that had once overwhelmed me when I thought of him.

Looking back now, I cannot recall a single instance where Akim Akimitch and I ever had a serious argument or quarrel. He was too mild and even-tempered for that, and over time, I learned to leave my grievances unspoken. Perhaps it was his unwavering calm that eventually helped to steady my own emotions, or perhaps I simply grew weary of battling against someone so immovable. Whatever the reason, the animosity I once felt toward him became little more than a distant memory, replaced by a quiet, if reluctant, sense of coexistence.

In addition to the three Russian nobles I previously mentioned, there were eight other nobles confined during my time in the prison. Among these, I developed a close friendship with a few, though even the best of them were difficult to deal with—often morbid, highly exclusive, and intolerant to an extreme. With two of them, I eventually had to sever all communication entirely. Of the group, only three had received a proper education: B—ski, M—tski, and the elderly J—ski, who had once been a professor of mathematics. The professor was a kind-hearted individual but highly eccentric and, despite his intellectual achievements, surprisingly narrow-minded.

M—tski and B—ski were vastly different from J—ski in both demeanor and character. From the very beginning, M—tski and I

346

established a strong mutual understanding. We never quarreled or disagreed openly, and I held him in great respect. Yet, despite my best efforts, I could never feel a deep or genuine affection for him. He had a reserved and mistrustful nature, tightly controlling his emotions, which created a barrier I could not cross. His soul seemed firmly closed off to others, a quality he made no effort to disguise. Perhaps I was mistaken, but I felt this so intensely that it hindered my ability to truly connect with him. Nevertheless, I must admit that his character was marked by undeniable nobility and inner strength.

M—tski's profound skepticism governed his interactions with those around him. He exhibited exceptional tact and skill in navigating social relations, demonstrating an impressive ability to manage his affairs prudently. Despite this skepticism, he was capable of unwavering belief and hope in certain areas, though these convictions were known only to himself. For all his social acumen, his relationships were far from harmonious—particularly with B—ski and B—ski's close friend, T—ski.

B—ski, in contrast, was an entirely different type of person. Physically frail and suffering from a consumptive disposition, he had an irritable temperament and an extremely delicate nervous system. Despite this, he was at heart a kind and generous man. His emotional volatility often resembled the whims of a child—erratic and exhausting to those around him. I found this aspect of his personality particularly challenging, and while I liked him deeply, I quickly realized I needed to maintain some distance from him for my own peace of mind.

My distancing from B—ski also caused a gradual estrangement from T—ski, whom I genuinely admired. Though T—ski lacked formal education, he was a man of great warmth and spiritual depth. His loyalty to and admiration for B—ski were profound, and anyone who distanced themselves from his friend was, in his eyes, an enemy. This unwavering devotion led to frequent disputes between him and M—tski, especially when it came to defending B—ski. Their animosity persisted for quite some time.

All of these men shared certain traits: they were irritable, mistrustful, and highly sensitive—both emotionally and physically. Their hypersensitivity was understandable given the extraordinary pressures they endured. Their sentences were harsh, often lasting ten or twelve years, and the conditions of their exile were particularly grueling. What intensified their suffering most, however, was their ingrained attitude toward the other convicts. They viewed these men as less than human, as wild beasts incapable of possessing even the most basic qualities of humanity. This prejudice ran deep, rooted not only in their upbringing and social class but also in their circumstances, which constantly reinforced these unfortunate perceptions. It was this inability to see the convicts as anything other than subhuman that left them isolated and perpetually at odds with their environment, making their imprisonment all the more unbearable.

Their life in the jail was an unending torment. While they were courteous and engaging in conversation with the Circassians, Tartars, and even Isaiah Fomitch, they could not extend the same to the other convicts. For the majority of prisoners, they harbored only disdain and aversion. The one exception to their blanket contempt was the aged "Old Believer," for whom they held genuine respect. Despite their exclusivity, I never once witnessed a convict reproach them for their noble birth, religious beliefs, or political convictions. This restraint surprised me, as it is typical for the Russian lower classes to ridicule or criticize those of differing backgrounds, particularly foreigners, whom they often regard with a blend of curiosity and amusement, as though they were figures of satire. However, in this unique environment, the convicts displayed more regard for the Polish nobles than they did for us Russians—a distinction that I doubt the Poles even noticed or cared about.

I mentioned T—ski earlier and must expand on his story. When T—ski and his close friend B—ski were forced to leave their initial place of exile and move to our fortress, T—ski carried his friend for much of the journey. B—ski, frail and in poor health, became utterly exhausted before even half of the first march was complete. Previously, they had been assigned to Y—gorsk, where their conditions were significantly better, and life was far less grueling than in our fortress. However, due to an exchange of seemingly innocuous letters with exiles in another location, the authorities decided to transfer them to our jail, placing them under stricter surveillance. Before their arrival, M—tski had endured his exile alone. Reflecting on the isolation and hardships he must have faced during that first year fills me with deep sympathy.

J—ski, the elder who devoted himself to constant prayer, was another of the Polish nobles. Unlike the others, who were young men, J—ski was well past fifty. He was a dignified and courteous man, though undeniably eccentric. Unfortunately, he was not well-liked by the others. Both T—ski and B—ski openly detested him, refusing even to speak to him. They claimed that he was insufferably obstinate and difficult to deal with—a point I found myself reluctantly agreeing with. Life in a convict establishment—or any place where people are forced into close and continuous proximity—seems to magnify tensions and breed animosities that might not arise elsewhere. The constant disagreements and disputes were exhausting, and J—ski's narrow-mindedness and peculiarities often made him the source of contention.

Although he and I never had a serious falling-out, we also never formed a close bond. Still, I could see that he possessed a sharp intellect. He once explained to me, in a blend of Russian and Polish, an elaborate astronomical theory of his own design. I later learned that he had written a scholarly work on the subject, which was reportedly met with scorn by the academic community. It seemed that his reasoning had taken some eccentric turns over the years.

One of his most striking habits was his devotion to prayer. He would spend entire days kneeling, immersed in his devotions. This unwavering piety earned him considerable respect from the other convicts, even if they found his personality difficult. Sadly, his health deteriorated during his time in the jail, and I witnessed his slow and painful demise. Despite his quirks and the general disdain he inspired, his steadfast spirituality left an impression on everyone.

J—ski's arrival at the prison was marked by an incident that earned him immediate recognition among the convicts. When he and the others were marched from Y—gorsk to our fortress, they were not allowed to shave during the journey. By the time they arrived, their hair and beards had grown long and unruly. This breach of discipline infuriated the Major, who erupted in a fit of rage when he saw them. Although the men themselves were not at fault, the Major's reaction underscored his obsession with enforcing order at all costs. This encounter with authority set the tone for J—ski's time in the prison and cemented his reputation among the other convicts.

"My God! Have you ever seen anything like it?" roared the Major, his voice seething with indignation. "They're nothing but vagabonds and brigands!"

J—ski, who had only a rudimentary grasp of Russian, misunderstood the Major's tirade. Believing the officer was genuinely asking if they were brigands or vagabonds, he replied calmly, "We are political prisoners, not rogues or vagabonds."

"So, you dare to answer back! Insolence! Clod!" bellowed the Major, his face flushing red with fury. "To the guard-house with him! A hundred strokes of the rod—immediately, this instant!"

The order was carried out without delay. J—ski, an old man with white hair, endured the punishment without resistance. He lay face down on the ground, his hand clenched tightly between his teeth to suppress any sound. Not once did he cry out or flinch under the brutal blows, his resolve unbroken and his body unmoving. His silence was as deafening as the cruel sound of the rods striking his back.

Meanwhile, B——ski and T——ski arrived at the jail just as this horrifying scene was taking place. M——ski, who had been eagerly awaiting their arrival at the main gate, rushed to greet them. Though they had never met before, M——ski embraced them both fervently, his relief and joy at finally having companions tempered by the appalling tale they brought with them. Disgusted and enraged, they recounted the Major's vicious treatment of J——ski, sparing no detail of the cruelty they had just witnessed.

M——ski later described to me the overwhelming fury he felt upon hearing their account. "I was consumed with rage," he told me. "I couldn't keep it in; I was trembling as though seized by a violent fever. I waited at the gate for J——ski, knowing he would be brought through there after his punishment. When the gate opened, there he was. His lips were pale and trembling, his face ashen, drained of all color. He didn't look at anyone—didn't acknowledge a single soul. He walked steadily through the groups of convicts who had gathered in the courtyard, every one of them aware that a noble had just been flogged."

J——ski's steps were heavy but resolute as he made his way to the barracks. Once inside, he went directly to his place, dropped to his knees, and began to pray in complete silence. The convicts who had witnessed his entrance were struck by the sight. They watched in astonishment as this man, humiliated and brutalized, sought solace in his faith. The sincerity and quiet dignity of his actions left a profound impression on everyone present.

"When I saw him kneeling there," M——ski continued, "an old man who had left behind a family—a wife and children—to endure such barbaric treatment, I couldn't bear it. I ran out of the barrack, my mind a whirl of rage and anguish. For two hours, I felt like I was losing my grip on reality, as though I were drunk or mad."

From that day forward, the convicts treated J——ski with newfound respect and reverence. What moved them most deeply was not just the fact that he had endured the punishment without a single cry or complaint, but the grace and strength he exhibited in its aftermath. His silent suffering became a symbol of resilience and dignity, and it commanded their admiration.

But to be fair and truthful, this unfortunate story should not be taken as representative of the general treatment of transported noblemen, whether Russian or Polish, by the authorities. It is an isolated incident and does not provide a solid foundation for passing judgment on how noble convicts are usually treated. This account merely illustrates that a bad or vindictive person can be found in any position of power. And if such a person happens to command a prison and holds a personal grudge against a particular inmate, that inmate's life can indeed become unbearably difficult. However, it is important to note that the higher administrative officials who oversee convict labor in Siberia, and from whom their subordinates derive both their directives and attitudes, often adopt a more considerate and differentiated approach when dealing with nobles. In some instances, nobles are even granted certain privileges that are not extended to convicts of lower social classes.

There are several reasons for this distinction. First, these administrative heads are themselves nobles and understand that members of their class cannot be treated with excessive harshness without risking severe consequences. There have been instances where nobles, refusing to endure corporal punishment, have reacted with desperate resistance, leading to serious repercussions. Additionally— and this might be the main reason—several decades ago, perhaps thirty-five years or more, a large number of noblemen were exiled to Siberia. These individuals conducted themselves with such dignity and irreproachable behavior that they set a precedent for how noble prisoners were to be regarded. The heads of departments began to treat noble convicts very differently from ordinary ones, and this approach became a norm that subordinate officials followed thereafter.

Of course, not all officials were pleased with this policy. Some resented the restraint it imposed and would have preferred to exercise unchecked authority. However, such opportunities were rare, as they were kept under strict oversight. I have ample reason to believe this and can explain why. I was assigned to the second category of hard labor, a classification that primarily included convicts who had been serfs under military control. This second category was notably more challenging than the first category (those assigned to mines) or the third category (those involved in manufacturing work).

The second category was harsher for nobles and common convicts alike because its administration was entirely military, and the governing methods were similar to those of Russian penal institutions. Officials in these establishments were stricter, and the treatment of prisoners more severe. Inmates were constantly kept in irons, always under the watchful eye of armed soldiers, and rarely—if ever—allowed outside the confines of stone walls. This stood in stark contrast to the conditions in the first and third categories, which, according to those with experience, were relatively less oppressive. Many convicts, including nobles, longed to be reassigned to the mines, which were officially deemed the harshest punishment under the law. For them, the mines represented a distant dream of escape from the rigidity of military-run prisons.

Those who had been confined in Russian convict establishments before being sent to Siberia often spoke with sheer horror of their prior experiences. They described Russian penal fortresses as nothing short of hellish and insisted that life in Siberia, despite its hardships, was akin to paradise by comparison. Their accounts painted a stark picture of the brutal conditions in Russian prisons, further underlining the comparative leniency of Siberian exile.

If it is true that we nobles were treated with special consideration in the establishment where I was imprisoned, which was under the direct control of the Governor-General and operated entirely on military principles, it follows that convicts in the first and third categories must have experienced somewhat greater leniency in their treatment. Based on all I heard from convicts in these other categories, I believe I can speak with some authority about the conditions throughout Siberia. In our prison, the surveillance and restrictions were notably stricter than what was practiced elsewhere. We were not granted any exemptions from the usual rules governing work, confinement, or the wearing of chains.

Unlike other prisons, our establishment offered no avenues for convicts to gain immunity from the regulations, and I understood well why this was so. Not long before my time, during what some might call the "good old days," intrigue and conspiracies aimed at discrediting officials had been so widespread that the authorities had grown deeply distrustful of informers. In such an atmosphere, any indulgence shown to a convict was regarded as a serious offense. As a result, both officials and convicts operated under a constant cloud of fear—fear of what might happen if they deviated from the rigid system of control. Consequently, we nobles were treated no differently than the other prisoners, save for one exception: we were generally spared corporal punishment.

Even this exemption, however, was conditional. I am convinced that had any of us committed an offense that warranted flogging under the regulations, we would not have been spared. The principle of equality in punishment was strictly enforced. That said, we were not subjected to random or unwarranted brutality, as many of the other prisoners often were.

When the Governor became aware of the punishment meted out to J—ski, he was furious with the Major and issued him a stern reprimand, instructing him to exercise greater caution in the future. This incident quickly became widely known. We also learned that the Governor-General, who held our Major in high regard for his strict adherence to legal boundaries and his perceived efficiency in service, had delivered a sharp rebuke. This reprimand appears to have left a lasting impression on the Major, as it likely prevented him from carrying out his long-standing desire to have M——ski beaten.

The Major had been heavily influenced by the malicious gossip spread by A——f about M——ski, and he seemed eager to act against him. However, despite his efforts to persecute and spy on M——ski, he could never find a legitimate excuse to justify such a punishment. Reluctantly, he had to abandon the idea, though it clearly rankled him to do so.

The story of J——ski's punishment spread rapidly throughout the town and drew widespread condemnation of the Major. Public opinion turned against him, and some people even went so far as to confront and reproach him openly for his actions. A few were bold enough to insult him outright. This backlash must have stung, as it came from a community that generally maintained a degree of deference toward authority figures. The Major, despite his outward composure, could not entirely escape the consequences of his actions in this case.

The first encounter I had with this man remains vivid in my memory, so I may as well recount it here. Before my arrival at the prison, both I and another nobleman sentenced alongside me had been warned about his dreadful character. While we were still at Tobolsk, several nobles who had been sentenced years earlier to decades of hard labor had visited us. These men, hardened by years of suffering, spoke kindly to us during our provisional confinement. They also took the time to caution us about the man who would soon have power over us. They painted a bleak picture of his cruelty and malice, warning us to prepare for the worst. Out of compassion, they promised to do what they could to mitigate his tyranny by reaching out to their contacts.

True to their word, they wrote letters to the three daughters of the Governor-General, who reportedly spoke to their father on our behalf. It seems they appealed to him to ensure we were not subjected to undue suffering. However, the Governor-General could do little more than instruct the Major to adhere strictly to the regulations and treat us fairly. His hands were tied when it came to curbing the man's more sinister tendencies.

It was around three in the afternoon when my companion and I arrived in the town under escort. Without delay, we were taken directly to the Major. We were left waiting in an ante-chamber while one of the guards went to summon the second-in-command of the prison. Not long after, the Major himself appeared. The moment he walked in, his presence felt oppressive. His face was flushed a deep red, as though it were permanently inflamed, and there was something about him that sent a shiver through me. He gave the impression of a predator, a spider about to pounce on flies helplessly caught in its web.

"What's your name, man?" he barked at my companion. His voice was rough and sharp, clearly calculated to intimidate.

My companion answered, giving his name.

"And you?" he said, snapping his attention to me and fixing me with a piercing glare from behind his spectacles.

I gave my name, my voice steady despite the unease coursing through me.

"Sergeant!" he shouted, without pausing. "Take them to the prison and have them shaved at the guard-house, civilian-style—hair off half their skulls. Tomorrow, see that they're put in irons." His tone was brutal, and every word carried the weight of disdain.

As he looked us over, his gaze landed on the gray cloaks we had been issued at Tobolsk. The cloaks had a yellow patch sewn onto the back, as was standard for prisoners. But his reaction to them was explosive. "What sort of cloaks are these?" he sneered. "A new uniform, eh? A new uniform! They're always coming up with something. That's a Petersburg trick if I've ever seen one," he muttered, inspecting us with a contemptuous air.

Then, without warning, he turned to the gendarme who had accompanied us and barked, "What have they got with them?"

"They've got their own clothes, your worship," replied the gendarme, standing rigidly at attention as though on parade. It was clear he was trembling slightly, though he tried to hide it. Everyone in the room knew exactly who the Major was and what he was capable of, and no one dared cross him.

This encounter set the tone for what we were to endure under his rule. His every word and action seemed designed to crush the spirit and assert his power, leaving no doubt that we were entering a new realm of suffering.

"Take their clothes away from them," he barked with the same ruthless tone. "They're allowed to keep nothing but their linen—their white underclothes. Any colored garments they have, take them, sell them at the next auction, and put the money into the prison account. A convict has no property," he added, his stern eyes boring into us as if daring us to argue. Then, with a voice even harsher than before, he continued, "And listen here! Behave yourselves, or you'll regret it. I won't tolerate complaints—none! The smallest infraction, and you'll feel the sticks. Cat-o'-nine-tails for the slightest offence!"

This reception, so alien to anything I had ever experienced in my life, left me shaken to my core. That night I felt almost physically ill, overwhelmed by the crushing reality of what lay ahead. To face such harshness at the very moment of entering this place of torment—it was more than my spirit could bear. I have recounted this part of my story before, but every detail of that day remains etched vividly in my memory.

From the very start, it was clear that we would not be spared a single ounce of the hardships endured by the other convicts. There were no exemptions, no easing of the burdens placed upon us. When it came to the forced labor, we worked shoulder-to-shoulder with the rest, enduring the same relentless grind. However, there were some friends among the officials who tried discreetly to make life a little less unbearable for us. For instance, B——ski and I were quietly assigned to

357

work in the bureau of the Engineers for three months, tasked with copying documents. This arrangement was done quietly, kept under wraps as much as possible to avoid arousing suspicion or resentment among the others.

This gesture of kindness came courtesy of the head engineers, and it was during the tenure of Lieutenant-Colonel G——kof, who, for six brief months, served as the Governor of our prison. His departure back to Russia shortly afterward was a great loss to us all, for he was like a ray of light in the suffocating darkness of that place. To the convicts, he seemed nothing short of an angel sent from heaven. The affection they held for him wasn't mere gratitude or admiration—it was closer to reverence. They adored him, and so did I.

Lieutenant-Colonel G——kof was a man of striking character, full of vitality and kindness. Though he was of short stature, his bold and confident demeanor made him seem larger than life. His every interaction with the prisoners radiated a warmth that none of us could quite understand. He treated the convicts as if they were his own children, not with condescension but with genuine paternal care. How he managed to connect so deeply with them remains a mystery to me, but his affection for these men was undeniable.

He seemed incapable of passing a convict without stopping for a moment of conversation, a kind word, or even a lighthearted joke. Yet his joviality never undermined his authority; there was nothing that felt dismissive or insincere in his demeanor. It was as if he had the rare gift of making each man feel seen, understood, and respected. And while he treated them with such approachable familiarity, the convicts never overstepped their boundaries. Quite the opposite—his kindness inspired an even greater respect. They regarded him with a unique mixture of reverence and affection, as though he were both a leader and a friend.

The mere sight of him approaching would light up their faces. Men who seemed perpetually hardened by suffering and hardship would suddenly smile with an unguarded warmth when he appeared. Their hands would snap to their caps, not out of fear but as a gesture of deep respect. A kind word or a pat on the back from him was considered an honor. It was extraordinary to witness how he transformed the atmosphere of the prison simply by being there. He was one of those rare individuals who seem born to win hearts, even in the bleakest of circumstances.

G—kof had a commanding, confident presence. His stride was long and purposeful, his posture straight and proud, earning him the nickname "a regular eagle" from the convicts. Although his position as overseer of engineering work gave him limited power to ease the prisoners' suffering—his responsibilities bound tightly by strict regulations—his small acts of humanity left an indelible mark on their hearts. When he encountered convicts who had completed their assigned work ahead of schedule, he allowed them to return to their quarters early, without waiting for the official dismissal marked by the drumbeat.

The prisoners adored him for the trust he placed in them and for his refusal to indulge in the petty, officious micromanagement that so many prison superiors delighted in. These minor but meaningful acts earned him a loyalty that few other authorities could command. It was said, and I have no doubt of its truth, that if G—kof had lost a thousand roubles in cash, even the most hardened thief among the convicts would have returned every note to him without hesitation. Such was the respect he inspired.

When the prisoners learned that G—kof was in open conflict with the despised Major—a feud that began about a month after G—kof's arrival—their joy was almost palpable. The tension between the two officers seemed to represent a battle of good versus evil, and the convicts couldn't hide their glee at the thought of their "eagle" standing up to the tyrannical "Eight-eyes."

The story of their quarrel became a source of endless speculation and amusement among the prisoners. The Major and G——kof had previously served together in the same detachment, and when they reunited after years apart, their initial camaraderie was short-lived. The differences in their characters were irreconcilable, and what started as a professional rivalry quickly escalated into personal enmity. Rumors swirled that their feud had gone beyond verbal disputes to an actual physical altercation—something entirely plausible given the Major's coarse nature and love of a brawl.

The convicts were wildly curious about the supposed fight. The mere idea of it thrilled them to no end, and they hungered for details, eager to know who had emerged victorious. Many were convinced G——kof had trounced the Major.

"The Commandant must have given him a proper thrashing!" they'd say. "He's small, but he's fierce—like a lion. Bet old Eight-eyes got so scared, he hid under the bed!"

Of course, no evidence ever confirmed that the fight had happened, but to the prisoners, it hardly mattered. The very thought of someone standing up to the Major, much less besting him, was enough to lift their spirits.

Unfortunately, G——kof's time with us was far too short. His departure was deeply felt by all, leaving an emptiness that took a long time to fill. The regret among the prisoners was universal; they spoke of him with genuine fondness and respect long after he was gone.

"We're never lucky enough to keep our eagles for long," the convicts lamented. "Especially not the good ones, the kind ones. They never stay."

The engineers who replaced him were also fine men, bringing with them a professionalism and decency that stood out against the backdrop of prison life. But G——kof was special, and his absence was a sore point for many of us. His brief tenure left a legacy of hope and humanity, a reminder that even in the bleakest of places, there are those who can inspire loyalty and respect simply by treating others with dignity.

It was G—kof who arranged for B—ski and me to work in his bureau, showing a particular fondness for exiled nobles. His decision provided a welcome respite from the grueling labor we had endured, and for a time, our lives were more tolerable. Even after he left, we were fortunate enough to remain under the care of another engineer who extended his kindness and friendship to us. During those days, we occupied ourselves with copying reports, our penmanship gradually improving through practice. But this relatively peaceful interlude did not last. An order soon came from the higher authorities, directing us back to hard labor. Someone, driven by spite or envy, had intervened to bring this about. Despite the seeming cruelty of the situation, B—ski and I found ourselves surprisingly untroubled by the decision. Truthfully, we had grown weary of copying.

For the next two years, I worked alongside B—ski in the workshops, toiling together day after day. Those long hours allowed us plenty of opportunities to talk, to exchange thoughts about the future, and to explore each other's beliefs and convictions. B—ski's mind was an unusual one, filled with peculiar insights and paradoxical ideas. There are people whose intelligence leads them to embrace contradictions boldly, but when they have suffered deeply and made immense sacrifices for their beliefs, those convictions become unshakable. To question or challenge such beliefs can feel almost cruel.

Whenever I disagreed with one of B—ski's ideas, he reacted with genuine hurt, sometimes lashing out with sharp retorts. Perhaps he was right more often than I was, though our arguments occasionally became heated. Over time, our differences proved too great, and we had to distance ourselves from one another. This saddened me deeply, for despite our disagreements, there was much we shared. We had built a foundation of mutual respect, and parting ways left a void in my already bleak existence.

As the years passed, I observed how prison life wore on M—tski. He descended into a gloom that seemed impenetrable, his spirit consumed by despair. When I first arrived, he was still approachable, even talkative. Having completed his second year of imprisonment, he was eager for news of the outside world. He bombarded me with questions, listened intently, and responded with visible emotion. At times, there was even a flicker of hope or curiosity in his eyes. But as time dragged on, his reserve grew stronger. He withdrew into himself, until it became nearly impossible to discern what he was thinking or feeling. The fire of his spirit seemed to be buried beneath layers of cold ash, and his temper soured with each passing day.

"Je hais ces brigands," he would often say, referring to the other convicts. I tried to reason with him, to share what little understanding or sympathy I had for the men we lived among, but my words never seemed to reach him. He would sometimes nod in agreement, as though conceding my point, but by the next day, his stance had not budged: "je hais ces brigands." We often spoke in French, a habit that puzzled the overseer, Dranichnikof, who took to calling us aides chirurgiens—assistant surgeons—for reasons known only to himself.

The only time I ever saw M—tski break free from his usual apathy was when he spoke of his mother. His face softened, and his voice grew quiet, tinged with an unmistakable sadness.

"She's old and frail," he confided to me one day. "She loves me more than anything in the world, and I don't even know if she's still alive. If she learns that I've been whipped..." His voice trailed off, the unspoken thought too painful to finish. It was clear that the mere idea of his mother discovering such a thing haunted him deeply, a rare glimpse into the tender heart that still beat beneath his hardened exterior.

M—tski was not of noble birth and had suffered the degrading punishment of the whip before his transportation to Siberia. The memory of that humiliation haunted him deeply. Whenever it came to mind, his face would harden, his teeth would clench, and he seemed unable to meet the gaze of anyone around him. As time went on and his imprisonment neared its end, he grew increasingly withdrawn, often pacing back and forth in silence, his thoughts locked away where no one could reach them. It became his habit to isolate himself, avoiding even those he once spoke to freely. His demeanor was a reflection of the inner torment he carried, a burden he seemed unable to share with anyone.

One day, at noon, he was unexpectedly summoned to the Governor's office. The Governor greeted him with an air of casual cheerfulness, a faint smile playing on his lips.

"Well, M—tski," said the Governor in a tone that seemed almost playful, "what dreams did you have last night?"

Later, when M—tski recounted the encounter to me, he described the moment vividly. "When he said those words," he confessed, "a shudder ran through me. It felt as though I had been struck straight in the heart. I thought he was mocking me."

Still, he managed to respond with dignity, "I dreamed that I received a letter from my mother."

"Better than that, much better!" the Governor replied, his smile widening. "You are free, M—tski. Your mother petitioned the Emperor, and her request has been granted. Here"—he handed over some papers—"is her letter, along with the official order for your release. You are to leave the jail without delay."

When M—tski returned to the barracks to tell us the news, he was visibly shaken, his face pale, and his hands trembling uncontrollably. It seemed he could scarcely believe that his long ordeal was finally over.

We gathered around him, offering our congratulations. He grasped our hands in turn, his cold, trembling fingers betraying the depth of his emotions. His voice was barely above a whisper as he expressed his gratitude, though the words were few. Many of the convicts came forward to wish him well, their genuine joy for his good fortune evident in their faces and gestures. Even those who rarely spoke or showed much warmth seemed moved by the moment, a rare instance of shared humanity in that grim place.

After his release, M—tski chose to remain in Siberia, settling in the very town where our prison was located. Before long, he found a modest position and began to rebuild his life. But he did not forget us, nor did he sever his connection to the world he had left behind. Whenever he could, he visited the jail, bringing with him news of the outside world.

It was clear that what interested him most was political news. He would eagerly share what he had heard or read, speaking with a fervor that reminded us of the man he had been before despair and imprisonment had dulled his spirit. These visits were brief, but they left an impression on all of us. For a few moments, he carried a piece of freedom back into the confines of our prison, a reminder of what might still be possible for those who dared to hope.

Besides the four Polish political prisoners I mentioned earlier, there were two others of the same nationality who had been sentenced to relatively short terms. Unlike the others, these two men were not well-educated but were kind-hearted, simple, and straightforward individuals. There was also another Polish prisoner, A—tchoukooski, who left no real impression on anyone. He was a remarkably unremarkable figure, lacking both individuality and presence. Finally, there was B—in, an older man who left an entirely different impression—one that was far from favorable.

B—in was a man of questionable character, vulgar in his demeanor and coarse in his mannerisms. He reminded one of a shopkeeper who had stumbled upon some wealth but had not acquired the refinement to accompany it. His lack of education was obvious, and he displayed little interest in anything beyond his trade, which was painting.

Specifically, he was a decorative painter, something akin to a scene-painter, and his skill in this area was undeniable. His talent quickly caught the attention of the prison authorities, who began assigning him to various projects around the town. Over time, he became something of a local celebrity among the officials, decorating walls and ceilings for nearly everyone in authority.

His reputation as a skilled decorator brought him a level of comfort few other prisoners could attain. His work was generously rewarded, and he was allowed to employ three other prisoners to assist him. Of these assistants, two became quite adept at the trade, and one, T—jwoski, eventually painted with nearly as much finesse as B—in himself.

One of B—in's most significant commissions came from none other than the Major. The Major, who lived in a government building, enlisted B—in to decorate the walls and ceilings of his quarters. The transformation was extraordinary. B—in's work was so elaborate and well-executed that the Major's modest house began to outshine the Governor-General's residence in terms of interior elegance. Though the building itself was old and decrepit, the vibrant and lavish designs created by B—in gave it the air of a palace.

The Major was beside himself with delight. He took every opportunity to show off the results, going so far as to declare that he could no longer remain single now that he lived in such splendor. "A fellow can't stay a bachelor in a place like this," he announced to anyone who would listen, and it was clear that he meant every word. His satisfaction with B—in and his assistants only grew as the project progressed. The work took a month to complete, and during that time, an extraordinary shift occurred in the Major's demeanor. For reasons known only to him, he began to show unexpected kindness toward us political prisoners.

This change was most evident in a surprising incident involving J—ski. One day, the Major summoned him to his office. When J—ski arrived, the Major spoke in a tone that was both serious and, astonishingly, remorseful.

"J—ski," the Major began, "I've done you wrong. I had you beaten for no reason. I regret it. Do you understand? I'm sorry. I, Major ——, am sorry."

J—ski, taken aback but composed, replied that he understood.

"Do you really understand?" the Major pressed, as if to emphasize the gravity of his admission. "I, who am set over you, have summoned you to ask for your pardon. You probably can't even comprehend that. What are you to me? A worm. Less than a worm. You're a convict, while I, by God's grace, am a Major—Major ——. Do you grasp that?"

Once again, J—ski replied calmly that he understood everything perfectly.

This moment was as bizarre as it was unexpected. It seemed as though the Major was attempting to reconcile his own conscience in the most theatrical manner possible. Whatever his reasons, the incident left a lasting impression on all who heard about it, though it did little to change the broader reality of life in the prison.

"Well, I want to be friends with you. But do you even understand the greatness of what I'm doing? Can you truly grasp and appreciate the nobility of soul I'm showing you? Just think about it—me, the Major!" and so on, and so forth.

J—ski shared this encounter with me afterward. It revealed that there was, indeed, some flicker of human feeling within this chaotic, tyrannical, and drunken tormentor. Taking into account the man's peculiar worldview and limited faculties, one could not entirely deny that this was a somewhat magnanimous act on his part. Perhaps he had been drinking a little less than usual that day—or perhaps a little more; who could say for certain?

The Major's grand plans of marriage, however, came to nothing. Despite his gaudy new living quarters, the long-awaited bride never materialized. Instead of walking proudly to the altar, he found himself summoned to answer for past deeds. Orders came down that he was to resign his position immediately. Some of his earlier misdeeds, committed during his tenure as superintendent of police in the same town, had caught up with him at last. The blow was as unexpected as it was devastating, descending upon him with no warning whatsoever.

The news of his downfall spread quickly, and the entire prison erupted in joy. Among the convicts, it was nothing less than a day of celebration, a rare moment of collective jubilation. Rumors circulated that the Major had broken down completely—sobbing, wailing, and lamenting his fate like an inconsolable old woman. But all his protests and tears were in vain. He was forced to vacate his position, sell his prized pair of gray horses, and part with nearly all his worldly possessions. The man who once ruled over us so imperiously now found himself reduced to utter destitution.

Occasionally, we would encounter him after his fall. Dressed in shabby civilian clothes, his cap adorned with a meaningless cockade, he was a pitiful sight. Whenever he passed us convicts, he would glare at us with venomous spite, his gaze as malicious as ever. But without his uniform, he no longer possessed even a shred of the authority or grandeur he once projected. The aura of superiority he had wrapped himself in was gone, stripped away along with his title.

To the convicts, his transformation was as stark as it was satisfying. When he had been in power, he strutted about like some divine being who had accidentally donned human clothing. Now, bereft of his military finery, he was laid bare for what he truly was—nothing more than a lackey, a disgraced and broken man, unworthy of the fear or respect he once commanded.

For men like him, the uniform is not just a garment; it is their entire identity. Once stripped of it, they are left with nothing, reduced to mere shadows of the figures they once pretended to be. And for the Major, there was no recovering from such a fall.

Chapter 9
The Escape

Not long after the Major's resignation, our prison underwent a significant reorganization. The system of "hard labour" and the accompanying regulations were abolished, and the institution was restructured to align with the military convict establishments of Russia. This shift brought about notable changes in the composition of the prisoners and the overall administration of the place.

Prisoners of the second category were no longer to be sent to our establishment. This category was comprised of individuals who, although sentenced, were still regarded as being on a military footing. These men had not permanently forfeited their civic rights and were still considered soldiers, albeit ones who had undergone corporal punishment. Their sentences were comparatively short, usually lasting no more than six years. Upon completing their terms or receiving pardons, they were permitted to rejoin the military ranks as before. Those who committed a second offense, however, faced much harsher penalties, including sentences of up to twenty years of imprisonment.

Prior to these changes, we already had a small section of soldier-prisoners among us, though their presence was more due to a lack of alternative accommodations than any deliberate administrative choice. With the reorganization, the facility was to house only military prisoners. Civilian convicts, who had been stripped of their civic rights, branded, cropped, and shaven, were allowed to remain to serve out the remainder of their sentences. However, no new civilian prisoners were to be sent to the establishment. Over time, as the remaining civilian convicts completed their terms, their numbers would dwindle. According to the plan, in about ten years, there would be no civilian convicts left at all.

The distinctions between the different classes of prisoners were maintained, though with some modifications. Occasionally, military criminals of higher rank and status were transferred to our prison temporarily, deemed too dangerous or prominent to be housed elsewhere. These individuals were usually kept here briefly before being sent on to Eastern Siberia to face harsher punishments.

In terms of daily life, not much changed for us. The work assignments and disciplinary practices remained largely the same, but the administrative structure was entirely overhauled and made considerably more complex. A commanding officer, holding the title of company commandant, was placed in charge of the prison. He was supported by four subaltern officers who rotated guard duties. The "invalids," who had previously served in administrative roles, were replaced by twelve non-commissioned officers and an arsenal superintendent.

The convicts were reorganized into sections of ten men each, and within these groups, corporals were chosen. However, the authority of these corporals over their fellow prisoners was purely nominal, as might be expected. Unsurprisingly, Akim Akimitch was among those selected for this minor "promotion," a role perfectly suited to his temperament and attitude.

The responsibility for implementing all these new arrangements was entrusted to the Governor, who continued to hold superior command over the entire establishment. However, the changes did not extend beyond these structural adjustments. Initially, the convicts were quite animated by the new developments, speculating among themselves about their new overseers and trying to deduce what sort of men they might be. But once it became apparent that the daily routine remained largely unchanged, their excitement waned, and life settled back into its familiar pattern.

One significant improvement was the departure of the Major, which brought a collective sense of relief. Everyone seemed to breathe easier, as though a heavy weight had been lifted. The omnipresent fear that had gripped the prison began to dissipate, replaced by a cautious optimism. For the first time in a long while, there was a sense that if grievances arose, one might approach the higher authorities to lodge a complaint. Moreover, the belief took root that punishment would only be meted out for valid reasons—or at least not arbitrarily, as had so often been the case under the Major's reign.

Brandy continued to find its way into the prison, despite the replacement of the "invalids" with subaltern officers. These subalterns were, for the most part, competent and conscientious men who understood their responsibilities and limits. Some initially attempted to assert their authority in an overbearing manner, treating the convicts as if they were mere rank-and-file soldiers under military command. However, they quickly abandoned such pretensions after encountering the stark realities of the prison environment. The convicts had their own ways of educating these officers, often through sharp and pointed lessons, which occasionally led to amusing or dramatic episodes.

One particularly memorable incident involved a sub-officer who allowed himself to be tempted by brandy, a commodity strictly prohibited but ever-present. After he sobered up, the convicts engaged him in a candid "discussion," reminding him that drinking with prisoners compromised his authority and left him vulnerable to certain expectations. From then on, he became significantly more agreeable and accommodating. In time, the subalterns turned a blind eye to the smuggling of brandy and even assisted the prisoners by purchasing goods on their behalf—white bread, meat, and other items—just as the invalids had done before them. This arrangement worked so seamlessly that I often found myself questioning why the authorities had bothered to convert the prison into a military institution at all.

This reorganization occurred two years before I left the prison, leaving me two more years to endure under the new system. While these changes added a layer of complexity to the prison's administration, they did little to alter the essence of our daily existence.

Reflecting on my time at the convict establishment, I find little value in recounting every minor detail or daily occurrence from those years. To do so would require writing twice or three times as many chapters as this narrative already contains, and I fear such an exhaustive account would only exhaust both myself and the reader. Most of what could be said about the life of a second-class convict has already been woven into this narrative, offering, I hope, a comprehensive picture of our conditions and struggles.

My aim throughout has been to depict the reality of life in the prison—its routines, its peculiarities, and its profound hardships—through the lens of my personal experiences. Whether I have succeeded in capturing this accurately and compellingly is for others to judge. For my part, I find myself reluctant to linger further on these memories. As I delve into the shadows of this dreadful past, the pain of those years resurfaces, gripping me with a force that feels almost suffocating. Perhaps it is time to let these recollections rest.

In addition, I cannot fully trust my memory regarding all the events of those final years of imprisonment, as my ability to recall them seems less sharp than my recollections of the earlier period. Some details have undoubtedly faded entirely from my mind. However, I remember all too vividly the oppressive slowness of those last two years—the unrelenting sadness, the way each day stretched endlessly, like water dripping monotonously, one drop at a time, into a vast abyss of sameness. I also remember the overwhelming longing for freedom, a desperate hope that became a powerful force within me, sustaining my resolve and giving me the strength to endure, to wait, and to hope.

Over time, I grew more hardened, more resilient. I clung to the passage of time as a source of solace, counting each day as it ended. If there were a thousand more days to endure, I found a measure of satisfaction in marking one off, leaving only nine hundred and ninety-nine ahead. Yet, amidst a hundred fellow prisoners enduring the same fate, I felt an ever-deepening solitude. This solitude, although painful, became something I began to cherish. Isolated within the sea of convicts, I turned inward, dissecting my past with an almost ruthless precision. I reviewed the chapters of my earlier life, revisiting my actions, my thoughts, and my choices with a critical eye.

Sometimes, I was harsh in my self-judgment, condemning my failings without mercy. Other times, I found myself strangely grateful to fate for granting me this enforced seclusion, for it was only in the silence and isolation of imprisonment that I could so thoroughly examine my life and its intricacies. In those hours of reflection, powerful and unexpected seeds of hope took root within my soul. I deliberated over the errors of my past, resolving to avoid the pitfalls that had once ensnared me. I began drafting a plan for the future, an outline of the life I vowed to lead upon gaining my freedom. There was a blind but absolute conviction within me that, once I escaped this purgatory, I would have the strength to implement every resolution I had so carefully crafted.

I yearned for freedom with a fervor that bordered on madness. The thought of engaging once more with life, testing my mettle against its challenges, filled me with both excitement and a kind of feverish impatience. There were moments when this longing became almost unbearable, gripping me like sharp talons, driving my pulse to race with frustration. Writing about these memories now is deeply painful. It is a raw and personal agony, a burden of recollections that likely holds little significance for others. Yet, I write because I believe there are those who will understand—those who have endured or may one day endure what I did: imprisonment, isolation, the cruel severance from life in the prime of one's strength and youth.

But enough of this introspection. Let me end these memoirs with a narrative that might capture the reader's interest, for I should not conclude so abruptly.

What shall it be? Perhaps some might wonder whether it was entirely impossible to escape from the prison, and whether, during my years there, any attempts were made to break free. I have previously mentioned that prisoners who have served two or three years tend to weigh the risks and often decide it is better to endure their sentence than to gamble on escape, particularly if their term is relatively short. These individuals focus on securing the modest settlement or opportunity for freedom that awaits at the end of their sentence.

However, for those facing many long years behind bars, the calculus is different. The prospect of freedom, no matter how slim, remains enticing, and they are more inclined to consider escape. Even so, attempts to break free were rare. Was this due to a lack of courage among the convicts, the rigid enforcement of military discipline, or simply the geographic isolation of the prison, surrounded as it was by the vast, open steppe? It is difficult to say, though likely all these factors played a role in discouraging escape. The odds were undeniably stacked against anyone daring enough to try.

During my time there, only two convicts made the attempt. Both were notorious criminals, men of considerable importance in their own circles. Their boldness and determination stand out in sharp contrast to the general atmosphere of resigned endurance that characterized the prison.

Once the Major was finally removed, A—v, the prison's infamous spy, found himself isolated, with no one to protect or support him. He was still relatively young, yet his personality only seemed to intensify as time went on. Bold, calculating, and sharply intelligent, A—v was the sort of man who adapted to circumstances with unsettling ease. Had he been granted freedom, I have little doubt he would have continued his duplicitous ways, using every opportunity to profit dishonestly. His methods—whether spying, forgery, or other illicit schemes—were honed to perfection. He would almost certainly have avoided getting caught again, applying the lessons learned during his years as a convict to refine his criminal craft.

Rumors circulated among the prisoners that one of his specialties was forging passports, a lucrative and dangerous skill in those times. It was apparent that A—v was willing to risk everything for the chance to improve his position. This desperate ambition provided me with deeper insight into the man's nature, and it was not a flattering picture. He was cold and methodical, his moral compass utterly warped, and his capacity for evil so calculating that it was chilling. My revulsion toward him was impossible to suppress. I came to believe that, had A—v needed a drink of brandy and his only means of obtaining it was by taking a life, he would have done so without hesitation—provided, of course, that the crime would go undetected. During his time in prison, A—v had perfected the art of detachment, learning to view every action, no matter how heinous, through a lens of pure self-interest.

This icy pragmatism made him an ideal accomplice for Koulikoff, a fellow prisoner from the special section, whose cunning plans would eventually intersect with A—v's own ruthless ambitions.

Koulikoff was an entirely different sort of man. Though no longer young, he possessed an unquenchable vitality, brimming with energy, confidence, and remarkable ability. He was a man who felt his own strength deeply and yearned for a life full of activity and richness, even as the years crept upon him. Men like Koulikoff, who seem to hunger for a boundless existence, cannot abide the stifling constraints of prison life. The jail was, for him, a slow suffocation, a place where his innate thirst for freedom and accomplishment could find no outlet. I would have been astonished had he not made some attempt to escape; it was simply in his nature. And, as it turned out, he did.

Whether Koulikoff or A—v held greater sway in their partnership was unclear. They were, in every sense, a perfect match—a pair of schemers who understood and complemented one another's strengths. It wasn't long before their shared goals brought them into a close alliance. I suspected that Koulikoff relied on A—v's skill in forging passports, an essential tool for anyone hoping to travel through Russia unnoticed. Moreover, A—v's noble background and knowledge of the upper echelons of society added an extra layer of utility to their plans. Together, they envisioned a future far from the grim confines of Siberia. What precise deals they struck, what schemes they envisioned, only they knew. Yet it was clear that their shared dream was to reach Russia, leaving behind the stigma of vagabondage and the indignities of exile.

Koulikoff was a man of immense resourcefulness, capable of playing multiple roles to suit any scenario. His natural adaptability and intelligence made him well-suited to a life on the run, and he likely believed he could thrive in freedom, no matter the odds. For men like him, life behind bars felt like slow strangulation—every moment a reminder of the opportunities slipping through his fingers. With this in mind, it was no surprise that Koulikoff and A——v soon began to plot their escape with the kind of fervor born from desperation and hope.

Thus began their clandestine collaboration, driven by the shared determination to leave the suffocating confines of prison behind and reclaim the freedom they had lost.

To escape without a soldier as an escort was entirely out of the question, so the first and most critical step was to secure a soldier's cooperation. In one of the battalions stationed at our fortress was a Pole named Kohler, a man in his middle years who possessed an intense energy and strength of character that seemed better suited for a higher calling than his current circumstances. Kohler was serious and courageous, qualities that had earned him respect even among those who held him captive. His backstory was well known: as a young recruit in Siberia, homesick and overwhelmed by his exile, he had once deserted his post. His flight ended in capture, followed by a brutal whipping. Afterward, he spent two years in the disciplinary companies, those punitive units reserved for military offenders. Eventually, he was allowed to rejoin his battalion, where his diligence and dedication to duty earned him a promotion to the rank of corporal.

Kohler was not without his faults. He was clearly a man who held a high opinion of himself, speaking in a way that hinted at no small amount of personal pride and self-importance. Yet, beneath his stoic exterior lay a simmering hatred, born of years of suffering and enforced separation from his homeland. I had observed him closely on several occasions when he was stationed among the soldiers guarding us. The Polish convicts had spoken of him often, and I came to believe that his homesickness had long since curdled into a cold, implacable resentment toward those who kept him in chains. Kohler was not the sort to shrink from dangerous schemes, and Koulikoff demonstrated both cunning and intuition by selecting him as an accomplice in his planned escape.

The partnership was struck, and the details of the plan meticulously arranged. The day was set—sometime in June, the hottest month of the year. The summer climate in our region was relatively mild and steady, which made it a more hospitable season for those seeking to travel by foot, whether fugitives or vagabonds. However, simply fleeing the fortress would not suffice; the geography of the area posed significant challenges. The fortress itself was situated on elevated, open terrain, with no immediate cover to conceal an escape. Though woods surrounded the region, they lay a considerable distance away, making them a poor choice for an initial hiding place. A successful escape would require not only careful planning but also the use of disguises, which would have to be procured from within the town.

Koulikoff had anticipated this need long before the plan was put into motion. He had, over the preceding months, carefully cultivated connections within the outskirts of the town, where he had prepared some sort of refuge or "den" for himself. Whether his associates in that area were fully aware of his intentions is unclear, though it seems likely they were involved. Among these contacts was a young woman who had recently settled in that part of the town—a striking beauty with a fiery personality, earning her the nickname "Fire and Flame." Her reputation preceded her, and she quickly became known for her charm and daring, attracting considerable attention wherever she went. Koulikoff had devoted significant time and money to winning her favor for over a year, suggesting that she played a key role in his plans. It is reasonable to assume that she assisted in organizing the escape, though the full extent of her involvement remains unknown.

When the morning came for the escape, the conspirators had arranged to be included in one of the work gangs sent out from the prison. Koulikoff and A—v, along with another convict named Chilkin—a stove-maker and plasterer by trade—secured assignments to renovate some abandoned barracks left empty as the soldiers moved into summer camp. Their role was ostensibly to assist Chilkin in transporting the necessary building materials. Kohler, the indispensable piece of the puzzle, ensured he was assigned to the escort detail for this particular work gang. According to regulations, three soldiers were required to accompany two prisoners, so Kohler brought along a young recruit he was training and drilling as part of his corporal duties.

The fugitives must have been highly persuasive to win over Kohler, a man of intelligence, seriousness, and forethought, who had so few years of service remaining in the army. To sway someone like him—a man who had endured so much yet still managed to climb back up the ranks—required not only eloquence and charisma but also a level of desperation and determination that could not be easily dismissed. That they succeeded in securing his loyalty speaks volumes about their resolve and resourcefulness. Thus, the stage was set for one of the boldest attempts at escape our prison had ever witnessed. The group reached the abandoned barracks around six o'clock in the morning. The area was desolate, with no one else around to supervise or interrupt their work. After an hour of laboring, Koulikoff and A—v approached Chilkin with a casual pretext. They told him they needed to step away briefly to visit the workshop, ostensibly to find someone and retrieve a particular tool required for the job. They had to approach this delicately, masking any hint of nervousness or haste in their voices, so as not to arouse suspicion in their companion.

Chilkin was no fool. A native of Moscow and a skilled stove-maker by trade, he was sharp, observant, and perceptive, though not particularly loquacious. His slight build and unassuming demeanor might have suggested an ordinary, unremarkable worker destined to spend his life in honest labor within some bustling Moscow workshop. Yet here he was, a convict in the "special section," having passed through the hands of some of the harshest military criminal systems. What twist of fate had led to such severe punishment for him? No one seemed to know. Chilkin himself never expressed bitterness or hostility about his situation, conducting himself quietly and inoffensively. He was known to indulge in bouts of heavy drinking on occasion, but aside from that, his behavior was generally irreproachable.

Unaware of the plan, Chilkin had to be thoroughly misled. Koulikoff hinted, with a sly wink, that their errand was to retrieve a bottle of brandy they had stashed in the workshop the day before. This explanation suited Chilkin perfectly. The idea of hidden brandy was entirely plausible, and he gave it no further thought. He remained behind with the young recruit, completely oblivious to the actual purpose of their departure. Meanwhile, Koulikoff, A—v, and Kohler slipped away, heading straight for the outskirts of town.

The minutes ticked by. Thirty minutes passed, and the men still had not returned. At first, Chilkin waited idly, but then he began to grow uneasy. Thoughts swirled in his mind, and slowly, he pieced things together. He recalled that Koulikoff had been acting strangely earlier, uncharacteristically guarded and secretive. There had been those quick, whispered exchanges between Koulikoff and A—v, accompanied by knowing glances and subtle gestures. The behavior of Kohler, the corporal, also struck him as unusual. Before leaving with the two convicts, Kohler had given the young recruit explicit instructions about what to do in his absence—a precaution Chilkin had never seen him take before. The more he considered these details, the more suspicious everything seemed.

As time dragged on and the trio failed to reappear, Chilkin's unease turned to outright alarm. A growing sense of dread began to take hold of him. It dawned on him that the convicts might have escaped and that their absence would inevitably lead to severe repercussions for himself. The authorities were bound to question him, and his proximity to the situation would make him an easy target for their suspicions. They might assume he had been complicit in the escape, and if he delayed reporting the incident, their doubts would harden into certainty. His own safety was at stake, and he realized he had no choice. He had to act quickly. Time was of the essence.

It occurred to Chilkin that Koulikoff and A—v had grown unusually close over the past weeks. He remembered seeing them huddled together behind the barracks, speaking in hushed tones. Their secretive behavior had caught his eye more than once, but he hadn't thought much of it at the time. Now, reflecting on their recent interactions, he felt certain they had been planning something.

He cast a sidelong glance at the soldier who stood as their escort. The young man seemed utterly unaware of anything amiss. He leaned lazily on his rifle, yawning and scratching his nose, a picture of innocence. Chilkin decided not to confide his growing suspicions to the soldier. Instead, he casually suggested they head to the engineers' workshop to check if anyone there had seen the missing men. The soldier, oblivious, followed him without question.

At the workshop, Chilkin asked around, but no one had seen or heard anything about Koulikoff and A—v. This deepened his unease. If they had simply gone off for a drinking spree in the outskirts of town, as Koulikoff had been known to do on occasion, they would have mentioned it to him. There was no reason for secrecy in such a case. No, this was something different—something planned and deliberate. Chilkin left the workshop and made his way back to the prison, his unease now a gnawing certainty.

By the time he reached the sergeant-major, it was nine o'clock. Still uncertain of the full truth, Chilkin hesitantly voiced his suspicions. At first, the sergeant-major seemed incredulous, reluctant to believe that something so serious could be underway. After all, Chilkin's report was based on little more than a vague sense of foreboding. But as Chilkin described the strange behavior of the two convicts and the unusual actions of Kohler, the sergeant-major grew alarmed. He rushed to inform the Major, who in turn hurried to the Governor. Within fifteen minutes, the entire prison administration was in motion.

The Governor-General was immediately notified, as the escape of these two convicts was no small matter. A—v had been loosely classified as a political prisoner, which meant his disappearance would be viewed seriously by the authorities in St. Petersburg. Koulikoff, on the other hand, was a convict from the "special section," marked as one of the most dangerous criminals. Worse still, he was an ex-soldier, making his escape particularly alarming. A glaring oversight came to light during the commotion: according to regulations, convicts from the special section were supposed to have two soldiers assigned as escorts whenever they left the prison. This rule had been blatantly ignored, exposing multiple officials to potential reprimands and punishments.

Panic spread quickly. Express messengers were dispatched to every district office within the municipality and the neighboring towns. Notices were sent out, describing the fugitives in detail, and warnings were issued to officials in surrounding regions. Cossacks were deployed to comb the countryside for any trace of the escapees, and letters were hurriedly sent to the authorities in adjoining governmental districts. The entire administration buzzed with a mixture of fear and frantic activity.

The commotion within the prison was just as intense. As the convicts returned from their daily labor, they learned of the dramatic escape. The news swept through the barracks like wildfire, sparking a mix of excitement and admiration. Despite the oppressive atmosphere of the prison, the convicts secretly rejoiced. The escape represented more than just a break in the monotony of their days—it symbolized defiance and hope.

For many, the audacious act stirred something deeply buried within: the possibility that their fate might not be as unchangeable as it seemed. It awakened dormant emotions, a flicker of possibility that their lives might yet hold room for freedom or at least resistance to their harsh reality. It was a spark that reignited their humanity, however fleetingly, amidst the endless grind of their imprisonment.

"Well, you see, they managed to get away in spite of all the guards and precautions! Why shouldn't we?"

That thought flashed through every convict's mind, lighting up their expressions with a mix of daring and satisfaction. It was as if the very air around them had shifted. Men who usually shuffled about under the weight of their chains now seemed to stand taller, their spines straighter, their gazes bolder. They exchanged looks of defiance, each silently confirming the same thought in the eyes of their comrades. Even the usually downtrodden seemed to carry themselves with a new sense of pride, their demeanor saying, "If they could escape, perhaps we could too."

The sub-officers, sensing the change in atmosphere, walked among the convicts with a stiff unease. The convicts, emboldened, met their gazes with subtle smirks or deliberately indifferent expressions. The unspoken message was clear: "You think you have us completely under control, but we can slip through your fingers whenever we choose."

Before long, the higher authorities arrived in a flurry of urgency, as though their mere presence could reassert control over the situation. The Governor himself appeared, flanked by his officers, their faces red with embarrassment and barely concealed anger. They looked at the convicts as if trying to root out the seeds of rebellion with their eyes alone. But the convicts stood firm, silent, and unwavering. Their expressions bore a trace of contempt, an unmistakable "We hold the upper hand now" attitude. The defiance was subtle but powerful, unspoken yet undeniable.

Everyone in the barracks knew what would come next. The convicts whispered among themselves, predicting a full-scale search. "They'll be rummaging through everything now, trying to prove they're still in charge," someone muttered. True to expectations, the authorities set about turning the place upside down. Every corner, every bed, every nook and cranny was subjected to a thorough inspection. Contraband was hastily hidden, tucked away into the most ingenious hiding spots, for everyone knew the officials would be desperate to prove their vigilance after the fact.

As predicted, the search yielded nothing. The officers found no hidden weapons, no tools for escape, no clues that might shed light on how the fugitives had managed to vanish. Their frustration grew with every empty-handed discovery.

The convicts, meanwhile, wore their indifference like armor. They maintained a calm and composed front, refusing to give the authorities so much as a flicker of satisfaction. When the time came to head out for afternoon work, they noticed their escorts had been doubled. Soldiers marched alongside them with an exaggerated show of vigilance, rifles at the ready, as though expecting the entire prison population to bolt at any moment.

When evening fell, the absurdity escalated further. Officers and sub-officers patrolled the barracks incessantly, bursting in at random intervals to catch the convicts unawares, their eyes darting suspiciously from man to man. Lists were checked and rechecked, names called out repeatedly. The convicts were counted no less than three times that evening—once in the yard, once in the barracks, and again just before lights out. It was as if the authorities believed they could will the fugitives back into the prison simply by verifying their absence enough times.

Despite all the commotion, the convicts remained remarkably composed. They knew better than to give the authorities any excuse to crack down harder. Conversations were kept light and inconsequential, and everyone seemed to move with exaggerated obedience. The atmosphere, tense as it was, remained orderly.

"It's not like those two fools would've left anyone here who knew what they were planning," someone remarked quietly. The others nodded in agreement. They knew that the authorities, for all their bluster and suspicion, were chasing shadows. The fugitives had covered their tracks too well, and no amount of frantic searching or interrogations would change that.

As the night wore on, the convicts allowed themselves a quiet satisfaction. The audacity of the escape had ignited something within them—a flicker of hope, a reminder that even in the most oppressive circumstances, freedom was not an impossibility.

"When you're about to pull a trick like that, you've got to stay quiet and keep your head down!"

"Koulikoff and A—v knew their stuff, no doubt about it. They must've covered their tracks perfectly. They've done it like real pros— kept their mouths shut, planned it right. They're gone now, the clever devils. Smart as whips, those two—like they could walk straight through locked doors!"

The feats of Koulikoff and A—v had already become the stuff of legend. Their daring escape had elevated them to almost mythical status among the convicts. Every man in the prison seemed to take pride in them, as if their success reflected on the whole group. Their names were spoken with reverence, their exploit celebrated as though it would echo down the ages and outlive even the prison itself.

"Those two are real live wires," said one convict admiringly.

"People keep saying nobody can escape from here," chimed in another. "Well, just look at those chaps—proves it can be done!"

"Yeah," added a third, with a tone of superiority, "but who is it that actually made it out? Men like Koulikoff and A—v—top-tier fellows. You can't compare yourself to them unless you're made of the same stuff."

Normally, a statement like that would have ruffled some feathers. The convicts were not the kind to let a challenge go unanswered, and someone would have snapped back with a sharp retort. But this time, there was only respectful silence. No one dared argue the point.

"True enough," muttered one. "Not everyone's a Koulikoff or an A—v. You've got to prove what you're made of before you earn the right to speak."

"Still," said another, a convict sitting by the kitchen window with a slow, deliberate drawl, "why do we stick around here, pals? What's the point? This isn't living—it's like we've been buried alive. Doesn't it feel that way to you?" He rubbed his cheek with the palm of his hand as if savoring the satisfaction of stirring the pot.

"Oh, come on now," grumbled another, more pragmatic fellow. "You think breaking out of prison is as easy as kicking off an old boot? You've got to be realistic. This place sticks to you like tar. What's the point in pulling a long face about it?"

"But look at Koulikoff," began an eager, younger prisoner, his voice full of hope.

"Koulikoff!" scoffed a grizzled old convict, cutting the lad short and casting a sharp glance his way. "Koulikoff! You think they churn out men like him in dozens? He's one of a kind."

"And what about A—v?" added another, his voice almost reverent. "There's a lad for you. Sharp as they come."

The conversation carried on, a mix of admiration, envy, and faint hope. Each man seemed to measure himself against the shadow of the escapees, wondering if he too might one day muster the courage, the cunning, or the sheer audacity to do what they had done. For the moment, though, they contented themselves with the shared thrill of knowing that someone—two of their own—had broken free from the chains that bound them all.

"Aye, aye, Koulikoff will handle things just fine. That man knows every trick in the book," someone said with a tone of admiration, his voice dripping with confidence in Koulikoff's abilities.

"I just wonder how far they've managed to get by now," another chimed in, his voice filled with curiosity.

From there, the conversation turned into an animated debate about the fugitives' possible progress. Did they manage to put a good distance between themselves and the town? Which route might they have taken? Which direction offered the best chance of success? Each theory sparked a lively exchange, and as some of the convicts were familiar with the surrounding area, their insights were listened to with eager attention.

Soon, the discussion shifted to the character of the peasants in the nearby villages, and it was clear the convicts held a very low opinion of them.

"Let me tell you, those peasants are no good at all—scoundrels, every last one of them!" one man exclaimed with a sneer.

"Peasants, ha! They're nothing but a pack of lowlifes!" added another, shaking his head in disdain.

"These Siberian villagers are the worst of the lot. They wouldn't hesitate to turn in a man, and if they had to, they'd kill you without blinking," someone else said, his voice heavy with contempt.

"Oh, come on now," another countered. "Our boys aren't easy to take down. You know that."

"True," someone agreed. "If anything happens, our guys will give as good as they get."

"Let's wait and see," another inmate said thoughtfully. "If they're smart and lucky, we'll hear news soon enough."

The discussion quickly veered into speculation about whether Koulikoff and A—v would truly escape capture.

"What do you think? Will they actually make it?" one asked, leaning forward as if his life depended on the answer.

"I'd stake my life on it—they'll never be caught," declared one of the more animated men, pounding the table with his fist for emphasis.

"Hm," another muttered skeptically. "That depends on how things go."

"I'll tell you this," said Skouratof, a wiry, animated convict with a flair for drama, "if it were me who got out, I'd bet my life they'd never catch me again. Not in a million years."

"You?" someone retorted incredulously, unable to hide his amusement.

The entire group burst into laughter, their mocking tones cutting through the room. It was clear they thought little of Skouratof's claim, but the man wasn't about to back down.

"Yes, me!" he snapped, his eyes blazing with determination. "I've thought it all through already. I'd find a way to slip through a keyhole if that's what it took!"

"Oh, sure you would," someone shot back, their voice dripping with sarcasm. "And when your stomach started growling, you'd crawl to the nearest peasant and beg for a bite to eat."

This prompted another round of laughter, louder and harsher than before.

"Beg for food from a peasant? You're a liar!" Skouratof shouted, his temper flaring.

"Pipe down, will you? We all know why you're here," someone jeered. "You and your Uncle Vacia—wasn't it for killing some poor peasant because you thought he'd bewitched your cattle?"

The laughter erupted again, echoing off the walls, but this time it was tinged with something sharper, more biting. The more serious convicts, those who held a grudging respect for the escapees, looked on with scowls of disapproval, their indignation simmering just beneath the surface.

"You're lying!" shouted Skouratof, his face red with indignation. "It was that rascal Mikitka who told you that story! I had nothing to do with it—it was all Uncle Vacia's doing. Don't drag my name into it. I'm a Moscow man through and through, been on the tramp since I was barely old enough to walk. I'll have you know, when the priest was teaching me to read the liturgy, he used to tweak my ears and make me repeat after him, 'Have pity on me, Lord, out of Thy great goodness.' Then he'd add, 'They've taken me up and brought me to the police-station out of Thy great goodness,' and make me chant it over and over. I tell you, that nonsense started when I was just a little kid."

The crowd roared with laughter, just as Skouratof intended. He basked in the attention, grinning like a jester who had hit his mark. But soon enough, the talk turned serious again, particularly among the older prisoners and those who had knowledge of escapes. The younger convicts, unable to contain their curiosity, leaned in, eagerly soaking up every word. A large group had gathered in and around the kitchen, and with no warders in sight, the convicts felt free to speak their minds.

Amidst the throng was a small Tartar convict named Mametka, his high cheekbones and comical expressions making him a standout figure. Though he barely understood Russian, his enthusiasm was infectious. He craned his neck forward, his face alight with childish glee as he tried to keep up with the conversation.

"Well, Mametka, my boy, iakchi—good, eh?" someone teased.

"Iakchi! Yes, iakchi!" Mametka replied, his words tumbling out in broken Russian as he nodded enthusiastically, his grin stretching from ear to ear.

"They'll never catch them, right? Iok?"

"Iok, iok!" Mametka exclaimed, his head bobbing furiously, his small frame practically vibrating with excitement.

"You don't even know what you're talking about, do you?" teased another convict, shaking his head in mock exasperation.

"That's it, that's it—iakchi!" Mametka answered, his voice full of eager agreement, oblivious to the laughter rippling through the group.

"All right, then, iakchi it is!" shouted Skouratof with a laugh, giving Mametka a playful thump on the head. The blow sent Mametka's cap tumbling down over his eyes, leaving him momentarily flustered as Skouratof swaggered out, clearly pleased with himself. Poor Mametka looked bewildered and crestfallen, much to the amusement of the crowd.

For about a week, the prison remained under tight scrutiny, with guards and officers on high alert. The surrounding area was thoroughly searched several times over. Yet somehow, the prisoners always seemed to know what the authorities were up to, as if they had an invisible network feeding them updates. According to the latest murmurs, things seemed to be going well for the fugitives. There was no trace of them to be found, and the convicts, feeling a surge of pride for their comrades, scoffed at the efforts of the authorities.

"They're wasting their time," said one, smirking. "Our boys are too clever for them."

Word spread that the local peasants had been mobilized, scouring the woods, ravines, and any other places where the runaways might hide.

"Bah! Nonsense," another convict retorted with a dismissive wave. "They're holed up somewhere safe, with people they can trust."

"Exactly," someone else agreed. "You think they'd just wander around like fools? No way—they planned this out perfectly."

The confidence in Koulikoff and A—v's escape was unshakable, and the prisoners wore it like a badge of honor, a silent declaration that even under the tightest constraints, the spirit of freedom could not be extinguished.

The general belief among the prisoners was that Koulikoff and A—v were still hiding somewhere in the outskirts of the town, perhaps in a cellar or some other concealed spot, waiting for the immediate alarm to subside and for their hair to grow back to a less suspicious length. It was thought they might remain in hiding for six months, or even longer, before daring to leave quietly under cover of night. These ideas were more than mere speculation—they were spun into intricate fantasies by the prisoners, who were caught up in an almost romantic enthusiasm over the escape. Everyone loved to imagine the fugitives outsmarting their pursuers, biding their time, and eventually slipping away to freedom.

However, just eight days after their daring breakout, a troubling rumor began to circulate: the authorities were on their trail. At first, the convicts dismissed the news with scornful laughter, confident that their comrades were far too clever to be caught so easily. But by evening, the whispers grew louder, and the mood began to shift. The next morning brought unsettling reports from the town—people were saying that the runaways had been captured and were being escorted back. The atmosphere in the prison became charged with nervous tension as the story continued to evolve. By the time dinner was over, the details were more concrete: Koulikoff and A—v had been apprehended in a hamlet seventy versts away from the town. The rumors reached their peak when the sergeant-major, fresh from speaking with the Major, confirmed that the fugitives were indeed caught and would be brought into the guardhouse that very night.

The convicts were thrown into a storm of emotions when the news was confirmed. At first, they were consumed by sheer fury, their disappointment laced with outrage. How could their heroes have allowed themselves to be caught? This quickly gave way to a deep sense of dejection, as though the capture represented a personal failure for everyone. Then, as is often the case with wounded pride, their anger turned bitter and sarcastic.

Instead of venting their frustration at the authorities or the circumstances that had led to the capture, the convicts redirected their scorn toward the very men they had glorified only days before. Koulikoff and A—v became the targets of biting ridicule and caustic remarks. It seemed the prisoners derived a grim satisfaction in tearing down the reputation of their fallen comrades, as though their capture was a deliberate affront to the dignity of those left behind. The blame-game spread like wildfire, with everyone joining in except for a small number of the more thoughtful and serious-minded convicts, who held their peace and seemed to look down on the rest for their petty behavior.

The scornful theories about how the escape had failed were as cruel as they were imaginative. The most popular opinion was that the fugitives had grown weak with hunger and, unable to bear it any longer, had foolishly approached a village to beg for bread from the peasants. Among the convicts, such an act was regarded as the lowest degradation, a violation of the unspoken code of pride that even vagabonds held dear. It was considered a betrayal of the spirit of their escape. Yet, for all the ridicule, the assumption was entirely wrong.

The truth, as it turned out, was much simpler and far more tragic. The authorities had managed to discover the trail Koulikoff and A—v had left as they fled the town. Their route led into a forest, where the fugitives had sought refuge. Unfortunately for them, the forest was soon surrounded by soldiers and peasants. With no way out and no chance of slipping through the encirclement, the two men were forced to surrender. Their flight, so full of promise and daring, had come to an abrupt and humiliating end.

That night, the fugitives were brought back to the prison, bound hand and foot, under heavy armed escort. The entire prison was abuzz with the news, and as soon as the sound of the carriages was heard, nearly all the convicts rushed to the palisades, craning their necks and jostling for position, desperate to catch a glimpse of what was happening. But there was little to see. The Governor's and Major's carriages stood ominously in front of the guardhouse, their dark forms silhouetted against the lamplight. The two escapees were hurried inside, where they were immediately shackled and placed in separate cells. Their punishment was delayed until the following day, which only heightened the sense of dread and suspense.

Back in the barracks, the mood among the prisoners shifted. Those who had scorned Koulikoff and A—v earlier now softened, their ridicule replaced by a quiet sympathy. The details of the capture spread like wildfire, and when the convicts learned that the two men had been surrounded in the woods and had no choice but to surrender, their attitudes changed. The harsh reality of their fellow prisoners' plight sobered everyone, and the barracks were soon alive with murmured discussions about the likely severity of the punishment.

"They'll get a thousand lashes each at least," muttered one man grimly.

"A thousand?" another scoffed. "You're dreaming. They'll beat the life out of them. Koulikoff is in the 'special section,' remember? They'll kill him. A—v might get off lighter, but not by much."

The speculations were endless, and each new theory seemed more brutal than the last. Yet, when the actual sentences were handed down the following day, the punishments turned out to be less severe than expected. A—v was given 500 lashes—a relatively lenient sentence, considering his previous good behavior and the fact that this was his first prison offense. Koulikoff, on the other hand, was sentenced to 1,500 lashes, a significantly harsher punishment, owing to his status in the "special section."

The convicts listened intently as the sentences were announced, their faces a mix of relief and resignation. Some whispered that the punishments were surprisingly mild, considering the magnitude of the escape attempt. But when the flogging began, there was no doubt about the brutal reality of their fate.

The two men bore their ordeal with stoicism and, in a show of loyalty that earned them some respect, refused to implicate anyone else in their escape. They insisted that they had gone straight to the woods after fleeing the barracks and had not sought refuge in anyone's home. This silence spared others from being dragged into the affair, and for that, at least, they were admired.

Despite the relative leniency of his punishment, A—v did not endure the full sentence. The prison doctors intervened after the first few lashes, declaring that continuing would endanger his life. He was taken to the hospital, where, true to form, he quickly regained his bravado. Soon he was boasting loudly about his plans for the future, claiming that he would not let this setback deter him and promising to stage an even more daring escape. His words, however, rang hollow to many; his failure had tarnished his once-daring reputation.

Koulikoff, in contrast, remained as composed and dignified as ever. He bore his punishment without a word of complaint, and his demeanor afterward gave no hint of the ordeal he had endured. Yet, despite his outward calm, the other convicts no longer looked at him with the same admiration. His failed escape had stripped him of the aura of superiority he once had. To them, he was no longer the untouchable figure they had once idolized but merely another man who had tried and failed, just as they all feared they might.

And so, the tale of Koulikoff and A——v's escape attempt ended not in glory but in disappointment. In the harsh world of the prison, success was everything, and without it, even the boldest dreams faded quickly. Koulikoff's star, once so bright, had dimmed, and he found himself back on the same level as the rest—a sobering reminder of the unforgiving realities of their lives.

Chapter 10
Freedom!

This incident took place during my final year in the convict prison, a year etched into my memory with the same vivid clarity as the events of my first years there. Yet, I feel I have already gone into sufficient detail about the hardships and peculiarities of my life in confinement. What stands out most about that last year is how, paradoxically, it was the least burdensome of all the years I endured. By then, I had become familiar with the routine, the people, and even the oppressive atmosphere of the place. Moreover, I had established a circle of acquaintances and even friends among the convicts, many of whom had, over time, come to regard me with genuine affection. It was a strange and humbling realization that amidst such grim surroundings, bonds of sympathy could still form.

Some of the men, hardened and mistrustful though they were, had entirely shifted their opinions about me. In the early years, they viewed me with suspicion or indifference, but as time wore on, many began to accept and even appreciate me. A few had grown so fond of me that when the day of my release came, they were visibly moved. One soldier, tasked with escorting both my companion and me out of the prison upon our discharge, was particularly affected. When the time came for us to leave, he was on the verge of tears, a touching and unexpected display of emotion in a place where tenderness was rarely shown.

Even after I had regained my freedom and was staying in one of the Government-provided rooms within the town, this same soldier came to visit almost daily. He seemed unable to fully part ways with us, his attachment to our shared experience persisting even beyond the walls of the prison. Yet, there were still others among the convicts with whom I could never establish any understanding or connection, no matter how much time passed or how hard I tried. For reasons unknown—perhaps rooted in their own insecurities, bitterness, or judgments—these men remained cold and distant to the very end, harboring the same aversion toward me on the day I left as they had shown the first time I set foot in the barracks.

That final year brought a few welcome indulgences that had been unimaginable earlier in my sentence. Among the military officials stationed in the town, I found some old acquaintances and even a few schoolmates from my youth. Their presence brought a sense of normalcy and connection to a world I had long been estranged from. Through their influence, I was granted small privileges: permission to have a little money, to correspond with my family, and, most wondrously, to have access to books. For years, I had been starved of literature, cut off from the written word that had once been such a vital part of my life.

The first book I received stirred emotions I can scarcely describe. It was nothing more than an old issue of a review, yet it felt like a treasure unearthed, a message sent to me from some distant, forgotten world. That night, I devoured its pages, sitting under the faint light in my corner of the barracks long after the doors were locked, until the faint gray of dawn began to seep into the room. The words on those pages seemed to pulsate with life, as if they were tangible things I could reach out and grasp. Each sentence brought memories flooding back—memories of a life I had lived before my imprisonment, a life that now seemed almost like it had belonged to someone else.

The experience of reading again was profound, but it also left me deeply unsettled. As I turned the pages, I couldn't help but feel the vast chasm that had opened between myself and the world beyond the prison walls. The ideas, events, and discussions reflected in the text felt foreign, as though they belonged to a realm I no longer understood. I wondered if I could ever catch up—if the years I had lost would forever separate me from the pulse of life outside. I tried to read between the lines, searching for clues that might connect me to what I had missed, but the more I sought, the more I felt that a new era had dawned, one that was alien to me in its entirety.

As this realization took root, it filled me with a strange, hollow sorrow. I began to see myself as a relic of a bygone time, a man left behind while the world moved forward. The isolation I had felt within the prison was now mirrored by an equally profound sense of estrangement from the world I had once known. I was, in a sense, suspended between two realms—neither truly part of the convict's world nor fully able to reclaim my place in the society I had left behind. This sense of displacement lingered, haunting me even as the end of my sentence drew near and the promise of freedom loomed closer.

Yes, there were arrears indeed, if one may call by such a modest name the immense gulf that had opened between myself and the world I had left behind. For the truth was stark: a whole generation had arisen, and I was no part of it; it did not know me, and I did not know it. The very currents of thought and the voices shaping them were alien to my ears. I remember coming upon an article that bore the name of someone who had once been dear to me. The sight of that name was like a spark, and I seized upon the paper with the utmost eagerness, hoping to bridge the chasm, if only for a moment. Yet, how strange and alien the rest of it seemed! The names at the foot of other pieces were unfamiliar, and the subjects they touched upon were like echoes from a distant shore. The new workers on the stage of life had already set their mark upon it, but their works, their thoughts, their lives were a mystery to me, and I was eager—desperately eager—to know them, to understand this new age into which I would soon be cast.

That hunger for understanding made the lack of books almost unbearable. To be starved of the written word, to live without the light that books could bring into that dark and desolate place, was a torment I could not describe. In earlier days, during the regime of the old Major, it was nearly impossible to get books into the prison. The mere attempt was fraught with danger, and if one was discovered during the routine searches, it caused such a commotion that the entire prison was thrown into turmoil. Every effort would be made to uncover how the contraband had found its way inside, and anyone suspected of complicity would be subjected to relentless questioning and indignities.

I dared not take such risks. Even if I had been willing, the futility of the attempt was clear. So I lived without books, retreating into myself, wrestling with countless questions and problems that had no resolution, tormenting my soul with thoughts that had no outlet. It was a barren, lonely struggle that words cannot fully convey.

I arrived at the prison in winter, and it was in winter that I was destined to leave—on the very anniversary of my arrival. How fervently did I await that winter! Every passing season became a milestone, a step closer to deliverance. I watched with an almost savage joy as the summer waned, the leaves turned brittle and gold, and the vast steppe began to shed its green mantle for the withering hues of autumn. Then came the winds, howling across the plain, and finally, the first flurry of snow. The long-prayed-for winter had come at last, and with it, the thought that freedom was no longer a distant dream but an imminent reality.

Yet, as strange as it may seem, the closer the day of my release drew, the quieter my soul became. Where I had once been consumed with impatience, I now found myself oddly calm, almost subdued. This serenity puzzled and frustrated me. Why wasn't I more elated? Why did I feel this strange, almost unnatural detachment? I even reproached myself for what seemed like cold indifference to the moment I had longed for with every fiber of my being.

In those final days, my fellow convicts began to look at me differently. There was a warmth, a humanity in their demeanor that had not been there before. They would stop me in the yard after the day's work, their faces softening as they offered their congratulations.

"Ah, little Father Alexander Petrovitch, soon you'll be free. You'll leave us poor devils behind to rot in this hell."

"What about you, Mertynof?" I would ask in reply. "How much longer do you have?"

"Me?" he would sigh, his voice heavy with resignation. "Oh, seven years yet. Seven long, endless years."

And then his eyes would drift away, gazing into the distant, unbearable horizon of those years yet to be endured. His sigh carried with it a sorrow so profound that it seemed to echo across the barracks.

Others, too, offered their farewells, but there was something different in their tone now. It was as though the nearness of my freedom had placed me on a higher plane in their eyes. They regarded me not just as a fellow convict but as someone who had been touched by a grace they longed for but could not reach. The light of freedom, faint as it was, had begun to shine on me, and in that glow, they saw something to hold onto, something to revere.

In this spirit, they bade me farewell. Their words, simple as they were, carried an unspoken depth of emotion, a recognition of the bonds we had shared and the gulf that would soon separate us. It was a farewell not just to me as a man but to the hope and dream of freedom that I now embodied for them.

K——schniski, a young Polish noble of a gentle and amiable disposition, often walked with me in the prison yard during those final days. The oppressive, stifling air of the barracks at night took a toll on his health, so he made a point of getting all the exercise and fresh air the restricted life of the prison would allow. There was something almost childlike in his determination to maintain his strength and spirit, a quiet rebellion against the crushing monotony and despair of our surroundings.

"I am looking forward impatiently to the day you are set free," he said to me with a kind smile one afternoon. "For when you go, it will feel as though I am one step closer to my own freedom. Just one more year for me to endure."

His words stayed with me, for they revealed a shared, unspoken truth among us prisoners: freedom, as we envisioned it, was something impossibly grand, something almost mythical in its promise. It existed as an ideal, something larger and brighter than anything it could ever be in reality. Our imaginations, constantly dwelling on it, exaggerated its beauty and power.

For us, freedom meant everything we were not. To see a free man, even the lowest servant of an officer, was to look upon a figure of near divinity. The simplest liberties that they possessed—a body unshackled by chains, a head untouched by the barber's brutal shears, the ability to come and go as they pleased, unguarded and unwatched—seemed to us the epitome of all human joy. The contrast between their world and ours was so stark, so painful, that it made their freedom appear almost unattainable, a treasure far beyond our grasp.

The night before my release, as the sun set and the prison grew quiet, I took a final, solitary walk around the compound. It was a ritual of farewell, a moment to confront the years I had spent there, to acknowledge them before I left them behind. How many thousands of times had I traced the same path around the palisades during those ten endless years? Each step seemed to echo with the weight of the past.

I paused at the rear of the barracks, where, during my first year, I had paced back and forth endlessly, lost in despair and solitude. How

vividly I remembered counting the days I still had to endure—
thousands upon thousands, stretching out before me like an unending
desert. That first year felt like a lifetime ago.

I lingered by the corner where the caged eagle had once lived, a
symbol of our shared captivity. I thought of Petroff, who so often
joined me there. During those final days, it seemed he could scarcely
bear to leave my side. He would walk beside me in silence, saying
nothing, yet conveying everything. His presence was both a comfort
and a reminder of all I was leaving behind. His face often held a strange,
almost childlike wonder, as though he were trying to understand what
freedom might feel like for me—and what its absence meant for him.

As I moved through the compound, I took countless mental
farewells of the barracks, their black, squared beams looming in the
dim light. Those walls had witnessed so much suffering, so much
wasted potential. How many youth and years, how much vitality and
strength, had been lost within them, swallowed by the merciless
monotony of prison life? How many lives, brimming with potential,
had been reduced to mere existence, their gifts squandered and
forgotten?

I could not help but think—and I must speak plainly of it—that
those men, my fellow prisoners, represented some of the strongest and
most capable individuals of our people. In body and mind, there was a
resilience in them that could have been a force for great good. Yet all
that strength, all that potential, was lost—hopelessly, irretrievably lost.
And for what?

Whose fault was it that these lives were wasted so utterly? Who
bore the responsibility for this colossal loss, this needless suffering?

Yes, whose fault was it?

The next morning dawned early and clear, bringing with it the
moment I had awaited for so long. Before the convicts were mustered
for work, I made my way through the barracks to bid a final farewell

to those who had shared my years of imprisonment. The atmosphere was thick with a mix of emotions—warmth, indifference, and even resentment. Many stretched out their hands to me, roughened and hardened by endless toil, with genuine goodwill. Some grasped my hand with a strength and fervor that seemed to convey their hearts in the gesture, as though they wanted me to carry a piece of their spirit into the world beyond the prison walls.

But these were the more generous souls among them. For most, there was a distance that could not be bridged. I had become, in their eyes, a man set apart—not by anything I had done but by the inevitability of my departure and the promise of freedom. They knew that, as soon as I left those gates, I would be among gentlemen again, seated at their tables, living in a world that was as far removed from theirs as the stars in the night sky. That knowledge hung heavy in the air, casting a shadow over our parting moments. For many of them, my hand was no longer the hand of an equal. I was already, to them, something different—a gentleman once more.

Some could not bear to face me and turned their backs, saying nothing to my parting words. A few, I thought, even looked at me with aversion, their expressions tinged with bitterness or pain. I could not blame them. The disparity in our futures was stark and undeniable.

At last, the drumbeat summoned them to their work. The yard emptied, the clamor of voices fading as the convicts filed out. I was left alone, save for Souchiloff. The poor man had risen even earlier than usual that morning to prepare for me a final cup of tea. His trembling hands betrayed his deep emotion, and when I gave him some of my clothes, my shirts, and a small sum of money, he broke down completely.

"It's not that, it's not that," he stammered, biting his quivering lips to keep from sobbing. "It's that I'm going to lose you, Alexander Petrovitch! What am I going to do without you?"

His words pierced my heart. He had been a constant presence in my life there, and now I was leaving him behind, bound to a world he could not follow.

I bid farewell to Akim Akimitch as well. The stoic man, who had borne his sentence with such quiet resignation, struggled to find his voice.

"Your turn will come soon, I pray," I said to him, trying to offer some measure of hope.

"Ah, no," he replied, shaking his head as he pressed my hand. "I shall remain here long, long, very long yet."

Emotion overwhelmed me, and I embraced him, our parting sealed with a kiss.

Soon, the yard was still, the convicts gone to their labors. Ten minutes later, my companion and I left the prison for the last time. We were escorted to the blacksmith's shop by a single sub-officer. No armed guards, no chains rattling—it was a quiet, almost understated end to my captivity.

The blacksmiths were convicts themselves, working methodically in the engineers' workshop. They attended to my friend first, their practiced hands removing his irons with precision. Then it was my turn. I approached the anvil and felt a strange mixture of anticipation and disbelief as they took hold of my leg, stretched it over the heavy iron block, and began their work.

"The rivet, man—turn the rivet first," the master smith instructed, his tone calm and measured. "There, so, so. Now, a stroke of the hammer!"

The metal clanged against the anvil, and then I heard it—the sound of my irons falling away. I bent down and picked them up, holding them in my hands. A strange impulse gripped me; I could not fully grasp that these heavy, cold chains had just been on my limbs, binding me to that place and its life of confinement. They felt alien now, a relic of a life I was leaving behind.

"Good-bye! Good-bye! Good-bye!" came the voices of the convicts, broken yet full of a strange joy. Their words were a mixture of farewell and blessing, and their faces, though hardened by suffering, carried a glimmer of genuine pleasure in seeing one of their own set free.

And so it was farewell.

Liberty awaited. A new life beckoned. It was a moment unlike any other—a resurrection, a rebirth from a living grave.

An unspeakable moment.

THE END

Thank you for Reading

You've Just Read a Piece of the Greatest Library Ever Rebuilt

Thank you for reading.

This book is one of thousands we're restoring, reimagining, and translating as part of the **Modern Library of Alexandria** — a global movement to preserve and share humanity's most important ideas.

What was once lost to fire and time is now rising again — not just as memory, but as living, breathing knowledge, freely accessible to all.

What You Can Do Next:

- **Keep Reading.**

  Discover more legendary works — in beautiful print, audiobook, or digital form — at LibraryofAlexandria.com.

- **Build Your Own Library.**

  Every title is available as a paperback, hardcover, or collectible boxset — at true printing cost. Craft a personal library worthy of display.

- **Spread the Light.**

  Share this book. Tell others about the movement. Help us translate every timeless work into every language, so no reader is ever left behind.

By finishing this book, you've already taken part in something extraordinary.

Join us at LibraryofAlexandria.com

Together, we're rebuilding the greatest library the world has ever known.

With appreciation,
The Modern Library of Alexandria Team

Visit:

www.libraryofalexandria.com

Or scan the code below: